STEP-BY-STEP

Picnics

Picnics

ROSEMARY WADEY

||| •PARRAGON• |||

First published in Great Britain in 1995 by
Parragon Book Service Ltd
Unit 13-17
Avonbridge Trading Estate
Atlantic Road
Avonmouth
Bristol BS11 9QD

ISBN 1-85813-661-X

Produced by Haldane Mason, London

Printed in Italy

Acknowledgements:
Art Direction: Ron Samuels
Editor: Joanna Swinnerton
Series Design: Pedro & Frances Prá-Lopez/Kingfisher Design
Page Design: Somewhere Creative
Photography: Joff Lee
Stylist: John Lee Studios
Home Economist: Rosemary Wadey

Photographs on pages 6, 20, 34, 48 and 62 reproduced by permission of
ZEFA Picture Library (UK) Ltd

Note:
Cup measurements in this book are for American cups. Tablespoons are assumed to be 15 ml.
Unless otherwise stated, milk is assumed to be full-fat, eggs are standard size 2
and pepper is freshly ground black pepper.

Contents

CHAPTER ONE

Elegant Picnics

An elegant picnic is suitable for many events, and lends a little grandeur to a special occasion. You could serve an open-air buffet at a garden party to celebrate a birthday or wedding; take one to a day at the races or an afternoon at the local regatta; or picnic during the interval at an open-air theatre on a warm summer evening – the possibilities are endless.

The essence of this type of picnic is that it should be lavish. The venue should be perfect, the weather beautiful, and most of all the food should be splendid. Everything that is needed to make it so is packed up and taken along too. A table with a pretty cloth and proper china, cutlery and glass – no plastic or paperware for this picnic. The food should be similar to that served at an elegant dinner party, but take care to choose dishes that will still look and taste good when they have been packed up and transported some distance before being set out and eaten – and remember that you will not have all the usual advantages of final preparations in your own kitchen!

All this can be done with a little extra thought beforehand, very special packing, a careful driver and then a beautiful setting for you and your friends. Don't worry about the washing up – simply pack everything away and leave that for the next day.

Opposite: *Even if you don't have such elegant accessories as a fully fitted picnic basket, little finishing touches like fresh flowers and a champagne bucket can turn even a simple picnic into a special occasion.*

STEP 1

STEP 2

STEP 4

STEP 5

STUFFED AUBERGINE (EGGPLANT) ROLLS

Long slices of aubergine (eggplant) are blanched and stuffed with a savoury rice and nut mixture, and baked in a piquant tomato and wine sauce to serve cold as a starter.

SERVES 8

3 aubergines (eggplants) (total weight about 750 g / 1½ lb)
60 g/ 2 oz/⅓ cup mixed long-grain and wild rice
4 spring onions (scallions), trimmed and thinly sliced
3 tbsp chopped cashew nuts or toasted chopped hazelnuts
2 tbsp capers
1 garlic clove, crushed
2 tbsp grated Parmesan cheese
1 egg, beaten
1 tbsp olive oil
1 tbsp balsamic vinegar
2 tbsp tomato purée (paste)
150 ml/¼ pint/⅔ cup water
150 ml/¼ pint/⅔ cup white wine
salt and pepper
coriander (cilantro) sprigs to garnish

1 Cut off the stem end of each aubergine (eggplant), then cut off and discard a strip of skin from alternate sides of each aubergine (eggplant). Cut each aubergine (eggplant) into thin slices to give a total of 16 slices.

2 Blanch the aubergine (eggplant) slices in boiling water for 5 minutes, then drain on paper towels.

3 Cook the rice in boiling salted water for about 12 minutes or until just tender. Drain and place in a bowl. Add the spring onions (scallions), nuts, capers, garlic, cheese, egg, salt and pepper, and mix well.

4 Spread a thin layer of rice mixture over each slice of aubergine (eggplant) and roll up carefully, securing with a wooden cocktail stick (toothpick). Place the rolls in a greased ovenproof dish and brush each one with the olive oil.

5 Combine the vinegar, tomato purée (paste) and water, and pour over the aubergine (eggplant) rolls. Cook in a preheated oven at 180°C/350°F/Gas Mark 4 for about 40 minutes until tender and most of the liquid has been absorbed. Transfer the rolls to a serving dish.

6 Add the wine to the pan juices and heat gently until the sediment loosens and then simmer gently for 2–3 minutes. Adjust the seasoning and strain over the aubergine (eggplant) rolls. Leave until cold and then chill thoroughly. Garnish with sprigs of coriander (cilantro) and cover with clingfilm (plastic wrap) and foil to transport.

8

THREE FILLET PARCEL (PACKAGE)

Fillets of lamb, pork and chicken are layered with sage leaves, wrapped in spinach leaves and a layer of cottage cheese and enclosed in puff pastry to bake and serve cold cut into slices.

STEP 1

STEP 2

STEP 4

STEP 5

SERVES 8

300–350 g/10–12 oz pork fillet or
  tenderloin
about 12 fresh sage leaves
250–300 g/8–10 oz lamb neck fillet
2 boneless chicken breast fillets (total weight
  about 300 g/10 oz)
2 tbsp oil
125 g/4 oz large spinach leaves
350 g/12 oz puff pastry, thawed if frozen
250 g/8 oz/1 cup plain cottage cheese
pinch of ground allspice
pinch of garlic powder
beaten egg or milk to glaze
salt and pepper

TO GARNISH:
sage leaves
cucumber slices

1 Layer the fillets beginning with the pork fillet, cover with half the sage leaves, then add the lamb fillet, more sage leaves and finally the chicken fillets. Secure with fine string and/or skewers.

2 Heat the oil in a frying pan (skillet) and fry the layered fillets for about 15 minutes, turning regularly until browned and partly cooked. Remove from the pan (skillet) and leave until cold.

3 Blanch the spinach leaves in boiling water for 2 minutes and drain thoroughly.

4 Roll out the pastry thinly into a rectangle large enough to enclose the layered fillets and allow for 5 narrow strips to be cut off the edge. Lay the spinach down the centre of the pastry, spread with the cottage cheese and season well with salt, pepper, allspice and garlic powder.

5 Remove the string or skewers from the fillets and lay on the cheese and spinach. Wrap up in the pastry, dampening the pastry edges to secure. Stand on a greased baking sheet and glaze with beaten egg or milk. Lay the strips of pastry over the roll and glaze it again.

6 Bake in a preheated oven at 200°C/400°F/Gas Mark 6 for 30 minutes until beginning to brown. Reduce the temperature to 180°C/ 350°F/Gas Mark 4 and bake for a further 20 minutes. Remove from the oven and leave to cool, then chill thoroughly. Serve in slices garnished with sage leaves and slices of cucumber.

STEP 3

STEP 4

STEP 5

STEP 6

SEAFOOD PASTA

This attractive seafood salad platter is full of different flavours, textures and colours.

SERVES 6–8

175 g/6 oz/1¹/₂ cups dried pasta shapes
1 tbsp oil
4 tbsp French dressing
2 garlic cloves, crushed
6 tbsp white wine
125 g/4 oz baby button mushrooms, trimmed
3 carrots
600 ml/1 pint/2¹/₂ cups fresh mussels in shells
125–175 g/4–6 oz frozen squid or octopus rings, thawed
175 g/6 oz/1 cup peeled tiger prawns (shrimp), thawed if frozen
6 sun-dried tomatoes, drained and sliced
3 tbsp chives, cut into 2.5 cm/1 inch pieces
salt and pepper

TO GARNISH:
24 mangetout (snow peas), trimmed
12 baby corn
12 prawns (shrimp) in shells

1 Cook the pasta in boiling salted water with the oil added until just tender – about 12 minutes. Drain.

2 Combine the dressing, the garlic and 2 tablespoons of wine. Mix in the mushrooms and leave to marinate.

3 Slice the carrots about 1 cm/¹/₂ inch thick and using a cocktail cutter, cut each slice into shapes. Blanch for 3–4 minutes, drain and add to the mushrooms.

4 Scrub the mussels, discarding any that are open or do not close when sharply tapped. Put into a saucepan with 150 ml /¹/₄ pint/²/₃ cup water and the remaining wine. Bring to the boil, cover and simmer for 3–4 minutes until they open. Drain, discarding any that are still closed. Reserve 12 mussels for garnish, leaving them on the half shell; remove the others from the shells and add to the mushroom mixture with the squid or octopus rings and prawns (shrimp).

5 Add the sun-dried tomatoes to the salad with the pasta and chives. Toss well and turn on to a large platter.

6 Blanch the mangetout (snow peas) for 1 minute and baby corn for 3 minutes, rinse under cold water and drain. Arrange around the edge of the salad, alternating with the mussels on shells and whole prawns (shrimp). Cover with clingfilm (plastic wrap) and chill until ready to transport.

PROVENCAL TOMATO & BASIL SALAD

These extra-large tomatoes make an excellent salad, especially when sliced and layered with fresh basil, garlic, kiwi fruit and onion rings together with dressed baby new potatoes.

STEP 2

SERVES 6–8

500 g/1 lb tiny new or salad potatoes, scrubbed
4–5 extra-large tomatoes
2 kiwi fruit
1 onion, sliced very thinly
2 tbsp roughly chopped fresh basil leaves
fresh basil leaves to garnish

DRESSING:
4 tbsp virgin olive oil
2 tbsp balsamic vinegar
1 garlic clove, crushed
2 tbsp mayonnaise or soured cream
salt and pepper

1 Cook the potatoes in their skins in salted water until just tender – about 10–15 minutes – then drain thoroughly.

2 To make the dressing, whisk together the oil, vinegar, garlic and seasoning until completely emulsified. Transfer half of the dressing to another bowl and whisk in the mayonnaise or soured cream.

3 Add the creamy dressing to the warm potatoes and toss thoroughly, then leave until cold.

4 Wipe the tomatoes and slice thinly. Peel the kiwi fruit and cut into thin slices. Layer the tomatoes with the kiwi fruit, slices of onion and chopped basil in a fairly shallow dish, leaving a space in the centre for the potatoes.

5 Spoon the potatoes in their dressing into the centre of the tomato salad.

6 Drizzle a little of the plain dressing over the tomatoes, or serve separately in a bowl or jug. Garnish the salad with fresh basil leaves. Cover the dish with clingfilm (plastic wrap) and chill until ready to transport.

STEP 3

STEP 4

TOMATOES

Ordinary tomatoes can be used for this salad, but make sure they are firm and bright red. You will need 8–10 tomatoes.

STEP 5

15

STEP 3

STEP 4

STEP 4

STEP 5

DOUBLE CHOCOLATE TERRINE

The blend of white and dark chocolate mousse laced with rum, set in a loaf tin (pan) for easy carriage and serving, is finished with a fresh raspberry coulis and fresh raspberries.

SERVES 6–8

WHITE MOUSSE:
250 g/8 oz/8 squares white chocolate
1¹/₂ tsp powdered gelatine plus 2 tbsp water
2 tbsp caster (superfine) sugar
2 egg yolks
150 ml/¹/₄ pint/²/₃ cup soured cream
150 ml/¹/₄ pint/²/₃ cup double (heavy)
  cream, whipped until thick

DARK MOUSSE:
175 g/6 oz/6 squares dark chocolate
2 tbsp black coffee (not too strong)
2 tsp powdered gelatine plus 1 tbsp water
2 tbsp rum
60 g/2 oz/¹/₄ cup butter, softened
2 egg yolks
300 ml/¹/₂ pint/1¹/₄ cups double (heavy)
  cream, whipped

RASPBERRY COULIS:
175 g/6 oz/1 cup fresh or frozen raspberries
about 1 tbsp icing (confectioners') sugar

TO DECORATE:
fresh raspberries
whipped cream

1 Line a 23 × 12 cm/9 × 5 inch loaf tin with food wrap (plastic wrap), leaving plenty of overhang.

2 To make the white mousse, break up the chocolate and melt in a bowl, either in a microwave oven on Medium Power for 2 minutes or over a pan of gently simmering water. Remove from the heat and stir until smooth.

3 Dissolve the gelatine in the water in a bowl over simmering water. Leave to cool slightly, then beat into the chocolate with the sugar and egg yolks, and then the soured cream. Fold in the double (heavy) cream. Pour into the tin and chill until set.

4 To make the dark mousse, melt the chocolate with the coffee, and dissolve the gelatine in the rum with the water, as above. Stir the dissolved gelatine into the melted chocolate, followed by the butter. Stir until dissolved then beat in the egg yolks. Fold the cream through the mousse. Pour over the white mousse and chill until set.

5 For the coulis, sieve (strain) the raspberries and sweeten to taste with the sugar. Turn the terrine out, peel off the clingfilm (plastic wrap) and decorate the top with the raspberries and whipped cream. Spoon the coulis around the base to serve.

STEP 1

STEP 2

STEP 5

STEP 6

ORCHARD FRUITS BRISTOL

An elegant fruit salad of poached pears and apples, oranges and strawberries in a wine and caramel syrup topped with crumbled caramel.

SERVES 6–8

4 oranges
175 g/6 oz/³/₄ cup granulated sugar
4 tbsp water
150 ml/¹/₄ pint/²/₃ cup white wine
4 firm pears
4 dessert (eating) apples
125 g/4 oz/³/₄ cup strawberries

1 Pare the rind thinly from 1 orange and cut into narrow strips. Cook in the minimum of boiling water for 3–4 minutes until tender. Drain and reserve the liquor. Squeeze the juice from this and 1 other orange.

2 Lay a sheet of non-stick baking parchment on a baking sheet or board. Heat the sugar gently in a pan until it melts, then continue without stirring until it turns a pale golden brown. Pour half the caramel quickly on to the parchment and leave to set.

3 Add the water and squeezed orange juice immediately to the caramel left in the pan with 150 ml/ ¹/₄ pint/²/₃ cup orange rind liquor. Heat until it melts, then add the wine and remove from the heat.

4 Peel, core and slice the pears and apples thickly (you can leave the apple skins on, if you prefer), and add to the caramel syrup. Bring gently to the boil and simmer for 3–4 minutes until just beginning to soften – they should still be firm in the centre. Transfer the fruits to a serving bowl.

5 Cut away the peel and pith from the remaining oranges and either ease out the segments or cut into slices, discarding any pips (seeds). Add to the other fruits. Hull the strawberries and halve, quarter or slice thickly depending on the size and add to the other fruits.

6 Add the orange strands to the syrup and bring back to the boil for 1 minute, then pour over the fruits. Leave until cold, then break up the caramel and sprinkle over the fruit. Cover with clingfilm (plastic wrap) and foil, and chill until ready to transport.

CARAMEL

The caramel will begin to melt when added to the fruit, so do this as near to serving as possible.

CHAPTER TWO

Winter Picnic Hamper

During the winter months there are often some lovely bright and sunny days. They may be chilly, but for those who like the outdoors, these are times to take advantage of. Everyone always gets hungry in the open air, so a picnic is just the answer for a day out in the country.

Begin the picnic with piping hot thick soup from a flask, so you will quickly warm up. For a really special day out, take mulled wine in flasks to start the meal. Provide food which is substantial but not too filling, and pack it in containers from which it can be served, with just the lid needing to be removed. That will both protect the food from the elements and cut the amount of space needed to pack it. Take good pottery mugs for the soup (and for coffee later), and either chunky china or good solid plastic-type plates. Remember to take a cake or biscuits (cookies) too, for everyone will get peckish later on, and these will go down well with a cup of tea or coffee.

A rug is a must, in fact several would be even better, for one can be used to sit on, and another used to wrap yourselves in if it is really cold! Food can be served from the hamper in the back of the car with very little preparation; there is no need to set up and lay a table, although a small portable table is always useful if space permits to stop things toppling over on uneven ground.

Opposite: A cold, bright day in winter is just as suitable for a picnic as a warm summer afternoon. Choose a sheltered spot in which to set up your picnic, and enjoy the fresh winter air.

CRAB BISQUE

This delicious creamy puréed soup, which is known as a bisque when made with shellfish or fish, is given a touch of brandy to warm up a cold day. Serve with bread rolls, such as the Cheese, Herb & Onion Rolls on page 24.

STEP 1

STEP 2

STEP 4

STEP 5

SERVES 4–6

1 fresh crab (about 500 g/1 lb) or 250 g/
    8 oz/1 cup frozen crab meat, thawed
1 onion, chopped
2 carrots, chopped
2 celery sticks, sliced thinly
1 bouquet garni
1.5 litres/2½ pints/6¼ cups water
45 g/1½ oz/3 tbsp butter or margarine
45 g/1½ oz/⅓ cup flour
1 tbsp lemon or lime juice
150 ml/¼ pint/⅔ cup dry white wine
¼ tsp ground allspice
30 g/1 oz/2 tbsp long-grain rice
3–4 tbsp brandy
6 tbsp double (heavy) cream or natural
    fromage frais
chopped fresh parsley
salt and pepper

1 Remove the brown and white crab meat carefully from the cleaned shell, smashing the claws to remove the meat from them; then chop the meat finely. Chill until required.

2 Break up the shell and put into a saucepan with the onion, carrots, celery, bouquet garni and water. Bring to the boil, cover and simmer for about 45 minutes. Strain the liquid and reserve 1 litre/1¾ pints/4 cups. If using frozen crab meat, use fish stock (bouillon) cubes.

3 Melt the fat in a pan, stir in the flour and cook for 1–2 minutes without browning. Add the crab stock gradually and bring to the boil. Add the lemon or lime juice, wine, allspice and rice, and simmer for 10 minutes, stirring occasionally.

4 Add the crab meat and simmer for a further 10–15 minutes, or until the rice is tender, stirring from time to time.

5 Add the brandy, reheat and adjust the seasoning. Finally, stir in the cream or fromage frais and 1–2 tablespoons chopped parsley, reheat and pour into a warmed vacuum flask for transporting.

6 Serve the soup in mugs, sprinkled with more parsley.

VARIATION

Smoked haddock can be used in place of crab; use the bones to make the stock.

STEP 4

STEP 5

STEP 6

STEP 7

CHEESE, HERB & ONION ROLLS

A good texture and flavour are achieved by mixing white and granary flours together with minced onion, grated cheese and fresh herbs such as tarragon, thyme or sage to make these bread rolls.

MAKES 10–12

250 g/8 oz/2 cups strong white flour
1¹⁄₂ tsp salt
1 tsp dried mustard powder
good pinch of pepper
250 g/8 oz/2 cups granary or malted wheat flour
2 tbsp chopped fresh mixed herbs
2 tbsp finely chopped spring onions (scallions)
125–175 g/4–6 oz/1–1¹⁄₂ cups mature (sharp) Cheddar cheese, finely grated
15 g/¹⁄₂ oz/¹⁄₂ cake fresh (compressed) yeast; or 1¹⁄₂ tsp dried yeast plus 1 tsp caster (superfine) sugar; or 1 sachet easy-blend yeast plus 1 tbsp oil
300 ml/¹⁄₂ pint/1¹⁄₄ cups warm water

1 Sift the white flour with the salt, mustard and pepper into a bowl. Mix in the granary flour, herbs, spring onions (scallions) and most of the cheese.

2 Blend the fresh yeast with the warm water or, if using dried yeast, dissolve the sugar in the water, sprinkle the yeast on top and leave in a warm place for about 10 minutes until frothy. Add the yeast liquid (or the easy-blend yeast, oil and water) to the dry ingredients and mix to form a firm dough, adding more flour if necessary, to leave the sides of the bowl clean.

3 Knead until smooth and elastic – about 10 minutes by hand or 3–4 minutes in a food processor with a dough hook. Cover with an oiled polythene bag and leave in a warm place to rise for 1 hour or until doubled in size.

4 Knock back (punch down) and knead the dough until smooth. Divide into 10–12 pieces and shape as you prefer – into round or long rolls, coils, knots or other shape of your choice.

5 Alternatively, make one large plaited loaf. Divide the dough into 3 even pieces and roll each into a long thin sausage. Beginning in the centre, plait to the end and secure. Turn the plait round and complete the other half.

6 Place on greased baking sheets, cover with an oiled sheet of polythene and leave to rise until doubled in size. Remove the polythene.

7 Sprinkle with the rest of the cheese. Bake in a preheated oven at 200°C/400°F/Gas Mark 6 for 15–20 minutes for rolls, or 30–40 minutes for the loaf.

RAISED TURKEY PIE

A filling of minced (ground) pork and bacon with diced turkey, pickled walnuts, mushrooms and herbs is enclosed in a hot-water pastry crust, to cut and serve in slices.

STEP 2

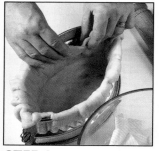

STEP 3

STEP 4

STEP 6

SERVES 6

FILLING:
350 g/12 oz raw turkey fillets
125 g/4 oz/¹/₂ cup lean raw pork, minced
125 g/4 oz/¹/₂ cup cooked ham, minced
    coarsely or chopped finely
1 small onion, minced
60 g/2 oz/²/₃ cup button mushrooms,
    chopped roughly
1 tbsp chopped fresh parsley
good pinch of ground coriander
6 pickled walnuts, well drained
beaten egg or milk to glaze
1 tsp powdered gelatine
150 ml/¹/₄ pint/²/₃ cup chicken stock
salt and pepper

PASTRY:
350 g/12 oz/3 cups plain flour
1 tsp salt
90 g/3 oz/¹/₃ cup lard or white shortening
6 tbsp water
3 tbsp milk

1 To make the filling, chop all the turkey fillets and mix with the pork, ham, onion, mushrooms, parsley, coriander and seasoning.

2 To make the pastry, sift the flour and salt into a bowl. Heat the fat in the water and milk until melted, then bring to the boil. Pour on to the flour and mix to an even dough.

3 Roll out about three-quarters of the dough and use to line a lightly greased raised pie mould or a loaf tin.

4 Put half the turkey mixture into the lined tin and arrange the walnuts over it. Cover with the rest of the turkey mixture. Roll out the reserved pastry for a lid, dampen the edges and position. Trim and crimp the edge. Make a hole in the centre for steam to escape. Garnish with pastry leaves and glaze.

5 Bake on a baking sheet in a preheated oven at 200°C/400°F/ Gas Mark 6 for 30 minutes. Reduce the temperature to 180°C/350°F/Gas Mark 4, glaze again and bake for a further hour. When browned, cover with a sheet of greaseproof paper (baking parchment).

6 Dissolve the gelatine in the stock, bringing just to the boil; season well. Leave the pie to cool for 10 minutes. Gradually pour in as much stock as possible through the hole in the lid. Leave until cold and then chill thoroughly for at least 12 hours. Unmould to serve.

WALDORF SLAW

This salad combines the best of a Waldorf salad and a coleslaw in a tart yogurt dressing with an attractive garnish of carrot sticks.

STEP 1

SERVES 4–6

4 celery sticks, preferably green
¼ white cabbage (about 250 g/8 oz)
60 g/2 oz/⅓ cup raisins
60 g/2 oz/½ cup walnut pieces
4–6 spring onions (scallions), trimmed and cut into thin slanting slices
2 green-skinned dessert (eating) apples
2 tbsp lemon or lime juice
4 tbsp thick mayonnaise
2 tbsp natural yogurt or natural fromage frais
2 tbsp French dressing
salt and pepper
2 carrots, trimmed, to garnish

1 Cut the celery into narrow slanting slices. Remove the core from the cabbage and shred finely either by hand or using the slicing blade of a food processor.

2 Put the celery, cabbage, raisins, walnut pieces and spring onions (scallions) into a bowl and mix together.

3 Quarter and core the apples and slice thinly, or cut into dice. Put into a bowl with the lemon or lime juice and toss until completely coated. Drain and add to the other salad ingredients.

4 Whisk together the mayonnaise, yogurt or fromage frais and French dressing, and season well. Add to the salad and toss evenly through it. Turn into a serving bowl.

STEP 3

5 To make the garnish, cut the carrots into very narrow julienne strips about 5 cm/2 inches in length and arrange around the edge of the salad.

6 Cover with clingfilm (plastic wrap) and chill until ready to transport. Alternatively, put the salad into a plastic food container with a secure lid.

STEP 4

VARIATION

This salad can be made using red cabbage for a change, and firm pears can be used in place of the apples.

STEP 5

29

STEP 2

STEP 3

STEP 4

STEP 6

MARBLED MOCHA CAKE

Chocolate- and coffee-flavoured cake mixtures are baked together into a marbled effect which is topped with a rich coffee icing (frosting).

SERVES 10–12

CAKE:
175 g/6 oz/³/₄ cup butter or soft margarine
125 g/4 oz/²/₃ cup light soft brown sugar
60 g/2 oz/¹/₄ cup caster (superfine) sugar
3 eggs
175 g/6 oz/1¹/₂ cups self-raising flour
2 tsp coffee flavouring (extract)
2 tbsp cocoa powder, sifted
1 tbsp water

ICING (FROSTING):
90 g/3 oz/¹/₃ cup butter
250 g/8 oz/1¹/₃ cups icing (confectioners')
  sugar, sifted
1 egg yolk
1–1¹/₂ tbsp coffee flavouring (extract)

1 Grease and line an 18 or 20 cm/7 or 8 inch round cake tin (pan) with greased greaseproof paper or non-stick baking parchment.

2 Cream the fat and sugars together until very light and fluffy and pale in colour. Beat in the eggs, one at a time, following each with a spoonful of the flour, then fold in the remaining flour.

3 Transfer half the mixture to another bowl and beat the coffee flavouring (extract) into 1 portion and the cocoa powder and water into the other.

4 Spoon alternate spoonfuls of the 2 cake mixtures into the prepared tin (pan) and then swirl together lightly and level the top. Bake in a preheated oven at 160°C/325°F/Gas Mark 3, allowing about 1 hour for the larger cake tin (pan) or 50 minutes for the smaller one, or until the cake is well risen and firm to the touch. Leave the cake to cool briefly in the tin (pan), then loosen and turn out on to a wire rack to cool completely.

5 To make the icing (frosting), cream the butter until smooth, then beat in half the icing (confectioners') sugar until smooth, followed by the egg yolk and 1 tablespoon coffee flavouring (extract). Work in the remaining icing (confectioners') sugar with sufficient coffee flavouring (extract) to give a piping consistency.

6 Using a large star nozzle (tip), pipe an attractive design of shells over the top of the cake. Leave to set. Place in a tin or rigid plastic container to transport.

STEP 1

STEP 3

STEP 4

STEP 5

RUM & GINGER TRIFLE

Individual trifles of boudoir biscuits (lady-fingers) steeped in rum, stem ginger and ginger syrup with raspberries and orange rind, topped with custard and cream.

SERVES 6

about 24 boudoir biscuits (lady-fingers)
6–8 pieces stem (candied) ginger, chopped
grated rind and juice of 1 orange
2–3 tbsp stem (candied) ginger syrup (from the jar)
4–6 tbsp rum
250 g/8 oz/1½ cups raspberries, fresh or frozen

CUSTARD:
450 ml/¾ pint/scant 2 cups milk
3 egg yolks
1 egg
few drops of vanilla flavouring (extract)
2 tbsp caster (superfine) sugar
1 tsp cornflour (cornstarch)

TO DECORATE:
300 ml/½ pint/1¼ cups whipping cream, whipped
few pieces stem (candied) or crystallized ginger, chopped
gold dragées
strips of angelica

1 Break each biscuit (lady-finger) into 3 or 4 pieces, divide between 6 individual serving bowls and sprinkle with the chopped ginger and grated orange rind.

2 Combine the orange juice, ginger syrup and rum, and spoon over the biscuits (lady-fingers).

3 Arrange the raspberries over the biscuits (lady-fingers), leaving the fruit to thaw, if frozen, when the juices will seep into the biscuits (lady-fingers).

4 To make the custard, heat all but 2 tablespoons of the milk to just below boiling. Blend the remaining milk with the egg yolks, egg, vanilla flavouring (extract), sugar and cornflour (cornstarch). Pour the hot milk on to the egg mixture and return to a heatproof bowl. Stand it over a saucepan of gently simmering water and cook gently, stirring frequently until the custard thickens sufficiently to coat the back of a spoon. Do not let it boil, or it will curdle.

5 Cool the custard a little then pour it over the fruit. Chill.

6 Pipe the cream over the custard with a large star nozzle (tip). Decorate with the ginger, dragées and angelica.

CHAPTER THREE

At the Seaside

A day at the seaside brings a smile to the faces of children and adults alike, and to complete the day, nothing is better than a delicious picnic with lots of food to choose from.

The beach, of course, means sand, which can get into everything all too easily, so make sure the food is packed into containers with tight-fitting lids and is wrapped in both clingfilm (plastic wrap) and foil to give extra protection. Make the food suitable for eating with fingers or forks, so it can be taken straight from the containers or transferred easily to paper or plastic plates.

Of course there are pebbled beaches and often grassy areas close by where the sand won't be as much of a problem, as well as breakwaters and sand dunes – the main picnic can be set out in the most convenient place, which needn't be right on the beach. As with all days spent outdoors, hunger pangs keep returning and people like to pick and nibble throughout the day, and this should be kept in mind when deciding on the menu. Don't take just one portion of everything for each person; it is much better to take lots of smaller amounts of items such as Samosas or Spanish Omelette Squares, and a salad containing large pieces of raw vegetables, like crudités, is always a good standby.

Opposite: *A picnic is the perfect meal to take to the beach, as all that fresh sea air makes people hungry, and even the simplest picnic will go down well.*

SPANISH OMELETTE SQUARES

An oven-baked omelette with diced potatoes, onions, peas, tomatoes, herbs and cheese is cut into small squares to make not much more than a mouthful.

STEP 2

STEP 3

STEP 4

STEP 6

MAKES ABOUT 36 SQUARES

2 tbsp olive oil
1 onion, thinly sliced
1 garlic clove, crushed
1 courgette (zucchini), trimmed and grated
   coarsely
1 red, green or orange (bell) pepper, halved,
   cored and deseeded
175 g/6 oz/1 cup cooked potato, diced
90 g/3 oz/²/₃ cup cooked peas
2 tomatoes, peeled, deseeded and cut into
   strips
2 tsp chopped fresh mixed herbs or 1 tsp
   dried mixed herbs
6 eggs
45–60 g/1¹/₂–2 oz/¹/₃–¹/₂ cup Gruyère or
   fresh Parmesan cheese, grated
salt and pepper

1 Heat the oil in a large frying pan (skillet) and fry the onion and garlic very gently until soft, but not coloured, about 5 minutes. Add the courgette (zucchini) and fry for a further 1–2 minutes. Turn into a bowl.

2 Place the (bell) pepper on a grill (broiler) rack skin-side upwards and cook under a preheated moderate grill (broiler) until the skin is well charred. Leave to cool slightly, then peel off the blackened skin and slice or chop the (bell) pepper flesh. Add the (bell) pepper to the onion mixture, together with the potato, peas, tomatoes and herbs.

3 Beat the eggs together with 1–2 tablespoons water and plenty of seasoning, then add to the vegetables and mix well.

4 Line a shallow 20–23 cm/8–9 inch square cake tin (pan) with non-stick baking parchment. Do not cut into the corners, just fold the parchment. Pour in the egg mixture, making sure the vegetables are fairly evenly distributed.

5 Cook in a preheated oven at 180°C/350°F/Gas Mark 4 for about 15 minutes or until almost set.

6 Sprinkle with the cheese and either return to the oven for 5–10 minutes or place under a preheated moderate grill (broiler) until evenly browned. Leave to cool. Remove from the tin (pan) and transport still wrapped in the baking parchment in an airtight plastic container, or cut into 2.5–4 cm/1–1¹/₂ inch squares and stack up in a plastic container.

CHICKEN SATAY KEBABS

Small kebabs of satay chicken with cubes of cheese and cherry tomatoes added are served on crisp lettuce leaves.

STEP 2

STEP 3

STEP 4

STEP 5

MAKES 8

8 wooden skewers, soaked in warm water
    for 30 minutes.
1 tbsp sherry
1 tbsp light soy sauce
1 tbsp sesame oil
finely grated rind of ¹/₂ lemon
1 tbsp lemon or lime juice
2 tsp sesame seeds
500 g/1 lb chicken breast meat, skinned
90 g/3 oz Double Gloucester (red) or Gouda
    cheese
16 cherry tomatoes
crisp lettuce leaves, such as Little Gem
salt and pepper

PEANUT DIP:
30 g/1 oz/¹/₃ cup desiccated (shredded)
    coconut
150 ml/¹/₄ pint/²/₃ cup boiling water
125 g/4 oz/¹/₂ cup crunchy peanut butter
good pinch of chilli powder
1 tsp brown sugar
1 tbsp light soy sauce
2 spring onions (scallions), trimmed and
    chopped

1 Combine the sherry, soy sauce, sesame oil, lemon rind, lemon or lime juice, sesame seeds and seasoning in a bowl.

2 Cut the chicken into 2.5 cm/1 inch cubes. Add to the marinade and mix well. Cover and leave for 3–6 hours, preferably in the refrigerator.

3 To make the dip, put the coconut into a saucepan with the water and bring back to the boil; leave until cold. Add the peanut butter, chilli powder, sugar and soy sauce and bring slowly to the boil. Simmer very gently, stirring all the time, for 2–3 minutes until thickened; then cool. When cold, stir in the spring onions (scallions), turn into a small bowl and cover with clingfilm (plastic wrap) and then foil to transport.

4 Thread the chicken on to 8 wooden skewers, keeping the chicken in the centre of each skewer. Cook under a moderate grill (broiler) for about 5 minutes on each side until cooked through. Leave until cold.

5 Cut the cheese into 16 cubes and then add one of these and a cherry tomato to each end of the skewers.

6 Stand each kebab on a crisp lettuce leaf, wrap in clingfilm (plastic wrap) or foil, or place in a plastic container. Serve with the peanut dip.

SAMOSAS WITH SPICY DIP

A spicy filling of minced meat and vegetables enclosed in a pastry crescent to deep fry and serve with a dip. They should be fried 2–3 hours before you leave for the picnic.

STEP 1

STEP 2

STEP 3

STEP 4

MAKES 16

FILLING:
1 onion, chopped finely
1 garlic clove, crushed
1 tsp freshly grated raw ginger root
2 tbsp oil
1 carrot, grated coarsely
1¹/₂ tsp garam masala
125 g/4 oz/¹/₂ cup cooked beef, pork or ham, minced (ground)
125 g/4 oz/³/₄ cup cooked peas
175 g/6 oz/1 cup cooked potatoes, diced finely
salt and pepper

PASTRY:
250 g/8 oz/2 cups plain (all-purpose) flour
¹/₂ tsp salt
30 g/1 oz/2 tbsp butter or margarine
about 100 ml/3¹/₂ fl oz/scant ¹/₂ cup cold water
oil for deep-frying

CURRIED DIP:
150 ml/¹/₄ pint/²/₃ cup thick mayonnaise
3 tbsp soured cream or fromage frais
1¹/₂ tsp curry powder
¹/₂ tsp ground coriander
1 tsp tomato purée (paste)
2 tbsp mango chutney, chopped
1 tbsp chopped fresh parsley

1 To make the filling, fry the onion, garlic and ginger root in the oil until soft. Add the carrot and fry for 2–3 minutes. Stir in the garam masala and 4 tablespoons water, season, and simmer gently until the liquid is almost absorbed. Remove from the heat, stir in the meat, peas and potatoes and leave to cool.

2 To make the pastry, sift the flour and salt into a bowl and rub in the butter. Add sufficient of the water to mix to a smooth, elastic dough, kneading continually. Cut the dough into 16 pieces and keep covered. Dip each piece into a little oil or coat lightly with flour and roll out to a 12 cm/5 inch circle.

3 Put 1–2 tablespoons of the filling on one side of each circle, dampen the edge, fold over and seal firmly. Keep the samosas covered with a damp cloth.

4 Heat the oil to 180–190°C/ 350–375°F, or until a cube of bread browns in about 30 seconds. Fry the samosas a few at a time for 3–4 minutes until golden brown, turning once or twice. Drain on paper towels.

5 To make the dip, combine all the ingredients, and pack separately.

GARDEN SALAD

This chunky salad includes tiny new potatoes tossed in a minty dressing, and has a mustard dip for dunking.

STEP 1

STEP 2

STEP 5

STEP 6

SERVES 6–8

500 g/1 lb tiny new or salad potatoes
4 tbsp French dressing made with olive oil
2 tbsp chopped fresh mint
6 tbsp soured cream
3 tbsp thick mayonnaise
2 tsp balsamic vinegar
1¹/₂ tsp coarse-grain mustard
¹/₂ tsp creamed horseradish
good pinch of brown sugar
225 g/8 oz broccoli florets
125 g/4 oz sugar snap peas or mangetout
(snow peas), trimmed
2 large carrots
4 celery sticks
1 yellow or orange (bell) pepper, halved,
cored and deseeded
1 bunch spring onions (scallions), trimmed
(optional)
1 head chicory (endive)
salt and pepper

1 Cook the potatoes in boiling salted water until just tender – about 10 minutes. While they cook, combine the French dressing and mint. Drain the potatoes thoroughly, add to the dressing while hot, toss well and leave until cold, giving an occasional stir.

2 To make the dip, combine the soured cream, mayonnaise, vinegar, mustard, horseradish, sugar and seasoning. Put into a bowl and cover with clingfilm (plastic wrap) and then foil.

3 Cut the broccoli into bite-sized florets and blanch for 2 minutes in boiling water. Drain and toss immediately in cold water; when cold, drain thoroughly.

4 Blanch the sugar snap peas or mangetout (snow peas) in the same way but only for 1 minute. Drain, rinse in cold water and drain again.

5 Cut the carrots and celery into sticks about 6 × 1 cm/2¹/₂ × ¹/₂ inch; and slice the (bell) pepper or cut into cubes. Cut off some of the green part of the spring onions (scallions), if using, and separate the chicory (endive) leaves.

6 Arrange the vegetables attractively in a fairly shallow bowl with the potatoes piled up in the centre. Cover with clingfilm (plastic wrap), and transport the dip separately.

STEP 1

STEP 2

STEP 3

STEP 4

ORANGE PECAN PIE

A really gooey and sticky pecan and orange pie, very moreish and just right for healthy appetites by the seaside.

SERVES 6–8

PASTRY:
175 g/6 oz/1½ cups plain (all-purpose)
flour
pinch of salt
90 g/3 oz/⅓ cup butter
1 tbsp finely chopped pecan nuts
4–5 tbsp iced water to mix

FILLING:
150 g/5 oz/1¼ cups pecan nuts, halved
2 eggs
175 g/6 oz/1 cup light soft brown sugar
175 g/6 oz/generous ½ cup golden (light
corn) syrup
grated rind of 1 large orange
1 tsp vanilla flavouring (extract)
icing (confectioners') sugar to decorate

1 To make the pastry, sift the flour and salt into a bowl, then rub in the butter until the mixture resembles fine breadcrumbs. Stir in the pecan nuts evenly, then add sufficient of the iced water to mix to a firm but pliable dough. Knead lightly until smooth.

2 Roll out the pastry and use to line a 20 cm/8 inch fluted flan ring, tin (pan) or dish.

3 Arrange the pecan halves evenly over the base of the pastry.

4 To make the filling, beat the eggs with the sugar, golden (light corn) syrup, orange rind and vanilla flavouring (extract). When evenly blended, pour or spoon over the pecans.

5 Stand the flan ring, tin (pan) or dish on a baking sheet and bake in a preheated oven at 190°C/375°F/Gas Mark 5 for about 40 minutes, or until the pastry is crisp and the filling firm to the touch.

6 Leave the pie to cool completely and then dredge lightly with sifted icing (confectioners') sugar. Cover first with clingfilm (plastic wrap) then with foil for transporting. Serve the pie cut into wedges.

WALNUTS

This pie can also be made with walnut halves for a change. It may be frozen for up to 2 months.

STEP 3

STEP 4

STEP 5

STEP 6

WHITE CHOCOLATE BROWNIES

These moist chewy brownies, full of chopped nuts and raisins, are made with white chocolate for a change and topped with swirled mixed chocolate – just right to munch on a beach picnic.

MAKES 8–12

60 g/2 oz/2 squares white chocolate
60 g/2 oz/¼ cup butter or margarine
175 g/6 oz/1 cup light soft brown sugar
½ tsp vanilla flavouring (extract)
2 eggs
75 g/2½ oz/⅔ cup self-raising flour, sifted
30 g/1 oz/¼ cup walnuts or other nuts,
    finely chopped
45 g/1½ oz/⅓ cup raisins

TOPPING:
60 g/2 oz/2 squares dark chocolate, melted
30 g/1 oz/1 square white chocolate, melted
icing (confectioners') sugar for dredging

1 Line a shallow 20 cm/8 inch square tin (pan) with non-stick baking parchment or greased greaseproof paper.

2 Break up the chocolate and place in a heatproof bowl with the fat. Melt in a microwave oven on Medium Power for 2 minutes, or over a pan of gently simmering water. Remove from the heat and beat in the sugar and vanilla flavouring (extract) until smooth.

3 Beat in the eggs, one at a time, until smooth, then fold in the flour.

4 Add the nuts and raisins and stir until evenly mixed.

5 Pour the mixture into the prepared tin (pan) and bake in a preheated oven at 180°C/350°F/Gas Mark 4 for 35–45 minutes, or until the mixture is well risen, firm to the touch and beginning to shrink away from the sides of the tin (pan). Leave to cool in the tin (pan), then remove carefully and peel off the paper.

6 Melt the chocolates separately for the topping. First spread the dark chocolate over the top of the brownies. As it begins to set, trickle the white chocolate over it and, taking a fork or skewer, swirl the chocolates together to give a marbled effect. Leave to set. Dredge with icing (confectioners') sugar.

7 Serve the brownies cut into squares or fingers and transport in an airtight container or wrap the whole tin (pan) in foil.

CHAPTER FOUR

In the Garden

A wrought-iron table or a wooden barbecue table makes an attractive setting for a garden picnic. A tablecloth looks nice with china and cutlery rather than plastic or paperware, but don't use the best silver. If you keep the numbers small, it makes the occasion more friendly for everyone.

Choose a fairly simple but interesting menu, but not one that takes days to prepare, as you may spoil your own enjoyment if you give yourself too much to do. Often this is a good 'spur of the moment' way to entertain friends, particularly when the day dawns fine and sunny or perhaps you have guests to stay. Another idea is to take this picnic to someone else's garden, perhaps as a surprise party or just to save them from doing the cooking.

Opposite: *The garden is an ideal place for a picnic, especially if you take a rug and a picnic basket and do the whole thing in style – it doesn't matter if you are only a few feet from the house!*

STEP 1

STEP 1

STEP 3

STEP 5

MELON WITH SMOKED SALMON MOUSSE

The refreshing flavour of the melon is offset beautifully by the rich salmon mousse and makes a most attractive and rather unusual starter.

SERVES 6

3 ripe small Charentais or Ogen melons

SMOKED SALMON MOUSSE:
175 g/6 oz smoked salmon pieces or slices
2–3 spring onions (scallions), trimmed and sliced
1–2 garlic cloves, crushed
175 g/6 oz/³/4 cup light cream cheese
2–3 tsp lemon or lime juice
2–4 tbsp natural yogurt or natural fromage frais
salt and pepper

TO GARNISH:
pitted black olives
sprigs of fresh dill

1 Halve the melons and scoop out the seeds. For an attractive finish, vandyke the edge by making short slanting cuts into the centre of the melon using a small sharp knife, creating a zigzag design round the centre of the melon.

2 To make the mousse, put the salmon pieces into a food processor with the spring onions (scallions) and garlic, and work until smoothly chopped. Alternatively, chop the smoked salmon,

spring onions (scallions) and garlic very finely, and mix together.

3 Add the cream cheese and process again until well blended, or beat into the chopped salmon mixture. Add lemon or lime juice to taste and sufficient yogurt or fromage frais to give a piping consistency. Season with salt and pepper.

4 Stand each melon half on a small plate, cutting a thin sliver off the base if it will not stand evenly.

5 Put the salmon mousse into a piping bag fitted with a large star nozzle (tip) and pipe a large whirl to fill the centre of each melon, piling it up in the centre.

6 Garnish each melon half with black olives and sprigs of fresh dill. When prepared, the melons may be chilled for up to 2 hours before serving.

VARIATION

Alternatively, halve a longer melon and cut into slices about 2.5 cm/1 inch thick. Arrange 3 or 4 slices on the plate and pipe the mousse at one end.

STEP 1

STEP 4

STEP 5

STEP 6

CHICKEN WITH LEMON & TARRAGON

Chicken fillets are cooked with saffron, white wine and stock flavoured with lemon rind and tarragon, then the sauce is thickened with egg yolks and soured cream and finished with mayonnaise.

SERVES 6

6 large boneless chicken breasts
¼ tsp saffron strands
250 ml/8 fl oz/1 cup boiling water
1 tbsp olive oil
30 g/1 oz/2 tbsp butter
1 garlic clove, crushed
125 ml/4 fl oz/½ cup dry white wine
grated rind of 1 small lemon
1 tbsp lemon juice
1–2 tbsp chopped fresh tarragon or 1 tsp
*   dried tarragon*
2 tsp cornflour (cornstarch)
1 egg yolk
6 tbsp soured cream or double (heavy)
*   cream*
4 tbsp thick mayonnaise
salt and pepper

TO GARNISH:
fresh tarragon
lemon twists

1 Remove the skin from the chicken and cut each breast almost horizontally into 3 thin slices. Season each piece well with salt and pepper.

2 Put the saffron strands into a bowl, pour on the boiling water and leave to stand until they are needed.

3 Heat the oil, butter and garlic in a frying pan (skillet). When foaming, add the pieces of chicken and fry for a few minutes on each side until well sealed but only lightly coloured.

4 Add the saffron liquid, wine, lemon rind and juice, and half the fresh tarragon or all the dried tarragon. Bring to the boil, then simmer gently for about 5 minutes or until tender. Lift out the chicken pieces with a perforated spoon and place on a serving dish in overlapping slices. Leave to cool. Boil the juices for 3–4 minutes to reduce slightly.

5 Blend the cornflour (cornstarch), egg yolk and cream together in a bowl. Whisk in a little of the cooking juices, then return to the pan and heat gently, stirring continuously until thickened and just barely simmering. Remove from the heat, adjust the seasoning and pour into a bowl. Cover and leave until cool.

6 Beat the mayonnaise and remaining fresh tarragon into the sauce and spoon over the chicken. Cover and chill thoroughly. Garnish with sprigs of fresh tarragon and lemon twists.

ROSTI POTATO CAKE WITH COURGETTES (ZUCCHINI) & CARROTS

A mixture of coarsely grated potatoes, courgettes (zucchini) and carrots with fried sliced onions cooked into a cake in a large frying pan (skillet), topped with cheese and finished off under the grill (broiler). Serve cold, cut into wedges.

STEP 1

STEP 2

STEP 3

STEP 4

SERVES 6

2 tbsp vegetable oil
1 large onion, sliced thinly
1 garlic clove, crushed (optional)
1 kg/2 lb potatoes
175 g/6 oz courgettes (zucchini), trimmed
125 g/4 oz carrots
1/2 tsp ground coriander
60 g/2 oz/1/2 cup mature (sharp) Gouda or Cheddar cheese, grated (optional)
salt and pepper

1 Heat 1 tablespoon of the oil in a large frying pan (skillet), add the onion and garlic, if using, and fry gently until soft, but only barely coloured – about 5 minutes.

2 Grate the potatoes coarsely into a bowl. Grate the courgettes (zucchini) and carrots, and mix into the potatoes with the coriander and seasoning until evenly mixed, then add the fried onions.

3 Heat the remaining oil in the frying pan (skillet), add the potato mixture and cook gently, stirring occasionally, for about 5 minutes. Flatten down into a cake and cook gently until browned underneath and almost cooked through – about 6–8 minutes.

4 Sprinkle the top of the potato cake with the grated cheese, if using, and place under a preheated moderate grill (broiler) for about 5 minutes or until lightly browned and cooked through.

5 Loosen the potato cake with a large palette knife (spatula) and slip it carefully on to a plate. Leave until cold, then cover with clingfilm (plastic wrap) or foil and chill until required. Serve cut into wedges.

ALTERNATIVES

This also makes a delicious vegetable accompaniment to any main course dish. Other vegetables can be used – parsnips, celeriac, leeks and fennel, for example.

STEP 1

STEP 3

STEP 4

STEP 5

RUSTIC CHEESE SCONES WITH CASHEW NUTS

Two kinds of flour, spring onions (scallions), chopped cashew nuts and cheese are baked into a scone bar to break off as required.

MAKES 8–10

175 g/6 oz/1½ cups self-raising flour
175 g/6 oz/1½ cups granary flour
½ tsp baking powder
pinch of salt
90 g/3 oz/⅓ cup butter or margarine
60 g/2 oz/½ cup cashew nut kernels, chopped
4 spring onions (scallions), trimmed and thinly sliced
3 tbsp freshly grated Parmesan cheese or 90 g/3 oz/¾ cup mature (sharp) Cheddar cheese, grated
1 egg, beaten
about 120 ml/4 fl oz/½ cup milk
1 tsp lemon juice
1 tbsp sesame seeds

1 Sift the white flour into a bowl and mix in the granary flour, baking powder and salt. Rub in the fat until the mixture resembles fine breadcrumbs.

2 Stir in the nuts and spring onions (scallions) followed by the cheese.

3 Add the egg and enough of the milk mixed with the lemon juice to mix to a soft but pliable dough. Turn on to a floured work surface (counter) and knead lightly until smooth.

4 Shape the dough into an oblong bar about 2.5 cm/1 inch thick and 10 cm/4 inches wide. Transfer to a well-floured baking sheet.

5 Mark the bar into 8 or 10 slices with the back of a knife, then brush lightly with milk or water and sprinkle liberally with the sesame seeds.

6 Bake in a preheated oven at 220°C/425°F/Gas Mark 7 for 20–25 minutes, or until well risen, golden brown and firm to the touch. Transfer to a wire rack to cool. When cold, wrap in foil for transporting, or until ready to serve, broken or cut into slices.

FREEZING

The scones may be frozen for up to 2 months.

STEP 3

STEP 4

STEP 5

STEP 6

FRUITS OF THE FOREST CHEESECAKE MOUSSE

Red wine jelly with fruits of the forest set in a layer over a cheesecake mousse in a loaf tin (pan) to turn out and serve cut into slices.

SERVES 6–8

1¹/₂ tsp powdered gelatine
4 tbsp water
2 tbsp caster (superfine) sugar
150 ml/¹/₄ pint/²/₃ cup red wine
250 g/8 oz/1³/₄ cups frozen fruits of the
forest (raspberries, blackberries,
redcurrants, blackcurrants), just thawed

CHEESECAKE LAYER:
500 g/1 lb/2 cups natural fromage frais
200 g/7 oz/scant 1 cup light cream cheese
finely grated rind of 1 lemon
finely grated rind of ¹/₂ orange
1 egg
60 g/2 oz/¹/₄ cup caster (superfine) sugar
1 tbsp lemon juice
1 tbsp powdered gelatine
3 tbsp water

TO DECORATE (OPTIONAL):
whipped cream
fresh raspberries and/or blackberries

1 Line a 23 × 12 cm/9 × 5 inch loaf tin (pan) with a double layer of food wrap (plastic wrap).

2 Dissolve the gelatine in the water either in a microwave oven set on Medium Power for 40 seconds or in a basin over a pan of gently simmering water. Leave to cool slightly, stir in the sugar and then mix into the red wine.

3 Pour a thin (about 5 mm/¹/₄ inch) layer of the wine jelly into the prepared tin (pan) and leave until just set. Add the fruits and any juice to the remaining jelly and spoon over the set layer, arranging the fruits attractively. Chill until set.

4 To make the cheesecake layer, beat the fromage frais, cream cheese and fruit rinds together until smooth. Put the egg, sugar and lemon juice into a heatproof bowl over a pan of simmering water. Cook gently, stirring continuously until thickened sufficiently to coat the back of the spoon. Remove from the heat.

5 Dissolve the gelatine in the water and stir into the lemon mixture, then fold this through the cheese mixture. Pour over the set jelly and chill, preferably overnight, until very firm.

6 To serve, turn out carefully and remove the food wrap (plastic wrap). Decorate with whipped cream and raspberries if liked.

STEP 2

STEP 3

STEP 4

STEP 6

FLORENTINE TWISTS

These famous and delicious Florentine biscuits (cookies) are twisted into curls or cones as they are removed from the baking sheets and then just the ends are dipped in chocolate.

MAKES ABOUT 20

90 g/3 oz/¹⁄₃ cup butter
125 g/4 oz/¹⁄₂ cup caster (superfine) sugar
60 g/2 oz/¹⁄₂ cup blanched or flaked (slivered) almonds, chopped roughly
30 g/1 oz/3 tbsp raisins, chopped
45 g/1¹⁄₂ oz/¹⁄₄ cup chopped mixed peel
45 g/1¹⁄₂ oz/scant ¹⁄₄ cup glacé (candied) cherries, chopped
30 g/1 oz/3 tbsp dried apricots, chopped finely
finely grated rind of ¹⁄₂ lemon or ¹⁄₂ small orange
about 125 g/4 oz/4 squares dark or white chocolate

1 Line 2–3 baking sheets with non-stick baking parchment; and grease 4–6 cream horn tins (moulds) or a fairly thin rolling pin, or wooden spoon handles.

2 Melt the butter and sugar together gently in a saucepan and then bring to the boil for 1 minute. Remove the pan from the heat and stir in all the remaining ingredients, except the chocolate. Leave to cool.

3 Put heaped teaspoonfuls of the mixture on to the baking sheets, keeping them well apart, only 3–4 per sheet, and flatten slightly.

4 Bake in a preheated oven at 180°C/350°F/Gas Mark 4 for 10–12 minutes, or until golden brown. Leave to cool until they begin to firm up. As they cool, press the edges back to form a neat shape. Remove each one carefully with a palette knife (spatula) and wrap quickly around a cream horn tin (mould), or lay over the rolling pin or spoon handles. If they become too firm to bend, return to the oven briefly to soften again.

5 Leave until cold and crisp and then slip carefully off the horn tins (moulds) or remove from the rolling pin or spoons.

6 Melt the chocolate in a heatproof bowl over a saucepan of hot water, or in a microwave oven set on Full Power for about 45 seconds, and stir until smooth. Either dip the end of each Florentine twist into the chocolate or, using a pastry brush, paint chocolate to come about halfway up the twist. As the chocolate sets, it can be marked into wavy lines with a fork. Leave to set.

CHAPTER FIVE

A Teenage Picnic

Young people seem to be continually on the move, always doing something or going somewhere, and they are always hungry. They find their entertainment in many ways; it may be playing or watching sport, a cycle ride or trip to an amusement park, or more simply just 'going out for the day – but please could we have some food'!

Forks, fingers and paper plates are the order of the day with bottles or cans of soft drinks to accompany a menu which should have plenty of choice to cater for all fads and fancies, as well as healthy appetites. If any food containers as well as the paperware can be discarded after the picnic, so much the better (use large margarine and yogurt cartons with airtight lids, for example) – simply provide a couple of bin bags for disposal of the rubbish.

Such food as crudités, small nutburgers and slices of pie are excellent as they are easy to eat and filling as well as tasty. If salad is included this can be put into individual bowls, and other items can be added at will. The general rule is that 'bits and pieces' in small amounts go down best of all, and allow for continual replenishments to satisfy those healthy appetites.

Opposite: Some simple, filling food and a suitable setting are all you need for an impromptu picnic.

STEP 1

STEP 2

STEP 4

STEP 6

VERONICA SALAD

A salad of strips of cooked chicken with grapes, celery and hard-boiled (hard-cooked) eggs in a lightly curried, minty dressing garnished with chicory (endive) and grapes.

SERVES 6

4 boneless chicken breasts, trimmed
2 tbsp olive oil
1 tbsp sunflower or vegetable oil
1–2 garlic cloves, crushed
1 onion, chopped finely
2 tbsp chopped fresh mint
4 green celery sticks
175 g/6 oz/1½ cups black grapes,
   preferably seedless
125 g/4 oz/1 cup large white (green)
   seedless grapes
30 g/1 oz/2 tbsp butter or margarine
1 tbsp plain (all-purpose) flour
½ tsp curry powder
3 tbsp white wine or stock
5 tbsp milk
2 tbsp natural fromage frais
2 tbsp mayonnaise or salad cream
1 head chicory (endive)
2 hard-boiled (hard-cooked) eggs
salt and pepper

1 Cut the chicken into narrow strips, removing any skin and gristle. Heat the oils in a frying pan (skillet), add the garlic and chicken and fry gently until well sealed. Add the onion and continue to fry until both the chicken and onion are tender.

2 Stir in the mint and plenty of seasoning. Drain off the oil and any juices immediately and put the chicken mixture into a bowl. Leave until cold.

3 Cut the celery into narrow slanting slices. Add to the chicken.

4 Reserve a few whole black grapes for garnish. If they are large or contain pips (seeds), cut the rest in half, remove any pips (seeds) and then add to the salad with the white (green) grapes.

5 Melt the fat in a pan, stir in the flour and curry powder and cook for 1–2 minutes. Add the wine and milk and bring to the boil, simmering until thick. Remove from the heat, season well, and stir in the fromage frais. Cover with clingfilm (plastic wrap) and leave until cold.

6 Add the mayonnaise or salad cream to the sauce and add to the chicken mixture, tossing evenly. Turn into a serving dish. Cut the chicory (endive) leaves into lengths of 5 cm/ 2 inches and arrange around the edge of the salad with the reserved grapes and quarters of hard-boiled (hard-cooked) egg. Cover and chill until needed.

STEP 1

STEP 2

STEP 3

STEP 4

NUTBURGERS WITH CHEESE

A delicious mixture of chopped nuts, onion, garlic, herbs, carrot and Parmesan cheese shaped into small balls, dipped in egg and crumbs to fry and serve cold.

MAKES 12

1 onion, finely chopped
1 garlic clove, crushed
1 tbsp olive oil
30 g/1 oz/¼ cup plain (all-purpose) flour
120 ml/4 fl oz/½ cup vegetable stock or milk
250 g/8 oz/2 cups chopped mixed nuts (including cashews, almonds, hazelnuts and walnuts)
60 g/2 oz/1 cup fresh breadcrumbs
2 carrots, coarsely grated
1 tbsp chopped fresh parsley
1 tbsp dried thyme
2 tbsp grated Parmesan cheese
1 tbsp lemon juice
1 tsp vegetable extract
1 egg, beaten
dried breadcrumbs
oil for deep-frying (optional)
mixed salad leaves (greens) to serve
salt and pepper

1 Fry the onion and garlic gently in the oil until soft. Stir in the flour and cook for 1–2 minutes. Add the stock or milk gradually and bring to the boil.

2 Remove from the heat and stir in the nuts, breadcrumbs, carrots, herbs, Parmesan cheese, lemon juice,

vegetable extract and seasoning. Leave until cold.

3 Divide the mixture into 12 and roll into even-sized balls.

4 Dip each piece first in beaten egg and then coat in breadcrumbs.

5 Place on a well greased baking sheet and bake in a preheated oven at 180°C/350°F/Gas Mark 4 for about 20 minutes, or until lightly browned and crisp. Alternatively, deep-fry in oil heated to 180°C/350°F for 3–4 minutes until golden brown. The oil is at the correct temperature for deep-frying when a cube of bread browns in it in 30 seconds.

6 Drain on crumpled paper towels and, when cold, arrange on a bed of salad leaves (greens). Cover with clingfilm (plastic wrap) or foil to transport.

VARIATION

These nutburgers can be made into miniature bite-sized balls if preferred, and they make excellent cocktail snacks.

POACHER'S PLAIT

An elegant puff or shortcrust (plain) pastry plait filled with a mixture of sausage meat, bacon, onion, mushrooms and sage to serve cut in slices, to eat with a fork or in your fingers.

STEP 2

STEP 3

STEP 4

STEP 4

SERVES 4–6

PASTRY:
250 g/8 oz/2 cups plain (all-purpose) flour
pinch of salt
60 g/2 oz/¼ cup lard or white shortening
60 g/2 oz/¼ cup butter or block margarine
cold water to mix
beaten egg or top of the milk to glaze
OR 350 g/12 oz puff pastry

FILLING:
500 g/1 lb pork sausage meat
175 g/6 oz/¾ cup lean bacon, derinded and
   chopped
1 onion, chopped finely
1 garlic clove, crushed
90 g/3 oz/1 cup mushrooms, chopped
1 tsp chopped fresh sage or ½ tsp dried sage
salt and pepper

1 To make the pastry, sift the flour and salt into a bowl and rub in the fat until the mixture resembles fine breadcrumbs. Add sufficient water to mix to a pliable dough. Knead lightly, then wrap in foil and chill.

2 To make the filling, combine the sausage meat, bacon, onion, garlic, mushrooms, sage, a little salt and plenty of pepper until evenly mixed.

3 Roll out the pastry on a lightly floured work surface (counter) to a 30 cm/12 inch square and place the sausage meat mixture in a block evenly down the centre, leaving a 2.5 cm/1 inch margin at the top and base. Make cuts at 2.5 cm/1 inch intervals down both sides of the pastry to within 4 cm/1½ inches of the filling.

4 Fold the top and bottom ends up over the filling and then cover the filling with alternate strips of pastry, first from one side and then the other, to make a plait.

5 Transfer the finished plait carefully to a lightly greased or dampened baking sheet and glaze thoroughly with beaten egg or milk.

6 Bake in a preheated oven at 220°C/425°F/Gas Mark 7 for 20 minutes, then reduce the temperature to 180°C/350°F/Gas Mark 4 and bake for a further 30–40 minutes until golden brown and crisp. Leave to cool, then wrap in foil and chill until ready to transport. Serve cut into slices.

CRUDITES WITH DIPS

Crunchy fresh vegetables, tortilla chips and snacks served with three very different dips are easy to dunk and munch. Transport the dips in small bowls covered with clingfilm (plastic wrap) and foil.

STEP 1

SERVES 6

¹/₄ cucumber
2–3 carrots
3 celery sticks
1 green (bell) pepper, halved, cored and
    deseeded
¹/₂ small cauliflower or head broccoli
1 bunch radishes, trimmed
1 × 250 g/8 oz packet tortilla chips
1 packet breadsticks, about 30

CURRIED DIP:
2 hard-boiled (hard-cooked) eggs, grated or
    chopped finely
4 tbsp natural fromage frais
2 tbsp thick mayonnaise
1 garlic clove, crushed
1 tsp curry powder
good pinch of ground mixed spice (apple
    pie spice)
salt and pepper

GARLIC CHEESE DIP:
200 g/7 oz/scant 1 cup light cream cheese
2 garlic cloves, crushed
2–3 tsp lemon or lime juice
4 spring onions (scallions), trimmed and
    chopped finely

SMOKED MACKEREL DIP:
1 tbsp very finely chopped onion

175 g/6 oz/³/₄ cup smoked mackerel fillet,
    skinned and flaked
finely grated rind of ¹/₄–¹/₂ lemon
2 tsp lemon juice
4 tbsp natural fromage frais or soured cream
1 tbsp chopped fresh parsley

1 Cut the cucumber, carrots and celery into sticks about 5 cm/2 inches long. Cut the (bell) pepper into strips and divide the cauliflower or broccoli into small florets. Put each vegetable separately into a small plastic bag for transportation.

2 To make the Curried Dip, combine all the ingredients, and season to taste.

3 To make the Garlic Cheese Dip, combine all the ingredients and season to taste.

4 To make the Smoked Mackerel Dip, blend all the ingredients together until well mixed and season to taste with salt and pepper.

5 To serve, stand the bowls of dips in the centre of a large platter and arrange the vegetables, tortilla chips and breadsticks around the bowls.

STEP 2

STEP 3

STEP 4

STEP 1

STEP 3

STEP 4

STEP 5

BANANA PICNIC LOAF

Mashed bananas with dried apricots or prunes and nuts are made into a delicious teabread to be cut into slices or fingers and eaten either plain or with butter.

MAKES 12 SLICES

175 g/6 oz/.1 cup light soft brown sugar
125 g/4 oz/¹/₂ cup butter or margarine
2 eggs
250 g/8 oz peeled ripe bananas (2–3 bananas)
grated rind of 1 lemon
2 tsp lemon juice
250 g/8 oz/2 cups self-raising flour
¹/₂ tsp ground cinnamon
¹/₄ tsp bicarbonate of soda (baking soda)
90 g/3 oz/¹/₂ cup no-need-to-soak dried apricots or prunes, chopped
60 g/2 oz/¹/₂ cup walnut pieces, roughly chopped
sifted icing (confectioners') sugar for dredging

1 Grease and line a 23 × 12 cm/9 × 5 inch loaf tin (pan) with greased greaseproof paper or non-stick baking parchment.

2 Cream the sugar and fat together until light and fluffy and pale in colour. Beat in the eggs, one at a time.

3 Mash the bananas with the lemon rind and juice, and beat into the cake mixture.

4 Sift the flour, cinnamon and bicarbonate of soda (baking soda) together and fold evenly into the cake mixture, followed by the chopped apricots or prunes and walnuts.

5 Turn into the tin (pan), level the top and bake in a preheated oven at 180°C/350°F/Gas Mark 4 for about 50 minutes or until firm to the touch and a skewer inserted in the loaf comes out clean. Leave to cool in the tin (pan) for 10 minutes, then turn out on to a wire rack and leave to cool completely.

6 Before transporting, remove the paper from around the cake, sprinkle the top with sifted icing (confectioners') sugar and wrap in foil to carry. Serve cut into slices or wedges.

FREEZING

This cake may be frozen for up to 3 months.

STEP 3

STEP 4

STEP 5

STEP 6

BELGIAN APRICOT TORTE

An unusual type of shortbread dough flavoured with orange and lemon rind which is grated into the tin (pan) with a rich apricot mixture in the centre. When cooked, it is dredged heavily with icing (confectioners') sugar and cut into wedges to serve.

MAKES 8–10

175 g/6 oz/³/₄ cup butter
60 g/2 oz/¹/₄ cup caster (superfine) sugar
1¹/₂ tbsp oil
¹/₂ tsp vanilla flavouring (extract)
1 egg, beaten
350 g/12 oz/3 cups plain (all-purpose) flour
1¹/₂ tsp baking powder
grated rind of 1 lemon
grated rind of 1 orange
175 g/6 oz/¹/₂ cup apricot jam
90 g/3 oz/¹/₂ cup no-need-to-soak dried apricots, chopped finely
icing (confectioners') sugar for dredging

1 Line an 18–20 cm/7–8 inch round cake tin (pan) with non-stick baking parchment or with greased greaseproof paper.

2 Cream the butter until soft then beat in the sugar and continue until light and fluffy. Beat in the oil, then add the vanilla flavouring (extract) and egg and beat well.

3 Sift the flour with the baking powder and gradually work into the creamed mixture with the grated lemon and orange rinds. Knead together

as for a shortbread dough. Divide the dough in half and coarsely grate one portion of it into the tin (pan) so it covers the base evenly.

4 Beat the jam until smooth then beat in the chopped apricots. Spread the apricot mixture evenly over the dough, taking it right to the edges.

5 Grate the remaining dough evenly over the jam and cook in a preheated oven at 150°C/300°F/Gas Mark 2 for about 1–1¹/₄ hours or until lightly browned and just firm. Remove from the oven and leave until cold.

6 Remove the torte from the tin (pan) and strip off the paper, then dredge heavily with sifted icing (confectioners') sugar. Either wrap in foil or place in an airtight plastic container to transport.

FREEZING

This cake can successfully be frozen for up to 3 months. Add the icing (confectioners') sugar when the cake has thawed. It will keep for at least a week in the refrigerator.

ORGANIZING A PICNIC

COOKED SALAD DRESSING

For those who like salad dressing rather than mayonnaise, this is an easy way to produce a delicious dressing. It will keep in an airtight container in the refrigerator for about 5 days.

1¼ level tbsp plain (all-purpose) flour
1½ tsp caster (superfine) sugar
1 tsp dried mustard powder
salt and white pepper
6 tbsp milk
30 g/1 oz/2 tbsp butter
1 egg, beaten
3–4 tbsp wine or tarragon vinegar
4 tbsp sunflower or vegetable oil

1. Mix together the flour, sugar, mustard and seasonings and stir in the milk gradually until smoothly blended.
2. Bring slowly to the boil, stirring all the time and simmer for 1 minute.
3. Remove from the heat and cool slightly, then beat in the butter until melted, followed by the egg. Return to a low heat and cook to just below boiling point, stirring continuously. Do not allow to boil or it may curdle.
4. Remove from the heat and beat in the vinegar gradually to taste, followed by the oil. Adjust the seasonings. Cover and leave to cool. Transfer to an airtight container and chill.

THE PERFECT PICNIC

A picnic can vary from a simple and impromptu affair, to a well-organized and thoughtfully planned outing. The occasion can vary: you might take a picnic to a sporting event, such as a cricket match or baseball game, to save having to find food when you get there, and to give an informal outing a sense of occasion. At the other end of the scale, you might organize a truly stylish, sophisticated and elegant picnic, which includes a proper table set with china, silver and glass, either as an event in its own right, held in your garden as an alternative to a dinner party, or to accompany a visit to the races, the opera, or perhaps to an open-air theatre. But whatever the occasion or style of the picnic, the pleasure of eating outdoors is always the same, and people's appetites and their appreciation of the food are always greatly enhanced by the fresh air and the unusual setting for a meal.

The location

When you have time to plan your picnic, do try to pick a pretty place with a certain amount of shade, reasonably level ground (particularly if you are taking a portable table) and some shelter, especially if you are on the beach, as even a light breeze can blow sand into your food. Many people like to find a tree, hedge, or similar landmark, rather than use an open spot in the middle of a field, particularly if you need shelter from the sun or wind.

Packing for the picnic

With a little thought and care, most food can be packed so that it arrives fresh and appetizing at its destination. Throughout this book you will find advice on how best to transport the finished dishes. However, if there is a bumpy drive to the venue, even more than the usual care will be needed with the packing.

Large picnic hampers or rigid boxes are essential when elegant picnics are to be transported, and often the glass and china need even more careful packaging than the food itself! Beware of using newspaper, as the ink can rub off on to your best china and glass, and make everything look grubby. Use brown paper or tissue paper first, and then newspaper or bubblewrap to cushion it further. If you are taking tea towels (dish cloths) and napkins, they can be put to good use by being wrapped around precious items, or used to fill a gap in the packing.

Remember to pack all the other essentials as well as the food and basic crockery. There is nothing worse than going to a lot of trouble with the food, and then arriving to find you have forgotten the condiments, the bread knife or, most important, the corkscrew!

Finally, always take some spare plastic bin liners and clear up completely when the picnic is finished. Take all your litter home to dispose of safely and properly.

The impromptu picnic

Even if your picnic is a last-minute affair, brought about by an unexpected hot and sunny day when a trip to the beach or the riverside suddenly becomes an excellent idea, the food can still be imaginative and delicious. Choose food that can be quickly prepared, that is suitable to eat with the fingers or possibly a fork, and that can be casually packed in foil or plastic containers which can also act as serving dishes. Choose food that will pack easily, so that it arrives intact and still looking its best.

The only accessories necessary for an informal picnic are perhaps paper plates, the odd paper napkin or some kitchen roll, plastic or paper cups or mugs for the ever essential flask of coffee, and a corkscrew if you are taking wine.

PLANNING THE MENU

If possible, a selection of food is best for a picnic, as appetites are always more healthy in 'the great outdoors' and even the most modest of eaters seem to consume enormous amounts of food. Having a selection of food will also help you to avoid any food dislikes or allergies and cater for all tastes, especially if some of the guests are unknown to you. You should in any case always cater for non-fish eaters, vegetarians and so on, and provide plenty of salads and simple food for those who prefer to eat lightly.

For impromptu picnics, sandwiches and rolls are excellent, as they can be assembled quickly, either before you leave, or at the picnic site, when people can choose their own combination of bread and filling. Most store cupboards and refrigerators will reveal something suitable for sandwich fillings, and if you have time, you could even take the opportunity to create something really special in addition to the classic standbys such as eggs, cheese and cold meat. You could even pick up freshly baked bread and rolls on the way to the picnic, especially as there are nearly always some shops open, wherever you are and whatever the day of the week.

Take salad ingredients cut into chunky pieces; carrots, cucumber, celery and courgettes (zucchini) are ideal, and so are the small hearty little gem type of lettuce, as the tiny leaves are strong enough to use for scooping up dips. Salad dressings can easily be taken separately in screw-top containers for dunking or spooning into a salad sandwich. Unless you are eating quite near to your home, it is better to add the dressing to a salad when you actually arrive and set up the picnic, as the dressing may make the salad soggy if left for too long.

Something sweet to finish off a picnic is always popular, but it needn't be an elaborate dessert; it can just as easily be fresh fruit, cakes and cookies, although pies and tarts always go down well. Consider taking individual yogurts, ice creams or sorbets, or even a frozen gâteau, if you have a freezer box to keep them in while the savoury food is being eaten.

Something to drink is essential and having a freezer box will definitely be an advantage. Sparkling drinks may get over-fizzed up if the trip is bumpy, so be very cautious when opening these, but wines, soft drinks, fruit juices and so on all travel well. Take some bottled water as well, as the drinks always seem to run out!

FRENCH DRESSING

The amount of olive oil used may be varied to suit your taste. Once made, store in a bottle or airtight container and keep in a cool place for up to 10 days. Shake vigorously before each use.

4 tbsp olive oil
4 tbsp sunflower, corn or
   vegetable oil
1 tbsp lemon juice (fresh or
   bottled)
salt and pepper
$1/2$ tsp dried mustard powder
$1/2$ tsp caster (superfine) sugar
1 garlic clove, crushed

1. Put all the ingredients either into a screw-top jar and shake vigorously until completely emulsified; or place in a bowl and whisk thoroughly until emulsified.
2. Taste and adjust the seasonings and store.

Variations:
Use a flavoured vinegar such as tarragon; or add 1–2 level tablespoons freshly chopped mixed herbs or one single herb; or add 2–3 tablespoons sieved (strained) raspberries, blackberries or blackcurrants for a fruit vinaigrette.

MAYONNAISE

Mayonnaise is not as difficult to make as it is often thought to be, but it is essential that all the ingredients are at room temperature before you start – chilled ingredients make curdling much more likely. The flavour can be varied widely by using a flavoured vinegar in place of wine or cider vinegar, and many flavourings can be added for variations. Once made, pack in a plastic, glass or other container with a secure lid and chill until required. It will keep in the refrigerator for about a week in prime condition. Use a fairly mild oil, but if you want to use olive oil, it is best to use only half olive and the remainder a lighter flavoured oil.

2 egg yolks
about 1 tbsp white wine
    vinegar or lemon juice
1/2 tsp made mustard
300 ml/1/2 pint/1 1/4 cups oil
    (vegetable, sunflower or
    olive oil)
salt and pepper
good pinch of caster (superfine)
    sugar

1. Put the egg yolks into a bowl with 1 teaspoon of the vinegar or lemon juice and the mustard and beat until thoroughly blended, using either a balloon whisk or hand-held electric whisk.
2. Whisk in the oil a drop at a time, definitely no faster, until

PACKING AND TRANSPORTING THE FOOD

Packing and transporting a picnic has been made much easier thanks to the huge range of rigid plastic and other containers with securely fitting lids that is now available. Along with clingfilm (plastic wrap) and foil, it is possible to transport almost anything, although some kinds of food will inevitably travel better than others. Lids and coverings are also important, for wherever you choose to picnic, a number of flies or wasps are almost certain to join you!

Foil is best for closely wrapping such things as meat, pastry items, pâtés, etc, but if the food is at all acidic this may cause pitting to the foil, and a layer of food wrap or greaseproof paper (baking parchment) should be used first, under the foil. If it is a food with a high-fat content, such as cheese, you should use a suitable food wrap and not just ordinary clingfilm (plastic wrap) for wrapping. Even rolls and sandwiches will arrive as if they have been freshly made when they are wrapped properly.

One or more good, sturdy insulated 'cold' boxes or picnic baskets will of course help greatly with the transporting of the food. Obviously begin by placing the heavier items at the bottom, but also try to put the desserts, fruit and sweet food there, so it can be unpacked and used more or less in the order it is to be eaten. Always stand up anything that might seep if it tipped over, wedging it between other items. It may be an idea to carry chilled wines, beers and other drinks in a separate cold box, as often these are required first and it will avoid

turning the food upside-down in the haste to find the drinks! It also means that the picnickers can enjoy a leisurely drink before the food is unpacked and laid out, which will ensure that your picnic is a civilized affair.

Individual insulated 'cold' bags or coolers, which can be used on a dinner table, are ideal for keeping wine or beer cool once opened. If you are picnicking by a river, take a net so the bottles can safely be dangled into the water for cooling.

Foods that do not have to be kept cool can be packed into shopping or carrier bags or boxes to stand upright in the back or boot of the car. It is a good idea to place small cardboard boxes inside larger bags, to help everything to stay upright when the bag is picked up. Don't pack the chilled food until the last minute – and don't forget to add the ice blocks to insulated boxes before you close the lids!

INCLEMENT WEATHER

When the weather is likely to be less than warm and sunny, take full advantage of the wide range of thermos and insulated flasks available. Many such flasks have wide necks, so it is quite easy to take a simple stew or casserole in one flask and hot cooked rice in another; and of course always take plenty of hot soup, coffee, tea and hot chocolate. Hot sausages can successfully be packed into thermos flasks, but alternatively they can be securely wrapped in foil, along with baked jacket potatoes, garlic bread, rolls etc., and stacked into an insulated box. This is usually used for keeping things cold but, like thermos flasks, is just as good at keeping things hot. Certain types of the ice blocks used for these boxes can be heated up in boiling water and added to the box to keep the heat in. Obviously this will not keep the food warm for hours on end, nor will the food taste its best if kept warm for too long, but the heat will last for several hours – we do this every year when taking a bunch of children on their ponies for a Christmas beach ride to be followed by soup, hot dogs and burgers.

Another idea is to take a portable calor gas stove for a kettle or saucepan of soup, but always be very careful where it is set up for if the wind increases, or if the calor gas stove falls over, it is a dangerous fire hazard. The safest way to set it up is to pile rocks around it, or bury it a few inches into the ground, and not to set it near bushes or trees, nor too near to the car.

OTHER ESSENTIALS

Depending on the type of picnic you are having, you will need one or two thick rugs or blankets to sit on or portable chairs, perhaps a portable table and tablecloth, along with paper napkins or a roll of paper towels. If the ground is a little damp, use a groundsheet under the rugs or the plastic bin liners to be used later for collecting the rubbish.

Whether to use paper, plastic or china plates is your own choice; food always tastes better off china, but of course paper is easier to dispose of and plastic is lighter and safer to carry than china.

Never leave litter behind, as it spoils the site for anyone else who uses it after you, and empty bottles, cans, polythene,

or clingfilm (plastic wrap) can cause immense damage and pain to animals and huge vets' bills to their owners. Plastic bin bags are also good for carrying home the dirty plates, cutlery and containers.

Don't take the best cutlery unless you are dining out in style (and probably will then have someone to help clear up afterwards!), but make sure you have at least one really sharp or serrated knife, condiments, scissors (most useful), a corkscrew and a bottle opener, and a damp cloth carried in a polythene bag with a couple of clean tea towels (dish cloths). It's not as if you are going to do the washing-up, but a clean cloth always comes in handy, particularly if there are small children around, who seem always to be covered in food, sand or dirt!

If you are planning a stylish picnic on a summer's day, it can be nice to take a large parasol, if it can be stuck in the ground, or has its own base that can easily be transported. When you are packing everything into the car, put the chairs, table and rugs in last, so they can be removed first and set up before the food is unpacked.

If you think your guests might feel energetic after eating, take along a frisbee, bats and balls, or just a tennis ball for an impromptu game of rounders or catch. If you are making a day of it, it is often nice to have something to do rather than simply lie around contemplating the remains of the food! And finally, don't forget to take the insect bite cream, and a basic first-aid kit, for if you are well equipped for all eventualities, they will probably not be needed!

about one third of the oil has been added and the mixture begins to thicken.
3. Add another teaspoon of vinegar or lemon juice and then continue to whisk in the oil, but now in a very thin trickle. It must be whisked briskly all the time, and when it begins to really thicken, the oil can be added a little faster.
4. Season to taste with salt, pepper and sugar, and add more vinegar or lemon juice if wished to give the desired flavour. If too thick, whisk in 1–2 tablespoons hot water. Store in an airtight container, in the refrigerator.

Variations:
Curried: add 1–2 teaspoons curry powder and, if liked, 1–2 tablespoons finely chopped mango chutney.

Green: add half a bunch of very finely chopped watercress with 2–3 finely chopped spring onions (scallions) if liked.

Horseradish: add 1–2 tablespoons creamed horseradish, or 2–3 teaspoons horseradish sauce, to the mayonnaise or to taste.

Mustard: add 2–3 tablespoons coarse grain mustard and a pinch of finely grated lemon rind.

Citrus: add the finely grated rind of 1 orange or $1\frac{1}{2}$–2 lemons.

INDEX

HEALTH PROFESSIONAL *and* PATIENT INTERACTION

Ruth Purtilo, PhD, FAPTA
Professor and Director
Ethics Initiative
MGH Institute of Health Professions
Boston, Massachusetts

Amy Haddad, PhD, RN
Director, Center for Health Policy and Ethics, and
the Dr. C.C. and Mabel L. Criss Endowed Chair in the Health Sciences
Creighton University Medical Center
Omaha, Nebraska

SAUNDERS

ELSEVIER

EDITION

7

SAUNDERS
ELSEVIER

11830 Westline Industrial Drive
St. Louis, Missouri 63146

HEALTH PROFESSIONAL AND PATIENT INTERACTION   ISBN: 978-1-4160-2244-2
**Copyright © 2007, 2002, 1996, 1990, 1984, 1978, 1973 by Saunders,
an imprint of Elsevier Inc.**

Notice

Previous editions copyrighted 2002, 1996, 1990, 1984, 1978, 1973

Library of Congress Control Number: 2007921588

Publishing Director: Linda Duncan
Acquisitions Editor: Kathryn Falk
Developmental Editor: Melissa Kuster Deutsch
Publishing Services Manager: Julie Eddy
Project Manager: Laura Loveall
Design Manager: Margaret Reid

Working together to grow
libraries in developing countries

www.elsevier.com | www.bookaid.org | www.sabre.org

ELSEVIER   BOOK AID International   Sabre Foundation

Printed in the United States of America

Last digit is the print number: 9 8 7 6 5 4 3 2 1

HEALTH
PROFESSIONAL

University of
Chester

ARROWE PARK
LIBRARY

This book is to be returned on or before the last date stamped
below. Overdue charges will be incurred by the late return of
books.

With gratitude to the patients, professional colleagues, friends, and students whose stories have enhanced the pages in this book—and enriched our lives.

Ruth and Amy

PREFACE

It is with anticipation that we present this seventh edition of *Health Professional and Patient Interaction* (HPPI). We believe that health care itself is in a period of profound transition. In the midst of change, basic foundations of the health professions become more important than ever. One such foundation is the health professional and patient relationship—the focus of this book.

We attempt in these pages to provide guidance in the complicated and challenging world of daily interactions that occur between health professionals and patients and to provide the tools to establish professional relationships built on respect.

This book should aid students to: (1) enhance critical self-reflection, (2) clarify the dynamics of the health professional and patient relationship, and (3) develop awareness of the larger societal and health care context in which the relationship takes place.

Respect is the thread that weaves together discussions regarding professional and patient encounters in the health care environment. Clarification of health professional and patient values sets the stage for exploring the context of interactions and the unique perspective that the health professional and patient bring to this relationship. HPPI includes resources from the foundational disciplines of the social sciences, humanities, communications, ethics, and current clinical research. The content is designed to apply to the everyday clinical experiences of health professionals.

In this new edition, we continue to direct our focus to themes that cross many professions. A case directed to the therapist, nurse, technologist, or physician is equally relevant to other health professionals as well. Part of the function of this book, therefore, is to show the extent to which the different disciplines share common challenges, opportunities for service, and goals.

In some instances, it is necessary to assign meaning to key terms. We mention three here: (1) *patient*—the recipient of a health service, (2) *clinical education*—the portion of the health professional's formal education that takes place at the type of worksite where he or she will practice, and (3) *clinical experience*—the composite of learning experiences to which a student is exposed.

The names of patients, health professionals, and other persons in the cases are fictitious.

When the last word of a manuscript has been written, its life has just begun. In sharing our ideas with you, the reader, we hope that in turn you will be stimulated to share yours with others, thus making us all more knowledgeable in the exciting venture of human interaction based on respect.

Ruth Purtilo
Amy Haddad

ACKNOWLEDGMENTS

One of the great joys of preparing this seventh edition of *Health Professional and Patient Interaction* has been the opportunity for us to work together in its development—again.

In the years since the sixth edition was released, we have received numerous letters from readers who have offered encouragement, suggestions, and critiques. Furthermore, both of us have discussed issues examined in the book with a large number of health professions students and faculty members around the country and the world. We thank them for the growth we experienced during those encounters. Our colleagues will recognize portions of those discussions that have been incorporated into this seventh edition.

Several persons at Elsevier have been outstanding in their guidance and support. Many people have asked who provided the original drawings, which have appeared consistently since the first edition. For this contribution, we gratefully acknowledge Grant Lashbrook.

We thank Justin Herrick and Rebecca Crowell for their able and efficient assistance in the preparation of this edition. It was a joy to work with them and each other. We also extend our heartfelt thanks to our husbands, Vard and Steve, who encouraged us through this preparation and numerous other projects.

CONTENTS

PART ONE

CREATING A CONTEXT OF RESPECT

As you know from your own life, relationships never take place in a vacuum! They are always challenged by forces that may or may not be in your control. Therefore, as you enter into the pages of this book about the health professional and patient relationship, the first thing we bring to your attention are some features of your personal life, the health care environment, and the larger society that we believe have a profound impact on that relationship.

Chapter 1 begins with a definition and discussion of respect. Respect is so central to a good working relationship between a health professional and a patient that you will meet the concept many times in your journey through this book. We describe how values—your own, those of the health professions and the institutions in which health professionals work, and society's—usually constitute a fertile oasis for respect to take root and grow. However, at times conflicts in these three arenas of value create rough terrain through which you must gingerly pass. Overall, the chapter is optimistic, as are we, about your opportunity to develop, maintain, and help foster respect in the health professions.

In Chapter 2 we direct your attention to some key elements of the organization and institutions of health care: how certain physical environments, laws, regulations, and policies factor into your professional life. This is not a thorough treatment of the institutional dimensions of your practice; rather, we pick areas that we judge to have the most influence on your relationships with patients, their families, and others. We show that respect is "institutionalized" through basic rights and responsibilities of health professionals and patients, and we address the pivotal legal/ethical notion of informed consent, by which you establish your basic contract with a patient.

1

In Chapter 3, the final chapter of Part One, we give you an opportunity to think substantively about the rich diversity of social characteristics that individuals and groups bring to relationships. We ask you to consider ways you can learn to appreciate differences, including those of culture and ethnicity, socioeconomic status, religion, age, and gender, and to show respect for people no matter what characteristics they have.

With these important considerations as a foundation, you will be prepared to proceed to the rest of the book.

RESPECT: THE DIFFERENCE IT MAKES

CHAPTER OBJECTIVES

The student will be able to:
- Give a brief definition of respect
- Describe why respect is so central to the success of the health professional and patient relationship
- Identify three spheres of values that constitute a person's "value system"
- Discuss the reasons why the professions today have become concerned about professionalism
- Distinguish collective professionalism from individual professionalism
- Describe autonomy as a value in modern day Western societies and how it affects decision-making within the health professions
- Discuss how professional values affect a professional who must treat patients whose values differ dramatically from his or her own
- List some values that have been proposed as being shared by all people, including "primary goods"

When I was small, there was a week when the whole country knew that every human life is irreplaceable. It was many years ago, but, as I recall, a child somewhere in the Midwest fell down an abandoned well, and for a week rescue teams worked to bring her out. This was a time before television, and radios were playing everywhere—in the stores, in the buses, even at school. Strangers met in the street and asked each other, "any news?" People of all religions prayed together.

As the rescue effort went on, no one asked if that was the child of a professor down there, the child of a cleaning woman, the child of a wealthy family. Was that child black, white, or yellow? Was that child good or naughty, smart or slow? In that week everyone knew that these things did not matter at all. That the importance of a child's life had nothing to do with those things. A person lost touched us all, diminished us all.[1]

Chances are you do not recall where you first encountered the idea that there is something about human beings that commands our attention and respect, something that goes beyond the differences that sometimes tend to separate us. The physician who wrote the above quote about her childhood experience goes on to say

FIGURE 1-1: Health professional with patient. *(© Getty Images/40111)*

that this experience was important because, as she would learn later, the idea that persons have a basic human dignity deserving of respect is at the heart of the health professional and patient relationship.

To get you started on your exploration of respect as it is expressed in your professional encounters, consider the picture of the health professional and a patient shown in Figure 1-1.

REFLECTIONS

What are the clues in this picture that show that respect, however you define it, is present? Some things we could draw from this simple example include the following:
- She looks like she is inviting the patient to express what she is feeling.
- Her body language says she cares.
- She has not created a physical barrier separating them.

You may see other features of this relationship that suggest the health professional respects her patient.

Whether you are preparing to enter a profession for the first time or are continuing to seek excellence in it through further study, being able to show and receive respect is a key to the satisfaction you will be able to realize over the course of your career as a professional. You might, in fact, think of respect as a linchpin that holds together your professional identity. Without respect for (and from) others, you will almost inevitably find the paths you are choosing in your professional life to be off course.

Fortunately, in this book you will have a chance to reckon with the primacy of respect—for yourself, for patients and their families, and for your professional peers. You will be reminded that you should expect respect from others in their treatment of you. You will have a chance to identify where it can be found in your attitudes, communications, and conduct or where its absence is creating a barrier to effectiveness. You will receive ideas from us (and through discussion of issues in this book, from each other) about how you can find, cultivate, and express respect in your everyday life as a professional.

WHAT IS RESPECT?

Respect comes from the Latin root *respicere*, which means to approach a person, group, idea, or object with regard or esteem.[2] It says, "you matter," "you are worth the trouble." Already one begins to see how tightly respect is woven into our sense of well-being as humans. No matter how extreme our circumstances, we hope that others will not discount our need to "be somebody," that we will be sympathetically accompanied through the most difficult and unlikable or threatening aspects of our struggles. And when we rejoice, we hope others will join us in our celebration of accomplishment. Throughout this book, when the discussion turns to respect between persons, there is an assumption that my respect must be directed toward something very fundamental in the other person, something that warrants my regard. Many writers who have tried to explain that humans have basic worth agree that we share a common essence, which they term *dignity*. Even the ancients, in their myths, described this common essence, a theme also explored in virtually all the world's major religious traditions.[3] The essence often is referred to as the *inherent dignity* of persons to help emphasize that it resides beyond the various physical, social, or psychological characteristics that distinguish us from each other.[4] The respect you show to another person ultimately is a reflection of your willingness to look past positive or negative attributes to the very core of what makes the person human.

The notion of inherent dignity is deeply ingrained into the idea of a profession, and there have been centuries of attempts to fully explain it within the health professions literature, an exploration that continues to this day. A recent document of the American Medical Association placed emphasis on the importance of seeing each patient as a fellow human being and stressed that to accomplish this, the physician must have a concern for humans *as such*.[5] What does the "as such" mean if not that there is a common thread of humanity that warrants basic regard no matter the variations that distinguish us? But because, taken by themselves, respect and dignity are abstract concepts, we will help you look for them in concrete shapes such as the tone of your voice when you address a patient, the adaptation of your pace and body language to meet the needs of a child versus an elderly patient, your trustworthy conduct, your presence during a crisis, and your willingness to work together with a patient's family and other professionals to reach a patient's health-related goal.

In the health care setting, respect is put into action as a response to the fact that patients are vulnerable in ways that do not exist outside of the health care context. Therefore, if you value respect, it is your responsibility to protect patients from exploitation or harm and to advocate for them in ways that will be to their benefit. To help you recognize and cultivate this type of respect, the first opportunity we give you is to examine your own values.

RESPECT AND YOUR VALUES

Values are deeply held attitudes and beliefs we have about the truth, beauty, or worth of a person, object, action, or idea. One criterion of a "true" value is that it has become part of a pattern of a person's life. In other words, values must not only be identified but also embraced and expressed. From what you have read so far you should be able to conclude that health professionals are expected to cultivate personal values that foster respect for themselves, patients, and others. Suppose you say, "Well, I value my freedom to make my own decisions. I value self-confidence, honesty, and efficiency. Are those values consistent with respect?" They most likely are. For example, it is possible that you may honestly and with full self-confidence exercise your autonomy to disagree with a patient's decision to forego your professional advice but still treat the patient with respect.

Taken together, your values constitute what can be called your *value system*. Some values in that system are highly specific to you. Some will be adopted through your cultural and/or professional subgroup. Still others are shared by humans because of our common "human condition." The unique value system for each person consti-tutes his or her idea of "the good life."

Values have their genesis in a variety of sources. We learn our early values from parents and other childhood friends, caregivers, teachers, religious beliefs and tradi-tions, and cultural influences such as TV and the Internet. Values are imparted, taught, reinforced, and internalized. We incorporate many of them into our lives as a personal value system. We also exist in a complex world of bureaucracies and institutions. These influence us too, so that as we mature our values evolve with us.

Personal Values

Personal values are strictly one's own. Most people cherish more than one personal good, or value. Literature provides striking examples of the exception: Ahab braved the high seas relishing the thought of getting revenge on the great white whale, Moby Dick; Sir Lancelot suffered many grave adversities in his relentless quest for the Holy Grail; and, before his change of heart, Ebenezer Scrooge treasured money. The lifestyles of Ahabs, Sir Lancelots, and Scrooges are not the same as those of most individuals. Most people have many personal values, some more clearly defined than others, and go through life trying to realize or balance several values simultaneously.

The process of developing self-consciousness about one's values is the focus of val-ues clarification exercises. Values clarification provides the means for us to discover what values we live by. An individual who is able to identify his or her own values is able to place worth on actions or objects that lead to personally satisfying choices. Conversely, if you are unclear about your values or the connection between values and choices, it is likely that there will be poor decision-making and dissatisfaction.[6]

> ◎ REFLECTIONS
>
> The following values clarification exercise is helpful in identifying personal values and how these values play themselves out in real life.
> - First, make a list of your 10 most important present values in order of importance.
> - Next, compare and contrast your own list of personal values with a peer's values.
> - Then, compare the list of your own highest ranking values with your own behavior.
>   To what degree is your behavior consistent with your stated values? If there is an inconsistency, why?
>   What are you going to do (if anything) to get your stated values and behaviors in closer alignment?

As we suggested, sometimes your personal values will conflict with each other. An example is the case of a person who is excessively obese. Although there are many factors contributing to obesity, consider the obese person who finds security in consuming food. Unfortunately, his habitual eating eventually causes his body to break down, and his physician tells him that he can expect a shortened life span. At this point his basic value of *life itself* is endangered by the competing personal value of *feeling secure*. Because both of these values are essential to good health, treatment often is directed toward helping this person derive security from aspects of life other than eating. Similar examples of clashing values surround challenges related to other life-endangering practices, such as smoking, alcohol and other substance abuse, or lack of exercise or good sleeping habits.

> ◎ REFLECTIONS
>
> Your choice to make a career in the health professions has come from a desire to act on some of your most cherished values. Can you name some personal values that you can recognize as consistent with your commitment to becoming and being a good health professional?

When patients seek your services it is almost always their own personal values that are driving them to do so. They believe rightfully that health professionals are there to help them be relieved of some forms of personal suffering. They value being or getting well. They seek comfort during chronic or life-threatening illness. They want you to help them maintain their value of health and optimize their functioning. Health care is, in fact, concerned primarily with personal values that are addressed through person-to-person relationships. Your professional preparation through the use of this book will include an opportunity to study and think about the challenges your own personal values pose and to identify many that facilitate your success.

Professional Values and Professionalism

Having chosen to become a health professional requires that you embrace values that are consistent with what being a professional means and what professional practice entails. Fortunately, many of these values overlap with your personal values or at least do not come into conflict with them. The word *professional* itself comes from the root *to profess*, or to declare something. When you adopt the values of your profession, as a professing person you are saying something important to society about your place in the community.

Many health professional organizations have articulated basic values that undergird their identity. The values help explain the reasonable expectations that society can count on regarding what that profession promises to do or not do. For example, seven essential values articulated by the American Association of Colleges of Nursing for nurses are altruism, truth, esthetics, equality, freedom, justice, and human dignity.[7] Another example is the list of values developed by the Education Section of the American Physical Therapy Association. In its document, *Professionalism in Physical Therapy: Core Values*, you will find the values of accountability, altruism, compassion and caring, excellence, integrity, professional duty, and social responsibility.[8] These two are just a sample—it is worth your effort to identify the values your own professional organization has generated. You will readily see areas of overlap among the professions and begin to observe a general profile of professional values.

The values arise in part from ongoing discussions of what constitutes a profession, making it special and distinct from other lines of work. Some themes appear over and over. For instance, professions have an organized body of specialized knowledge and skills that are prized by society. This may result in the profession listing the values of professional autonomy, competence, and skill in professional judgment. Society can expect members of a profession to be able to exercise wise judgment consistent with their area of special knowledge and skills and to apply it unsparingly to patient problems. In addition, being a "profession" involves having knowledge and skills that are judged by society to serve some basic human need. Basic need often renders a person or group vulnerable, so a profession's values of altruism and compassion are its promise to treat the patient's vulnerability with due care. Another mark of a profession is that it has a code of ethics to which its members are expected to conform. It is not surprising, then, that some of the professional values observed in the literature focus on ethical ideals of selfless conduct, trustworthiness, and accountability.

In recent years professional organizations have devoted growing attention to the idea of "professionalism;" as you prepare to enter your profession, you will surely encounter it. The initiatives geared to professionalism share the common goal of identifying, protecting, and fostering the appropriate focus of the professional's role in society and what it is that gives meaning to professionals' work. As one book subtitle summarizes it, the goal is to create and sustain "a culture of humanism" in the health professions.[9] The underlying concern is that forces outside of the professions themselves (such as changes in the health care system and pressures from society to conform to its whims) may place undue pressure on professionals.

Professional responsibility is a dominant theme in professionalism. It emphasizes that the professions must be responsive to today's societal changes and demands. At the same time, William Sullivan, in his probing analysis of the role of the professions in today's society, advises the professions to be careful not to lose their own core values in their attempt to mold themselves to society's expectations. More than ever, he notes, they "have become responsible for key public values." It is this responsibility that sets off professionals from other workers. Although professionals are engaged in generating or applying new ideas and technologies, they are all directly pledged to an ethic of public service.[10]

Of course, reflection by the professions on the values they uphold (and why) is by no means an entirely novel phenomenon unique to the present age. Such reflection has been the focus of lively study and debate since the delineation of three traditional professions (law, medicine, and the clergy) during the Middle Ages. Today many still refer to a profession as a "calling" that requires total devotion, specialized knowledge, and extensive academic preparation. From these root terms and interpretations, the professions today are identified as groups whose members have responded to an opportunity to hold a special place in society, differentiated from those who simply hold a job or have an occupation. It is from that long history of reflection that the current emphasis on professionalism finds it historical niche. What is important about the present emphasis on professionalism, as Sullivan and others observe, is that it is a response to a specific set of claims from the public for professional accountability. Their claims derive from society's values and society's beliefs.

Swisher and Page point out that the emphasis on professionalism is what can be called "collective professionalism" because it applies to all members of a professional group.[11] The challenge for you, the individual professional entering today's health care system, is to tailor the guidance from your profession to fit the requirements of your own specific professional practice. As these authors note, this further reflection provides the basis for the necessary step from collective professionalism to individual professionalism.[11] In other words, the task is to incorporate appropriate values of professionalism into your personal value system. It is hoped that this section of the chapter demonstrates that a large part of your professional role requires that you negotiate with society to determine what works for you and to understand which of society's values you welcome as a part of your own value system.

Societal Values

One well-recognized characteristic of "the human condition" is that we, as human beings, organize ourselves into complex interactions as groups of individuals called societies. You belong to many communities within the larger society already. Each subgroup has values that you are aware of and may accept, reject, or question in regard to how they support your attempt to lead a good life.

ⓢ REFLECTIONS

Take a minute to name some of the societal subgroups you are most influenced by such as your extended family, neighborhood, ethnic community, part of the country where you live, school you attend, religious affiliation, and social or civic organizations. Can you name one or two values you have absorbed from your membership in each of these subgroups? If not, where did your values come from other than from these common sources?

In Chapter 3 you have an opportunity to consider in more depth the rich variations and opportunities that our membership in various subgroups affords us. Only in recent years has the richness of diversity been brought to self-consciousness in the professions.

The scope of influences on society's more provincial range of value choices also has expanded greatly in the last few decades due to the information and transportation revolutions. Millions have immediate access to the World Wide Web, radio, and television. We can travel extensively or meet those who do. These broadening circles of access and influence have led some to conclude that we are all indeed members of a global society; to survive, we must come to grips with the common values that will help all lead a good life. As you will see in Chapter 9, patients have taken advantage of the World Wide Web, TV commercials, and other means of data gathering to gain clinical information not previously available to them.

In spite of the increasing exposure to new and ever-expanding sources of values, some dimensions of our humanity seem to cut a wide swath across cultural, ethnic, religious, and other subgroups. With our ability to communicate and reflect, humans value being able to share their thoughts and ideas with each other. Humans are technological beings who value the use of tools to assist in the completion of daily tasks. We are historical beings who value building cultures based on the wisdom, mistakes, and knowledge of those who lived before us. We are political beings who value our laws that govern interaction, and aesthetic beings who create nonfunctional objects and value them for their beauty alone. Humans also perform rituals and are ethical beings, able to distinguish between right and wrong and to adjust behavior accordingly.[12] Human beings are social beings and therefore rarely find satisfaction outside the social context of living in a society.

Because the individual identifies so strongly with his or her societal affiliation, and in some places and times is identified entirely by it, it is not surprising that some values seem to be held in common by most or all of humanity. However, it is difficult to find full agreement beyond the most general values. Literary and philosophical writings are replete with suggestions.

◎ REFLECTIONS

Consider whether you believe the following are universally held societal values:
- Protection of human life
- Rights and liberties
- Having power and opportunities
- Income and wealth
- Self-respect
- Health and vigor
- Intelligence and imagination
- Character traits such as courage, compassion, a desire to do justice, honesty
- Faith and hope
- Love
- Autonomy, having say-so, self-governance

All of these values have been proposed to be universal, though the list of such values is much longer.

The laws of most societies seem to be organized on the principle that *human life* itself is a basic value and therefore ought to be protected and nourished. Philosophers are an ongoing source of reflection on societal values. For instance, John Rawls, one of the most influential American philosophers of the 20th century, argued that humans value several primary goods. *Social* primary goods include *rights, liberties, powers, opportunities, income, wealth,* and *self-respect.* (Self-respect is necessary for a person to have a sure conviction that his or her life plan is worth carrying out or capable of being fulfilled.) The realization of these goods is at least partially determined by the structure of society itself. *Natural* primary goods, also partly determined by societal structures but not directly under their control, include *health, vigor, intelligence,* and *imagination.* Together, he says, these social and natural primary goods provide a sort of "index of welfare" for individuals in any society.[13]

Other writers suggest certain character traits as the basic societal values that can produce a good life for the larger community; however, there is dispute over which character traits are the central ones. For instance, in ancient Greek thought, the *cardinal virtues* of temperance, prudence, a desire to do justice, courage, and fortitude (or moral strength to do what is right) were considered central to being able to lead a good life in any societal context. Early Christian thinkers argued that these alone were not sufficient for a good life and that faith in God, hope, and love were crucial. Other world religions and schools of philosophical thought also have contributed their lists.

A good example in modern Western societies of a value that has retained its hold and primacy is the value placed on individual autonomy. In fact, it seems to have a monopoly on our moral attention. At no other time in history has there been such an emphasis on the importance of having control over one's own life, of independent functioning, and of radical self-reliance. Failure to succeed is often interpreted as not trying hard enough to be independent and in control of one's life and of subsequently becoming a burden.

A changing ethnic and cultural milieu in Western societies is calling into question the primacy attributed to individual autonomy. For example, we are learning that the social value placed on individual adult autonomy understandably places an immense burden on persons whose independence has been diminished by illness or injury as well as distorting the opportunity for meaningful relationships in such situations.[14] We also are learning that in many highly developed ethnic, religious, and other subgroups, their decision-making processes involve highly evolved patterns of communal decision-making.[15] Moreover, due to the changing population demographics of the United States, Canada, and Western Europe, these countries are being challenged to adjust their autonomy-laden approaches to incorporate insights from a more diverse society.[16] Of course, there are values other than those of autonomy and conformity to accepted norms that spring from the idiosyncrasies of a given society. Any time a person is placed in a position in which it is impossible to live up to society's expectations and the values it dictates, he or she may experience tremendous anxiety (Figure 1-2).

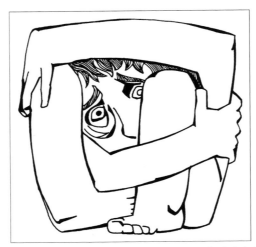

FIGURE 1-2: When a person is placed in a position in which it is impossible to live up to society's expectations, he or she may experience tremendous anxiety and discomfort.

Whatever one's lot in life, the need to be accepted within the societal realm of values influences the well-being of almost everyone.

THE GOOD LIFE AND YOU

In this chapter, you encountered examples of three sets of values—personal, professional, and societal. Their differences have been highlighted, but in everyday life, a person adopts a set of personal values that overlap in part and are harmonious with role-related and the larger society's values. A schematic representation of such a person's value system is shown in Figure 1-3.

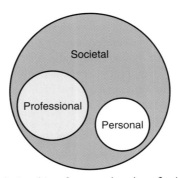

FIGURE 1-3: Relationship of personal and professional societal values.

Here, the person has internalized social and role-derived values so that he or she cannot distinguish them from what is perceived simply as personal preferences. Motivation for doing so usually arises from choosing to live harmoniously in society (and for the health professional, in her or his work role) and experiencing personal benefit from it. One can live harmoniously by the valuing of mundane things such as obedience to traffic and other laws, adherence to practices of etiquette, and willingness to pay taxes. Personal benefits from internalizing societal values may include the opportunity for friendship and collegiality, economic independence, and help in cultivating certain virtues such as courage and compassion. In short, persons need personal values to individualize themselves. Most adhere to role-related and societal values to feel like an accepted part of their society and of humankind. It is possible to say of anyone who lives according to his or her values system, "That person has a good life." However, when a person's value system includes values that help to uphold and further society as well, we say, "That person *leads* a good life."

Of course, not everyone adopts a set of personal values compatible with societal values or even with those of his or her own social or cultural subgroup. Such a person's value system is represented in Figure 1-4.

In the extreme form, this person has not internalized any societal values. Such a person either desires not to live in harmony with society or, more likely, believes that there are no benefits to be derived from doing so. Some examples of people whose values clash with societal values are the hermit, the criminal, and the saint or martyr. The hermit and criminal reject societal values and replace them with their own; the saint or martyr rejects societal values and replaces them with some "higher" set of values.

There are varying degrees to which such persons divorce themselves from societal values. On the one hand, the woman who drives through a red light to make it to her tennis match on time is replacing a societal value of obedience to traffic rules with the personal value of reaching her destination to play that game of tennis. On the other hand, the conscientious objector who performs alternative service is refusing to accept the societal value of engaging in war to protect one's country on the basis of following the antiwar dictates of a higher law. *Most* people experience some such conflict from time to time.

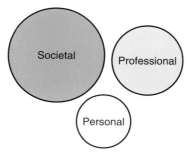

FIGURE 1-4: Fragmented values-in-conflict situation.

This is a serious matter. It is well known that as humans we have a tendency generally not to rock the boat, no matter how unsatisfactory the situation. There is a powerful passage in *Dead Man Walking* when Sister Prejean, the narrator of the book, understands suddenly after hearing a political activist speak that she is going to have to rock the boat, as it were, regarding justice and the poor. The speaker challenged Sister Prejean and the rest of the audience to reflect on their own values and actions.

> What were we to do about such glaring injustices? She knew her facts and I found myself mentally pitting my arguments against her challenge—we were nuns, not social workers, not political. But it's as if she knew what I was thinking. She pointed out that to claim to be apolitical or neutral in the face of such injustices would be, in actuality, to uphold the status quo—a very political position to take, and on the side of the oppressors.[17]

For the health professional, a disconnect can also occur when professional values come into conflict with personal values (or what the professional believes are appropriate societal values). Anytime a professional does not conform to the norms of his or her profession it can become a source of discomfort to the majority who accept the status quo. It requires courage and self-knowledge to stand out as a change agent when professional values do not honor the ultimate values the dissenting professional believes are being compromised. At the same time, as in all situations, the person who dissents from accepted social norms bears the burden of showing why. In the process it may also become clear that the dissent was misplaced.

The ultimate standard by which such conflict can be measured is the extent to which each position honors the widely accepted value in health care that respect for all persons is required, even though a patient's specific values may differ dramatically from one's own. The professional value of respect for persons reminds us that all persons deserve to be treated fairly and in a humane manner.

RESPECT FOR CHANGES IN VALUES

A first step toward respect in any circumstance is to learn more about a person. In your role as a health professional, not all patients will be eager to talk with you about what they consider to be important. However, if they know you are treating them with respect, you will probably be successful in learning what is important to them.

Family and friends, when available, are also good sources. They are usually eager to assist, and an alert health professional will detect clues from casual conversation (e.g., "I'll tell you one thing; the fishing trip just wasn't the same this year without Joe."). Additionally, the patient's clinical record offers information about the patient's social and medical history. All this information may help you understand the patient, even though you may not, in the end, like him or her any better.

⊚ REFLECTIONS

Can you think of types of people whose personal (or societal subgroup's) values differ so radically from your own that you would have difficulty feeling respect for and showing respect to the person?

What avenues do you have open to you to be sure due respect is shown to this person?

In addition to being able to identify one's own and others' values, health professionals must work on the premise that everyone's values change from time to time. Unexpected opportunities, tragedy, and new insights all act as controls in a person's notion of what is considered valuable in life. However, the circumstances that force or enable most people to change their values usually evolve slowly, whereas those that force a patient to do so may appear in a matter of minutes or hours! We discuss this phenomenon in more detail in Chapters 6 and 7. A brief glimpse at the course of one patient's evolving values is illustrated in the following case:

> Daniela Janowski was the star soccer player on her college team at Midtown State College. It came as a terrible surprise when in her mid-twenties she began to experience the debilitating symptoms of multiple sclerosis.
>
> It is 6 years later. She is almost totally unable to walk. Her weight has dropped to 90 pounds from her previous 125. She suffered one period of deep depression. She says that many people pity her, but she now has come to the happy conclusion that she "has much to live for."
>
> ▶ What types of values might Daniela have that would allow her to feel as if there is "much to live for" when so much has radically changed in her life?

The process of reclaiming and replacing values may take weeks, months, or years for any of us. The person who becomes a patient must learn what the illness or injury really means in terms of long-term impairment. Another woman who, like Daniela, had multiple sclerosis told one of the authors that it took her years to stop doing silly things that overstressed her. She said, "It was because I didn't *know* my disease; now I *know* it, like a friend, strange as that may sound. Not knowing was the hardest part. ..."

As we reiterate in later chapters, the success of adjustment and acceptance to inevitable change is also based on the support of family, friends, and health professionals whether it be you who is undergoing inevitable change or patients and others with whom you come into contact. Health professionals can be instrumental in identifying possible new interests for a patient, especially when he or she is attentive to the fact that any person's quality of life is far more than the values he or she may have at the moment. One of the greatest gifts a health professional can offer is to be present as a person "tries on" a new identity with the values that will be fitting for the new situation.

SUMMARY

Respect for others and receiving respect from them are essential ingredients for a successful professional practice. Respect involves both attitudes and behavior that acknowledge your regard for another person's dignity, no matter what his or her attributes and circumstances are.

Our values are determinants of whether we will want and be able to express genuine respect for patients, their families, and other professionals. Some values arise from personal preferences while others become internalized over time through the influences of affiliations and societal forces. Professional values are transmitted through the educational, clinical, and research institutions of health care. You can make good progress on your road to respectful interaction by identifying your own values, by developing a genuine interest in others' values, and by appreciating why both may change over time.

REFERENCES

1. Remen RN: *My grandfather's blessings: stories of strength, refuge and belonging,* New York, 2000, Riverhead Books.
2. *Webster's New Collegiate Dictionary,* Springfield, MA, 1974, G and C Merriam-Webster.
3. Purtilo RB: New respect for respect in ethics education. In Purtilo RB, Jensen GM, Royeen CB, editors: *Educating for moral action: a sourcebook in health and rehabilitation ethics,* Philadelphia, 2005, FA Davis.
4. Kilner JF: Human dignity. In Post SG, editor-in-chief: *Encyclopedia of bioethics,* ed 3, Vol 2, New York, 2004, Thomson, Gale.
5. American Medical Association: *Declaration of professional responsibility: medicine's social contract with humanity* (website): http://www.ama-assn.org/ama/pub/category/7491.html. Accessed December 4, 2001.
6. Brown D, Grace RK: Values in life role choices and outcomes: a conceptual model, *The Career Development Quarterly* 44:211-223, 1996.
7. *Essentials of college and university education for professional nursing, final report,* Washington, DC, 1995, American Association of Colleges of Nursing.
8. American Physical Therapy Association: *Professionalism in physical therapy: consensus document of the American Physical Therapy Association,* Alexandria, VA, 2003, American Physical Therapy Association.
9. Wear D, Bickel J, editors: *Educating for professionalism: creating a culture of humanism in medical education,* Iowa City, 2000, University of Iowa Press.
10. Sullivan M: *Work and integrity: the crisis and promise of professionalism in America,* ed 2, San Francisco, 2005, Jossey-Bass.
11. Swisher LL, Page CG: *Professionalism in physical therapy: history, practice and development,* St Louis, 2005, Elsevier.
12. Adler MJ: *The difference of man and the difference it makes,* ed 2, New York, 1993, Fordham University Press.
13. Rawls J: *A theory of justice,* ed 2, Cambridge, 1971, Belknap Press of Harvard University.
14. Kitay EF: Vulnerability and the moral nature of dependency relations. In *Love's labor: essays on women, equality and dependencies,* New York, 1999, Routledge.
15. Bonder B, Martin L, Miracle A: Negotiating cultural differences in working with clients. In *Culture in clinical care,* Thorofare, NJ, 2002, Slack.
16. Wells SA: An ethic of diversity. In Purtilo RB, Jensen GM, Royeen CB, editors: *Educating for moral action: a sourcebook in health and rehabilitation ethics,* Philadelphia, 2005, FA Davis.
17. Prejean H: *Dead man walking,* New York, 1994, Vintage Books.

RESPECT IN THE INSTITUTIONAL SETTINGS OF HEALTH CARE

CHAPTER OBJECTIVES

The student will be able to:

- Compare the perspectives of people viewing health care from each of Glaser's three realms: individual, institutional, and societal
- List four major forces that have resulted in our present organizational structure of health care
- Compare public- and private-sector relationships and describe why health professional and patient interactions are public-sector relationships
- Compare the characteristics of total institutions and partial institutions of health care
- Identify two aspects of administration that are likely to have a direct impact on the organizational environment in which you work
- List several types of laws, regulations, and policies that have a bearing on how you will practice your profession and what you should be able to expect from the institution in which you work
- Discuss the idea of patient's rights documents and the purposes they are designed to serve
- Describe the basis for and two major components of informed consent

The VA Medical Center was wonderful and exactly what I needed, but, as I was repeatedly told while I was there, "This isn't a hotel. You'll have to work here, but this is a good hospital." I was blessed the day I slammed into the front door and was admitted. Whatever modesty I may have had I should have left at the front door when I was admitted. Over the coming month I would be poked, prodded and felt up like a prom date after drinking too much Sloe Gin.[1]

As you now have begun to see, this book is about your work with people who need your services and how respect can be shown to them in your everyday interactions. In the process of learning what is required for respectful interaction, the organization and institutions of health care must be taken into account, but the individual patient's values and well-being should never be lost in the maze of these other considerations.

Some of you have seen paintings by the French impressionist painter Marc Chagall. His weightless figures hover in space, supported by clouds and celebrated by

FIGURE 2-1: Chagall, Marc (1887-1985) © ARS, NY. *The Journey of the People.* 1968. Oil on canvas, 128 x 205 cm. Private Collection. *(Courtesy Scala/Art Resource, NY.)*

ethereal musicians. The heavenly environment Chagall creates suggests mystery, romance, bliss, and promise (Figure 2-1).

His work speaks to a deeper meaning: our environments always create certain expectations and evoke powerful feelings. They influence our attitudes and conduct in ways that sometimes we do not understand. But in some health care environments, patients may not find bliss or promise. They may experience unfamiliarity and even danger.

Today almost all health care is provided, administered, and managed through institutions. It follows that with rare exceptions every student reading this book will be employed within an institution. All individuals who are acting as a part of an organization (e.g., a health care institution) must take into account the well-being of the institution.

Many times contracts for positions will include promises that one will abide by policies or specific behaviors for the good of the organization. Policies may include details about finances, ethical conduct toward other individuals and institutions, management issues, marketing, and loyalty to the institution. Your professional preparation will also include ways to prepare yourself to abide by specific laws, regulations, and other institutional dimensions of your work. In addition, you will need to know how to respond when conflicts arise because of legitimate claims made on you by the patient and your employing institution. Throughout this book reference is made to how various types of institutional facilities (e.g., nursing homes, industrial or school clinics, institutions for mentally ill persons, and health maintenance settings) affect what you as a health professional will face in your attempt to provide high-quality professional service.

Glaser's Three Realms

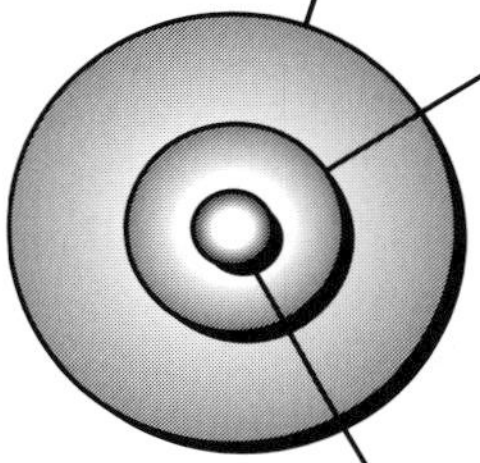

Societal | **The good and virtuous society**

Its values reflect the common good—the overall and long-term good and goodness of society (city, state, country). It attends to the health, vigor, balance, and equity of society's key systems and structures—political, economic, legal, educational, etc.—so that society increasingly is and continues to be an environment in which persons can be born, grow, labor, love, flourish, age, and die as humanely as possible. *Societal ethics deals primarily with the key systems and structures of society through which it achieves its purpose and in which we read its ethical character.*

Institutional | **The good and virtuous institution**

Its values reflect the overall and long-term good and goodness of institutions (families, agencies, corporations). It attends to the health, vigor, balance, and equity of the institution's key systems and structures so that the institution can accomplish its mission, vision, values, and goals while attending to its rights and duties vis-à-vis the individuals who make it up and the larger society in which it exists. *Institutional ethics is concerned primarily with the key systems and structures of an institution through which it achieves its purpose and in which we read its ethical character.*

Individual | **The good and virtuous individual**

Its values reflect the good and goodness of individuals. It attends to the balance and the right relationships among various dimensions of a single individual (spiritual, mental, physical, emotional, etc.) as well as the values that support rights and duties that exist between individuals.

FIGURE 2-2: Glaser's Three Realms.

Glaser maintains that to understand the role of institutions in the health professional's everyday life, you must first recognize that they are situated at the interface of the individual and the larger society. There are, he says, "three realms," each having an impact on the other two (Figure 2-2).[2]

One observation is that institutional policies and practices must respond to societal values but also be responsive to values that guide health professions practice. However, success as health professionals depends not only on interpersonal relationships but also relationships with institutional policies, management, and administration, as well as being able to reckon with the values of the larger society.

The institutional realm of health care is not easy to characterize. It is a complex web of ideas and values. These values are expressed in numerous types of health care facilities whose functions vary widely. Moreover, the institutional organization of health care is not completely a "rational system." Rational systems are oriented expressly to the pursuit of one specific goal and have a highly formalized social structure designed to meet that goal.[3] An example is an airport, where the single goal is to move people and goods from place to place. The institutions of health care are more illustrative of an "open system" in which shifting and sometimes competing interest groups negotiate for their goals to be met. At the same time, there are some silver threads of continuity that lend themselves to generalizations so that you can begin to understand your work environment. You will need to know what it might look like to the patients who enter it, to health professionals who spend their days working in it, and to the larger community that supports it.

What are some key values of institutions? Efficiency of operations is important. In the United States, freedom from undue regulation *(autonomy)* and freedom to compete favorably in marketplace competition *(free enterprise)* are two others. Facilities that focus on underserved populations are driven by considerations of justice.

As you consider the institutional environment, paying attention to Glaser's three realms should help you to identify areas where individual, institutional, and societal values overlap and where they create conflicts that will require your best ethical reasoning, courage to resist inhumane institutional or societal policies, willingness to affirm policies and practices that uphold important professional values, and commitment to implementing strategies of change in your workplace.

FINDING YOUR INSTITUTIONAL HOME

When you enter a program of professional preparation, the choice about the institutional setting where you will work may already have been made by the focus of your profession. Maintenance and prevention activities include careers in health spas, schools, industry, and free-standing clinics that provide prenatal or well-baby check-ups. If you want to engage in rehabilitation activities or respond to acute or chronic health or end-of-life care needs, it is likely you will work in a hospital, rehabilitation center, nursing home, or hospice or in-home care. The opportunities for where you will practice are many and varied. As you enter the health professions, the idea that you will work in a hospital is far less likely than it was even a decade ago. In thinking about your career, therefore, it is important to also consider the type of institution in which you will practice.

 REFLECTIONS

- Are you at the point in your professional development at which you have decided on the type of practice you want?
- If so, take a few minutes to visualize the physical environment. What do the rooms look like? What kind of equipment is in the area? What other functions are served in the same building? Are other types of professionals present? Who are they?

Other characteristics of facilities offering health care services have continued to evolve too. For instance, most health care facilities in the United States, Canada, and Great Britain are not restricted to one kind of service. There are tertiary care facilities such as burn hospitals or oncology centers and free-standing clinics for vaccinations, cardiac evaluations, dental care, diabetes and cholesterol tests, or other preventative measures, but the trend is toward comprehensive buildings housing "health plans" and away from institutions with one particular function. One large managed care organization (MCO) may have facilities and professionals to respond to the whole continuum of care. This approach represents a move toward more population-based models of care in which the goal is to define a target population of patients, define the health needs of this particular population, and then develop a community-based set of services to address that community. Not unusual today are complexes that involve many types of facilities and services. There may be a hospital, a nursing home, a clinic, or several clinics housing various levels and types of care for ambulatory patients, home care services, supplier sources for durable medical equipment, and a pharmacy.

Why have we moved from a system at the beginning of the 20th century in which whoever could afford care was treated at home to the beginning of the 21st century to massive networks of facilities (Figure 2-3)? Many have commented on this movement, identifying it with the efficiency sought through:

- Industrialization: The industrial revolution and its compartmentalization of public and private life functions
- Urbanization: The movement of people to the cities and the resulting potential for increasing efficiency by offering a more centralized site for services

FIGURE 2-3: Aerial view of a large medical center. *(Courtesy Massachusetts General Hospital, Boston, MA.)*

- Specialization: The emergence of specialized medicine necessitating a centralized site for coordination of care
- Team-oriented management: The evolution from the single professional and patient to teams of professionals sharing information, equipment, and other institutional resources

In short, the institutional value of efficiency has dramatically influenced the style and design of the institutions where you will practice.

There are many critics of the present approaches. For one thing, in spite of the movement toward larger health care networks such as MCOs in the United States and elsewhere, critics maintain that our current organization results in fragmentation of services rather than continuity. Such critics suggest that these phenomena may be compatible with a free market economy in some regards but compromise some important social values such as access to health care services based on need rather than on factors such as ability to pay. You will have an opportunity to help shape the new health care environment that will continue to develop as you enter your profession.

CHARACTERISTICS OF INSTITUTIONAL RELATIONSHIPS

The ability to show and receive respect in the work environment requires an understanding of several characteristics of relationships that take place in health care institutions compared with other types of relationships. In this section we examine two aspects of health care institutions; namely, their public rather than private nature and their role as partial rather than total institutions, each of which will help you better understand how to express respect in your role in the institutional setting.

Public- and Private-Sector Relationships

Public-sector relationships are interactions reserved for public life. Therefore, individuals generally separate their lives into a private world of family and friends and a public world of other relationships designed to serve a useful purpose and then dissolve. Friendships are private-sector relationships; whereas, student and professor or patient and health professional relationships belong to the world of institutional interactions (i.e., public-sector relationships). Understandably, both parties enter public-sector relationships with different expectations than would friends or two people preparing to become partners in marriage. For example, the social boundaries that are maintained in a public-sector relationship permit rapid introduction and rapid separation when it is over, all the while promoting periodic cooperation. All public-sector relationships are characterized by abrupt changes from extreme remoteness to extreme nearness and the expectation that the relationship will be temporary. An illustration from the academic setting is that of a class of students who have become very close during their years of preparation but are now graduating. For example, a public sector relationship that you will experience in your professional life is attendance at continuing education offerings sometimes lasting a day or two. Participants come from a variety of places, work closely together focusing on specific learning goals, and then depart back to their own practice settings.

⊚ REFLECTIONS

- Think about the ways in which your relationship with your academic and clinical educators is consistent with public-sector relationship criteria. Jot them down for further reflection as this chapter unfolds.
- Are your relationships with your fellow students more akin to private- or public-sector relationships? Why?

The opportunities for involvement in each other's lives and well-being and the boundaries that must be honored with patients, families, and peers in the goal of maintaining respect are addressed throughout this book, especially in Part Five.

The physical structure of an institution helps to enable an effective private- or public-sector relationship. Hospitals or schools, for instance, unmistakably are public buildings. What are some of the clues for this conclusion? Sometimes the environment where health care is administered mingles private- and public-sector environments. For instance, a lounge where patients or residents can gather fosters private-sector friendships within the public-sector assisted care or nursing home facility. On a different scale, a home visit to a client requires that you go to his or her residence, knock on the door and be welcomed in as a guest would be, make your way across the living room among discarded pages of the morning paper, trip over the sleeping dog, and move a bathrobe from a comfortable overstuffed chair to sit down. You have entered a profoundly private-sector environment. However, the fact that your presence represents the type of public-sector relationship that takes place within health care institutions usually suffices to adequately set the tone for measures that show appropriate respect for a public-sector interaction. Your conduct and attitudes give important clues, as is emphasized throughout this book. At the same time, the type of institution can greatly enhance your effectiveness if it is designed to bring about the specific goals of health care as well as provide a humane and efficient environment overall.

Total and Partial Institutions

Another aspect of professional life is the ability to exert a certain kind of authority regarding your area of knowledge and respect for the authority that other health professionals and administrators have because of their own respective areas of expertise and roles. The design of institutions can enhance this appropriate exercise of authority. To illustrate, recall your experience in a campus dormitory, airport, hospital, or other type of institution. Each has its physical design and function accompanied by certain rules, regulations, policies, and other constraints. We judge such constraints as legitimate if they seem to serve understandable goals of the institution. Almost 50 years ago sociologist Goffman advanced the understanding of institutions based on these observations, suggesting basic distinctions that are still useful today in dividing them into "total" and "partial" institutions.[4]

Total Institutions

Total institutions are those in which personal autonomy is totally or seriously compromised. They are places where, as Goffman describes it, "a large number of like-situated individuals, cut off from the wider society for an appreciable period of time, together lead an enclosed, formally administered round of life."[4] Usually professional and supportive personnel are the sole authority: they "run" the institution, and the assumption is that either the individual or society (and in some cases, both) benefit from the arrangement. Often a ritual act of donning the clothing of the institution (e.g., a nun's habit in a cloistered convent or a prison jumpsuit) further signifies the surrender of identity and autonomy and "the acquisition of a new identity oriented to the authority of the professional staff and to the aims and purposes and the smooth operation of the institution."[4] Although their functions vary, examples of total institutions are many: monasteries, nursing homes, Alzheimer's units, long-term care facilities, hospitals for severely mentally ill or developmentally challenged persons, and prisons.

Only a small percentage of health professional and patient interactions take place within the highly codified and rigid structure of a total institution. When they do, the patient's autonomy is compromised by illness, injury, lack of decision-making capacity, or some social factor such as committing a crime. In this situation of uneven authority, every precaution to respect the dignity of the person must be rigorously undertaken. Recognition of the vulnerability of such persons to abuse at the hands of even well-meaning individuals often necessitates writing special precautionary guidelines and policies for health care. For instance, there are especially stringent guidelines for protecting persons in such environments from abuses carried out in the name of clinical research.

We believe that May summarizes the issue of total institutions in health care settings well, using the nursing home as an example:

> The nursing home occupies the same place in the psyche of the elderly today that the poorhouse and the orphanage played in the imagination of Victorian children. Even those who never set foot in such a facility fear it as fate.
>
> The deprivations that total institutions impose hardly argue for dismantling them. They have their place. But planners must give serious thought to their design, particularly to what might be called the moral significance of "turf."[5]

At several places in this book, particularly in Part Three, we revisit the idea of *turf*, those aspects of a personal living space and those dimensions of self-determination that can help to lend dignity in the midst of serious constraints as a result of health-related confinement to an institution.

Partial Institutions

Along the continuum of institutional arrangements, most health care institutions can be classified as *partial institutions* because they constrain patients' autonomy in some important ways but also allow for varying degrees of self-determination.

People entering such institutions are very concerned about the potential constraints they will face.

 REFLECTIONS

Suppose you are entering a health care facility for a serious injury that will involve surgery and, possibly, several weeks of inpatient rehabilitation. Of the following questions, which ones do you think would be of concern to you?
- Will I be able to go home from time to time during a long-term institutionalization and, if so, under what conditions?
- Are my children allowed to visit?
- May I see or be allowed to see my pet?
- What will I be allowed to eat, and what kind of "time off" from a heavy schedule of tests and treatments might I be able to negotiate?
- How much input will I have into changes in my diagnostic or therapeutic regimen?
- May I wear my own clothes?
- May I change doctors or other health care professionals without fear of retribution if there is reason to doubt their competence?

These concerns will vary according to the type of condition and the values system of the individual. However, the important point is that the patient will have concerns about what restrictions the institution will impose.

Your own autonomy in the institution where you work as a professional also will be constrained by policies for securing employment, regulations regarding employee conduct, expectations regarding the number of people in your care, and the other institutional peculiarities that will either enable or inhibit your ability to satisfy your professional and personal goals.

Health professionals are key sources of institutional change who can help create ways that respect can be expressed in humane and person-centered environments. As people talk about ways in which their autonomy and other values can be honored within the confines of partial institutions, you can think of ways to help realize those changes. Obviously a crucial component of your professional choices is to find an institution that is consistent with your personality and values system. In many areas of this book the authors assume that most interactions between health professionals and patients take place within an environment consistent with the characteristics of partial institutions.

WORKING WITH THE ADMINISTRATION

All employees in institutions have the opportunity and challenge of working well with their administrators. The administration involves those persons whose role it is to safeguard the interests of the institution and all of its components. In health care institutions the administration comprises a wide range of groups and individuals, including institutional trustees, boards of directors, and the central administration (including a chief executive officer [CEO] and chief financial officer [CFO], personnel or human resources director, and departmental and unit supervisors responsible for operations or services). The range and duties of the administration should be shaped according to the needs of the institution as determined by its mission, goals, and functions. It is not surprising, then, that in health care institutions one finds departments devoted to quality care, to assurance that patients and families will be treated with respect, and to holding health professionals accountable and ensuring that they get due reward for excellence. It is also not surprising that, like other institutions, there will be departments devoted to oversight, financial solvency, legal issues, public relations, and efficiency.

In health care institutions these administrative supports always must be prepared to work with professionals to ensure their mutually shared goal of good health care for the parties to whom they are accountable. At the same time, differences in the scope of accountabilities determined by their respective roles lead to understandable conflict at times. To illustrate how differently administration and health professionals might look at the same set of challenges, we invite you to consider the following case, first from the point of view of the professional-patient relationship and then from the administrator's point of view.

> Mary Jacobs is the coordinator of the large pediatric division of Metro Rehabilitation Center. She is single, the mother of two children. She has mortgage payments and car payments to make, but thanks to her job, she feels quite secure financially.
>
> Mary has worked at the Center for 15 years. The first 12 years she worked as a staff professional in the adolescent unit, with increasing supervisory and student clinical teaching responsibilities. Three years ago she was tapped by the administration for her present position, which includes departmental administrative responsibilities as well as a patient load. While it has many benefits, she realizes her primary concern still lies with the patients and their parents. At the same time she liked the idea of being able to further shape a service with an excellent reputation and took seriously the administration's belief that she was the right person for the job at a time when two competing pediatric rehabilitation units were opening up in the vicinity. She has to admit that the 3 years overall have been both personally and professionally rewarding.
>
> Mary reports directly to the Vice President for Patient Services (Carole Nash), though most of her day-to-day activities revolve around the team, support personnel, and patients. She meets with Carole once a month. She is painfully aware that the pediatric unit has been under increasing financial duress, due to the competition's aggressive tactics to attract private-pay patients. She is not entirely surprised when Carole tells her that due to financial pressures at Metro, she must lay off two professional staff and six support staff by the end of the fiscal quarter (within the next 6 weeks). But as she walks back to her unit she begins to resent having to upset such a well-working team and deal with the inevitable crash in morale. Central to her concern is that the upset will have a detrimental effect on patient care quality. She has to admit that she also resents her unit being asked to make cuts when she is aware that overall the census is down at Metro Rehab.

The next morning Mary calls the Vice President's office to ask if she can discuss this situation with Carole. The administrative assistant replies that he will check but wants to warn Mary that Carole herself did not make the decision independently, and he believes "the final decision already has been made." About a half hour later Carole drops in to see Mary. She says that she appreciates how difficult this is for Mary and her staff, but adds, "With the present situation in the pediatric unit, there should be no question in your mind, either, what had to be done. As you know, I, too, come from a clinical background, so I'm sure you feel torn. I wish we had the resources to launch an aggressive campaign to counter our competition, but we don't. So, I finally agreed with the board that one area we can afford to downsize is yours. Ethically speaking I am torn, but it's the kind of hard decision administrators sometimes have to make. I am sorry."

As is often the case in health care settings, the clinical and administrative roles are not entirely separate, so that at some level both Mary Jacobs and Carole Nash can see the others' point of view. Viewed from Mary's perspective as a health professional who identifies with her caregiving role more than her administrative one, reflect on the following:

	Strongly Agree	Agree	Not Sure	Disagree	Strongly Disagree
1. Mary has a right to expect that her concerns be listened to by the higher administration.					
2. If Mary can show that patient care quality in her unit will be compromised, Carole should go back to the board to advocate their finding another place to cut personnel.					
3. Mary's concern that a decrease in team morale might have a detrimental effect on patient care is a legitimate concern.					
4. If Mary does not succeed in making her case, she should resign.					

▶ What values, duties, and other considerations are appropriate for Mary Jacobs to consider in preparing for her discussion with Carole Nash?
▶ At what point should she share her problem with others, and who should they be? Why?

▶ What alternatives are open to her other than resigning if she is unsuccessful in reversing Carole's decision?

Viewed from Carole Nash's perspective as an administrator, reflect on the following from the point of view of institutional loyalties:

	Strongly Agree	Agree	Not Sure	Disagree	Strongly Disagree
1. Carole's major responsibility is to be sure Metro Rehab Center stays viable, even though some difficult decisions must be made.					
2. The board's plan to cut personnel to help sustain the viability of Metro Rehabilitation Center outweighs Mary's concern that team morale will be compromised in the unit.					
3. Carole should meet with the members of Mary's unit prior to giving Mary the task of laying off personnel.					
4. Better administrative decisions would be made if administrators in high positions like Carole's did not have a health professions background, because there is too much risk of a conflict of interest between what the institution needs overall and their worry about what might happen to individual patients or professionals.					

▶ What governing values, duties, and other considerations are appropriate for Carole to consider in her position as she responds to this administrative problem?

▶ Should Carole have shared the information with Mary that the decision came from the Metro Board of Directors instead of representing it as being her decision alone? Why or why not? What, if any, alternatives are open to Carole to help ensure that the positive aspects of the outcome will be optimized and the damage minimal?

This case is just one type of situation in which health professionals and administrators may have to negotiate decisions that are not 100% acceptable to either party. The better the communication channels and the more transparent the policies and processes for mediating difficult decisions, the more likely it is that the highest possible level of satisfaction will be reached.

HONORING THE INTERFACE OF INSTITUTIONS AND SOCIETY

In addition to the constraints and opportunities you, your colleagues, and your patients will experience from the design of the institution and its administrative practices and policies, your daily professional life in that institution will be affected by some laws and regulations that govern all types of health care settings. The following pages illustrate some of the most widespread and important categories.

Laws and Regulations to Maintain Competence

In an effort to protect society from quacks and incompetent practitioners, all health care institutions that want to remain accredited by national and regional accrediting boards must take steps to ensure that their professional staff is well qualified to do the work they say they can do. In the United States, laws of every state include professional licensing, certification, and registration mechanisms whereby a person must pass a test and meet other qualifying characteristics to practice in that state. In other countries, provincial or national laws may be the rule. Some institutions go beyond the minimum requirements established by the government bodies by adding continuing education requirements for their own professional employees. Also, national certifying bodies (such as specialty boards in medicine, nursing, and other professions) will have requirements pertaining to continued competence. Today many health professionals are personally responsible for negligence and other types of conduct that lead to malpractice claims, so institutions increasingly are requiring individuals to maintain personal malpractice insurance. These requirements should not have a negative impact on your work and may even have a positive effect, since they have been developed over the years to help ensure that the basic tenets of respect are maintained for all who need your services. However, as is true of all laws and regulations, having a legal "license" to do something does not alone ensure adherence to society's expectations of what it has given permission for a person to do.

Laws and Regulations to Prevent Discrimination

Several nondiscrimination laws have direct bearing on health care institutions in the United States. Some of these apply directly to health professionals as employees. Consider a few key examples:
- Title VII of the Civil Rights Act (1964) prohibits employers from refusing to hire an employee on the basis of race, color, sex, religion, or national origin.
- The Equal Opportunity Act buttressed and expanded Title VII in 1972.
- The Equal Pay Act of 1963 required that men and women receive equal pay for performing similar work.
- The Age Discrimination and Employment Act prohibiting discrimination against persons 40 to 70 years old was passed in 1967.

THE FAR SIDE®   By GARY LARSON

**"Well, I'll be darned ... I guess he does
have a license to do that."**

- The Rehabilitation Act (Section 504) of 1973 required all employers to have an affirmative action plan that includes handicapped persons. Superseding this act was the Americans with Disabilities Act of 1990, which states that institutions with more than 25 employees cannot use a physical examination to deny employment.

  Other laws have a direct bearing on your relationship with patients. For instance, prohibitions against some types of behavior, such as touching a patient without his or her consent or sexual intercourse with patients often are written into licensing laws as well as being reiterated in institutional policies and the ethical codes of professional organizations.

Other Laws and Regulations

With the advent of the AIDS epidemic, numerous laws and policies have been implemented nationally and within institutions to try to decrease the accidental transmittal of infection through body substances to health professionals, among patients, or to others. The most notable of these in the United States is the Universal Precautions, a federal mandate requiring all health professionals to protect themselves and others by wearing certain types of gowns, gloves, goggles, and other equipment while treating any patient and by adhering to strict methods for handling and disposing of body fluids and needles. The requirements for the amount and type of protective clothing vary according to the likelihood of body fluids being transferred from patient to health professional or vice versa. For instance, an orthopedic surgeon may become splattered from head to toe with blood during surgery and may receive a puncture wound from the slip of a scalpel or from a splintered or protruding bone. A dietitian or an occupational therapist, in comparison, is not likely to be in a situation of direct and extensive contact with body fluids. Some health professionals have worried that the "space capsule" appearance of the protective garb is damaging to health professional and patient rapport, although everyone agrees with the necessity of minimizing transmittal of the AIDS virus and other pathogens that reside in body fluids.[6]

Depending on your area of service as a health professional, you may be regulated by other laws and regulations. In the United States, if you work in a clinical or laboratory area where blood and other body fluids are handled, you will be subject to an institution's standards as set out by the Occupational Safety and Health Administration (OSHA) for limiting your exposure to these potentially pathogenic substances and safe disposal of these materials.

If you work with patients or clients who have sexually transmitted or other infectious diseases, you will be required to report this information to your state's department of health or similar governing body. In some instances this may create an ethical conflict for you if you do not want to break the confidence of this matter entrusted to you by a patient.

Laws and regulations regarding the documentation of patient status, patient progress, and other patient information will affect you every day of your practice. The medical record (whether electronic or hard copy) is a legal document, as are many other types of reports and statements you prepare for billings, quality assurance reviews, and other activities requiring data about patients and clients (Figure 2-4). Sometimes professionals treat documentation as a means of protecting their own interests legally. We prefer that you think of your documentation as a kind of travelogue of the journey you and the patient are taking during your professional encounter. Therefore, preparation of your documentation, like all other aspects of your interaction within the institution, should be undertaken first with respect for the patient's dignity and rights and then with respect for the type of professional you want the world to know you are.

Although this sampling of regulations and policies is not intended to be exhaustive and focuses on laws of the United States, it illustrates the many types of constraints that come with the health professional's inevitable need to develop institutional affiliations with health care facilities.

Laws, Regulations, and Change

We conclude this section with a short reminder that laws and regulations are always in a state of flux. If, upon review, you judge that the laws and regulations that you are asked to abide by in your place of employment will enhance your capacity to be respected and show respect in all areas of your professional interaction, they deserve

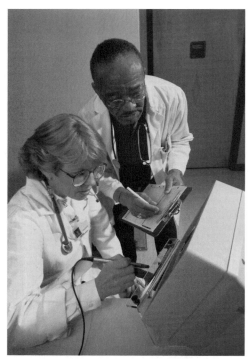

FIGURE 2-4: Health professionals at a computer entering data into electronic medical records. *(© Corbis.)*

to be followed. If they present major difficulties for you practically or ethically you should reflect seriously on how you can help bring about change. Like every generation of health professionals before you, you have an opportunity throughout your career to help shape a better environment for the health professions by working to change unworkable, unfair, or otherwise inadequate laws, regulations, and other policies. Good patient care is the ultimate goal of health care institutions, and all institutional activities must reflect that goal.

Policy change is a complex process. Sociologist and American policy analyst Campbell suggests that policy change comes when a certain set of "policy windows of opportunity" open due to the coming together of ideas and people over time: "Participants have different goals or preferences; the process is some sort of fight or bargaining; the result is determined by each participant's relative power, or by the amount of energy each is able and willing to expend on that issue, and how skillfully resources are deployed."[7]

The process of changing unacceptable laws, regulations, and policy requires willingness, persistence, and courage. Some steps toward that end include:

- Documenting problems diligently
- Gaining an understanding of the informal opinion leaders and formal authorities in the type of situation you wish to change

- Identifying colleagues with whom you can link arms to develop effective strategies for addressing your issue
- Being flexible and preparing to negotiate anew as new information comes your way
- Staying with the project until change is accomplished or you understand why it cannot be

RIGHTS, RESPONSIBILITIES, AND YOUR WORK ENVIRONMENT

The rights and responsibilities you will face in the institutional setting where you work will be spelled out in your contract and in the standing documents of the institution (e.g., bylaws and employee manuals). We have already mentioned some rights that are protected and responsibilities that are mandated by law. Like laws and regulations, additional guidelines detailing your rights and responsibilities should be examined carefully for their potential to foster or hinder respect for you, your colleagues, and patients.

PATIENTS' RIGHTS DOCUMENTS

In health care institutions patients, too, have rights and incur responsibilities. Some that are protected by law have been mentioned. However, other rights not addressed by legal guidelines have come to be accepted as important. Among the most helpful documents for understanding what they are is the American Hospital Association's list of patients' rights first published in 1975. They have been updated several times but still are used as a prototype for many other health care institutions and groups today.[8]

Among rights often listed are the rights to considerate and respectful care, accurate and complete information, participation (directly or through a legally appointed spokesperson) in health care decisions, privacy, and confidentiality (within constraints of the law). There are rights to information about the institution itself (e.g., who owns it and what its overall services are) and the right to have continuity of care.

All U.S. readers of this book have been—or will be—introduced to HIPAA regulations. This set of regulations is based on the tenets of the Health Insurance Portability and Accountability Act of 1996. The regulations themselves are called the New Federal Medical-Privacy Rule and are designed to help protect patient privacy. Because of the complexity of their requirements, they did not go into effect until 2003. They are having a profound effect on health professionals and health care institutions regarding the type of confidential information that can be transmitted into medical records and other information systems. The Rule also contains new requirements regarding information about research subjects. The following types of details are among the most important that may not be photocopied or faxed without specific authorization to do so by the patient: psychotherapy records, counseling about domestic violence, sexual assault counseling, HIV test results, records regarding sexually transmitted diseases, and social work records.[9]

REFLECTIONS

What rights and responsibilities would you like to see included in nationally binding documents in your country of employment?

Grievance Mechanisms

In recent years several professional organizations and institutions have created mechanisms to assist patients who believe their rights or other reasonable expectations are not being honored. Some institutions employ patient representatives, or ombudsmen, whose job it is to listen to patients' problems and try to help solve them. Institutional ethics committees, highly encouraged by the Joint Commission on Accreditation of Health Care Organizations, the accrediting body of U.S. health care facilities, are often useful for bringing together health professionals and patients and their families as they try to determine what to do next in complex life-and-death decisions or to help resolve conflicts among various members of the group. There have been recommendations that health care institutions hire mediation specialists to try to reach consensus about areas of conflict or dissension.

Grievance mechanisms for employees also are available. Disputes about policies or practices, salary increases, work hours, and termination of employment are frequent reasons employees seek recourse through institutional mechanisms. An important area of employee protection has been implemented in recent years for personnel who report wrong-doing. In the past the desire to "blow the whistle" on an incompetent, unethical, or impaired colleague often was suppressed by the realistic fear of reprisal. However, as Glaser notes in the graphic of his three realms, the good and virtuous institution "attends to the health, vigor, balance and equity of the institution's key system."[2] To uphold this goal, adequate mechanisms must be in place to help ensure its success.

INFORMED CONSENT: THE BASIC INSTITUTIONAL CONTRACT GUIDING INTERACTION

We conclude this chapter on the institutional settings of health care with a close look at informed consent in the health professional and patient relationship. An institutional mechanism for gaining informed consent (or refusal) from patients or their surrogates will be found in virtually every health care institution in the United States. It is *sine qua non* the most basic contract guiding institutions and professionals in their interaction with patients and their surrogates.

The need for mechanisms ensuring informed consent rests on the assumption that both health professionals and the institutions of health care themselves place patients in a potentially vulnerable position. The patient's say-so or "agency" is threatened by this imbalance of power and the goal of informed consent is to help level the playing field between health professional and patient.

Informed consent involves disclosing to a patient what is to be done to him or her, including the potential risks and desired outcomes, and obtaining the patient's consent to (or refusal of) the procedure.

Disclosure of Relevant Information

Over the years a debate has ensued over how much information must be provided to enable a person to make an intelligent decision regarding treatment. One school of thought in health care maintains that it is impossible to provide the information in all of its detail. Members of this group base their argument on the complexity of treatments, which, they say, patients cannot understand. A second school maintains that it is inadvisable to provide information; that to do so can only harm the patient. This is a particularly delicate issue in the matter of treatments for mental illnesses for which the therapist believes a favorable outcome can be attained only by keeping certain information from the patient. Providing information is problematic, too, for health professionals who wish to give a placebo to a patient who is finding no relief from pain killers. As soon as the patient knows a sugar pill or other inert substance is being substituted for a "real" medication, the placebo becomes ineffective.

Proponents of a third view argue that information does not harm, but rather that knowledge sets a person free by allowing the patient to retain control over the events of his or her life. In a context of a total or partial institution, the goal should be to maximize the patient's autonomy, or say-so, as much as possible. The language a health professional or other employee of the institution uses to describe the details should be personalized to maximize each person's comprehension. In other words, the standard used for determining the type and amount of disclosure should be one derived from the knowledge of each individual patient and the practices regarding individual or collective decision-making consistent with his or her culture, sometimes referred to as the "subjective person standard." Although dispute lingers about the depth of information that health professionals must give to a patient, there is agreement about the type of information that must be shared. A patient should be told the proposed treatment in terms he or she can understand. This includes information about the diagnosis and prognosis, the recommended types of interventions, and the desired outcome. The patient should also be given information about alternatives to the proposed treatment, which may include doing nothing, and the risks involved for each. Finally, the patient should be aware that he or she may request that any diagnostic or treatment regimen be discontinued without fear of retribution.

Giving or Refusing Consent

The patient's consent or refusal is the sign that he or she is not being coerced into any course of action. Obtaining consent is also a means of enforcing the implicit rules of the relationship, which is to say that the health professional will neither harm the patient nor be unfaithful to the task of helping the patient.

Although informed consent is a potent mechanism for honoring patients' preferences, it is not a fail-safe protection from difficult decisions or even outright conflict among health professionals themselves or between them and patients or families. Unfortunately, such conflict often ensues around important end-of-life decisions or other moments of high stress.[10] One form of difficulty is that sometimes what the patient considers best for himself or herself is not consistent with what the health professional considers best. Consider, for example, the following case:

> You work in a long-term care facility that recently experienced an outbreak of scabies (a highly communicable skin disease caused by an arachnid, *Sarcoptes scabiei*, the itch mite). When the usual public health measures fail to prevent new and recurring cases, the decision is made by a committee of senior health professionals in the facility to treat all patients and staff with lindane. One patient, Cora Grosklaus, who is 82 years old, alert, and oriented, refuses the treatment that consists of a prolonged hot bath or shower with a thorough scrubbing followed by the application of the medication, particularly in the pubic area. Regardless of the explanations the staff have provided about the importance of the treatment for her well-being and that of others, Mrs. Grosklaus will have none of it stating, "I will not submit to such humiliating treatment."[11]
>
> ▶ If you were a member of the team caring for Mrs. Grosklaus, how might you have gone about explaining to her the importance of the application?
> ▶ Where might a breakdown in communication have occurred, and what could have been done to possibly prevent this unhappy state of affairs?
> ▶ The measure being undertaken should benefit Mrs. Grosklaus as well as serve an important public health measure. What should be done if, like the team described above, you got nowhere in convincing her?

Sometimes health care institutions feel trapped by patients (or, in this case, long-term care facility residents) who refuse treatments that health professionals believe are necessary. Sometimes individuals do just the opposite of Cora—they insist on treatments that health professionals believe are inappropriate. At other times patients insist on going home before the health professionals believe they are ready. In the latter case, they are said to have left "AMA"—against medical advice. They may be asked to sign a document confirming that they have been informed of the physician's judgment but are choosing to act contrary to his or her advice.

Much more refinement of the concept and limits of informed consent and related mechanisms still is needed. Great strides have been made toward recognizing and honoring patients' preferences as an integral aspect of decision-making in health care institutions. At the same time, problems do remain. The process of gaining informed consent is designed to ensure that the health professional's and institution's promises to help and to not inflict harm are kept. However, daily interaction with the patient cannot depend on acquiring the patient's (or family's) written consent every step of the way. Trust must underlie the consent process and whatever else goes on in the setting; it promotes feelings of relatedness and allows the procedures to flow smoothly. In short, if informed consent mechanisms are substituted for other aspects of a humane environment, institutions will not succeed in respecting the patient's dignity.

SUMMARY

This chapter highlights that a respect-filled health care environment requires the cooperation and responsible participation of individuals, institutional leaders, and society as a whole. Your own efforts will be fruitless without institutional support. At the same time, respect is so fundamental that you have an opportunity and duty to exercise it at all levels: as an individual professional, as an employee of the institution, and as a citizen. When institutional policies, practices, and processes threaten a respectful environment, your obligation extends to helping change the situation in a constructive manner. We ended this chapter with a focus on informed consent—a basic legal and ethical process employed by institutions whereby respect is brought down to the most personal level of your interactions with the people you are preparing to serve in your professional role.

REFERENCES

1. Little ME: *Stranger in the mirror*, Bloomington, IN, 2006, Author House.
2. Glaser J: *Three realms of ethics*, Kansas City, MO, 1994, Sheed and Ward.
3. Scott WR: *Organizations: rational, natural and open systems*, Englewood Cliffs, NJ, 1981, Prentice Hall.
4. Goffman E: *Asylums*, Garden City, NY, 1961, Anchor Books.
5. May W: *The patient's ordeal*, Bloomington, 1991, Indiana University Press.
6. U.S. Department of Health and Human Services, Public Health Service, Centers for Disease Control: *Morbidity and Mortality Weekly Report* 36(suppl 25):55-65, 1987.
7. Campbell JC: *How policies change: the Japanese government and the aging society*, Princeton, NJ, 1992, Princeton University Press.
8. American Hospital Association: *A patient's bill of rights*, Chicago, 1992 [1975], American Hospital Association.
9. l Register 2002. 67:53182-53273.
10. Bloche MG: Managing conflict at the end of life, *N Engl J Med* 352(23):2371-2376, 2005.
11. Smith M and others: *Pharmacy ethics*, Binghamton, NY, 1991, Pharmaceutical Products Press.

RESPECT IN A DIVERSE SOCIETY

Why, a cabdriver would go the wrong way down a one-way street to pick up a white woman. White women are the best fares. Don't cause you no trouble. Don't hassle you. Worst fares are young black men. I call 'em "yo" boys. Nothing but trouble. I won't pick them up, and *I'm* black, in case you hadn't noticed.

—Washington, DC, cabdriver, July 2000

The first two chapters discussed the value context of individuals, as persons and professionals, and the institutional environment. Respect also involves sensitivity to individual and group differences. Thus, you may discover that, even with deep understanding of your personal values and clarity about the goals and values of the place where you work, respectful interaction still does not result. Yet to be considered is the fact that each person interprets actions, facial expressions, choice of words, and other forms of communication according to his or her cultural conditioning and past experience. All of these interactions take place within a society that, at least within the United States, has been described as a "melting pot" in which all of the various cultures and beliefs blend together. Some hold that the melting pot description of the United States is no longer accurate and that it is more like "chunky stew," a stew savored both for the character of the individual ingredients (ethnically-derived differences) and for the delicious melding of flavors (social integration).[1] Others liken society to a mosaic with each person comprising an integral part of a complex but comprehensive picture.[2]

In this chapter, we examine some of the differences you will encounter in clinical practice and the barriers (e.g., personal and cultural biases, prejudices, and discrimination) that get in the way of appreciating differences and inhibit respectful interaction.

BIAS, PREJUDICE, AND DISCRIMINATION

A *cultural bias* is a tendency to interpret a word or action according to a culturally derived meaning assigned to it. Cultural bias derives from cultural variation, discussed later in this chapter. For example, some cultures view smiles as a deeply personal sign of happiness that is only shared with intimates. Others view smiles as an indication of general friendliness to be shared with any and all. It is quite possible that another can interpret a friendly smile on the part of one person as disingenuous or inappropriate. Regarding health care, attitudes toward pain, methods of conveyance of bad news, management of chronic illness and disability, beliefs about the seriousness and causes of illness, and death-related issues vary among different cultures. These different kinds of beliefs about disease and illness have an impact on health care-seeking behavior and acceptance of the advice and intervention of health professionals. Understanding a patient's concept of health and illness is critical to the development of interaction strategies that are acceptable to the patient.

A *personal bias* is a tendency to interpret a word or action in terms of a personal significance assigned to it. It is found largely in what is commonly called *prejudice*. Personal bias can derive from culturally defined interpretations but can also originate from a number of other sources grounded in personal experience. The individual internalizes the cultural attitudes until he or she believes them to be entirely personal. Put another way, a personal bias is an individual's feeling about a particular person or thing that colors his or her interpretation of it. The bias can lead to more favorable or less favorable judgments than are deserved. This process is similar to that of internalizing societal values described in Chapter 1.

Understanding the way personal biases influence us and their effect on our attitudes and conduct is important to the health professional. Whenever bias is present, it affects the type of communication possible between the persons involved and therefore must be recognized as one determining factor in respectful interaction. None of the documents outlining patients' rights support an ethical or legal right permitting professionals to refuse care or show any kind of disrespect on the basis of their personal biases.

The Washington, DC, cabdriver quoted at the beginning of this chapter expresses a negative personal bias based on his experience with certain passengers. How does it show up in his comments? How might this bias show up in his actions?

The cabdriver's comments also show another side to his judgments: in some cases, personal bias may produce a positive personal bias or "halo effect" on certain individuals; that is, two people may have common interests or characteristics, and their camaraderie is immediately apparent. How is the halo effect at work in the comments of this Washington, DC, cabdriver? While showing favoritism on this basis alone is not permissible in the patient and health professional relationship, common interests can, of course, have legitimate positive effects on the relationship between two persons working together.

Consider, again, the *negative personal biases* of the cabdriver. He is discriminating against young, black, male passengers. Discrimination is negative, different treatment of a person or group. Usually it is derived from prejudice. *Prejudice* is "an aversive or hostile attitude toward a person who belongs to a group, simply because he belongs to that group, and is therefore assumed to have objectionable qualities ascribed to that group."[3] In this way we see how prejudicial attitudes manifest themselves in discriminatory behavior.

In short, every exchange between a patient and health professional undoubtedly will be influenced by cultural differences and other sources of personal bias. Sometimes these feelings will create an attitude of prejudice and a desire to discriminate. In Chapter 2, you were introduced to some of the laws that help define the legal limits to which discrimination can be pushed within the health care environment. However, despite legal guidelines, discrimination occurs craftily and evasively. You must watch for it in yourself and others because both parties involved are inevitably injured by the interaction. Consider your initial reaction to the cabdriver's statement. Were you offended? Were you perhaps a little sympathetic to the driver's situation? Whatever your reaction, it should give you a glimpse into your own prejudices.

Gordon Allport, in his definitive work, *The Nature of Prejudice* (which, although written over 50 years ago, is still widely considered an authoritative study), warns, "It is a serious error to ascribe prejudice and discrimination to any single taproot, reaching into economic exploitation, social structure, the mores, fear, aggression, sex conflict or any other favored soil. Prejudice and discrimination… may draw nourishment from all these conditions and many others."[3] It should be emphasized that treating people differently because of race, religion, ethnicity, gender, or other attributes does not necessarily imply prejudice and discrimination. Respect for differences includes understanding when those differences should count, how they inform the responses of people, and the process of caring for them.

What can you learn from the previous pages? One thing you can discern is that the cultivation of respectful attitudes and conduct begins with self-examination and consideration of what cultural differences mean to you. This is not as easy as it may seem at first glance. It requires that you enter into a "difficult dialogue;" that is, you are asked to reconsider long-held assumptions about individuals and groups that raise questions about your values and beliefs. Engagement in this type of activity may lead to feelings of discomfort and uneasiness.[4] These uncomfortable feelings result from the limited experience most of us have in interacting and talking with individuals different from ourselves.

We explore here a variety of differences, both obvious and subtle, that exist between people, such as differences in language, one of the most basic reasons for miscommunication—why, for example, even when we speak the same language, we may hear what a patient says but not understand its true meaning. Once you become aware of your often unconscious biases you can more easily avoid being controlled by them in your interactions with others. Furthermore, by becoming aware of your hidden biases, you will be less likely to form inappropriate judgments about patients, colleagues, and others and more likely to remain sensitive and open to differences that influence your interactions with them.

RESPECTING DIFFERENCES

We live in a multicultural society. Sensitivity to cultural differences today has increased owing to the various minority rights movements over the last several decades and the fact that there is an ever-growing percentage of ethnic minorities in the United States (Figure 3-1). According to the 2000 census, the national population was 281,422,000; of this total, 12.5% self-identified as Hispanic or Latino; 12.3% as black or African American; 3.6% as Asian; and about 1% as American Indian or Pacific Islander.[5]

This growing diversity has strong implications for the provision of health care. There is a significant underrepresentation of minorities in the health professions, which contributes to the disparity in the health status of minority groups—African American, Hispanics, Asian Americans, American Indians, Alaskan natives, and Pacific Islanders. "A singular challenge facing health care institutions in this century will be assisting an essentially homogeneous group of health care professionals to meet the special needs of a culturally diverse society."[6]

Depending on where you live, you may be more or less aware of the percentage of persons from cultural and racial backgrounds that are different from your own who

FIGURE 3-1: *(Used with permission of Chuck Asay and Creators Syndicate.)*

are living in your community. One way to identify the various cultural groups in your area is to use data from the U.S. Census Bureau, which is organized by state. You can access the most recent information by going to the home page of the U.S. Census Bureau (http://www.census.gov). There are tables for each state and you can find the cultures represented, the languages spoken, and other information about where you live and work.

In almost every health care setting, you will interact with patients of backgrounds different from your own. Certain differences are obvious; others are hidden. The iceberg model illustrates how much remains below the surface in our interactions with others (Figure 3-2).

Health professionals generally believe they know a patient's race or gender merely by interacting with a patient, but, as you will see from further discussion in this chapter, we may not be as accurate as we think in determining exactly who the person is sitting in front of us. With this limited information about potential differences, a professional can adjust communication patterns and approaches accordingly. However, it is more difficult to assess a patient's socioeconomic status or place of residence, two differences that can have as profound an effect on a patient's health beliefs or behavior as do visible attributes such as race and gender. The differences that are hidden may create more stress than those that can more readily be identified.

Even with experience, you may sometimes fail to appreciate significant differences in others with whom you interact. It is a continual challenge to look below the surface at the differences that affect interactions with patients and devise strategies to overcome barriers and facilitate communication. Many such differences have come to be viewed collectively as being characteristics of a person's "culture." Using a broad definition, we describe *culture* as the beliefs, customs, technological achievements, language, and history of a group of similar people.[7] So you can think of culture in terms of primary characteristics such as race, gender, age, and ethnicity and secondary

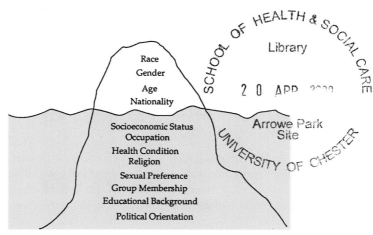

FIGURE 3-2: Iceberg model of multicultural influences on communication. *(From Krepp GL: Effective communication in multicultural health care settings, New York, 1994, Sage Publications. © 1994. Reprinted by permission of Sage Publications, Inc.)*

characteristics such as place of residence, sexual orientation, and socioeconomic status. Cultural practices and beliefs can have a significant effect on the following health related issues: diet, family rituals, healing beliefs, communication process and style, death rituals, spirituality, values, art, and history. Because culture has such a broad impact on health and because of the increasing diversity in the United States, "cultural competence has gained attention as a potential strategy to improve quality and eliminate racial/ethnic disparities in health care."[8] We turn your attention to a difference that is the root of numerous conflicts between social groups—race.

Race

Race is one characteristic of culture almost always mentioned in discussions about cultural differences and is perhaps the characteristic most fraught with controversy. However, even the distinctions used by the U.S. Census Bureau constitute a system based on outmoded concepts and dubious assumptions about genetic difference. "In fact, race is poorly correlated with any biologic or cultural phenomenon other than skin color, which makes it a useless classification for biomedical or social research."[9] An editorial in *Nature Genetics* flatly stated, "scientists have long been saying that at a genetic level there is more variation between two individuals in the same population than between populations and that there is no biological basis for race."[10] One of the authors was visiting South Africa during the apartheid years, where laws were based on "racial" distinctions. A geneticist and anthropologist with whom she worked noted that the most accurate way to talk about races was to say that so-and-so was "classified as" white, black, or another race. They wanted to emphasize the social construction of this potent label. At present the idea of race has social meaning, assigns status, limits opportunities, and influences interactions between health professionals and patients.[11] Take a moment to reflect on the race categories listed in Box 3-1 that are presently being used to classify people by the U.S. Census Bureau.

◎ REFLECTIONS

- Which race category do you most closely claim as your own?
- Would someone meeting you for the first time place you in the same category or categories you chose for yourself?

The same difficulty with racial identification can occur with your patients as well.

Although it is generally true that patient treatment and counseling are more effective when obtained from members of one's self-identified racial group, it does not mean that patients must be treated by members of the same race. First of all, this would not be possible because there are so few minority health professionals. Second, it is possible to learn how to appropriately handle the health care of minority groups different from our own racial and ethnic backgrounds through sensitivity, knowledge, and skills in cross-cultural communication.

BOX 3-1

HOW ARE THE RACE CATEGORIES USED IN CENSUS 2000 DEFINED?

"White" refers to people having origins in any of the original peoples of Europe, the Middle East, or North Africa. It includes people who indicated their race or races as "White" or wrote in entries such as Irish, German, Italian, Lebanese, Near Easterner, Arab, or Polish.

"Black or African American" refers to people having origins in any of the Black racial groups of Africa. It includes people who indicated their race or races as "Black, African Am., or Negro," or wrote in entries such as African American, Afro American, Nigerian, or Haitian.

"American Indian and Alaska Native" refers to people having origins in any of the original peoples of North and South America (including Central America), and who maintain tribal affiliation or community attachment. It includes people who indicated their race or races by marking this category or writing in their principal or enrolled tribe, such as Rosebud Sioux, Chippewa, or Navajo.

"Asian" refers to people having origins in any of the original peoples of the Far East, Southeast Asia, or the Indian subcontinent. It includes people who indicated their race or races as "Asian Indian," "Chinese," "Filipino," "Korean," "Japanese," "Vietnamese," or "Other Asian," or wrote in entries such as Burmese, Hmong, Pakistani, or Thai.

"Native Hawaiian and Other Pacific Islander" refers to people having origins in any of the original peoples of Hawaii, Guam, Samoa, or other Pacific Islands. It includes people who indicated their race or races as "Native Hawaiian," "Guamanian or Chamorro," "Samoan," or "Other Pacific Islander," or wrote in such entries such as Tahitian, Mariana Islander, or Chuukese.

"Some other race" was included in Census 2000 for respondents who were unable to identify with the five Office of Management and Budget race categories. Respondents who provided write-in entries such as Moroccan, South African, Belizean, or a Hispanic origin (for example, Mexican, Puerto Rican, or Cuban) are included in the "some other race" category.

From United States Department of Commerce, US Census Bureau, Population Division, Population Projections Branch, Washington, DC, 2000.

There are other barriers to be overcome between patients and health professionals that are, unfortunately, deeply tied to notions of race. In a national study conducted by the Institutes of Medicine on disparities in health care, evidence indicated that stereotyping, biases and uncertainty on the part of health care providers can all contribute to unequal treatment.[12] Additionally, there are ample historical reasons for minorities to mistrust the health care system. For example, in the not-too-distant past, black patients were refused treatment at "white only" hospitals. Some were under-treated and deceived in the infamous Tuskegee syphilis study. Gaining the trust of patients whose race is different from one's own is a challenge but not an insurmountable one if a health professional can show that her or his aim is to provide optimal care personally and minimize and eventually eliminate disparities in care.

One of the first steps in reducing disparities in the health care setting is to be aware that they exist. For example, not long ago one of the authors participated in an ethics consultation regarding an extremely ill newborn. The black parents of the baby looked around the table of health professionals gathered for the meeting. The father quietly commented, "I'd feel a whole lot better about this if there was one black face other than ours at this table." Although everyone present was there for the good of the baby and his family, the lack of representation of someone of the parents' racial group was a significant barrier to the discussion and, ultimately, to the decisions made. If the father had not made the comment, the health professionals involved probably would never have noticed the circle of white faces surrounding the black couple.

The preceding example indicates that there may be justifiable reasons to consider social categories of race when making clinical decisions. Another situation in which race (and ethnicity) may be a reason for differential treatment is when certain medications are prescribed because both can affect disease pathophysiology and drug metabolism.[13,14] "Certain genetic variations may well correlate with groups whose ancestors lived in particular regions (e.g., the sickle-cell trait is found in areas of western Africa, the Mediterranean, and southeast India where malaria has long been prevalent). These correlations can help in identifying and treating diseases. Directly correlating genetic differences to social categories of race may, in the short run, help to address certain health problems. In the long run, however, it opens to [sic] door to a wide range of potentially devastating discriminatory practices—some overt, others subtle and hard to see or anticipate."[15]

Race and ethnic background can also influence dietary habits and other activities of daily living that have a direct impact on health care outcomes. Although different treatment based on race or ethnicity may be justified in special cases such as those mentioned, it is the exception, not the rule. You must remain alert for unjustified differences in care based on race or ethnicity.

Gender

Gender issues interact with other primary and secondary characteristics of culture to shape a person's identity. There are many implications for assessment and treatment of patients based on differences in gender. Gender inequities exist in health care just as they do in society at large. Women in the United States have a history of unequal access to sources of economic and political power.[16] This is especially true for black women or older women who experience the combined impact of race, gender, and age discrimination. Gender inequities in health care are inexcusable and should be remedied. At the same time it is also important to simultaneously acknowledge differences that should be taken into consideration and accommodated in planning and delivering care.

Let us take as an example the preferences of patients regarding the gender of their physician. Numerous studies have documented the fact that 20% to 56% of women explicitly prefer a female physician for women's health problems.[17,18] Because many women feel uncomfortable and perhaps embarrassed during a gynecological examination, they may prefer female physicians because they are familiar with the female body and have firsthand experience with the examination. If women are more comfortable with the examination, then they will be more likely to follow through with checkups and follow the recommendations of the physician. A recent study shows that outside of the specialty of obstetrics and gynecology, communication skills was the most important factor for women patients regarding their interaction with a physician.[19] The challenge for all health professionals is to adopt behaviors and communication styles to compensate for any differences from their patients.

A patient's preference for a health professional of the same gender may not only be a personal but also a cultural or religious one. Many cultural groups are very concerned about modesty and may require that only a female health professional examine a female patient's genitalia or be present when the patient is undressed. Gender differences regarding modesty can have direct implications for diagnosis and treatment, as is evident in the following case:

> A 50-year-old female peasant from Mexico is seen in the clinic. The patient's 35-year-old son accompanies her. The woman has been coming to the clinic for some time. Her son usually interprets because she does not speak English. An interpreter who is employed by the clinic is called because the son has to leave for work and cannot stay and translate for his mother. Before they enter the room, the physician discloses to the female interpreter that he is concerned about whether the health problems claimed by this woman are real or imagined. She has been in the clinic three times before, each time with different vague and diffuse complaints, none of which make medical sense. The physician learns through the translator that the woman has a fistula in her rectum. In her previous visits, she could not bring herself to reveal her true symptoms in the presence of, and therefore to, her son as he interpreted for her. She was so embarrassed that she invented other symptoms to justify visits to the physician. She wanted someone else to interpret, but did not know how she could ask since she would have to speak through her son.[20]

Although some problems in this example occurred because of differences in gender, they were compounded by language barriers. The case offers insight into the problems that can arise when language is a primary barrier. Since 1999, federal and state laws require that full language access to health care services be available in health care institutions receiving federal funds.[21] If an interpreter is needed, one should be provided whether it is an actual certified interpreter or another model of service such as telephone or remote interpreting. If you have to rely on a chance interpreter such as a family member for translation, you should pay attention to the gender of the translator as well as to the translator's relationship to the patient, because this can affect what the patient is willing to share. Language barriers are a critical stumbling block to the delivery of health care. The Institutes of Medicine report on health disparities also called for an increase in the availability of interpretation services to help with the language barriers that can lead to poor health outcomes.[22] There are several websites, such as http://www.omhrc.gov/CLAS and http://www.hhs.gov/ocr/lep, that provide national standards for culturally and linguistically appropriate interpretation services in health care.

Age

The particular form of stigma associated with being old is related to the prejudices of an ageist society. The word *ageism* was coined to designate the discriminatory treatment of old people (as *sexism* was coined to describe the systematic devaluation of one sex on both an individual and a societal basis).

Older adults are constantly confronted with ageist conduct. Unfortunately, ageist conduct occurs in the health care environment as well. Older patients often receive less attention or are denied services based on their age alone. Physical and psychological problems may not be addressed because health professionals assume that they are normal for an older person. Older patients are often overmedicated and experience the effects of poorly coordinated care. Regardless of his or her state of health or physical ability, an elderly patient is commonly met with a patronizing attitude. Ways in which you can overcome the tendencies to engage in ageist behavior are discussed in more detail in Chapter 16.

Ethnicity

Ethnicity refers to a person's sense of belonging to a group of people sharing a common origin, history, and set of social beliefs. Recall from the broad definition of "culture" earlier in this chapter that ethnicity counts as one of the primary characteristics of culture along with race, age, and gender. Ethnicity may also refer to an individual's place of geographical or national origin, one of the secondary characteristics of culture. For example, the U.S. Census Bureau states that Hispanics may be of any race.[5]

It used to be very easy to identify an ethnicity-based cultural variation because one could readily distinguish between the various ways of doing things in different parts of the world. Frequently, early explorers were stunned by the practices they encountered as norms in cultures, and all too often they used the occasion to demean or diminish the importance of the cultural practices of other societies. Even 100 years ago, the "American way" differed significantly from the "European way," and these two were easily distinguished from the "African way" or the "Far Eastern way." Today, in most parts of the world, a large variety of influences such as telecommunications, the ease of global travel, and the presence of foreign visitors impact what used to be traditional, homogeneous cultures. Although the United States has a history of immigration from various parts of the world, "Never before has the United States received immigrants from so many countries, from such different social and economic backgrounds, and for so many reasons."[23] A result is that it is often more challenging to sort out and identify specific cultural differences that modify behavior in various ethnic groups.

Sometimes as a health professional you may have a difficult time remembering that members of an ethnic group cannot be expected to be homogeneous. Their ethnicity is only one characteristic of the culture or cultures they bring to their present experience. For example, an outstanding physician and friend of the authors grew up in rural Nigeria, studied as an undergraduate in Scotland, took her medical training at Johns Hopkins University in Baltimore, Maryland, and now practices in the heart of Midwest America. When asked if she had difficulty "adjusting" to the Midwest, she said that she simply brought along to "this new culture" the best of what she had the opportunity to accumulate along the way! At times, each of us becomes aware of cultural beliefs held by an individual that, on the surface, seem to be incongruent.

For example, a Chinese American may be highly assimilated into the majority culture and seek mainstream health care for a gastrointestinal disorder yet also seek care from a traditional Chinese healer who might prescribe herbs, teas, or other forms of therapies appropriate for his culture. Because we can identify with individual variations in our own cultural beliefs and the blending of seemingly opposite beliefs that can occur within us as individuals, we must appreciate the profound variability that can exist within cultural groups.

One of the widest cultural gaps you will encounter in your role as a health professional is that created by the "ethnocentrism" of health professionals. (Although separate professions often are not thought of as cultures in themselves, they are.) *Ethnocentrism* is the belief that one's own cultural ways are superior. Health professionals often believe that their way is best and so are guilty of medical ethnocentrism. In fact, while you are a student you are learning and adopting the culture of your chosen health profession. The culture of a health professional encompasses the interrelationships of professional values, beliefs, customs, habits, and symbols. You are learning the cultural meaning that your profession gives to concepts such as pain, disability, disease, and illness. You will find that even within the culture of the health professions, there are different meanings and understandings of identical phenomena. Thus, as an individual you may share the same ethnic origin, race, and gender as the patient you are working with and yet not hold the same beliefs and perspectives about some important things related to what his or her care should involve.

The following poem, used here with the author's permission, demonstrates how difficult it can be to reach across the ethnic and other cultural gaps between health professional and patient:

4/2

She came into the room smiling.
"This is the real thing," said the interpreter.
"Sientese," I said, gesturing to the chair, grateful for my limited Spanish.
I asked her questions about cancer and illness.
"Only Americans talk of dying of cancer," she said.
I asked her questions about cancer and illness.
"Look in the eyes, you can tell by the eyes," she said.
I looked in her eyes.
I asked her questions about cancer and illness.
"The curanderas use objects and herbs for healing.
They have their own way of speaking.
No one else understands them."
She looked at me.
"That's all," she said. She stood.
that's all that's all that's all
whispered ancestor spirits
holders of ancient wisdom
written in Aztec
kept in jars and pots

herbs animals
stones
goat's milk
"That's all," she said.
she smiled
she left the room.
          —*Jolene Siemsen*

Socioeconomic Status

The vast majority of U.S. and Canadian health professionals are white, with average incomes that are in the middle to high economic range when considered globally. The income level and accompanying higher social status of health professionals tend to create barriers in their relationships with patients. "Ethnic minority groups and economically disadvantaged individuals may have particular difficulty feeling in control within a setting dominated by well-educated professionals."[24] The difference in socioeconomic status may hinder patients from asking you important questions, hinder you from empathizing with patients, and limit your knowledge of the practical everyday obstacles that prevent or facilitate the ability of patients to pursue medication or treatment regimens.[25] The following case highlights the challenges some patients face just getting to a medical appointment.

> A young mother and her two small children, a toddler and a 3-month-old, leave their apartment at 7:00 A.M. for a 9:00 A.M. clinic visit. With the baby in a stroller and the toddler at his mother's side, they head for the bus stop that is four blocks from their home. The first bus is late because of icy conditions. She will have to transfer three times to get to the clinic and walk two blocks to the clinic building. She arrives at the clinic 45 minutes late for her 9:00 A.M. appointment. The medical assistant at the intake desk looks at the clock as the mother signs in and says, "Couldn't you have called if you were going to be late?"

We will address different interpretations of time in Chapter 9, but in this case there is no disagreement about what is "on time." The medical assistant does not understand the complications that arise from having to be dependent on public transportation or the hassle of using a pay phone while juggling two small children in the cold. The fact that this patient actually made it to the clinic is testament to her desire to receive care. Yet, this fact becomes lost in complaints about the patient's tardiness and lack of consideration for the clinic staff. Health professionals may take for granted owning a car or a cell phone, items that could be completely beyond the financial means of some patients.

The difference in social class and economic status also affects the type and frequency of interaction between patient and health professional outside the health care setting. The informal networks that exist in neighborhoods and communities provide opportunities to establish cooperation, exchange information, and determine appropriate behavior. "For instance, minority patients might be described as 'noncompliant' by clinicians (who mainly have been socialized in a white urban middle-class milieu) when, in fact, the patients are 'following the rule,' but rules that are based on a different set of principles."[26]

Outsiders can make unintentional errors in judgment because they underestimate the effects of ethnicity, age, or class on insiders' responses or actions; that is, the responses and actions of individuals born or socialized into membership of the group. Outsiders must work to "get in," to gain, build, and maintain trust with a group.[27]

Level of education is another difference between health professionals and patients related to socioeconomic status. Although patients may respect education in the abstract, they may also be suspicious that you will use your education to take advantage of them rather than to assist them. Patients may also be too intimidated to admit when they do not understand something. For fear that they will be seen as ignorant or superstitious, patients may neglect to mention that they are also seeking alternative methods of care or providers. Even when patients are well educated, they may not speak the dominant language well enough to adequately express themselves. For example, a French tourist in the United States was in a minor accident that required an emergency room visit. The patient, an attorney, spoke some English, but told the nurse in the triage unit that she would feel better if she could talk to someone in French because, "I lack eloquence in English." You may understand what the French patient means if you have struggled to make yourself understood across a language barrier. It is important to remember that the "language" of health care is often foreign to patients as well. In Chapter 9 we discuss in more detail how language and vocabulary, which are partially a result of education, can facilitate or block what patients perceive as respect from you.

Occupation and Place of Residence

One of the first questions we often ask a new acquaintance in a social setting is, "What do you do?" We deeply identify with our occupations in mainstream American culture. Some would go so far as to say that their occupation defines who they are more than their ethnicity or other primary characteristics. Occupations shape how people see the world and what they value. The importance of a person's occupation is sometimes seen more clearly when injury, illness, or retirement forces a change in occupation. How patients occupy themselves, whether they spend their time in the formal workforce or not, can give important cultural clues that have an impact on health care beliefs and decisions.

We do not often think of place of residence as a cultural variable in our interactions with patients, yet there is increasing evidence that place of residence has an impact on how patients think about health. For example, certain health beliefs and practices sometimes differ between urban and rural patients. Rural patients, because of their environment, must often travel a considerable distance to see a health professional. Thus, rural patients are more independent than their urban counterparts. Another significant difference between rural and urban dwellers is the way health needs are viewed. Rural dwellers, both male and female, from a variety of locations, tend to determine health needs primarily in relation to work activities.[28] The make-up of rural communities in the United States is becoming more diverse with an influx of immigrants from many parts of the world because of job opportunities. So, previously homogeneous rural communities are experiencing changes. "For many rural residents, experiences with cultures different from their own are rare, sometimes creating barriers to those from different cultures who settle in the community."[29] Thus, it is important to consider not only where someone lives but the other cultural values that they bring to their place of residence.

A striking example of the impact the values held by rural dwellers can have on health decisions is evident in the following case:

> Michael T. is a 61-year-old wheat farmer. He maintains his large and profitable family farm with the help of his wife, three sons, and occasional hired help. He has managed and actively worked on the same farm for almost 40 years. Mr. T. attended the state university for 2 years, studying agribusiness. By his state's standards he is well educated; he is in the middle-income bracket. During the harvesting season, he often works parts of the fields alone with the help of rented heavy farm equipment. Two years ago while working in this way, he caught the middle finger of his right hand in a moving part of his equipment while he was adjusting a machine component. He could not pull his finger free, and the injury was quite painful. Mr. T. realized that it might be some time before anyone would come to his aid. The weather was changing, and he needed to complete the harvesting work in the field to avoid damage to the wheat crop and prevent additional equipment rental costs. He decided to pull his hand free, severing his finger at its base. He was able to control the bleeding with a tightly bound handkerchief, and he completed harvesting the field.
>
> When he returned home, his son drove him to the nearest town, 57 miles away, where he sought care in the hospital emergency room.
>
> Before continuing with the rest of the case, consider what your reaction might be if you were the first health professional to interact with Mr. T. when he arrived at the emergency room.
>
> ▶ Do you think Mr. T. is brave, stupid, shortsighted, practical, hard-working, frugal, or a combination of these characteristics?
>
> ▶ If you had been in his position, what would you have done?
>
> ▶ How might these personal values and cultural beliefs affect your ability to interact with Mr. T.?
>
> Let us return to the case and see how the health professionals involved responded to the situation.
>
> The physician who saw Mr. T. was very distressed that he had not retrieved the digit and sought care immediately. While dressing Mr. T.'s wound, the physician explained that, with prompt action and air ambulance transport to the state's major medical center, it might have been possible for the finger to be reattached.
>
> Fortunately, Mr. T. did not develop an infection or other serious complication after his injury. He was able to manage his farm as usual once he healed. When he tells neighbors about the story of this event, he often comments, "It simply goes to show you that, if you go to those doctors too soon, you end up with lots of unnecessary treatment and bills."[30]

Whether a patient lives on a farm, in the inner city, or in the suburbs, you will show respect when you are mindful of the impact place of residence can have on interactions with patients. This is especially true when the patient does not have a permanent place of residence or is homeless. The challenges of working with patients whose only home is the streets include major issues such as ensuring the safety and basic well-being of the patient, but also practical considerations unique to this environment such as the need for access to a bathroom or to a source of drinking water. Persons who live on the street either by choice or necessity are part of a subculture that is often hidden from view and require openness and understanding from health professionals.

Religion

Another feature of culture that influences your relationship with patients is religious beliefs. Religion gives meaning to illness, pain, and suffering. Religious beliefs are often most apparent when a patient is seriously injured, critically ill, or dying. For example, the Christian faith, with its valuing of human life and belief in eternal life, states that whereas a struggle for health can be meaningful, a struggle against death at all costs to the point that the effort becomes a torment is nonsense.[31] The Christian cultural view of the dying process and death itself influences treatment decisions and may promote requests for symbolically meaningful activities such as receiving the sacraments.

A different view of illness is evident with believers in Islam. "The word *Islam* means to submit; that is, to submit their lives to the will of God (Allah). A fatalistic worldview is common whereby the person attributes the incidence and outcome of a health condition to 'inshallah.' This belief can make preventive health behaviors or self-care programs difficult to institute. Because God is perceived to be in control of the outcome, what can humans do?"[32] Christian and Muslim beliefs are widespread and relatively well known; therefore, health professionals may not find much difficulty in recognizing them. Religious beliefs that are far removed from mainstream religious traditions may challenge health care professionals' understanding, tolerance, and willingness to make accommodations.

Sexual Orientation

In modern society, sexual orientation is yet another characteristic of culture that may elicit biased responses to a person. Gay, lesbian, bisexual, and transgender patients are often treated differently because of sexual orientation. One commonality among gay men and lesbians is that they may hide their lifestyle for fear of prejudicial attitudes and discrimination. Thus, the sexual orientation of patients may be somewhat invisible. However, given the number of men and women who report being homosexual (and that number is probably an underestimate of the actual total), it is highly likely that most health professionals provide care to gay, lesbian, bisexual, or transgender patients.

In an interesting study, undergraduate health professions students focused on their discomfort with a variety of persons from differing cultural groups. The students reported the most consistently negative attitudes toward lesbian, gay, and bisexual people.[33] Because of unexamined homophobia, many health professionals react with shock or thinly veiled unease when they learn that a patient is not heterosexual.

In addition to the negative attitudes expressed by health professionals toward patients with a sexual orientation different from their own, gay, lesbian, bisexual, and transgendered patients find themselves in a health care system that is built on hetero-sexual assumptions to the extent that women who seek gynecological or obstetrical care may not even be asked about their sexual history. Lesbian and gay patients' part-ners may not be formally acknowledged. Providing sensitive, culturally appropriate care requires taking the patient's sexual orientation fully into account and assuring that the information is used to optimize his or her quality of care.

CULTURAL HUMILITY

The overall lesson to be gleaned from the preceding description of various cultural characteristics is that the atmosphere in health care must rest on fully appreciating what each culture brings to the richness of our society and on acceptance, not on fear and misunderstanding.

What is needed is an approach to each patient, client, and colleague that takes into account cultural differences. Rather than focus on cultural competence as if there were a discrete skill one could master much like reading a sphygmomanometer, we propose the idea of cultural humility. Cultural humility is a process that requires humility[34]:

- as individuals continually engage in self-reflection and self-critique as life-long learners.
- in how health professionals bring into check the power imbalances that exist in the dynamics of communication by using patient-focused interviewing and care.
- to develop and maintain mutually respectful and dynamic partnerships with communities on behalf of individual patients and communities in the context of community-based clinical and advocacy training models.

It is often difficult to grasp our own views, so one method of obtaining this infor-mation is to interview family members, parents, or grandparents to understand where your attitudes toward health originate. Here are some sample questions to get you started:

1. When faced with an injury or illness, did your family member first seek out the help of a health professional or someone else?
2. If someone else, who and why?
3. How does your family view pain? Are you supposed to be "good" and keep quiet about pain, or are you supposed to complain so that pain will be relieved?
4. What home remedies are used for everyday health problems such as headaches, minor burns, or stomach upset?

In Chapter 1, you were reminded to approach each patient with respect. This means, among other things, consciously avoiding unfair judgments about other people's traditions, values, and beliefs. We are much more likely to respect a patient's decision or action if we understand its rationale. Misunderstandings can result in harm to the patient in that he or she may hesitate to seek medical attention or follow the advice of someone so out of touch with his or her beliefs.

One barrier to respectful interaction is the tendency for health professionals to adopt stereotypes and expect certain behaviors from patients from a particular culture simply because they are from that culture. Avoid scripted remarks such as "Jewish patients believe ..." or "All Chinese patients practice ..." because it is impossible to generalize from one patient to an entire culture. "Although some behaviors may appear similar within an identified cultural group, the astute health provider must assess for differences both within and between groups to plan appropriate care."[35]

In the face of cultural differences you will need basic negotiation skills. This means finding a place where you can feel confident in the exercise of your professional judgment yet incorporate the beliefs and values of patients into their treatment plan to achieve mutually desirable outcomes.

Culturally sensitive care is knowledge about, and sensitivity to, the different experiences and responses individuals may have because of a variety of characteristics of their lives.[36] The goal of cultural humility is to provide care characterized by respect. Such care is meaningful and fits with cultural beliefs and ways of life for those involved. Since diversity in society is likely to increase rather than decrease in the coming years, access to the most current statistics regarding demography and tools to assist in providing culturally appropriate care is vitally important. Box 3-2 provides a list of web resources to assist you in obtaining the most current information.

BOX 3-2

WEB RESOURCES FOR DELIVERING CULTURALLY APPROPRIATE CARE

Hispanic Serving Health Professions	www.hshps.com
NMA Cultural Competence Primer	www.askme3.org/pdfs/NMAPrimer.pdf
National Center for Cultural Competence	http://gucchd.georgetown.edu/nccc
U.S. Administration on Aging	www.aoa.gov
Office of Minority Health	www.omhrc.gov
Stanford Geriatric Education Center	http://sgec.stanford.edu
American Society on Aging	www.asaging.org
Center for Applied Linguistics	www.cal.org
ALTA Language Services	www.altalang.com
Center for Cross-Cultural Research	www.ac.wwu.edu/~culture
The Cross Cultural Health Program	www.xculture.org

SUMMARY

The issues relevant to showing respect in the midst of diversity must continually be examined and reflected upon. Any time cultural variations and personal biases become a basis for prejudice or discrimination, these destructive tendencies and conduct will be increased by other distinguishing differences among individuals as well. The only constructive approach to evaluating human differences with the goal of showing respect is to take each experience as an opportunity to learn more about the rich diversity of the human condition and to take what one learns as a gift that will enrich one's own life.

REFERENCES

1. Spencer M, Markstrom-Adams C: Identity processes among racial and ethnic minority children in America, *Child Dev* 61:290-310, 1990.
2. Suh EE: The model of cultural competence through an evolutionary concept analysis, *J Transcult Nurs* 15(2):93-102, 2004.
3. Allport G: *The nature of prejudice*, Reading, MA, 1954, Addison-Wesley.
4. Baldwin D, Nelms T: Difficult dialogues: impact on nursing education curricula, *J Prof Nurs* 9(6):343-346, 1993.
5. United States Department of Commerce, U.S. Census Bureau, Population Division, Population Projections Branch. Washington, DC, 2000, (website): http://www.census.com.
6. Jones ME, Cason CL, Bond ML: Cultural attitudes, knowledge and skills of a health workforce, *J Transcult Nurs* 15(4):283-290, 2004.
7. Johnson FA: Contributions of anthropology to psychiatry. In Goldman H, editor: *Review of Psychiatry*, ed 2, Norwalk, CT, 1988, Appleton & Lange.
8. Betancourt JR and others: Cultural competence and health care disparities: key perspectives and trends, *Health Affairs* 24:499-505, 2005.
9. Hahn RA: The state of federal health statistics on racial and ethnic groups, *JAMA* 267: 268-271, 1992.
10. Editorial, Genes, drugs and race, *Nature Genetics* 29:239-40, 2001.
11. Pinderhughes E: *Understanding race, ethnicity, and power*, New York, 1989, Free Press.
12. Smedley B, Stith A, Nelson A, editors: Committee on understanding and eliminating racial and ethnic disparities in health care, Institutes of Medicine, *Unequal treatment: confronting racial and ethnic disparities in healthcare*, Washington, DC, 2003, The National Academies Press, page 1.
13. Hines SE: Caring for diverse populations: intelligent prescribing in diverse populations, *Patient Care* 34(9):135-136, 139-140, 142, 2000.
14. Lin KM, Smith MW: Psychopharmacotherapy in the context of culture and ethnicity. In Ruiz P, editor: *Ethnicity and psychopharmacology, vol 19(4), Review of Psychiatry*, Washington, DC, 2000, American Psychiatric Press.
15. Kahn J: Getting the numbers right: statistical mischief and racial profiling in heart failure research, *Perspectives in Biology and Medicine* 46(4):473-83, 2003.
16. Conway-Turner K: Older women of color: a feminist exploration of the intersections of personal, familial and community life, *J Women Aging* 11(2/3):115-130, 1999.
17. Kerssens JJ, Bensing JM, Andela MG: Patient preferences for genders of health professionals, *Soc Sci Med* 44:1531-1540, 1997.
18. Delgado A, Lopez-Fernandez LA, Luna JD: Influence of the doctor's gender in the satisfaction of users, *Med Care* 31:795-800, 1993.
19. Mavis B and others: Female patients' preferences related to interpersonal communications, clinical competence, and gender when selecting a physician, *Acad Med* 80(12):1159-1165, 2005.

20. Haffner L: Translation is not enough: interpreting in a medical setting, *West J Med* 157(3): 256, 1992.
21. Executive Order 13166, "Improving Access to Services for Persons with Limited English Proficiency," August 16, 2000; 65 Fed. Reg. 50121.
22. Smedley B, Stith A, Nelson A, editors: Committee on understanding and eliminating racial and ethnic disparities in health care, Institutes of Medicine, *Unequal treatment: confronting racial and ethnic disparities in healthcare*, Washington, DC, 2003, The National Academies Press.
23. Portes A, Rumbaut R: *Immigrant America: a portrait*, ed 2, Berkeley, 1997, University of California Press.
24. Ramer L and others: Multimeasure pain assessment in an ethnically diverse group of patients with cancer, *J Transcult Nurs* 10(2):94-101, 1999.
25. Waitzkin H: *The politics of medical encounters: how patients and doctors deal with social problems*, New Haven, CT, 1991, Yale University Press.
26. Fineman N: The social construction of non-compliance: implications for cross-cultural geriatric practice, *J Cross-cult Gerontol* 6:219-228, 1991.
27. Kauffman KS: The insider/outsider dilemma: field experience of a white researcher "getting in" a poor black community, *Nurs Res* 43(3):179-183, 1994.
28. Bushy A: Rural determinants in family health: considerations for community nurses. In Bushy A, editor: *Rural Nursing*, Vol 23, Newbury Park, NY, 1991, Sage.
29. Wrigley P: The challenge of educating English language learners in rural areas (website): http://escort.org/files/active/1/Challenges%20Article.pdf. Accessed July 26, 2006.
30. Long KA: The concept of health: rural perspectives, *Nurs Clin North Am* 28(1):123-130, 1993.
31. *Care of the dying: a Catholic perspective*, St Louis, 1993, The Catholic Health Association of the United States.
32. Haddad LG, Hoeman SP: Home healthcare and the Arab-American client, *Home Healthc Nurse* 18(3):189-197, 2000.
33. Eliason MJ, Raheim S: Experiences and comfort with culturally diverse groups in undergraduate pre-nursing students, *J Nurs Educ* 39(4):161-165, 2000.
34. Tervalon M, Murray-Garcia J: Cultural humility versus cultural competence: a critical distinction in defining physician training outcomes in multicultural education, *J Health Care Poor Underserved* 9(2):117-125, 1998.
35. Bechtel GA, Davidhizar RE: Integrating cultural diversity in patient education, *Semin Nurse Manag* 7(4):193-197, 1999.
36. Meleis AI: Culturally competent care, *J Transcult Nurs* 10(1):12, 1999.

PART ONE

Questions for Thought and Discussion

1. In what important ways is professional education similar to and different from other types of formal education?
2. Review the characteristics of a profession. Apply these characteristics to your particular profession. Which do you meet? Which do not seem to apply? Why?
3. You are the supervisor of an ambulatory clinic. You recognize an increase in the number of Sudanese immigrants in your patient population. What should you do to prepare your staff to care for these patients?
4. A 13-year-old girl from Saudi Arabia, who does not speak English, is badly burned over her face, arms and legs. Her father has brought her to the United States to receive care. As the male therapist caring for her in your hospital's burn unit, how should you proceed to provide her with culturally competent care?[1]
5. Your first encounter with a health care institution is in your professional education program. It has policies and regulations regarding your interactions with faculty and peers. Obtain copies of these documents and discuss how they facilitate or hinder respectful interaction.
6. You are treating a 24-year-old woman whose diagnosis is cervical cancer. You do not know if she is aware of her diagnosis. One day she asks you to get her medical chart for her from the nursing desk. "The 'Bill of Rights for Patients' in this hospital says that I have a right to accurate information and I figure that is where I will get it." What will you say to her? What will you do? Why?

REFERENCES

1. Lehana, C: Interpreter services in pediatric nursing. *Ped Nurs* 31(4):292-296, 2005.

RESPECT FOR YOURSELF

Part Two focuses on you, the health professional, as an individual, because a key to all respectful human interaction lies in respecting yourself. When you and your colleagues enter the health professions, you bring with you your own unique combination of abilities, needs, values, and dreams. Understandably, you expect to incorporate these into the positions you will assume as a health professional.

Chapter 4 focuses on your student experiences and the opportunity to cultivate self-respect during this period. The questions asked in this chapter are fundamental to promoting respect for yourself throughout your career in the health professions: "What is professional education?" "What is expected of me during this period of professional preparation?" "How does it affect me as a person?" "What habits reflecting respect for myself can I cultivate as a student that will serve me well throughout my professional career?"

Chapter 5 focuses on respect for yourself as you assume your professional role. Although not all health professions place people in the role of direct patient contact, some of the most challenging aspects of professional life are in the clinical setting, where you will be acting as a professional advocate. A health professional's attitudes toward and understanding of the clinical setting influence the effectiveness of interaction with patients. The role of the health professional as one of a whole matrix of persons caring for a patient is examined with attention devoted to the importance of being a good player on the health care "team." Newer dimensions of interaction (e.g., through computer technologies) also are examined. Chapter 5 concludes with suggestions about how to utilize the strengths of the community of persons with whom you will work.

By the end of Part Two, you should be better able to view yourself as respectfully as others will in your several roles as a health professional.

CHAPTER 4

RESPECT FOR YOURSELF: THE STUDENT YEARS

CHAPTER OBJECTIVES

The student will be able to:

- Identify three kinds of learning that take place during professional preparation and the environment in which each takes place
- Explain similarities and differences between the classroom and clinical settings of professional preparation
- Identify four types of skills associated with professional practice
- Name eight steps in acquiring skills needed for professional practice
- List five procedures that should assist the student in adjusting to the clinical education phase of professional preparation
- Describe the characteristics of critical thinking and their role in professional problem-solving
- Evaluate several sources of student anxiety and some methods of addressing it effectively
- List some positive goals students can realize by attending to their own needs and sources of satisfaction
- Distinguish the strengths of a Sisyphus-type approach to professional tasks from those of a Pandora-type
- Identify some characteristics of solitude and why it is important
- List four ways to help ensure that you will make time for leisure, play, creativity, and solitude

"I'm a student nurse," I began by way of introduction. "Could we sit down somewhere and talk?"

Ann led the way with shaky steps to a small table and two chairs. Ruth followed us and stood behind her mother and played with her necklaces.

I asked Ann, "How long have you had this shakiness?"

"Started two days ago," Ann replied.

"Has this happened before?"

"Sometimes, but not this bad."

I had seen a few patients react to antipsychotic drugs this way, but not this severely. At least I thought it was a reaction to the medication. Maybe Ann drank as well, I didn't know how to ask her if she did. ...

—A. Haddad[1]

SELF-RESPECT AND THE DESIRE TO CONTRIBUTE

Most students know that they would like to be able to make a contribution to others in society. It is a motivator for applying to an education program in the health professions. The desire to help others is so central to your role as a professional that it will help sustain your self-respect over the years. Often, although not always, this desire arises because students have had an experience of their own illness or injury and have been helped by a professional whom they have come to admire, or a friend or loved one was ill and dying and health professionals showed able assistance and compassion in caring for the person. Students also know that they may have moments when they will feel very uncertain of how to proceed to make the kind of contribution they have admired in others, like the student nurse who is in his or her first semester of working in a home setting.

Sometimes the desire to make a contribution is nurtured by a student's recognition that he or she has a talent for being a good listener or for helping friends when they are in trouble. Other students have had an opportunity to save another person's life or in other ways have intervened constructively, and that experience has been instrumental in their desire to be of service.

The desire to help is not always the primary or only factor that leads people to choose a career as a health professional. Love of science, the desire to be in a "people-oriented" line of work, the desire for status, and a career that promises to provide a good salary and high satisfaction are other important and understandable motivators. However, the desire to make a significant contribution in life is very important in helping you stay true to your course of study when the going gets rough. One good approach is to identify early on a teacher or other professional role model who manifests attributes you admire (Figure 4-1).

 REFLECTIONS

Have you identified classroom or clinical educators whose manner, conduct, attitudes, or skills you admire? What, specifically, are the traits that caught your attention?

HOW DO I BECOME COMPETENT IN MY FIELD?

The phrase you will hear dozens of times during your preparation to become a health professional is that you must become competent in your field. Competence means that you are prepared to be and do what reasonably is expected of you in your role insofar as your formal education, licensing and other requirements placed upon you can prepare you. To help you know when you are achieving this ultimate goal you will be introduced to "competencies" that have been developed by the leaders in your field in response to your profession's own and society's expectations of every member of your field.

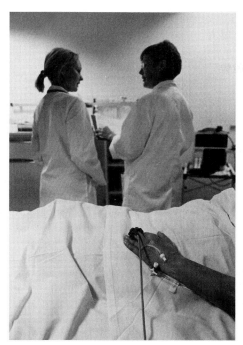

FIGURE 4-1: Identifying a professional role model can enable a student to remain true to his or her course of studies. *(© Corbis.)*

You will gradually become aware that preparation for becoming a health professional is different from that for other fields. While students in other programs of study are partying on Friday afternoon, the health professions student may be at the clinic or laboratory carrying out an education internship or field work requirement; while roommates are still trying to get out of bed in the morning, it is not unusual for the health professions student to be on the way out the door; and, while most careers do not require students to adopt a set of professional attitudes, behaviors, and ethical guidelines, the health professions do.

Education in the health professions prepares you to competently carry out a lifelong commitment and realize a certain type of lifestyle. You have already learned that your identity as a health professional carries with it expectations on the part of society, as well as privileges and responsibilities. You will be considered an "expert" in your field, but as a professional you will be looked on as a person whose special knowledge, skills, and attitudes can make the world a better place and improve individuals' lives. In choosing to be a health professional, you are accepting that competence involves not only what you will do but also who you will become in your own eyes and in the eyes of patients and others.

What can you expect during your years of formal education? On the following pages we discuss three types of learning experiences that will predominate: the acquisition of basic concepts and theories (knowledge), the mastery of professional skills, and the attainment of attitudes appropriate to your role as a health professional. Each will support your self-respect for your choice of profession, preparing you for effective and respectful interaction with patients, colleagues, and society.

Knowledge (Theoretical Concepts)

Traditionally, education in the health professions required knowledge of the classics and, as the scientific age developed, basic sciences. Today, the foundation of required knowledge is much broader.

What knowledge do you need to become a competent health professional? Knowledge in the sciences still provides a foundation for understanding the body and the natural forces acting on it, and knowledge in the behavioral sciences of psychology, sociology, and anthropology provides understanding of people's needs and behaviors and of how these needs and behaviors affect interaction. Knowledge in the liberal arts exposes one to the great political, religious, and philosophical ideas and establishes one's own link with history. An awareness of pertinent economic and legal concepts allows one to understand in the complex world of how the delivery of health care is financed today and some basic guidelines governing the activities of health care institutions today. Knowledge of statistics and information technology furnishes a baseline for research design, data analysis, and communication functions. Knowledge of policies at the institutional, local, and national levels helps you to understand the links between practice and the larger social context in which you work.

Theoretical knowledge regarding the techniques relevant to your profession explains the rationale for adopting practices consistent with evidence-based information. If the only type of learning for professional competence were acquisition and integration of knowledge, there would be no need to include extensive laboratory experience or clinical education in the preparation of health professionals like yourself. Already you begin to see that education for the health professions differs from the formal preparation for most other careers.

Skills

At the time they enter their professional curriculum, most students are more accustomed to classroom learning than to laboratory and clinical learning. In the years of professional preparation, more time in the laboratory and clinic is required for the acquisition of skills. Only with experience will full mastery of a skill be realized, but all components for enabling that mastery must be presented in your professional preparation.

The acquisition of skill often requires long, tedious hours of practice. This is where your instructor's skill as an educator and your willingness to persevere really count.

---

⑥ REFLECTIONS

The frustration that often accompanies mastering a skill was illustrated recently when one of the authors decided to learn to fly fish. She read several books, watched a video, and studied the types of flies and equipment, then hired a guide to take her to a trout stream in northern Maine. The first half-day was spent far from the water, in a field, learning to cast the fly out. At least half the time the fly caught in trees, bushes, and other overhanging obstructions. After lunch, finally in the water, she learned that the coordination required to lay the line flat and cast the fly out far enough from her boots to attract anything other than shore line weeds was a far cry from the pictures in the video. That night, nursing a sore shoulder and wrist, she remembered her instructor's encouragement to rest up and "with practice you'll see yourself improving day-by-day." She wondered. Hundreds of casts later it still wasn't perfect, but the fly more often landed in the stream where she was trying to set it.

Consider four basic skills needed for competence in a health profession:

Technical Skill

Technical skill is the ability to safely and effectively apply a given technique to secure a diagnosis, conduct an evaluation, or provide a treatment intervention. The medical technologist analyzes the contents of a sample of blood or other body fluids. The physical therapist conducts a gait analysis. The pharmacist identifies and prepares the proper dosage of medication. The speech pathologist assesses voice sounds. In each case, technical expertise includes an intricate coordination of mind and body, as well as the exercise of sound informed judgment. The application of techniques requires skillful management of oneself and of the technical equipment of one's profession.

Skill in Interpersonal Relationships and Communication

As a health professional you will interact with a wide variety of people during the course of a day: other health professionals, support personnel, patients and their families, students, visitors, administrators, and business contacts such as professional equipment salespersons. This activity demands that you understand appropriate conduct in different types of relationships. It means being able to accept responsibility as a supervisor and constructive criticism when supervised. It involves learning how caring is expressed in the professional role and demands tact, diplomacy, consistency, and forthrightness. It also requires listening as if your patient's life depended on it—and it may! Many areas of this book describe means whereby you can express respect through your communications skills, and Part Four focuses specifically on it.

Teaching and Administrative Skill

Education of individual patients or clients and the larger public is essential in virtually every health field today. Whatever your choice of profession, you will be required to engage in educational activities geared to patients, families, students, other health professionals, and support personnel. Administrative skills also are essential. You will be expected to organize and implement workable solutions to potential problems; set reasonable short- and long-term goals in your workplace; engage in fair, objective evaluation of yourself and others; engage in policy formation and review; and do your share to maintain a cost-effective operation.

Research Skill

Research advances the knowledge and skills of your field. Skill in *quantitative* research approaches requires that you develop a research question, design a project, formulate a hypothesis, and collect and analyze data to determine whether your hypothesis is correct. *Qualitative* research is conducted utilizing in-depth interviews or other narratives designed to highlight important areas of understanding about the type of problem or phenomenon at hand. Honest, accurate reporting of findings is imperative. As today's students enter practice, their reimbursement will be based on evidence-based practices, i.e., those confirmed by research to be effective.

 REFLECTIONS

- From your studies so far name some areas of current research in your field.
- Even though you may not yet have had much experience in your field, try to think of an area of your future practice where you can imagine doing research yourself.

To understand better how students acquire skills for professional practice, consider the following steps your professional program will guide you through. You will:
1. Acquire knowledge related to the skill
2. Experience the skill applied to yourself
3. Apply the skill to a classmate
4. Observe a professional person using the skill
5. Assist the professional person in using the skill
6. Be closely supervised in the first attempts to apply the skill alone
7. Satisfactorily use the skill in a variety of situations, with decreasing amounts of direct supervision
8. Be tested for basic competence in applying the skill

Note the progression from classroom to professional setting in this process. Step 1 can easily take place in a classroom or online, while steps 2 and 3 must take place in the skills laboratory. Steps 4 through 8 take place in the workplace setting where a variety of situations are available, perhaps initially in simulated patient situations and then with real patients and decreasing amounts of direct supervision. Thus, the basics needed to assume eventual mastery of professional skills require that only a part of the training be in the classroom.

As a student, you have a right to expect the faculty's commitment to your learning, appropriate teaching styles, and type and amount of supervision and guidance during the various steps of your professional preparation. The greatest challenge to educators is to shape their approaches to guarantee that you have an opportunity to acquire the skills you will need, but it is their moral and legal obligation to do so.

Attitudes and Character

During your student years, your professors are expected to teach and reinforce attitudes and character traits consistent with respect in your professional role.

 REFLECTIONS

Consider the following questions related to attitudes:
- Do you consider yourself a helper? Under what conditions might you resent having to help? How do you expect people to respond to you after you have done your best to help them?
- How do you respond to a person who is mentally or physically impaired? Do you feel pity? Embarrassment? Discomfort or disdain? Compassion?
- What qualities make life worth living? Would some people be better off dead?
- If you were to become seriously ill or have a serious accident, what changes in your present status would be the most difficult to accept? Why?

Your attitudes toward helping, the qualities that you believe make life worth living, and your own personal integrity are among the most central to your success as a professional.

One important attitude to acquire or cultivate during your student years is a love of learning; it is best planted during this period if it is to flourish in later years. This attitude can actually have a strong bearing on your success as a professional. May identified ten characteristics required for success in the health professions, one being a *commitment to learning,* which he described as the ability to self-assess, self-correct, and self-direct, as well as the willingness to continually seek new knowledge and understanding.[2] Unfortunately, the competitive nature of some academic programs and many students' drive to succeed may take the joy out of learning and replace it with attitudes of anger or resentment for having to study all the time. In the best educational environments faculty and students work together to avoid this catastrophe. The physical environment should be an encouragement. Institutions in which professional education takes place must take responsibility to make your work and leisure environments conducive to learning through appropriate design of the building inside and out. Students have a responsibility to help maintain it too, by treating it respectfully, as a resource.

You should now be familiar with three kinds of learning that take place during professional preparation: knowledge, skills, and attitude/character formation. In addition, you know the environments in which each kind of learning most efficiently and effectively takes place. With this baseline, you are ready to explore the nature of the relationship between classroom and clinical professional education.

CLINICAL EDUCATION: SPECIAL CHALLENGES

Clinical education is called by different names in different professions: *clinical education, clinical fieldwork, clinical clerkships, rotations*, or *internships*, to name some. This aspect of your education provides you with an opportunity to demonstrate that you will succeed in your future work environment. The quality and quantity of teaching that take place are determined by such wide-ranging and unpredictable variables as the availability of patients and the availability of other professionals who can monitor and guide the students. New smells, sounds, and sights combine with new tasks to present an exciting challenge to students, and almost all students find it the most stimulating part of their educational preparation. Faculty who work as teachers and supervisors benefit from the opportunity, too.

Refinement and synthesis are important functions of clinical education. Refinement implies that you now have the basic materials with which to work and must learn to use them optimally. Synthesis is the work of putting together, in a meaningful way, the many details you have learned in your professional preparation up to this time. At this juncture you encounter:

- Large numbers of patients with different problems
- Several manifestations of a single clinical condition
- Time limitations
- Multiple professional responsibilities related to the work environment (e.g., documentation and participating in staff meetings)
- Work with members of various health care teams
- Assimilation of particular techniques into workable evaluation or treatment programs

The desired outcome is a competent professional person ready to enter practice.

There is inherent wisdom in getting off to a good start in any new venture, and a few practical guidelines apply to students beginning the new venture into clinical education. A general rule is to acknowledge that you are entering an environment that has its own players, peculiarities, and habits. Respect for the fact that you are in someone else's territory is key. Fortunately, most educators in this setting extend themselves to try to help students feel accepted, but you may find the situation awkward anyway, at least initially. It is rather like going into someone else's home and being told to "make yourself at home." It takes time to be able to feel "at home" no matter what the host or hostess says. We remember a medical student telling us about her awkwardness at the nurse's station at the onset of her first clinical education placement. She had received a thorough orientation from her physician supervisor, who then left.

I just stood at the nurse's station waiting for someone to ask me what I wanted or tell me what to do. Nobody paid any attention to me. My supervisor was nowhere to be seen. I felt like I was at the grocery store waiting to check out but nobody noticed that I was there. It was awful.

Fortunately, she eventually became more at ease and enjoyed it so much that upon graduation she returned there to do her residency. This student could have been helped over her initial unease by following a few simple suggestions:

- Always introduce yourself to the key players, even those who do not seem to be "important."
- Try to assess in advance the usual protocols and ways of doing things in this setting.
- Ask explicit questions about the expectations of your supervisor.
- Assume that occasionally someone may be suspicious of or perplexed by a newcomer in "their" environment, and prepare to respond to their questions or comments in a nondefensive and instructive manner.
- Assume that everyone basically wants to assist in your learning. If you have any reason to believe otherwise, you should discuss it with your faculty advisor.

⊙ REFLECTIONS

If you have already begun your clinical education, reflect on what you felt and found in this new environment when you first arrived, and what, if anything, had changed by the time you left. Do you have insight into why the changes took place?

Try to recall a recent situation not in your professional preparation where you felt awkward in your new environment. In retrospect, what things could you have done to make the situation more pleasant for yourself? Jot them down here. Would they apply to clinical education?

In short, be attentive to the opportunities and challenges of this new environment. Busy staff do notice when someone shows genuine interest in their work, their professional challenges, and especially in the patients' well-being. Politely but firmly hold your clinical educators to high standards of their instructional tasks so that they will succeed as educators and you as the learner. In this phase of your education, you are gaining the self-confidence and self-respect for your role that will enable you to proceed deftly towards full professional participation in your chosen workplace.

CRITICAL THINKING: PREPARATION FOR THE UNEXPECTED

No matter how good a student you are or how committed and excellent your faculty, you will not become fully prepared for every situation you will encounter. To successfully meet challenges that are novel or unexpected in the clinical setting requires that you acquire the ability to think critically. It goes beyond the purpose of this text to provide training in critical thinking, but you should receive it elsewhere in your curriculum. To complement that learning we invite you to consider the following dimensions of the art of critical thinking:

Critical thinking requires time and silence. Just as we exercise our bodies, we need time to exercise our minds. Initially, you might find that your mind is quite undisciplined and jumps from one idea to the next with little pattern or coherence. After a while, it is possible to see familiar themes in your thoughts. This creative work counters the common misconception that merely thinking is wasting time. With so much new happening in the clinical setting, it is crucial to take time to think about it.

Critical thinking entails being neutral toward a situation at the outset. This does not mean that you are disinterested. It means that you are able to view the place and people in a situation objectively and to take in the whole of the experience. Health care settings are often highly stressful. The essence of critical thinking is the ability to calmly survey a situation and think about what is happening as clearly as you can.

Critical thinking involves sizing up a situation, getting to the point of what is happening, and observing general principles behind the specifics of circumstances. Keen observation and attuned listening is essential to critical thinking to move from personal perspectives to the perspectives of others involved in a clinical situation.

Critical thinking requires discernment to identify credible, logical reasons that people use to justify their views or recommendations, distinguishing them from those that are strictly illogical and emotional. This is not to say that emotions are trivial or should be suppressed. However, without thought, feelings can cause you to lose perspective. A common device used to avoid rational arguments while trying to persuade others emotionally is to engage in a logical *fallacy*, an incorrect way of reasoning.

Although there are several types of fallacies, two of the most common are being ambiguous and jumping to hasty conclusions. One commits the fallacy of ambiguity by not defining key terms. Complex problems require complex terms that need clear definition for the parties involved to understand each other. Individuals who do not listen well in the first place may hear only the last thing that has been said and, thus, steer the argument in a totally different and unconnected direction, resulting in a hasty, and perhaps harmful, conclusion.

These components of critical thinking—keen observation and listening skills, the ability to see and apply general principles in specific circumstances, and sensitivity to fallacies—can be learned and practiced in all facets of life, but they are critical for success in professional life and must be cultivated during professional preparation.

FINDING MEANING IN THE STUDENT ROLE

The stresses that students face often are directly related to the transitional nature of their position: they are not fully professional but go beyond being a lay person. The process of progressing from a classroom student to a full professional means that your role is constantly evolving. In trying to find your exact function on the health care team, you may find that you are sometimes "put in your place" by patients and professionals alike. A case in point involves a clinical imaging student who mustered the courage to call a physician to clarify a referral. Although the student had identified herself at the outset of the call, when she finished sharing her concerns the physician responded, "Okay, you may have a point. Now put a real professional on the line and let me talk with her." That kind of response hurts, no matter how confident you might have felt when you made the call. This grey zone of being "betwixt and between" gives rise to some of the types of anxiety we explore next.

Why Do I Feel Anxious?

The bad news is that most anxiety directly arising from the pressures of student life is difficult to avoid completely since much is due to the transitory role of students. The good news is that most of it will pass for the same reason! However, for many students at least three serious questions may be the focus of anxiety, and each is worth attending to. The first is "Am I/Can I get prepared well enough to pass the courses and complete the degree requirements?" This type of insecurity is most evident just before an exam, and when you can attach your anxiety to something as concrete as an exam, it is possible to deal with it. The second question, "Do I have what it takes?" is rather like the first but is more fundamental. It may arise from the troublesome suspicion that other students and your professional models have qualities that you seem to lack or from the fact that you have responsibilities that compete for your attention.

Both questions may be related to your assessment of your intellectual or moral capacities as well as to your physical or emotional limits. They are questions often asked by students who fail an exam or experience the rather common reaction of feeling faint the first time they see a badly injured patient, observe surgery, or are unexpectedly overwhelmed by a noxious odor.

The third question is "Can I afford to stay in school?" Many students feel burdened by the financial demands that an education places on them and their families. Anxiety about having to take another loan or find a job or the possibility of having to drop out of school altogether is more common than is sometimes supposed.

Anxieties related directly to student life affect many students' performances. However, anxieties arising from nonstudent issues also can impinge on student success. An impending divorce, either one's own or that of one's parents or child, an unwanted pregnancy, the news that a loved one is seriously ill—these and many other problems can influence a person's performance dramatically.

Some students worry about their choice of profession. This is understandable: it is a big decision. Pressures on young people to decide what they are going to be lead many to choose a career early in life, sometimes as early as junior high school. At the same time, a growing number of students who have raised children or spent many years in another line of work also are choosing formal education in the health professions. Their anxiety often springs from the belief that they are acting on their last chance to realize a dream, may be too old to compete competitively in a job market apparently geared to the young, or are not giving enough time to other obligations of midlife. Much is at stake in making the correct judgment about a field of study. Whatever background brings students to their studies, each may not only ask, "Is this what I want?" but also ponder, "Is this what I want more than the other good opportunities open to me?"

How Can I Respond Constructively to Anxiety?

Most students do go through a skeptical, questioning phase, but if anxiety persists it should be addressed. We provide some suggestions here about what you can do to respond well and go on to enjoy your choice of life's work.

Identify the Source

One of the most important steps in dissipating the destructive tension associated with anxiety is to identify its source if you can do so on your own. Is it directly school-related? Is there some other obvious reason that anxiety has descended on you, or is the source too diffuse to identify? Are there times when you are free from it, and if so, when? What activities seem to help allay it?

Share Feelings with a Friend or Trustworthy Classmate

The sting of anxiety is that it can alienate you from others who know that something is wrong but do not know what or why (Figure 4-2). They may even think it is something they have done. In sharing your anxiety with a trusted person, you have overcome the isolation of the experience and in most cases have gained an ally who can help you address it. An unintended side effect of this process is that you may find out how common your feelings are. By knowing that others, too, are feeling the anxiety, you feel less "out of joint" with the rest of the world.

"I'm not eating. I'm self-medicating."

FIGURE 4-2: *(© The New Yorker Collection 2001. William Haefeli from cartoonbank.com. All rights reserved.)*

Seek Professional Help

When talking with a friend is not adequate, you deserve the benefit of help from a professional. In such cases, an instructor or counselor can help you discover why you feel anxious. In other instances, the treatment for anxiety may require an extended course of intervention over weeks or months. Your well-being is at stake, and this is an area of caring for yourself that, when acted upon, will help foster your self-respect for what you took the time to do.

In all of these methods, the key to decreasing anxiety, once its source is identified, is to attend to it so that it does not ruin what would otherwise be the exciting adventure of professional preparation.

SELF-RESPECT THROUGH NURTURING YOURSELF

Nurturing yourself is not limited to addressing worrisome problems such as anxiety. In Chapter 1 you were introduced to the idea that persons' well-being depends in part on their ability to identify and shape their lives in a manner consistent with their own values and those that help to build a stronger community. The basic question we ask for your reflection is, "What kinds of attitudes and activities can you cultivate during your student years to stay authentically *you*—healthy, satisfied with your job, and able to integrate your professional and personal goals?"

Today there is a general belief that individuals are ultimately responsible for their own health. Do you agree? It certainly is the case that people feel better, look better, and are able to function more fully when nurturing their own sense of well-being, seeking balance in their lives, and mapping a life course that has opportunity for changing priorities. None of these goals ever comes easily! For example, studying for your professional degree means giving up other pleasures as well as dealing with competing responsibilities.

The challenge of keeping life-affirming goals in the forefront of your life plan as new situations arise has long been recognized. However, acknowledging the benefits of nurturing yourself to stay healthy physically, mentally, and spiritually and actually being successful in doing so are not the same! In this section, insights and suggestions are offered to help you succeed in staying healthy.

Overcoming Illusions of Invulnerability

Many health professionals are so used to being helpers that they perceive themselves as "the strong ones," immune to illness or debilitation. This illusion begins in student years when pressures of study and achievement increase. Goethe, in his *Elective Affinities,* illustrates that everyone has a potential for organizing a world that fits his or her illusions: "And so they all, each in his own way, reflectingly or unreflectingly, go on with their daily lives; everything seems to have its accustomed course, for indeed, even in desperate situations where everything hangs in the balance, one goes on living as though nothing were wrong."[3]

To make matters worse for health professionals, most ethical codes and oaths in the health professions do not provide encouragement to health professionals to take good care of themselves. It is as if they, too, deny the health professional's vulnerability.

Throughout history, the major codes have been duty-oriented and have emphasized the health professional's responsibility to *others,* with a striking degree of negligence in talking about responsibility to one's own self. This is not surprising, since, as you also learned in Chapter 1, a professional by definition is one who provides an important service to others. In fact, there was so much emphasis on serving others that some early documents in nursing and medicine suggested that one's dedication might lead to death in times of plague or other danger. Medical historians tell us that the physician Galen suffered nightmares for the rest of his life owing to his feelings of guilt after he fled the plague of Rome to protect his own life and that of his family. The good news is that today martyrdom is out! However, ethical codes of the health professions have been slow to incorporate the importance of taking good care of yourself as a value, even though you are obviously in a better position to serve others when you are acting from a position of strength yourself.

 REFLECTIONS

The need to respect your own limits seems to be a blind spot in most writings guiding professionals. Review the ethical code of your chosen field to see if your leaders have incorporated this important aspect of professional life into the code.

In the presence of psychological reasons for adopting a feeling of invulnerability and in the absence of clear ethical guidelines to foster self-care, your challenge is to forge a path during your student years that will serve you well over the years. We offer two general suggestions: the first is to adopt generative approaches to your tasks; the second is to take time for yourself. Although they may be obvious, the particulars of how to go about each of these deserve attention.

Adopting Generative Approaches

Personal strengths and habits are reasonable starting points for developing health-supporting work habits during your student years that will help sustain you throughout your career. Two characters from Greek mythology, Sisyphus and Pandora, offer contrasting models for approaching tasks. Whereas neither taken alone is adequate, some aspects of the two models taken together can create a balanced approach to stresses and problems you will encounter:

One model is Sisyphus.[4] He is portrayed as possessing competence, single-mindedness, and perseverance. As a king, being "held responsible" required that Sisyphus willingly place himself in a position of decision-making and accept as an integral aspect of his role the consequences that would follow if he did not complete his job well. In the Sisyphus approach, the major challenge is to pursue the completion of a task with due diligence.

Although he is portrayed as a male figure, his approach is by no means limited to male students and health professionals today! The Sisyphus type of individual is decisive, acts autonomously, competes with vigor, but generally sees little need for input from others. Things are going well when he is "in control."

The person who adopts this approach fosters and values efficient decision-making and conduct. The Sisyphus-type health professional also places a high value on competence. One can see that Sisyphus-type traits support expertise in the professions, in which each contributor must be highly competent. The emphasis of the Sisyphus model on holding oneself fully responsible makes this type of health professions student supportive of accountability-oriented tasks such as completing assignments on time and with high quality. An entire social workers' code of ethics is organized around the concept and language of "responsibility" and ethics codes of numerous health professions place it centrally in their ethical guidelines.[5] In fact one might ask if the Sisyphus approach has any shortcomings at all.

The answer is yes. As in many Greek tragedies, his major strength was also his downfall. His activities were such that during his tenure as king of Corinth he incurred the wrath of Zeus, who doomed him to Hades. There his strengths determined his eternal punishment. Sisyphus has to forever roll uphill a heavy stone, which forever rolls down again (Figure 4-3). He keeps pushing, never reflecting, never getting help, never trying an alternative route, and never attempting to renegotiate the terms—always pushing up the same path again and again and again ... *ad infinitum.*

FIGURE 4-3: Sisyphus' major strength was also his downfall; he never realized that his goal may have been attainable by trying a different route or method. (© *Art Resources, NY, 2006. The Myth of Sisyphus. Detail of black figure vase. By Acheloos Painter [6th BCE] located in the Staatliche Antikensammlung, Munich, Germany. Photo provided by Picture archives Foto Marburg.)*

His accountability is awesome. The fastidious persistence with which he exercises his task is exhausting. He is rigorously responsible. *But he never succeeds.* What would happen if only once, just once, Sisyphus would break away to try the alternative route up the back side of the mountain, or better yet, around it? Suppose if only once he'd say, "Phooey, this isn't going to work. I'm going to bed!" Although his dogged persistence generates much activity, the tragedy of Sisyphus is his inability to recognize that his goal may be attainable by some other route.

There is another problem with the Sisyphus model. Modern-day Sisyphus-type health professionals are becoming immortalized, too—in the literature of "burnout." *Burnout* is the term applied to a person's state of emotional and physical exhaustion due to extreme duress. The demands of professional life can be exhausting, and most leaders today are not placed in immortal bodies with immortal minds and spirits. The dogged persistence of an overwhelmed Sisyphus can diminish competence, produce a closet substance abuser, or cause chronic rage and depression. Burnout, as it is called, destroys some of the most committed leaders in the professions.[6] There is mounting evidence that their destructive habits leading to incompetence, unethical corner cutting, and impairment all too often have their start during the years of preparation for a profession.[7] Because there is such a high price to pay for many who adopt a Sisyphus approach only, it is worthwhile to consider alternative or additional modes of professional functioning. It seems that some of the serious difficulties accompanying a strictly Sisyphus approach can be mitigated by weaving them skillfully with Pandoran traits. Therefore, let us consider this model.

Pandora was a leader in her own right, being the first mortal woman in Greek mythology (Figure 4-4). She was playful, imaginative, and mischievous. Her inquisitiveness was unbridled. Her optimism and ingenuity were a delight to behold.[4]

Virtues required for operating within this model include the acknowledgment of surprise, ability to embrace rather than to oversimplify ambiguities, willingness to accommodate uncertainty, courage to act in the face of the unknown, optimism, risk-taking, love of the lyrical, a propensity for dancing rather than for marching, and a comfort with improvisation.

One can readily see the contrast with Sisyphus and begin to assess this model's strengths (which, again, may be expressed by members of both genders). To be a Pandora requires imaginative exploration to overcome the uselessness, in some situations, of trying old—even time-tested—routes for today's changing health care system demands. The weakest link in the chain of the Sisyphus approach is the inability to see the promise of anything new and uncertain; Pandora's approach welcomes such challenges.

Preparation for dealing with uncertainty seldom is addressed adequately in formal professional programs of study. Still, uncertainty faces the health professional almost every day. One physician observes:

> In my own practice, I came to dread the simple complaints such as colds, viruses, and headaches, not so much because I was worried that I was missing something serious, but because people seemed so disappointed with the indefinite results of my examination and treatment. I am sure that if the time were all accumulated and tallied, I have literally spent days trying to explain the uncertainty of medicine to often understandably unwilling patients.[8]

FIGURE 4-4: Imaginative exploration, such as Pandora's, can help the young health professional meet new challenges. *(© Art Resources, NY, 2006. Pandora by Rosso Fiorentino, located in the Ecole des Beaux Arts, Paris. Photo provided by Snark.)*

This physician's discomfort is understandable! Without accurate knowledge you may cause harm to a patient, a peer, or your institution. At the same time, no one can know everything about how to reach the ends worth achieving through professional interventions. Even for the most knowledgeable health professional, the problem of uncertainty rests in the variability of the human condition. When an error is made, this fact can threaten one's self-respect because it is so closely identified with the mandate not to cause harm to the patient. Because everyone errs at some time, Blustein and others have urged that from the time you are a student you must cultivate the (neglected) virtue of self-forgiveness. Self-forgiveness is not sweeping problems under the rug; rather, it requires confronting the issue, taking necessary steps to seek forgiveness of the harmed person, and then forgiving oneself.[9]

What these insights highlight is that old paths up the mountain, however deeply worn by those before you, are not ensured routes to success in uncertain moments. Given the uncertainty that characterizes large areas of the practice of the health professions, health professionals necessarily must be creative strategists, risk takers, innovators.

However, many readers know that Pandora is not remembered mostly for her vitality, optimism, and ingeniousness, but rather for her mistake. Impulsively, she opened a box—the wrong box—and all human resources escaped and were lost, leaving only hope. Clearly, the Pandora mode needs "tempering," just as the Sisyphus approach does. Flexibility and a wide range of resources will be needed for you to settle on an appropriate response that will preserve your equanimity when challenged by something new and uncertain, but allow you to explore new options as well. Pandora and Sisyphus represent two extremes of approach. Ideally, you will avoid the detrimental effects of each while capitalizing on their considerable combined strengths, utilizing them during your student years in preparation for a lifetime career that is successful and self-fulfilling.

Respecting Your Need for Solitude

No matter how wisely you choose a lifestyle that allows ample doses of both Sisyphean and Pandoran traits, you still deserve to claim time to be alone. A vital strategy for survival is solitude.

Solitude is a positive, active state of being, although the experience of solitude is not identical to happiness and may even be "bittersweet" (accompanied by sorrow or anger); nonetheless, it is *sought out* as a need in itself, not foisted upon one as a result of feeling rejected or "out of contact." It is respecting your need to not always be responding to other people. Unlike loneliness, which is a form of suffering, solitude can be wonderful.

⊚ REFLECTIONS

List here the things you most like to do by yourself. If you do not currently make or have enough time for these activities, make two columns, one listing the reasons you do not do them, the other making some suggestions to yourself about how you might make more opportunities to enjoy them.

Pooh Bear, the most philosophical and reflective member of Winnie-the-Pooh's community, sought solitude often (Figure 4-5). He understood that solitude is a time to be *with yourself only,* not with others, and to engage in reflections and activities that can better prepare you for relationships. Some people are active in their solitude, finding walking, jogging, biking, reading, or other solitary activities a time for reflection. Others prefer the stillness of meditation or just sitting quietly Pooh Bear style. Yet, many health professionals do not in fact respect their need for time alone enough. Do you? If not, your student years are a good time to begin building such time into your daily routine.

Many students find that the structure of educational institutions tends to create barriers to the important work of solitude. Health care institutions too are seldom environments where there is encouragement to stop and reflect, take time off for a quiet walk, or in other ways take time quietly alone to regroup and relax. Some ideas to help you make time for yourself include the following:

- Set a time and place and rigorously adhere to it.
- Become bold in identifying to others what you are doing.

FIGURE 4-5: "And He sits and thinks of the things they know; He and the Forest, alone together … " (From Winnie-The-Pooh *by AA Milne, illustrated by EH Shepard, copyright 1926 by EP Dutton, renewed 1954 by AA Milne. Used by permission of Dutton Children's Books, an imprint of Penguin Books for Young Readers, a division of Penguin Putnam Inc.)*

- Take notes on your reflections or keep a log of your activities.
- Remind yourself often that a basic minimum requirement upon which many other health-supporting activities depend is to take time to be with yourself.

In addition, you can help others to have their own time alone by learning to recognize this need in colleagues and encouraging it.

REAPING THE REWARDS OF PERSEVERANCE

This chapter would be incomplete without a short note to you on the rewards of persevering.

The health professions continue to be among the most rewarding and challenging careers available today. Most educational programs select from a large pool of applicants, ensuring that you will spend your professional career with highly qualified and interesting colleagues. The opportunity for personal growth and professional advancement is high in almost all health profession fields. The daily work is varied and engaging. When you complete your formal study, there will be an awareness of how you can help to make the life of another person, indeed the lives of many other persons, better. Fortunately, students usually do learn how to celebrate the successful completion of various aspects of their journey by end-of-term parties, post-exam indulgences, and other markers. The educational programs themselves help mark your milestone through such events as celebrations after board exams, pinning or "white coat" ceremonies, honors convocations and, of course, commencement activities. Because the rewards of persevering to the end are many, the remaining chapters are designed to assist you in maximizing the wealth of experiences open to persons in the health professions. Read on, and plan for a fine future.

SUMMARY

This chapter highlights how self-respect for your choice of profession and your movement through your student years can be cultivated. You will face some challenges, anxieties, and anticipations but this chapter provides guidelines for helping to get past the barriers when the going gets rough. The emphasis on preparedness through the acquisition of knowledge, skills, and ennobling attitudes should help you remain focused on why you are here reading this book in the first place. Exercising critical thought skills, reckoning with your vulnerability, and making time for yourself will sustain you and set good habits for the long haul. Your goals should be to enjoy the student role, be prepared for its challenges when they come, understand them, and then leave the student years respectfully behind for your new life as a professional. All along, your self-respect and the habits it generates are cherished resources that are being nurtured each day.

REFERENCES

1. Haddad A: Spring semester. In Haddad AM, Brown KH, editors: *The arduous touch: women's voices in health care,* West Lafayette, IN, 1999, NotaBell Books/Purdue University Press.
2. May W and others: Model for ability-based assessment in physical therapy education, *J Phys Ther Educ* 9:1-2, 1995.
3. Goethe JW: *Elective affinities,* New York, 1978, Penguin Books.
4. Pinsent J: *Greek mythology,* London, 1969, Hamlyn Publishers Group.
5. National Association of Social Workers, Inc.: *Code of ethics of the National Association of Social Workers,* Washington DC, 1993, National Association of Social Workers.
6. Kapp MB: Impaired professionals. In Post SG, editor: *Encyclopedia of bioethics,* ed 3, New York, 2004, Macmillan.
7. Boisaubin E, Levine R: Identifying and assisting the impaired physician, *Am J Med Sciences* 322:31-36, 2001.
8. Hilfiker D: *Healing the wounds,* Omaha, NE, 1999, Creighton University Press. (Originally published New York, 1985, Pantheon Books. Reprinted with annotations.)
9. Blustein J: Doctoring and the (neglected) virtue of self-forgiveness. In Thomasma DC, Kissell JL, editors: *The health care professional as friend and healer,* Washington, DC, 2000, Georgetown University Press.

RESPECT FOR YOURSELF IN YOUR PROFESSIONAL CAPACITY

The student will be able to:
- Distinguish between the characteristics of being an intimate and a personal helper
- Compare important aspects of social and therapeutic helping relationships, describing why maintaining this distinction in everyday practice affects your self-respect as a professional
- List four criteria for referral of patients
- Identify and discuss two respect-enhancing goals that the interdisciplinary health care team approach is designed to meet
- Compare the values realized through team decisions that are hierarchy-derived and those that are community-derived
- Identify bonds among health professionals that are created by several forms of common language

In the profession of health care, proficient and effective delivery requires a "therapeutic use of one's self" while interacting with clients. If health care consisted of "working on bodies" alone, perhaps a consideration of the self would not be necessary. But the fact remains that health care involves people interacting with people. ...

—C.M. Davis[1]

This chapter continues on the course of moving from your role as a student to your role as a professional (Figure 5-1). We introduce you to several specific capacities that, if nurtured, will serve you well in this professional role. These include being prepared to offer help in a special way, being able to engage in skilled activities that distinguish your everyday relationships from your professional ones, and learning the strengths of working on interdisciplinary health care teams. You will have an opportunity to consider some ways that you can learn to show respect to other members of your team and what to expect in terms of their support of you. Together these capacities will help ensure that you will experience deep satisfaction and self-respect in your professional roles.

FIGURE 5-1: A health professional with her patient. *(© Corbis.)*

DEVELOPING YOUR CAPACITY TO HELP

In the traditional use of the term, the "helping professions" referred only to those that provided prolonged, one-to-one contact with patients. Today, the usage has been expanded to include all health professionals, whether their skills are used in direct person-to-person contact or in working through others, because the overall goal is to benefit individuals in society. Therefore, whatever your choice of profession, the way you use your capacities to help others will affect the self-respect you will enjoy over the course of your professional life. Some steps towards achieving the goal of being a professional helper are to learn to distinguish between intimate and personal modes of helping and to recognize important differences between social and therapeutic helping relationships. We will address each for your consideration.

Intimate versus Personal Help

Helping ranges from performing highly intimate acts to performing simple, personal ones, depending on the depth of involvement in which you engage another person. *Intimate help* is what you offer to someone you love or for whom you are willing to do a big favor. The offer of intimate help in its most extreme form means that you would be willing to risk danger to yourself for this person. In contrast, *personal help* is what you are willing to offer acquaintances or strangers when giving directions, assisting a person physically, or donating money to a good cause. Personal help demands an investment in the well-being of others but should be distinguished from intimate involvement, the latter of which is reserved for families and close friends.

Professional helping falls within the category of personal rather than intimate help-ing. Maintaining the respectful conduct that characterizes personal helping in the health professional and patient interaction is the focus of this book. A more in-depth description of its characteristics is the focus of Part Three.

 REFLECTIONS

Reflect on the last couple days of your encounters with family, friends, and others with whom you have come into contact.
- Which of the encounters were intimate?
- Which ones met the general criteria of personal helping?
- Why?

Social Helping Relationships

A related way to view helping relationships concentrates on the activities rather than on the degree of involvement with the other person in a social setting. Any help in which your resources for providing help are not specific, well-defined professional skills can be called *social helping*. Social helping takes many forms because the num-bers of resources you can use are as numerous as your imagination and your willing-ness to extend yourself for someone else's benefit. One helps a child cross the street, one helps lessen an old man's loneliness by paying him a visit, or one helps a neigh-bor in need by lending her 5 dollars. This type of helping stems from an unselfish or "altruistic" motive of wanting to benefit someone else. There is an interesting and growing body of literature in the field of evolutionary psychology that debates whether we have an *inherent* inclination to express caring or compassion.[2]

Offers of help are not always welcomed by the recipient and in fact may not be interpreted as help at all. This seems especially true if the recipient perceives the offer as being motivated by the helper's desire to fulfill his or her own needs.[3] Persons with functional impairments often are victims of this displaced motive. Consider the following case recounted by a student:

> On weekends, the student cared for a 13-year-old boy with paraplegia who ambulated with the help of a wheelchair. One Saturday, the student and boy were shopping in a large department store and paused at a vending machine for a coke. First the student bought a soft drink for his young friend and then turned to buy one for himself. The boy had just taken the first sip and was resting the can on the arm of his wheelchair when a woman laden with bundles rushed up and dropped a dollar in his lap. She patted the astonished boy on the head and exclaimed, "Poor, poor boy. I hope that helps you get better." She then gathered up her packages and scurried away.

It seems to us that a little reflection on the part of the woman would have quickly exposed her conduct as being inappropriate and maybe even a source of belittlement and bewilderment to the recipient (Figure 5-2).

FIGURE 5-2: A woman patting a boy in a wheelchair on the head.

In short, the helper in the social helping relationship may use any available means to offer assistance rather than depending on special skills, but how the help is perceived by the recipient will be determined in part by what the motive seems to be. There is another kind of help available; it can be termed *therapeutic help* and takes place within the "therapeutic helping relationship."

Therapeutic Helping Relationships

A therapeutic helping relationship develops when a health professional performs professionally competent acts designed to benefit the person who needs his or her services. Therapeutic helping is personal, not intimate, and your primary resources are specific, well-defined professional skills. For instance, the prosthetist may measure the stump of a patient's amputation and then competently fashion a prosthesis, a dietitian may need to interview the patient only once to be able to evaluate nutritional status and plan the dietary regimen, or a medical technologist may remain in the laboratory to perform extensive laboratory analyses. All of these health professionals are helping in a therapeutic manner because they are drawing on competence that can be classified as professionally appropriate, designed to benefit the patient.

- Name some unique therapeutic activities that members of your chosen profession engage in during their interactions with patients.
- Name some that are not necessarily unique to your profession but fall within the boundaries of therapeutic helping as it has been described above.

The therapeutic helping relationship does not necessarily require prolonged contact. Of course, more than competence is required for full respect to be expressed toward a patient. In the accompanying cartoon you see one example of a professional whose competence does not equate to full caring (Figure 5-3)! You will learn about additional dimensions of genuine caring as the book progresses.

FIGURE 5-3: *(Peanuts: © United Feature Syndicate, Inc. Reprinted by permission.)*

The most important information you should take away from this discussion about the therapeutic helping relationship is that it takes place between a person who has a special problem and another person skilled in techniques that can alleviate or diminish that problem. The relationship can be established at the first meeting and is therefore as pertinent to health professionals who see a person and family only once as it is to those who see them over a prolonged period of time. Specific limits are imposed by the relation between the individual's problem and the health professional's skills; for example, a speech pathologist cannot enter into a therapeutic helping relationship with a patient who has no speech or language problems. The differences between helping as a social relationship and helping as a therapeutic relationship are summarized in Box 5-1.

BOX 5-1

COMPARISON BETWEEN HELPING AS A SOCIAL AND AS A THERAPEUTIC RELATIONSHIP

Helping as a Social Relationship
May be an intimate or personal act
Helper utilizes a wide variety of resources
Helping as a Therapeutic Relationship
Is a personal but not an intimate act
Helper primarily utilizes well-defined, specialized professional skills

Within the therapeutic helping relationship the patient's personality, motives, and other characteristics have power to influence how health professionals respond, as is evident in the following case:

> When Eddy Underhill was admitted to the Veterans Affairs Medical Center again, no one was surprised. He was well known to the staff in the emergency room and to most of the personnel who had been there for any length of time, and none of them were glad to see him. Eddy lived in a furnished room in the poorest section of town, where his veteran's pension was enough to cover his rent plus enough alcohol to keep him drunk almost all the time. Occasionally, he would spend money on food, but never if it meant going without booze.
>
> This time he was admitted with impending delirium tremens, a life-threatening condition resulting from alcohol withdrawal. Often such admissions would occur toward the end of the month when his money ran out, and scavenging could not net him enough money to keep him drinking. Other times he was admitted for pneumonia, contracted after spending a winter night unconscious in the gutter, or bleeding from esophageal varices, or trauma from falling on the street or being beaten up by thugs.
>
> Jesse Sampson, a young chaplain who had recently begun working at the hospital, started to visit Eddy after his acute withdrawal symptoms had subsided. Eddy had some degree of brain damage from chronic alcohol abuse but was garrulous and enjoyed "shooting the breeze" with this young man who came to see him every day. Chaplain Sampson was very different from the doctors and nurses at the hospital, who spent as little time as possible with Eddy. The chaplain would sit down in a chair next to the bed as if he were not in a hurry to be somewhere else. He would ask Eddy questions about himself and his life as if he really cared about the answers. Eddy told Jesse that booze was his only friend and that his life was lonely, but he seemed warmer and more convivial when he was drunk. He had no family. His friends were the other people on skid row. He had no ambitions. Life was hard and pretty senseless, and he just wanted to get through it as easily as he could. He appreciated being brought to the hospital when he was in really bad shape. There it was warm, and he got decent food, but most of the people treated him with thinly veiled disgust. This often made him angry. "I'm a gomer (get out of my emergency room), you know. They hate my kind, but they can't come right out and say so, so they try to ignore me. They wish I would die, and some time I will. Would serve 'em right. But they won't care—they'll just keep on goin' about their prissy and proud ways. They think they are so good-hearted, but they don't know what it's like to live on the street. To be alone with your only friend, the bottle. It's my life, and I got a right to do what I want. I served my time in the war, and I got a right to be in this hospital, to come in here and get dried out and get a little food. I'm an old man. I got a right."[4]

Mr. Underhill is the type of patient who can cause much consternation for health professionals. The example set by the chaplain is not always easy to follow, although most would applaud the chaplain's caring approach.

> How many sources of potential negative bias can you identify in this story?
> What would *you* do to try to help this patient?
> What things about him would you find difficult to accept?

This dramatic instance is not the only type of challenge you will encounter. For example, some patients who initially seek your services seem to resist any kind of help, even though you judge that the services offered should benefit them. For these patients, receiving help may be seen as a sign of weakness, even though their suffering or troubling condition has driven them to your door. Other types of patients might surprise you. Sometimes people who are lonely do not comply with your efforts to help because if they do they will lose the benefit of your company. (For some major challenges that patients face, see Chapter 6.) These and other examples highlight the fact that the wish to help is not always easily accomplished.

BEING AN EXPERT HELPER

Chapter 4 introduced you to steps that are required to become competent, an expert. Everyone who enters the health professions has had the opportunity to provide competent help to someone who needs it. Doing a job well is closely tied to feelings of self-respect, so making sure you are in a situation in which your best self can be expressed is extremely important.[5]

Being an expert helper in the health professions usually necessitates working closely with people. Occasionally a student gets as far as the clinical setting before discovering how much time must be spent in actual patient or client contact and/or with professional colleagues and others. For some, this is not what they anticipated and they conclude that while being an expert is great, being an expert helper entails demands that do not suit their personality.

It is difficult for someone who has already entered a program in the health professions to concede that he or she does not like working closely with people. The good news is that a person is usually not in the wrong profession, but rather may become one of those professionals who pursue the relatively scarce but rewarding careers in areas in which little ongoing contact with other people is required. Such careers include some types of laboratory work, research, design (of equipment or departments), and some areas of management and writing. What better way is there to demonstrate a concern for others than to contribute to the high standards and productivity of the health professions by working in these less socially demanding areas?

SHARED RESPONSIBILITY FOR OPTIMAL CARE

As we noted above, a clinician's role traditionally was geared to helping a patient over a period of time. This role can now be expanded to include limited contact with individual patients or, in some instances, indirect contact through supervision of assistants and referrals to other professionals. In the next few pages you will examine two mechanisms available to you to help you succeed in providing optimal care.

What About Working with Assistants?

The *assistant* is someone who works together with a professional to help accomplish the patient's goals insofar as they are understood by the health care professional. The term itself sometimes adds confusion because some assistants, such as physicians' assistants, are health professionals themselves and may enjoy the benefit of assistants who aid them. Other assistants are trained to become a part of the support staff for nurse practitioners, therapists, technologists, or other more highly educated professionals. What difference do assistants make? Professional assistant programs were introduced to help provide lower-cost optimal care and to alleviate serious personnel shortages in many health fields.

Some individuals who entered a health profession with the understanding that they would provide help through direct interventions with patients are finding that treatment interventions they thought were a part of their professional responsibility are now being carried out by assistants. In this case professionals may fear that they will experience less satisfaction with their career choice than they had hoped for. When assistants were first introduced, some health professionals needlessly feared that assistants would entirely take over treatments or procedures that put them in direct contact with patients, leaving the professional with evaluation and administrative tasks only. This has not proven to be the case.

Assistants are in the health care system to stay. This allows more deeply trained professionals to share the tasks involved in and extend the resources available for providing the best care possible at the lowest cost. In some cases, this means that your professional responsibilities will include being a competent, respectful supervisor to persons performing procedures previously performed directly by health professionals in your field. For the assistant it will involve respectfully accepting such supervision.

When Is Referral Appropriate?

Referral is a time-honored method of ensuring that a person who seeks professional services will receive optimal care while not having to depend completely on one professional's capabilities and resources. It acknowledges that you cannot always single-handedly manage a person's health care needs, even those that warrant skills that fall within the scope of what your profession provides. Sometimes health professionals are reticent to refer a patient to someone else, even though she or he can do the job more effectively and it is in the patient's best interest. Reasons are that health professionals take their jobs seriously, become attached to patients with whom they have been working, and find it painful to admit what feels like "failure." None of these reasons justify holding on to a patient who would benefit more from the help of another colleague.

You should take steps to implement referral when the patient's progress is at risk of being hindered because (1) you are not experienced in appropriate techniques, (2) you do not have adequate equipment for providing proper services to that particular person, (3) you and the patient have a serious and irresolvable personality conflict, (4) you experience a negative bias toward the person (or group to which the person belongs) to the extent that you believe it may interfere with providing competent care, or (5) your attachment to the patient is resulting in helping conduct more akin to intimacy than the conduct appropriate for a therapeutic helping relationship.

Optimal care, then, entails using the time-honored referral system to extend your professional resources. It requires self-knowledge: knowing when and where to refer the patient for further evaluation or treatment. In this manner, your integrity as a professional helper can be maintained, and your self-respect will be enhanced because of your good judgment.

TEAMS AND TEAMWORK

Work with assistants and the practice of patient referral are two examples of how teamwork can enhance your self-respect through improving patient care by these means. However, to understand the extent to which your work will involve teamwork, we turn now to a description of how patient care is enhanced through your participation on interdisciplinary health care teams. Almost all health care today is provided through such teams.

 REFLECTIONS

Take a minute to think about the different types of teams you have participated on.
- What were the criteria for being chosen to be on the team?
- Was it designed to cooperate with other teams or compete against them?
- What were the goals of the team?
- What activities were required of team members to meet these goals?

   By referring back to your previous experience, you may get a better idea of how your participation as a member of interdisciplinary health care teams will be similar or different from those situations.

Patient-Oriented Goals of Teams

Interdisciplinary health care teams were developed to try to effect several important goals in patient care. First, because of specialization, it became obvious that professionals must band together to provide coordinated and comprehensive care. One goal of teamwork was to provide protection against the complete fragmentation of services that could result from more specialization.

A second goal grew from the belief that team-coordinated care is more likely to ensure that the patient's many needs are met in a manner that shows respect for that person as a *unique individual.* In other words, despite the importance of coordinated and comprehensive care, no one today judges this as the sole criterion of good health care. Health professionals must also fulfill the stringent requirement of tailoring care to suit the individual who receives it. The hope is that the deeply held moral ideal of respect for persons (including yourself) is best realized by the team approach because it allows the patient to be viewed from many different perspectives and by also drawing on others' resources when appropriate. This multi-faceted perspective is an advantage not only because it can expand the range of technical skills available but also because it allows the patient's caregivers to consider several points of view regarding the larger picture of what is best for the patient. Consider the following case.

Jack came back from military duty with one arm, the result of a mine explosion that killed four of his buddies with whom he was on the mission. Being one of only three survivors in the incident, he said over and over again that he felt very lucky to be alive and planned to live life to its fullest. Following his shoulder disarticulation amputation, he was sent back to the United States to recover and begin rehabilitation. He seemed determined to prove that he was ready to take life on as he participated with vigor in his rehabilitation regime.

So it came as a surprise when, some weeks into his rehabilitation program, he abruptly announced that he was now leaving the hospital, having decided not to wear an upper extremity prosthesis after all. He said that he had been online talking to various people with amputations, and lots of them didn't wear their prostheses. He himself had just begun to be fitted and could "tell" it was going to be cumbersome. "I'll do better without that thing," he said.

Most of the therapists involved in his care were convinced that this 23-year-old man was absolutely doing the wrong thing whether from the point of view of reduced function, poorer trunk balance, or esthetics. But some of the other health professionals, especially some of the nurses, a resident physician, and his social worker were not so sure he was making the wrong decision. For one thing, they believed that he had the psychological makeup to fall into the group of patients most likely to discard their prostheses after a while. The social worker reflected on a discussion with Jack in which he said he felt that going through life with one arm would give him a greater opportunity to tell others how he lost it. That way people would know he believed in the United States and "was proud of losing his arm for his country." "Besides," he added, "those artificial arms aren't real."

To tell the truth, none of the professionals were 100% comfortable with his decision. Their team meeting lasted longer than usual with the result being that they decided on the following courses of action: First, the physical therapist (whom Jack seemed to like) would probe further as to the reasons Jack made this decision. Second, the staff liaison psychiatrist would talk with him to determine if he had issues that he did not want to raise with the other team members, or if this was a result of depression. Third, the social worker would ask his permission to talk with other family members, none of whom could afford to visit him in a state more than 1000 miles from their home, though they talked with him often by phone. His mom and brother had even talked to the social worker a couple of times. Finally, everyone would continue to show him as much support as possible while trying to keep him from bolting right away and also find other areas of his life at the rehabilitation center where he could exercise his say-so.

This interdisciplinary health care team was honoring that a good intervention must fit within the context of the patient's needs, hopes, and fears. Some would have had experience in amputee care and would know that, following a shoulder disarticulation, a person who is well qualified medically to be fitted with an upper extremity prosthesis may be opposed to it on esthetic, financial, or religious grounds. Assuming that the patient understands the ramifications of each of the options, withholding the prosthesis would be judged a morally permissible course of action despite the technical advantages of the prosthesis. Thus, Jack's well-being became the reference point for deciding what steps could be taken individually and collectively to be sure he was making the right decision.

What happened in Jack's situation? After doing their homework, the team met again. The social worker said that her call to Jack's mom and brother had concerned them enough that they decided to borrow money to come out to visit him. The others agreed that they would urge Jack to hang in there until the family visit had taken place. The visit seemed to turn him around, and he decided to remain in the program. This convinced the team members who had had doubts about encouraging him to try the prosthesis that they should support such a trial.

Institutional Goals Served by Teams

In addition to the patient-oriented goals that interdisciplinary health care teams serve, the team approach has been welcomed by institutions because teams can help meet the goals of efficient health care delivery while enjoying a sense of equality and mutuality among themselves. Health care institutions are made up of two broad categories of actions: actions flowing from hierarchy-derived decisions and those flowing from community-derived decisions.

Within a hierarchical pattern of decision-making, decisions flow from very few persons to affect very many. The authority and responsibility weigh heaviest at the top. A value realized by this mode of functioning is institutional efficiency, some aspects of which you learned about in Chapter 2 during your introduction to policies. Health care teams implement policies and other decisions made by the administration.

Within a community framework of decision-making, decisions arise more equally throughout the institution. Some theorists call this a "bottom up" approach; it has gained in popularity in recent years. Authority and accountability are shared across the institution by its various constituents. Power differentials are less obvious. Professionals with different skills function together with mutual support and as task-sharers. Values realized by this approach are equality and mutuality. Health care teams not only help to implement policies and practices created by others but also may generate them.

Therefore, different but essential institutional values are realized in the two forms of activity served by interdisciplinary health care teams. All team members can work together efficiently and cooperatively to help meet professional *and* institutional goals.

Looking back at the patient-oriented goals realized through team work and combining them with an understanding of how teams help contribute to an institution's goals, it should be easy to see how the team environment helps each member become a means of growth and increased effectiveness for the others. However, growth and increased effectiveness over your professional lifetime obviously require more than dependence on and support of teammates.

It is to this larger context of resources that the last section of this chapter points you.

SHOWING RESPECT WHILE ENJOYING SUPPORT

In Chapter 4 you were introduced to some ways to engender and preserve self-respect that are particularly relevant to the unique situation of being a student. We also emphasized that many of the general themes in that chapter continue to be relevant considerations throughout your professional career. We turn now to several considerations that you can add to what you learned in Chapter 4—considerations for maintaining your self-respect through your professional career. Part and parcel of this challenge is that people providing this support also experience your respect. Family and friends are at the top of the list. Professional colleagues are close behind.

Putting Family and Friends First

Needed for success and satisfaction in your career are persons with whom you can share joys, dreams, fun, and frustrations. Because professional life can be so involving, family and friends outside of your work environment are at risk of being left out of your life in very important ways unless you make conscious efforts to include them (Figure 5-4). They are your most precious and immediate source of support, but often they are taken for granted and may get the leftover part of your days, the

FIGURE 5-4: Health professionals should remember to make time for family and friends. (© Getty Images/100069.)

majority of which is spent in professional activities. This excerpt from a day in the life of a physician reflects a routine that many health professionals will identify with regarding the amount and quality of time spent with their families:

> It is now seven o'clock. I drive home. The day of work is finished. I know that I shall not have any more calls as I sign my phone out to the telephone answering service. I sit down to dinner with my wife and three school-age children. I listen to the children recount the activities of the day. It is March, and my wife and I begin to talk about possible vacation sites for this summer. After dinner I go to my study and take a journal from a pile of unread periodicals. I thumb through it, unable to concentrate enough to get interested in any one article. I turn on the television and begin to watch an NBA game. Later, my wife wakens me.[6]

⊚ REFLECTIONS

- What do you find encouraging about this scene as you think about your own professional life? Troubling?
- What habits do you have that will serve you well in terms of nurturing your most important relationships?

Your job is to establish habits early that will reflect the rhythms needed for your family members and friends to be *able* to support you when you need it. A young lawyer recounts the choices he began to exercise when he felt himself being consumed by his work:

> There were a few things that helped to restore my sense of equilibrium. The first was to make a conscious effort to spend time with my wife. In the beginning, I resisted when my wife would plead, cajole, and sometimes push me out the door of our apartment so that we could spend a few hours watching a movie or going to dinner. Eventually, I realized how important this time was. It strengthened our relationship by keeping the lines of communication open between us. Not only that, it also made me a *better* worker by giving my anxious mind a much needed rest.
>
> A second source of balance came from getting together with other people who were facing similar pressures at work. Two or three times a month I would meet with a few friends from law school who were working in other firms around town. Our get-togethers were combination lunches and b.s. sessions. These meetings did wonders for my perspective. I found myself becoming less anxious and self-absorbed as I discovered that my friends were dealing with the same worries and concerns I was facing. We helped ourselves by helping each other.
>
> Another thing that helped was to take ten or fifteen minutes during my morning commute to sit quietly, reflect about my life, and say a few prayers. This helped center me for the day. It gave me a sense of perspective. It allowed me to see the ways in which my work was an integral part of my spiritual life. …

Together, these small things helped bring my life and my work back into balance. They let me see my work more realistically. They stopped me from investing too much of myself in my work. And they reminded me that I was more than a worker and that my work was only work.[7]

In short, this young professional utilized the resources of family, colleagues, and his own form of spiritual reflection to create the balance he felt slipping from him. In the process he created a support network. He just mentions in passing that he realized his immediate professional colleagues also were a resource. It is so important that we examine it in more detail.

The Ties That Bind

One source of support, which is often overlooked, is that persons working in a health care situation have several common bonds, all of which help to establish rapport and support among them.

The Bond of Caring

Health professionals share the motivation to express caring—about a patient's problems, prognosis, and progress; about the department; about what is happening in their field; and about health services in general. You voluntarily place yourself in the mainstream of human suffering, thereby showing that you care. No neon lights beckon you in. No one commits you to this role. There are no locked doors preventing your departure. You choose to be there because you care enough about human well-being and the relief of suffering to want to effect certain changes by the use of professional skills.

Sometimes overlooked, and to the detriment of everyone involved, health professionals may take less time telling one another directly that they care about one another than they do sharing their concerns about patients, policies, or other external factors. Creating an atmosphere of shared care transforms a workplace from a site only to a true community.

Technical Language as a Bond

Another silver thread that creates a bond among health professionals is the technical language of each specific profession and the shared language of health care. Although this may seem irrelevant at first glance, it should not be overlooked as a means whereby potential tensions can be diverted. For example, an older professional who feels she has nothing in common with a young recent graduate may see him in a much different light after discussing with him newer approaches to the treatment of diabetes mellitus or a better method of analyzing cholesterol levels. Similarly, the younger professional probably will gain new respect for the older one who bothers to explain a new piece of evaluative equipment or the value of an interesting technique that was not covered in school.

Cross-cultural encounters occasioned by movement of health professionals across national and other cultural boundaries depend on this shared technical language too. You will have opportunities to attend international meetings or be host to professionals in your workplace who bring cultural characteristics entirely new to you.

The Bond of Gratitude

Gratitude or appreciation is expressed too seldom by persons working together. A simple word of thanks can create more good will than months of competent work together during which neither person makes an effort to express appreciation to the other. There are many ways to say "thank you," from an affirming smile or nod to placing a small surprise on your colleague's desk as a way to show your gratitude. Remembering another person's birthday or the anniversary of a special event and performing other "random acts of kindness" creates a general environment of congeniality in which the language of mutual respect for the efforts and gifts of one another's presence can flourish.

Environments That Encourage Support

The three bonds—of caring, technical language, and gratitude—can help to reduce tensions among co-workers and foster a sense of "belongingness" among them. Together they can encourage the realization of mutually shared goals and values. However, as you learned in Chapter 2, it is not enough for individuals to have a desire to create a supportive environment—it must also be reflected in the entire structure and values of those who have policy authority. In other words, each person must help create mechanisms that will maintain supportive interactions.

It is a good idea, then, when you look for a position in a new setting, to seek at least one person who appears to be a potential source of support. If no one person promises to be such a resource, it is better to look elsewhere. In addition, you should be bold in asking questions that will allow you to gain some understanding of how support is expressed within the department and larger institution. To make an assessment, the following guidelines may be useful:

- Inquire of your future employer whether there are meetings or other sessions where problems associated with the everyday stresses of health care delivery are discussed.
- Ask some of the people you will be working with what they believe to be the sources of the most intense stress in that environment and how *the group* handles them.
- Ask some of the people you will be working with how each as an individual deals with the stress of his or her position, and whether, as a whole, the environment is a supportive or divisive one.
- Make a mental note of those who appear to be potential sources of support, or if no one appears to be. If everyone denies that problems exist or becomes defensive about such questions when they are tactfully posed, this probably signals a setting in which stresses are dealt with alone, without the support of one's colleagues.[4]
- Fortunately, only in rare situations are no support mechanisms available. In fact, being a support to others often is the key to finding support from them when it is needed. The old adage, "To have a friend is to be one," holds true in the workplace.

Play: Enjoying One Another's Company

If you were to complete this section on support systems with what the authors have said so far, you would probably conclude that the work environment is heavy with tension and problems 24-7. No one could—or should—put up with constant doom and gloom. In fact, health professionals are fortunate to be in a line of work in which they know that their work usually is making a positive difference in patients' lives. That in itself is reason to take the opportunity to enjoy the work setting.

One colleague said that for him work and play were the same thing. He called it "plork." Although it is a good thing to enjoy one's job and the work required to do it well, in our estimation this is shortchanging the joy that can come from remembering to put some levity and fun into the environment, too. Pressures on health professionals to use their time well clearly create stresses at times, but the curse of stress is that one sometimes forgets to use the time still available to take advantage of a cartoon, a good joke, a lighthearted story that a colleague or patient is trying to tell, or some other type of pleasure. One author, himself a health professional, observes:

> Joy is only possible for persons who are attentive to the present. One cannot be happy if one is continually ruminating about what might have been or fretting over whether wishes will come to pass. Americans have a tough time with real joy. Americans are oriented toward outcomes, expectations, and the future; toward ever more competition in proving that they deliver the best results, and anxiously pondering how things might have turned out if only they had chosen differently. This makes it hard to be happy. In health care, these tendencies are exaggerated. Worries about what will happen next to the patient and worries about their own future careers blot out the possibility of joy for many health care professionals. Joy is a present tense phenomenon. It is possible only if one attends to the moment.[8]

Sometimes activities outside of work hours enhance the ability to enjoy one another in a more relaxed environment. There are the usual afternoon coffees or parties or sports teams, but the activities need not stop there. For instance, the authors are part of a writing group. We meet regularly with several other health professions colleagues after work. We write about our work experiences in the form of short stories, poetry, and essays. At first all of us were scared to share anything, believing it would not be good enough. However, as we became more comfortable with one another, we started looking forward to hearing one another's stories. In addition to writing about some very serious problems, we find our gathering to be a great vehicle for laughing at ourselves and good-naturedly at one another, as well as an "excuse" to get to know one another better. One delightful outcome was that we were able to publish some of our work for others to share too.

In your own search for finding a congenial group, you can use some of the same approaches that we suggested above to assess the type of situation you are getting into. Ask yourself:

- Does everyone look like they have just heard the worst news of their lives as they rush around?
- Are there cartoons, lighthearted comments, and funny pictures anywhere?

- Do you see any photos of the group having a good time together at a picnic or some other event? (In our present work situation the group has an annual "day away together" as well as tea for all members of the group on Thursday afternoons.)
- What kind of response do you get when you ask if the group has fun together? Is it treated as a good question? An inappropriate one?
- Is there a common area where colleagues and staff can relax when they do get a moment? Is there a congenial place away from the patient care or other professional areas for conversation, relaxation, or a snack?
- Do the people who are interviewing you seem to have good dispositions?

Obviously the professional who substitutes a good time for good work is not one who will, or should, last long in a position. However, finding and helping to further create a positive work environment can do much to enrich the situation for everyone involved, and not the least important, for yourself.

SUMMARY

When you become a health professional you will assume many roles in the course of your chosen career. Self-respect is an essential component of satisfaction over the course of that career, and to maintain and nurture it requires several capacities. Understanding the appropriate nature of the help you proffer is one key resource. Maintaining your competence, remaining compassionate, and learning to work with assistants and on teams are important conditions for the self-respect you will attain in your lifelong efforts. The ideas in this chapter also help you to remember that showing respect to and support for family, friends, and the people you work with daily will help sustain you. Their support is essential to break your fall should you ever feel like you are losing your footing.

REFERENCES

1. Davis CM: *Patient-practitioner interaction,* ed 3, Thorofare, NJ, 1998, Slack.
2. Wright R: *The moral animal: why we are the way we are: the new science of evolutionary psychology,* New York, 1994, Pantheon Books.
3. Cassell E: Recognizing suffering, *Hastings Cent Rep* 21(3):24-31, 1991.
4. Purtilo R: *Ethical dimensions in the health professions,* ed 3, Philadelphia, 1999, WB Saunders.
5. Purtilo R: New respect for respect in ethics education. In Purtilo R, Jensen G, Royeen CB, editors: *Educating for moral action: a sourcebook in health and rehabilitation ethics,* Philadelphia, 2005, FA Davis.
6. Reynolds RC, Stone J, editors: *On doctoring: stories, poems, essays,* New York, 1995, Simon and Schuster.
7. Allegretti J: *Loving your job, finding your passion: work and the spiritual life,* Mahwah, NJ, 2000, Paulist Press.
8. Sulmasy DP: *The healer's calling: a spirituality for physicians and other health care professionals,* Mahwah, NJ, 1997, Paulist Press.

PART TWO

Questions for Thought and Discussion

1. What are some skills that are more important to your particular profession than to the health professions as a whole?

2. You go to a patient's bedside to perform a procedure. Before entering his room, you read his clinical record. Then you go in, greet the patient, ask how he feels, explain the procedure, make certain he is comfortable, carry out the procedure, get him a drink of water that he requests, bid him good-bye, and make notations in the record.

   a. What components of this interaction could be classified as social helping? Why?

   b. What components could be classified as therapeutic helping? Why?

3. You have been asked by members of your class to run for office in the national student organization of your profession. You are already very busy with school-work and your personal commitments. List your most important priorities and decide what would be compromised the most by taking on this new position. What values will determine whether you will choose to run for this office?

4. John B. has been diagnosed as having sickle cell anemia and is a patient in the unit where you are working. Such patients are sometimes labeled as drug-seeking when in fact they are in severe pain during a crisis. What characteristics of the team approach can help to ensure that this mistake is less likely to be made when he appears in the emergency room in acute pain?

5. When you are looking for a position, what sorts of activities would you look for that would make you feel confident that this is a supportive environment for the stresses you might face? What would make your work more enjoyable?

PART
THREE

RESPECT FOR THE PATIENT'S SITUATION

Part Three examines closely the person who seeks professional help—the patient. Almost everyone becomes a patient at some time, and you can undoubtedly recall some fears and problems you have experienced as one, as well as the sympathy and special attention you received in that situation. Obviously, your understanding of a patient's predicament is a resource that can help you respond more effectively and respectfully.

In most cases, a person's role in society during a period of illness and its accompanying incapacity differs in significant ways from before the person became ill. Part Three examines how the situation affects him or her and the health professional's function in helping the patient. The result can be a return to health, learning to live with incapacity, or preparation for death. Chapter 6 discusses special challenges faced by patients. Chapter 7 examines the patient in his or her relationships as a member of the larger society, whether or not recovery occurs.

Ask yourself the following questions as you read about the patient as a person:
- How do my professional attitudes and conduct convey respect toward a patient?
- What do I need to know about a patient to help him or her set reasonable goals?
- What should I look for in a patient's responses to give me a clue to his or her own set of values?
- To what extent are values constructive tools for building a patient's future?

CHALLENGES TO PATIENTS

CHAPTER OBJECTIVES

The student will be able to:
- Describe common conditions that create barriers to maintaining wellness
- List the most important changes experienced as losses by persons who become inpatients and some challenges of reckoning with such changes in health care facilities
- Compare challenges facing inpatients, ambulatory care patients, and patients who are treated in their homes
- Identify several types of privileges or accommodations patients may enjoy
- Describe key characteristics of Molière's *Imaginary Invalid* that are similar to those of patients today who seem to benefit from remaining ill

Ten years ago, if I were setting out to make a film about catastrophic illness and subsequent disability, I would not have cast myself in the lead role. In my pre-stroke ignorance, I probably would have looked for someone stronger and braver than I—not yet knowing that we are all capable of much more bravery than we think.

—B.S. Klein[1]

Most challenges facing patients are related to their transition from everyday routine to the altered role that sick or impaired persons assume in society. The role includes physical, psychological, and spiritual challenges, whether the condition is short- or long-term. Fortunately, these challenges have received considerable attention in health professions literature and curricula in recent years, so it is likely that you will have one or more courses in which they are discussed. Some common themes are presented here as a basis for your ongoing thought and reflection.

MAINTAINING WELLNESS

It is fitting that a chapter on challenges to patients begins with some reflections on maintaining wellness, because in recent years much emphasis has been placed on maintaining and fostering a healthy lifestyle—on "staying healthy." Staying well seems to be to everyone's advantage—the individual, his or her loved ones, and society. Wellness ensues from maintaining health-supporting habits over a lifetime. As you know, a healthy life ultimately depends on many things including a safe and health-inducing environment. Good nutrition, sleep, exercise, and other health-fostering habits are essential. Freedom from basic want and violence are too. Today thousands of health professionals build practices based on preventative approaches—teaching people some of the essentials of how to remain healthy. A few examples are nutritionists who are involved in school nutrition programs, nurses and nurse practitioners who may work in perinatal or other community education and screening clinics, physicians and occupational and physical therapists who focus on safety and health maintenance in the workplace or hold positions in sports or recreational settings. A growing body of literature suggests that the mind and body can develop and grow stronger over an entire lifetime (Figure 6-1), a topic we take up in more detail in Chapter 16.

At the same time, lifelong wellness is not a goal completely within an individual's own control, even with the help of a safe and health-inducing environment. Almost weekly there are discoveries of new genetic predispositions to illness; scientists have identified scores of environmental toxins, and other health hazards are appearing on

FIGURE 6-1: An older person exercising. (© *Getty Images/10293.*)

the horizon; many people live in conditions of poverty, lacking basic public health and safety conditions, while others suffer unavoidable work-related stress symptoms. Accidents and other misfortunes dash dreams, alter possibilities, and modify relationships. Moreover, most of us today have periods of less wellness or more wellness. For example, a person with mild pneumonia or late-onset diabetes or severe atherosclerotic heart disease may function mostly as a healthy person but still may need the intervention of a health professional for serious symptoms related to the condition. At best, each of us moves through life on a continuum between maximal health and life-threatening illness or death.

RECKONING WITH CHANGE

The transition from being relatively well to becoming ill or impaired almost inevitably entails change in the form of losses. The loss may take the shape of decreased physical or mental function, as reflected in this excerpt from a young woman who has been working energetically to recover from stroke and then "bottoms out":

> One Saturday morning, you can't bring yourself to get out of bed. Jim [her husband] hears you weeping, comes into the bedroom, and lies down next to you,
>
> "What's wrong?"
>
> "I don't feel like myself. I don't want to get up and face another day in this damaged body. Everything is so hard and I'm just tired of trying to do basic shit, like getting dressed. I just don't think I can live this way. I can't do it."
>
> "Can't do what? Get dressed? Come on, I'll help you."
>
> "No. ... I don't think I can do all the things that I keep telling everyone I'm going to do. I think I've been saying I'm going to do all this stuff to convince myself. Jim, I can't even put a sock on."
>
> This is not who you are. You feel even worse now, because you've unloaded all your fears and insecurities on Jim. All he wants is positive energy from you, and you can't even give him that. ...[2]

Persons who lose their sight or other senses, those who lose control of movement or vital body functions, and those who through illness become incapable of making competent judgments may experience a similar sense of loss. The loss may also involve a change in physical appearance, such as the person who undergoes an amputation or is scarred after a severe burn.

The significance of these changes for each person is determined by a complex interweaving of several factors, including the physical and emotional effects of the pathological process itself, the alteration in the person's environment or social roles, and the coping mechanisms the patient has developed throughout his or her life. The concert pianist who loses an index finger in an accident will have a more profound loss than most of us who might experience a similar trauma, illustrating that the degree of loss is highly personal.

Patients will react to you in ways that express their concern about their losses. For example, upon entering a patient's room, the phlebotomist may catch the brunt of

---

⊙ REFLECTIONS

Reflect on losses you might incur that you think would *most* threaten your identity and sense of well being. Name a:

Sensory loss _____

Physical function loss _____

Body part loss _____

Mental capacity loss _____

- Why do you think these specific losses would affect your sense of well-being (and of being "well") more than some other losses you might sustain?
- Do you think your list is similar to that of most people your age? Of persons 20 years older or younger than you? Why or why not?

---

the patient's anxiety through comments such as "Here comes the vampire!" The radiological technologist may be accused of destroying cells with the imaging equipment. Professionals whose diagnostic and treatment procedures require patients to engage in physical or emotional exertion can be accused of sapping a patient's strength. These expressions of anger or fear reflect the challenge a patient is facing in trying to protect his or her body and sense of well-being from further loss.

Loss of Former Self-Image

A natural extension of loss of function or previous physical appearance is the belief by some that one has literally lost one's old self. This is especially likely when physical or mental change promises to be prolonged or permanent. You have probably had the feeling sometimes that you just "weren't yourself" that day or that what you did in a particular situation was not typical of the "real you." For most people, this sense of self-alienation is temporary; however, it may become more long-lasting for a person experiencing significant losses associated with injury or illness.[3]

A patient's feeling of having lost herself or himself may result in part from the conviction that what one *is* is largely determined by what one looks like. In other words, one's *self*-image depends to a large extent on *body* image (Figure 6-2).

There is a close relationship between appearance, accompanying body image, and sense of self worth.[4] This is not surprising in a society with a multibillion dollar advertising enterprise stressing appearance above all else, and with it the idea of physical beauty and vitality depicted within very narrow norms. Despite the proverb's bidding, most of us still do "judge a book by its cover."

Have you encountered anyone today you thought was exceptionally fit, beautiful, or graceful? Our stereotypes of success and assurance of acceptance often depend on physical appearance. Painful sanctions are imposed on those whose appearance deviates too far from some societally determined standard of normality. A person who encounters illness or impairment must face daily the changes that depart from these

FIGURE 6-2: The patient's fantasies about the distortion of her former appearance may override what she sees in the mirror.

stereotypes of success and beauty. The work that accompanies developing a new sense of one's physical self after change in physical bodily appearance brought about by surgery has been explored by one of the authors through poetry:

FRENCH WEAVING

I piece together the tattered edges
with illusion net,
laying just the right size squares
over the gaping holes.
Carefully,
arduously
embroider the net to the original.
Trying to match the pattern,
tie up loose ends,
mimic the original curve and detail.
I pick up a thread
of who I once was,
try and attach it,
here,
here,
and here.
My clumsy attempts

only approximate the intricacy of the design.
Yet the untrained eye
cannot see my repair.
Run your fingers over my skin
to feel the flaws.
—Amy Haddad [5]

◎ REFLECTIONS

- What is this poet saying? (The title, "French Weaving," is named for an embroidery technique used to repair damaged lace or crochet work. If done by an expert hand, it is hard to see areas of repair though another expert would always be able to tell.)
- Does this apply to the work patients have to do to help "repair" themselves?
- Name some skills that your health profession has as resources to assist in such repair work.

As you may expect, part of the health professional's success depends upon an adeptness at helping the patient either reclaim his or her old image as recovery occurs or, when necessary, discover a realistic and satisfactory new body image. Timing is one important element in your work with patients who are adjusting to changes in body image. There is no preestablished time frame for a man to accept his colostomy or a woman to look at the scar where her breast used to be. Each patient will move in his or her own way and at his or her own pace into this new life territory.

INSTITUTIONALIZATION

Although not all people who become ill or injured spend time in hospitals or other health care institutions, the most seriously involved are admitted as inpatients.

The necessity of spending time confined in a health care facility may significantly disrupt an individual's personal life, as well as the lives of family, occupational associates, and friends. The challenges associated with the disruption may be primarily social, but it is likely that they will also be economic, owing to loss of work, health care–related expenses, or both. The economic burden is especially acute for a person who is self-supporting or is the breadwinner in a family. A single parent has the burden of finding and paying for suitable caretakers for children. A child, teenager, or other student loses valuable instruction and may fall behind or have to drop out of school. A professional person may have to forego participation in an important project. Whatever the individual's personal responsibilities, he or she is likely to be affected socially and economically.

Psychological stresses compound the social and economic ones. A person often believes that entering an institution for care signals that he or she is not winning the battle of coping with an illness or impairment. This psychological defeat can be as deleterious to her or his welfare as the physical manifestations of the illness itself.

In submitting to confinement in an institution, the person finally is admitting openly that the problem is "out of control" and that people professionally qualified to provide certain services are needed on a continuous basis. The patient understandably is anxious about leaving his or her health, and perhaps life, in the hands of strangers, but judges that there are no other good alternatives. Sometimes the awareness that the institutionalization took place because of severe stress on family and other caregivers adds to the discouragement.

Losses Associated with Institutional Life

The disruption of normal life patterns and coping mechanisms that may accompany patients' admissions is exacerbated by the fact that suddenly they are robbed of both home and important basic privacies. Therefore, having met the initial challenge of admitting to illness or impairment, patients now have to face other changes.

Home

Most people view their home as a safe haven in a complex, fast-paced world. Of course, there are some exceptions, notably people for whom home is a place of loneliness, strife, abuse, or boredom. Occasionally, a person will feign illness to be admitted to—or exaggerate symptoms to remain in—a health care facility just to escape threats to their well-being. These patients require special consideration by health professionals and are discussed later in this chapter.

What makes home so desirable for most people when they are away from it? The answer is that the physical, psychological, and social comforts of home are missed by most patients in health care facilities.

Physical comforts take a number of forms. You have undoubtedly walked into someone's room or home where everything is in incredible chaos and disarray. In the midst of the pandemonium, the person or family members appear perfectly at ease; this is their idea of "really living!" Undoubtedly, you have also entered a home where even the teacups seem to sit primly on shelves, where dust *dares* not settle, and curtains never ruffle. In the midst of this porcelain perfection, these family members also appear perfectly at ease!

The physical comfort of home may best be described as freedom to extend oneself naturally and completely into one's immediate environment: to do (or not do) what one wishes, when one wishes, and how one wishes. The environment within the home, whether it contains 1 or 40 rooms, can be changed to conform to one's own needs, habits, and desires.

The bed is a good example of how health care facilities often are unable to adequately accommodate the needs and habits of a person. Almost anyone would agree that a good night's rest greatly determines one's outlook on life the next day, and most people acknowledge that their own bed is one of the most important comforts of home. The standard hospital bed is of a given height, width, length, and firmness. Although the hospital personnel stop short of treating patients in the manner of Procrustes, the culprit in Greek mythology who invited his guests to sleep in his guest bed and responded by chopping off the legs of those who were too tall, institutions usually are limited to offering a standard "hospital bed."

The obvious difficulties of totally personalizing every patient's health care setting are readily apparent. Hospice is a notable exception, with many hospices giving high priority to encouraging patients to have familiar objects around them. Many nursing homes and long-term care facilities, "home" to residents unable to return to their own home, are also devoting much more attention to providing familiar, comfort-enhancing "props." The more that can be done to optimize physical comfort for the patient who is away from home, the more readily he or she will be able to direct energies toward healing, adjusting to dying from a life-threatening illness, or living with impairment.

Psychological and *social comforts* of familiar surroundings also are sacrificed. A favorite chair for relaxation, a magnifying mirror for applying makeup, a family picture, or a ragged toy may all be symbols of security to the person. The mere arrangement of furniture in a room or the sight of a tree or birdbath in the yard may give a person a sense of well-being. We are told that many patients, upon returning home, burst into tears upon being welcomed by a beloved pet or when noting that a flowerbed has blossomed in his or her absence. All too often these comforts are left behind when the person goes to a health care facility.

Psychological and social comfort also may be experienced in the routine associated with being "at home." It is not at all unusual for a patient who enters a health care facility to become confused about what day of the week it is because important, regularly scheduled events are missing. The person who likes to start the day with a cup of coffee and the morning paper will be unsettled when, in a health care facility, the coffee is served with breakfast and the morning paper arrives just before he or she is scheduled to undergo the first diagnostic test or treatment session of the day. A child who is used to a bedtime story may have great difficulty sleeping without it.

Familiarity is most significantly embodied by people and pets in the home. An older woman may literally live for the companionship of a small granddaughter. A single person may look forward to the weekly visit of a bridge group or housekeeper. Children have the familiarity of family and playmates. The harsh restrictions regarding visiting hours, number of guests admitted, and, most of all, the exclusion of children or pets from the presence of institutionalized patients, may be a source of sorrow in itself.

All of these examples highlight serious but often unstated problems that patients in health care facilities face—to find basic comforts that they have experienced in their homes. In fact, patients do try to retrieve a little bit of home. A remarkable sign is the contents of their rooms and bedside stands. Contents of a stand tell one as much about the patient as the contents of a small boy's pocket does about him (Figure 6-3). Generally, the tabletop is cluttered with greeting cards, photos, or stuffed animals. In the top drawer are stamps, writing paper, religious books or objects, assorted ointments, a Swiss Army knife, a cell phone, and more! One of the authors once found a smoked herring in the back of a drawer after a roommate complained that the patient in the next bed was sneaking fish into his bland diet, and the smell was telling all.

A health professional who has the opportunity to see into an open drawer will glean much information about the patient's personality and life.

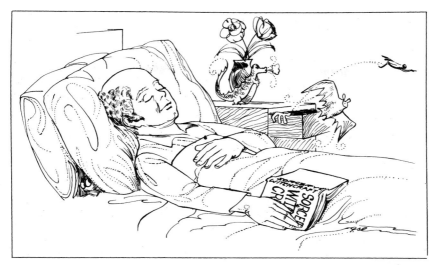

FIGURE 6-3: The bedside stand will reveal untold mysteries about the patient.

You will also learn something about the patient if the room is devoid of personal objects. An empty room may indicate that the patient is not willing to be sick enough to stay too long or is too ill to have even thought about his or her surroundings. Dying patients may want to divest themselves of possessions or get rid of reminders that they will not "get well." Empty rooms may also mean these patients have no one to bring them anything.

Note, however, that a patient understandably may be sensitive about having a health professional snoop around the room, even if only to read a card attached to a bowl of roses or to linger while hanging up a bathrobe in the closet. Their sensitivity about these seemingly innocent gestures is due to the fact that, in addition to missing the comforts of home, the patient also is robbed of privacy in many ways and may count this additional invasion as inappropriate or annoying.

Privacy

The need for individual privacy may vary from person to person depending on his or her ethnicity, age, other cultural traits, and past experience. Whatever the individual boundaries of comfort, every patient in an institutional setting will experience less control over his or her privacy needs than at home.

---

⑥ REFLECTIONS

Picture this—you are a patient uprooted from your home and placed in a health care facility room. Which of the following do you think will bother you the most?
- You are forced to be in a double room with a stranger as a roommate.
- "Walls" are curtains through which health professionals and others can listen or intrude without warning.

Continued

Ⓖ REFLECTIONS—CONT'D

- There is no opportunity to hold a confidential conversation.
- You can't have a good cry, pray aloud, have an angry outburst, or use the commode without others hearing.
- You can't lock the door to your room or to the bathroom.
- Love-making with a sexual partner seems out of the question.
- Light switches are out of your reach and can be switched on and off only by persons entering the room.

This scenario illustrates that except in rare circumstances, at least some of your most cherished privacy "props" are removed during institutionalization. For some, privacy is necessary to succeed in certain activities such as sleeping or urinating. If a patient feels that he or she is being watched constantly because of monitors or windows from the hallway, it may be well nigh impossible for him or her to conduct the most basic hygienic and other activities of daily living.

Lack of privacy has many cultural nuances that all too often are neglected. In some cultures, the most profound shame would be experienced by a person whose body or bodily functions are exposed to a member of the opposite sex, even a health professional. In some instances a woman would be banned from her community. Overhearing a conversation of someone else may be a sign of extreme rudeness. Passing gas or belching, vomiting, or crying out in pain may be considered unseemly and cause for great embarrassment. All of those are potential causes for anxiety due to the lack of privacy alone!

The hallmark of the loss of privacy is the hospital gown. Even presidents and kings are not spared the potential indignity of walking down the hall in that garment with the gaping back! You can help patients by making sure they are covered adequately to preserve their modesty.

Whatever the source, the patient robbed of privacy is likely to feel intense discomfort. Health professionals must be diligent in helping patients meet the challenge of maintaining their right to privacy.

Loss of Independence

Challenges related to the loss of home and privacy are rooted in the far more basic loss of independence. The institutional value of efficiency, which is important so that the facility can be responsive to the many demands of its functioning, creates serious problems for the patient who needs time for solitude or religious observance, variety in a schedule, or other resources he or she uses to keep a sense of balance and perspective. Most health facilities impose profound restrictions on independence, many of them unnecessary. For instance, almost every minute of the day is scheduled for patients, their preferences often being unnecessarily compromised in the name of staff efficiency. For others, their choices about how and where they would like to spend their unscheduled time are ignored, and usually are significantly limited anyway by policies or institutional practices. Patients are transported or accompanied from place to place for therapy, diagnostic procedures, and other activities, often not knowing where they are headed, how long it will take, or what is going to happen. In many facilities visiting hours are fixed, and the telephone switchboard may prohibit calls from going through after a certain hour at night.

Often the patient's (or other patients') safety and well-being are factors in restricting independence. However, for many patients it is a challenge to sort out when and how much restriction of their independence is warranted. For example, in some cases, the patient may be on a restricted diet, may not be allowed to have a drink of an alcoholic beverage, may be required to exercise (or to rest) at given intervals, and may not leave the facility. For acutely ill patients, this is a temporary frustration. In the worst case, for chronically ill or permanently institutionalized patients it becomes a way of life. Fortunately, we are in a period when health care institutions are taking a hard look at how respect can be honored more fully while still maintaining a high level of efficiency and patient safety. You will be in a good position to help suggest changes in institutional structures, policies, and functions that will allow its occupants to realize a maximal degree of independence.

AMBULATORY CARE SETTINGS

More and more procedures are being performed in ambulatory settings. Here institutionalization is very brief. In many cases it does not involve an overnight stay.

 REFLECTIONS

Have you ever been treated or taken a friend or family member to be treated in an ambulatory care setting such as an outpatient clinic, "Doc in a Box" office in a strip mall, or emergency room?

If so, reflect on the environment of that setting and how it differed from, say, a hospital, nursing home, or a rehabilitation center.

Jot down some notes about it before reading on and then compare your observations with the authors' observations below.

Ambulatory care patients are in the awkward position of sitting on the fence between two worlds. They may appear completely well and therefore not be treated as "sick" or "impaired." However, they are definitely *patients* for the following reasons: physical or mental function is impaired enough to produce discomfort in the person or to result in his or her inability to proceed with some activities formerly taken for granted; symptoms are severe enough to have been openly acknowledged by the person and confirmed by a physician or other health professional; the person has agreed to participate in a treatment or diagnostic regimen that requires regular trips to the health care facility, and the visit takes high enough priority in the patient's life so that other competing activities are sacrificed. For example, ambulatory care patients who receive radiation or chemotherapy must visit the clinic for many weeks, which requires serious disruptions in their schedules and repeated trips to and from the facility. Each cancellation of an ordinary event and each trip is a shrill reminder of their condition (Figure 6-4).

FIGURE 6-4: A patient entering an ambulatory care setting. *(© Corbis.)*

From your perspective as a health professional, challenges facing such patients may appear almost indistinguishable from those facing patients who are admitted to a facility as inpatients. We believe there are notable differences. For instance, ambulatory care patients may suffer from the loss of self-image even more keenly than inpatients. The person admitted as an inpatient to the health care facility becomes surrounded by others in a similar predicament and is allowed to look and act the part, whereas ambulatory care patients are more like "drop ins" or "visitors" and do not feel as if they have this license; the latter come into the treatment setting for a brief period only and then return to their everyday surroundings where colleagues, families, and others may have no sympathy for what they are facing. The person who is ambulatory also may feel excluded from the "action" that appears to be taking place in the health facility, like a spectator at a game he or she would benefit from knowing how to play but doesn't. The inpatients know the lingo and can find their way around. The worry about being "out of the know" grows in part from the feeling that the institutionalized patients recognize one another, understand the rules, and have a better chance of winning the professionals' attention. Ambulatory care patients may feel jealous of those who are in closer contact with the health professionals, aides, and others.

There are other practical challenges for the ambulatory care patient, too. In some instances patients have to fight for time off from work, have difficulty finding—and paying—someone trustworthy to care for children or attend to a homebound spouse or parent. They may lose precious pay or vacation time. The trip to and from the health facility can be so arduous and expensive that the person questions the worth of the visit, especially if when they arrive there is a long wait before being seen.

If you as a health professional observe that a person receiving ambulatory care is feeling socially isolated, you can help the person overcome this alienation, become acquainted with others, and in other ways help him or her find a sense of belonging in the health care environment. At the same time, you and your colleagues can also help the person see the gains of being able to remain uninstitutionalized rather than having to be admitted as an inpatient to a health care facility.

THE HOME CARE ENVIRONMENT

Although home care patients do not have to suffer the trauma of adapting to a strange institutional environment, there are different challenges for persons receiving health care services in their homes (Figure 6-5).

The presence of skilled health professionals who come to provide sophisticated therapy and professional care is a relatively recent phenomenon. Thus, there is always tension between the true purpose of the home (i.e., a refuge from the outside world) and the home as a site where patients receive technical interventions and care from strangers. Furthermore, homes are not hospitals and are not designed to be mini-intensive care units, rehabilitation centers, or long-term care facilities, so they lack equipment, space, and in some cases even electrical or other resources required for equipment that must be brought into the home setting.

The presence of health care professionals in the home often is met with mixed emotions by patients and families. On the one hand, there is a sense of relief that assistance with foreign equipment and procedures is at hand and that family caregivers can be relieved temporarily of the burden of continuous care. On the other, professional care in the home inevitably involves an intrusion into personal space, routines, and behaviors. Patients may not know how to treat health care professionals in their homes and thus cannot truly relax or be themselves while the health professional is present. Should they treat them as guests and offer them social courtesies such as coffee and cookies? Or should they treat them as hired help, much as one would treat

FIGURE 6-5: A home care patient. (© *Corbis.*)

a plumber or electrician who comes to the home to perform a specific task and then departs without an expectation of social pleasantries?

In short, home care is clearly unique in that professional services are carried out on the patient's turf, in an environment designed for very different purposes than health care. Here the rules and dynamics of a household are the standards for behavior rather than the rules of a bureaucratic organization. It is not surprising, then, that the challenges of maintaining a true level of the comforts that often are lost during institutionalization also face the patient who now must receive care at home. Furthermore, maintaining one's privacy takes a different form in the home care setting than it presents in institutions.

> The Kimura family had been constant companions to their son Noby during his acute recovery and rehabilitation following a train accident that initially left him comatose and then paralyzed. When it was time to take their 20-year-old quadriplegic, ventilator-dependent son home, they wanted him to be a part of the family's life. They and he agreed it would be terrible if he were placed away in a second-story bedroom, so they cleared the dining room of furniture except for the family's small Shinto shrine in the corner to make room for the bed and equipment.
>
> ▶ What are the strengths of this arrangement for this family?
> ▶ What difficulties can you predict for the family because of this arrangement?
> ▶ In order to fully assess the challenges for Noby and his family, what else would you like to know about their home? Their family dynamics? Other details?
>
> Let's go to the next step in the Kimura family's adjustment to this dramatic change in their lives:
>
> After 2 months with this arrangement, both Noby and his parents decided this was a poor decision. The family had little privacy when professional caregivers were in attendance. The patient felt like he had no privacy at all. They talked over the situation and came to a new solution: Noby would be moved to the lower-level family room where he could still be a part of the family life but not the center of all activity. Health professionals as well as his friends could come and go without coming through the rest of the house. He could invite his parents to watch TV or just sit in the room to talk and he could still enjoy some private time as young men of this age normally need and want.
>
> ▶ What new challenges do you predict for the Kimuras in this arrangement?
> ▶ What family values do you identify in their attempt to be a family again?

Their story illustrates that patients and their families may not appreciate the long-term stress the home care arrangement can cause because initially they are so elated to be together again in their own home environment.

Home care personnel can work with family and patients to plan their schedule and care delivery so that the patient can have enough privacy and the family can develop a sense of appropriate psychological, if not physical, distance between themselves and the caregivers in their home.

WEIGHING LOSSES AND PRIVILEGES

It sounds curious to talk of patients as having "privileges," especially in light of the previous sections in which you were introduced to serious challenges that patients face. At the same time, certain accommodations are reserved for anyone who temporarily is struck down by illness or physical or mental impairment. A major feature is that others relieve him or her of certain roles and responsibilities. In Chapter 2 you were introduced to various rights, laws, and social policies that express respect for this accommodation.

 REFLECTIONS

What privileges did you have as a child when you were sick or sustained an injury? What changes did you experience?
Which of the following common answers by students also were true of your experience?

- Meals were brought to me in bed.
- I didn't have to go to school.
- I had first choice of the toys.
- I was exempt from doing the dishes.
- I could watch television/listen to the radio/play video games in my room.
- I was given a cold washcloth for my forehead.
- I got ice cream or chicken soup (or some other special food or home remedy).
    Now think about the "negotiation tools" your parents, sitter, or other person in authority used to be sure you were doing all you could to "get well" enough to go back to school, etc.

Support for a stricken person is an understandable part of the care extended to him or her out of respect for the difficulties that accompany being sick or otherwise laid low. However, inherent in the granting of such privileges is a message that these accommodations are also an encouragement to keep up the good fight back to health if that goal is possible. In other words, the privileges are not designed to convey permission for the person to remain in the patient role indefinitely if he or she is capable of recovery. And if recovery is not a reasonable goal, the person is expected to begin to learn the challenge of living well with impairment or preparing for impending death.

The increasing emphasis on the patient's role as an active agent in the process and not just as a passive recipient of the health professional's services is highlighted by the amount of information shared on the Internet, in the daily news, and through other public media sources. Patients today believe that some of the "help" they need is to seek professional intervention, but also that they must have information about their own health that will assist them in the process of healing or adjustment.[6]

It is easy to conclude that a patient who has a lot of information about her or his conditions will be better equipped to prepare for whatever lays ahead. This is not necessarily so. A woman who previously had been treated for life-threatening adenocarcinoma of the lung, and who was now undergoing new tests because of a persistent cough, lends insight into how difficult it is to feel confidently in control of one's health or life, especially when there is an underlying threat:

> Bending over the table as a doctor inserted a needle into my back to extract some fluid I started to think about what I would do if a presumably innocent cough turned out to be the sound of the other shoe dropping. I had once had a good reason to listen for that other shoe; I'd had malignant lymph nodes in my mediastinum—the middle of my chest—as well as a tumor in my lung. I had always been amazed at how little time I'd spent listening for it, and what I most disliked about having the needle stuck into my back was that it began to awaken what I'd come to think of as the dragon that sleeps inside anyone who has had cancer. I'd written once that we can never kill this dragon, but we go about the business of our daily lives—giving our children breakfast, putting more mulch on our gardens—in the hope that it will stay asleep for a while longer. What I hadn't said was what I'd do if the dragon woke up. But, even as I braced myself for the insertion of the needle, it seemed unlikely that lung cancer, a notoriously aggressive disease, would hang around for so long only to reassert itself in the guise of a cough that interfered with my dreams of seeing the Bosporus.[7]

Many patients are very resourceful in maintaining hope and participating in their treatment. But failure to do so may signal an awareness that the privileges in the form of accommodations by other people usually are short lived. The arduous preparation for coping with challenges of longer illness or impairment or preparing for death involves more serious losses and understandably fills many with dread. Paul Tillich, a theologian who escaped imprisonment and almost certain death in a Nazi prison camp, wrote a treatise on what happens when all one knows is thrown into disarray. He titled it *The Courage to Be*.[8] This seems an apt way to think about patients.

CHOOSING TO REMAIN A PATIENT

We invite you to focus your attention now on the rare person who could but does not want to move beyond the patient role or who even relishes being in it. Clearly, for them, the privileges they receive while they are struggling or incapacitated outweigh those granted them when they are well. One extreme way a person remains in the patient role is to feign symptoms long after they are gone or to fabricate them. Such a patient is engaged in *malingering*.

It behooves us to send a word of caution at this point. Sometimes patient problems are complex in other ways that can lead to mistakenly labeling the patient a malingerer. The patient may have symptoms of organic illness in the absence of organic pathological signs. This patient is not necessarily a malingerer but may have physical symptoms of a mental illness: He may have a "hysterical symptom" or have undergone a conversion reaction (i.e., a psychological problem has been converted into an organic, or physical, symptom) that for all practical purposes mimics malingering. Sometimes the organic basis of a condition is very difficult to diagnose, and the person may be treated as a "malingerer" only to later find the cause.

Unfortunately, such people are treated as "faking it" for months or years when a serious reason for their symptoms and suffering is diagnosed. Then there are "borderline" cases: A recent issue of *The New Yorker Magazine* profiled a man who woke up after a stint in the hospital, having been hit on the head.[9] When he "came to" he was completely amnesic. However, in the absence of neurological findings substantiating his symptoms, and his apparent contentedness to be taken care of by others while relearning virtually everything, questions have begun to surface about whether he ever was, or any longer is, amnesic. If not, he would qualify as a malingerer, but no one is certain enough to label him one. A fourth complex situation is the so-called "non-compliant" patient, meaning the patient who refuses to follow clear and necessary measures prescribed by the health professionals. Studies of apparent lack of cooperation in following a treatment regimen show that this behavior has many sources, some of which have little or nothing to do with the patient's desire to participate in his or her treatment and healing. Only those who intentionally refuse to take necessary measures when able to do so, intentionally undermining treatment attempts to return the patient to society, would qualify as a malingerer.

Escape or Financial Gain

You may wonder what patients who malinger gain by their behavior, considering the advantages of a healthy, independent, and active life. For some, they see protection from the threatening outside world as one advantage of remaining in the patient role. A woman who lives on the streets as a homeless person may find refuge in being in a health care institution, as may persons in abusive or neglectful home situations. Fear of going back to the front lines of war after an injury or, in the days of the draft, of ever going to the front lines may be cause for malingering. But the range of people who malinger goes well beyond persons in situations as extreme as these.

Financial gain may also be a desired advantage. Malingering patients are seen often in clinics that treat work-related injuries, which cost society millions of dollars each year in labor losses. Their situation has resulted in an increasing number of programs in the workplace, such as "work hardening" and other approaches, that have as their goal to return persons to work after they have been absent because of illness or injury. This is accomplished through positive incentives to stay at or return to work. Many of these patients have jobs that are boring or dangerous or offer no opportunity for advancement; therefore, they welcome any means of escape from the job, hoping that workers' compensation or some other form of disability insurance will help meet basic needs. In the United States, similar attempts to gain early retirement or to receive extensive disability support often are settled through the court system. The solutions to these issues are complicated and require thoughtful approaches by governments, the health care system, employers, and workers.

Social Gain

Social gain is a third possibility of a gain desired by patients who choose to remain in the patient role and receive the privileges afforded to people in that role. They are able to manipulate the attention of family, friends, and their professionals when they perceive that this approach is successful. If the results are rewarding enough, an individual may decide that it is not worthwhile to be restored to his or her former symptom-free life.

A perfect example of such a patient is Argan, the malingering patient in Molière's play, *The Imaginary Invalid*. He controls everyone in his life by virtue of his "weakened" condition. When his daughter Angélique is old enough to be married, he chooses a physician as her husband. Toinnette, the maid, asks Argan why the physician has been chosen when Angélique is obviously in love with someone else:

> Argan: My reason is that, in view of the feeble and poorly state that I'm in I want to marry my daughter into the medical profession so that I can assure myself of help in my illness and have a supply of the remedies I need within the family and be in a position to have consultations and prescriptions whenever I want them.
>
> Toinnette, boldly: Well that's certainly a reason and it's nice to be discussing it so calmly. But master, with your hand on your heart, now, *are* you ill?
>
> Argan: What, you jade! Am I ill! You impudent creature! *Am I ill?*
>
> Toinnette: All right then, you *are* ill. Don't let's quarrel about that. You *are* ill. Very ill. I agree with you there. More ill than you think. That's settled. But your daughter should marry to suit herself. *She* isn't ill so there's no need to give *her* a doctor.
>
> Argan: It's for my own sake that I'm marrying her to a doctor. A daughter with any proper feeling ought to be only too pleased to marry someone who will be of service to her father's health.[10]

The world thus revolves around Argan's medicines and body functions. His emotional dependency is revealed in his continual tattling to his wife about the annoying Toinnette, who is the only one who confronts him with his hypocrisy. His brother Béralde observes, "One proof that there's nothing wrong with you and that your health is perfectly sound is that in spite of all your efforts you haven't managed to damage your constitution and you've survived all the medicines they've given you to swallow."

Argan quickly counters, "But don't you know, brother, that that's just what's keeping me going. Mr. Purgon [the physician] says that if he left off attending me for three days I shouldn't survive it."[10]

Audiences for 300 years have been laughing at Argan's obvious self-deluding rationalizations. They laugh because they can identify with Argan's reluctance to give up the privileges of the patient's position in society. However, most differ from Argan in that they do not enjoy these privileges enough to create a lifestyle around their symptoms and debilitating disorders.

Respectful Responses to Malingering

You will occasionally meet a person who is malingering and should be prepared to respond constructively and respectfully to him or her. It is understandable that most health professionals become frustrated when confronted with a patient who apparently does not want to improve but who wants the attention of treatment, often at the price of attention that you and your colleagues judge should be going to other patients. The following case will help you reflect on what you can do:

> Marilyn Siegler is a 19-year-old woman who has long had "family problems." Her father is a successful businessman, and her mother is very much involved in the charitable and social activities of the large city in which they live. From the time she was a child Marilyn has felt that her parents favored her older brother, who now has decided to become a partner in their father's business.
>
> Marilyn has been seen by numerous counselors and psychiatrists since her teen years, when she made a suicide attempt. All agree that her feelings of rejection are the basis for her unhappiness. Several attempts have been made to bring the parents in for family counseling, but they have always been too busy.
>
> Marilyn is a freshman medical student. She went from boarding school to a prestigious private college in a state distant from her home and, upon admission to medical school in this Midwest university, chose to live in a dormitory with other medical school and health professions graduate students. She is very friendly and outgoing, though as the year has progressed she has seemed to grow increasingly demanding of those around her. During the past 3 months she has developed a rapidly progressing weakness in her legs and is now confined to a wheelchair. Extensive tests have revealed no physical basis for the disabling symptoms to date. Recently her parents have decided it would be best for Marilyn to return home, where they plan to employ a private tutor for her with the hopes of her being able to complete her first year of medical school.
>
> Jane is living in the dormitory where Marilyn lives. Marilyn has been a patient in the clinic where Jane is currently working as part of her professional on-site preparation. She has observed numerous costly diagnostic procedures being performed on Marilyn to get at the root of her problem and, therefore, knows much more about Marilyn's elusive clinical history than any of the other people in the dorm. She has, of course, never disclosed it to anyone, but it gives Jane a special affection for Marilyn. She does not fully share the feeling of some of her dorm mates who are relieved that Marilyn may be leaving the dorm, saying they are tired of being increasingly called on to assist her.
>
> Last Monday morning the clinic area was unusually full when Marilyn wheeled into the clinic complaining about how exhausted she was. The receptionist took Marilyn to a remote area of some unused private treatment cubicles near the storeroom and an unused bathroom. She asked Marilyn if she could get herself undressed for the test she was about to undergo. Marilyn said she thought she could.
>
> A few minutes later Jane started down the long corridor to check on Marilyn's progress and was astonished to see Marilyn scurrying back from the bathroom to her curtained changing area. Jane could not believe her eyes. Marilyn was walking briskly— and with apparent great ease!
>
> ▶ What should Jane say and do next?
> ▶ What should the staff supervisors and others do, having this uncomfortable issue to deal with?

Every situation has its own challenges; however, the following principles can guide you when you are a health professional responsible for the care of a patient you suspect is malingering:

▶ *Principle 1*. Believe the patient until all reasonable evidence that there is a physical basis for the patient's complaint of symptoms has been legitimately discounted.

This requires diligence on everyone's part to be thorough in diagnosis. To do less is to stigmatize the patient unfairly as well as help set a course that may be clinically harmful. In Jane's case even her simple observation needs to be confirmed. For instance, might Marilyn's symptoms be decreased by medication or other clinical factors? This is especially critical because once a person is definitively identified as a malingerer, he or she needs professional counseling. The patient cannot be coerced into wanting to return to society or previous roles and responsibilities until their underlying problems are addressed. Health professionals like yourself often become involved in this problem-solving process by working closely with the psychologist or psychiatrist and by reinforcing conduct that contributes to helping the patient welcome the opportunity to reclaim the degree of healthfulness available to him or her.

▶ *Principle 2*. Effective teamwork and team respect toward the patient are essential.

Inform and employ every team member to assist in the discovery process; if malingering is verified, continue to treat the person respectfully under these unusual circumstances. Respect does not mean that the patient's behavior is acceptable, rather that it warrants the type of care mentioned above. Malingering is a stigmatizing label and once suspected, the attitude of health professionals can turn to neglect or retribution because the patient is "faking it." A common example is seen in the treatment of patients with pain for which no objective basis can be found. If patients are given placebos instead of analgesics to prove that their pain is illusory, they are invariably angry and hurt when they find out about the deception, even though they may have received complete pain relief from the placebo. To avoid the development of an adversarial relationship, the whole team must be prepared to treat the malingering as part of the patient's care package.

▶ *Principle 3*. Pay attention to comments from family and friends.

Family and friends who have brought concerns about the patient's condition to your attention can be helpful in the discovery process and also should be counted as potential resources for the course that follows. For instance, one of the authors found that a critical conversation had been opened by the wife of a patient when the wife asked whether it was "unusual for daytime wrist pain like her husband's to be so severe that he could not work but it didn't seem to bother him in the evening." When asked what she meant she said he told her he had been diagnosed with "daytime" pain, but the doctors and others could not find the basis for it. (This last part was true.) It turned out upon further conversation with this wife that the pain disappeared in the evening to the extent that he could spend most nights at the bowling alley using the same arm that kept him from working at a job he had come to despise. That led to additional inquiry of the patient that finally resulted in his being referred for counseling once he was identified as a malingerer, and he eventually went back to work.

▶ *Principle 4.* As with all sensitive patient issues, confidentiality must be judiciously guarded.

Even in the story of the wife's "disclosure" described in Principle 3, one of the most difficult areas of exploration in this husband-wife situation was to take seriously the information gained from the wife but to use as much skill and caring as possible in getting the patient to raise the bowling issue himself. Even after the patient's malingering had been discovered, the health professionals were bound to honor the patient's right not have the findings of his malingering shared with his wife until and unless he was prepared to do so.

SUMMARY

In this chapter you have had an opportunity to focus squarely on some peculiarities of the patient's challenges during changes that virtually everyone finds unwelcome and difficult in one way or another. Whether the transition involves real or feared losses and adjustments, they involve some degree of a patient's disruption from long-established patterns. Special accommodations the patient receives may be short-lived, especially if he or she seems not to be participating actively in recovery or adjustments that must be made. Some things will be viewed with disdain, distrust, or impatience by persons who make up the fabric of the patient's life. Malingering is one of the special situations you may encounter, but the principles of good patient care apply to this and other unusual challenges. Your role and skills cannot be divorced from this larger real-life picture that the patient brings to your doorstep. Their challenge then becomes your challenge too—and one worth meeting well.

REFERENCES

1. Klein BS: *Slow dance: a story of stroke, love, and disability,* Berkeley, CA, 1998, Page Mill Press.
2. Garrison JF: *P.S. Julia*, Middleton, MA, 2005, Pinhead Press.
3. Dudzinski D: The diving bell meets the butterfly: identity lost and remembered, *Theory Med Bioeth* 22:33-46, 2000.
4. Wendell S: *The rejected body: feminist philosophical reflections on disability*, New York, 1996, Routledge.
5. Haddad A: "French weaving," 2001, unpublished. (With permission of the author.)
6. Purtilo R: Professional-patient relationship: ethical issues. In Reich W, editor: *Encyclopedia of Bioethics,* ed 3, Vol 4, New York, 2004, Macmillan.
7. Trillin AS: Betting your life, *The New Yorker* Jan 29, 2001.
8. Tillich P: *The courage to be*, New Haven, 1952, Yale University Press.
9. Friend T: Backstory. new man. *The New Yorker* Feb 27, 2006.
10. Molière JB: *The misanthrope and other plays,* London, 1959, Penguin Books. (Translated by J Wood.)

RESPECT FOR THE PATIENT'S PERSONAL RELATIONSHIPS

CHAPTER OBJECTIVES

The student will be able to:

- Identify three major questions patients and their loved ones may ask as they experience increased fragility in their close relationships during illness or after a serious injury
- Describe three key ways that patients, their family, and others close to them express their concerns to the health professional regarding their fear that they are losing the support of friends, colleagues, and others they count on
- Explain how uncertainty also affects the patient's relationships with loved ones and the health professional's role in attempting to alleviate undue anxieties and concerns
- Identify several barriers that family or other nonprofessional (volunteer, informal) caregivers face in trying to live their commitment to caregiving and what the health professional can do to be a positive influence
- Discuss ways the health professional can be an advocate for patients and families faced with financial burdens related to health care
- Describe opportunities for health professionals to assist patients in their attempts to strengthen and revitalize important relationships

A special pattern of communication developed between Robin and Mark (her father) during his hospitalization. Each morning Mark phoned home to tell her about the animal picture on the sugar packet that he had saved from his breakfast tray. One morning Robin explained to Mark that she had a cold, and then, with three-year-old directness, asked, "What do you have, Daddy?"

After a pause he replied, "I have cancer."

She handed the phone to me and said, "I think Daddy's crying." Though he had never hesitated to discuss his illness with others who asked, he was deeply shaken by the weight of Robin's question and the implications of his answer.

—S.A. Albertson[1]

The personal life of a patient includes the personal relationships he or she brings to the health professional and patient encounter. Respect for this fact is immensely important if you are to reach the goal of maintaining the patient's dignity during your professional interactions with her or him. Some ways in which patients' personal relationships are affected include topics addressed in the previous chapter:

- loss of the familiar surroundings in which relationships are most easily nurtured
- loss of the capacity to participate in his or her usual fashion
- granting of privileges to the patient by others with conditions attached
- unmet expectations of others that the patient will return to former roles

This chapter focuses directly on patients' personal relationships, with an emphasis on some ways illness or injury can change them. Most of our attention is beamed on the patient's relationship with family; however, the patient identifies who "family" is. For instance, many people consider their family to include life partners outside of a marriage relationship, or cousins, uncles, aunts, and others related by blood and marriage (Figure 7-1). We also acknowledge that the patient's relationships with close friends, long-time business associates, and others who are important to the patient often are deeply affected. Special attention in this chapter is devoted to family members or other persons who become caregivers for the patient because their personal relationship often is dramatically challenged by the new situation. We offer suggestions about how and when you can become a source of support and encouragement to a patient and those close to him or her as they go through the hard times.

FIGURE 7-1: A patient's personal relationships with family members and friends can be affected by illness or injury. (© Getty Images/AA051759.)

FACING THE FRAGILITY OF RELATIONSHIPS

Any significant change in a person has the power to alter his or her status and roles in various close relationships. Like a mobile, when one person in a relationship changes, every component necessarily moves, and everyone has to pull together to find a viable new balance point. As patients become aware of changes, they often express concerns of abandonment or fears that they will be unable to contribute to their key relationships in meaningful ways. In this section we ask you to consider three questions that plague many:

• Will others lose interest in helping to sustain my dearest relationships?
• Will we weather the winds of change?
• What certainties can I count on to sustain and nourish my relationships?

Loved ones and friends who are thrust into the role of caregiving often grapple with similar questions.

Will Others Lose Interest?

We all hope that our families, friends, and associates will take our problems to heart—fortunately, they usually do. However, sometimes patients are unpleasantly surprised by the degree of indifference they feel many people show to the struggle they went—or are going—through. You know from your own experience that this feeling is not limited to persons who become patients. More generally speaking, it can be dismaying to realize that, no matter what momentous event you have been through or are still experiencing, the majority of people in your life do not want to know very much about it!

There may be a lot of reasons for others' apparent lack of interest. For instance, when there is good news to share, some might be jealous of your good fortune or feel that their security is threatened by your success; when the news is bad, some may be threatened by that, too, thinking, "There but for the grace of God go I." For that matter, some really do not care much in the first place, even though it was easy and enjoyable to show interest when things were moving along in the usual familiar groove.

In extreme circumstances most people do turn more inward and become self-absorbed, and patients are no exception. Therefore, sometimes the patient becomes extremely boring or demanding, driving others away. Friends and loved ones may assume that the patient no longer really cares about them and lose interest in maintaining the relationship for that reason.

The truth is that most people expect at least their family and close friends to be there for them when difficult times arise, and it is a shock when that doesn't happen. One of the authors recounts elsewhere the moment when a 20-year-old patient named David, who was quadriplegic as a result of diving into a shallow pond when he was 19, told her the bad news about his older brother Jim and David's fiancée, Jane. Noticing that something seemed to be troubling David this particular Monday morning, she tried unsuccessfully to encourage the usually loquacious David into conversation. Finally she asked if he had been "on a weekend binge or something."

"No. But I need a drink."
"What do you mean, you need a drink?" [long silence] "David! *What's the matter?*"
   His shoulders sagged lower and I saw the flaps of skin on his chin and belly. ... Eighty pounds lighter too quickly for his young skin to keep up with his diminishing bulk.

He raised his head, barely, and whispered hoarsely from somewhere way back in his throat, or life, "Jane is going to marry Jim."

For the first time ever, I was without words with David. He looked straight into my eyes, locked in that moment of recognition that we had both lost our footing and were falling.[2]

As a health professional, sometimes you are really affected by a terrible event in a patient's life, and, like the therapist in this excerpt, you feel stunned into not knowing what to say or do. She probably did the right thing just then by letting David see that this news was very difficult for her to hear because of the enormity she knew it held for David. Later he told her that the tears in her eyes convinced him that she really cared. Fortunately, few patients have to absorb blows like those David endured, but over the years the authors have learned never to be surprised when a patient suffers a profound emotional blow due to a breakdown of an important relationship.

However daunting it may seem, it is always worthwhile to try to offer comfort and hope in such situations. For instance, if you see it coming, you can try to help prepare patients for a disappointment they might encounter in their expectations and make suggestions for renewed participation in their other communities of support. Just by talking directly to the patient about an obvious absence of someone who was present on a regular basis previously may give the person an opening to discuss his fears or the reality of what is happening. Of course, to pry deeply into the particulars of a personal relationship (or the apparent increasing dissolution of one) also can be an unwelcome intrusion into the patient's privacy if the timing is not right. The point is that gentle probing may lead to an opportunity for the patient to talk through and think more expansively about the situation. In fact, sometimes allowing a patient to talk about family, friends, or other social contacts will help him or her start remembering things about the relationships that are treasured and help the patient's focus to turn to strengthening those relationships during this unusual time.

Family members, partners, or friends who become caregivers often go through their own worries about whether others are losing interest in the patient or are becoming indifferent to the stresses on the relationship the patient and caregiver(s) are experiencing. Their concerns are founded on their observation that longtime friends and associates are backing off. This seems to be especially true in situations when the one being cared for has undergone a serious and long-standing change in appearance or abilities.

The social functions and activities that partners, families, and friends enjoy with others often dwindle, isolating the patient and caregivers from familiar sources of enjoyment and their feeling of belonging within their larger communities. The loss of a job can further distance them from longtime associates and patterns. We surmise that others' fears that "this could be us," combined with the awkwardness of being with a couple or family who are dealing with momentous changes, often result in their finding it easier to stay away than to face the hard realities with the affected persons. Internal divisions within families also may erupt, often over differing hopes and expectations about who will take responsibility for various aspects of caregiving.

The patient may begin to feel as if he or she has caused all the stress and withdraw further from contributing to the vitality of key relationships.

Unfortunately, a special burden falls on relationships when the patient has a condition that carries a social stigma of some sort. People who have AIDS are prime examples of such a group who (by virtue of their illness) may lose their social life, job, and health insurance. Although great strides have been made in the United States and elsewhere to educate about AIDS, this disease still has the power to marginalize patients and their loved ones from their communities and important relationships. Suspicion or confirmation about the source of the HIV infection may be knowledge that some people close to the patient cannot accept. Others may find their commitment to the relationship stretched thin by negative responses to the patient or themselves from neighbors, former friends, or acquaintances.

The range of conditions for which a patient and those closest to him or her may be led to believe they should feel shame will vary according to the social values of the patient's culture and subcultures. In Christina Lee's excellent book, *Women's Health: Psychological and Social Perspectives,* she points out that depending on their environment, women may be expected to be ashamed of reproductive conditions such as premenstrual syndrome, menopause symptoms, infertility or postpartum depression, excess weight or physically "disfiguring" conditions that lay outside the norms of beauty, and of age-related symptoms.[3]

Sometimes people close to the patient also are expected to feel ashamed for having a role in causing or worsening a patient's condition.[4] An example was relayed to us by a colleague who was teaching a 3-week summer course in another city when her husband had a serious heart attack. She recalls the following conversation upon hearing the news that her husband was in the cardiac intensive care unit:

Cardiologist: Your husband has had a serious heart attack and is in the cardiac care unit.
Woman: Oh no! What happened?
Cardiologist: [Explains some medical details.] Was he well when you left?
Woman: He seemed fine! We have known his heart is bad but we thought it was under control since he has been under your care. [More questions about his condition.]
Cardiologist: You know he has trouble staying on his diet. Has he been eating correctly?
Woman (still shaken): I think so! I've been gone for three weeks but…
Cardiologist: Oh, yes. Husbands often eat things they shouldn't when their wives are gone.

The woman said that although she never could tell whether the doctor was intentionally trying to shame her for not being there when her husband had a heart attack, she could not figure out why he would have said such a thing for any other reason.

What can health professionals do to help decrease the deleterious effects of others' intentional or unintentional blaming of the patient or loved one? At the very least, this physician's comment is a reminder that health professionals must always listen to their own comments with a reflective third ear to think about how they might be coming across to the other person. Putting them in contact with patient and/or family support groups of similarly affected persons may help them succeed in guarding against shame. Beyond that, any time you can speak up to counter destructive, shame-inducing attitudes and behaviors in the larger society is time well spent.

Can We Weather the Winds of Change?

Patients also justifiably worry about other relationship-related effects of serious illness or impairment from injury. Unfortunately, the change a person undergoes during illness or injury may cause him or her to become almost a stranger to loved ones.[5] In extreme cases, the original form of old relationships becomes unrecognizable in the present situation. For example, a spouse who sustains a traumatic brain injury may become like a child; a long-time business partner who becomes mentally ill may become suspicious or abusive toward family, trusted associates, or clients; or a young man known for his bravado may become fearful of hanging out with the guys after a heart attack, fearing they will see him as a has-been. However, usually the changes are more subtle, like a chill wind that slices through an otherwise refreshing fall breeze, sending an unexpected shiver of worry across all those in the relationship. One man, a physician named Owen, writes insightfully and sensitively about his increasing sense of disorientation, dread, and fatigue as he watches his wife of almost thirty years, Lezlie, succumb to a fast-growing (and spreading) ovarian cancer—and his inability to "fix it," even though she is in one of the best hospitals in the world where he is a respected physician. He sees the person he knew during their many years together slipping away from him as her symptoms and complications take their toll on her. These sources of suffering are compounded by guilt when Owen begins fantasizing about a beautiful nurse named Natalie who is one of his wife's caregivers:

> So it occurred to me then that this was part of something that had been willed … perhaps ordained … that Natalie and I would become lovers. There would be this transition as there might be—at least in fictional accounts—when bereaved husbands fall in love with their late wife's caretaker …
>
> [Natalie accompanies him to a professional presentation he is making in another town. He learns later that their friends and his wife are so worried about his state that they arrange for her to find a reason to go with him. She attends his presentation.]
>
> After the talk, I walked from the conference room with Natalie at my side. I had always been scrupulously faithful to my wife and would remain so. Still, it pleased me to have an attractive woman at my side. Natalie's appearance was striking and there was a seductive quality about her that she was unaware of and that made one think that no one in her life was more important. I craved like an alcoholic in withdrawal. I don't remember what I said to Natalie. … It was something to the effect that I, while alone the previous night, had imagined that she and I had married and that she, too, had become ill. There was a silent moment in which I watched Natalie's face change. She said I had misinterpreted her feelings.
>
> We flew back separately to Boston.[6]

This family member is able to reflect on his situation and regain his bearings so that he can endure the upheaval he, his wife, and their children are living through.

He credits their ability to see this through as a couple and family as having been dependent in large part on friends, family, and colleagues who quietly, and sometimes assertively, intervened to provide them support.

⊚ REFLECTIONS

> Think about a relationship you hold very dear—and would count on the most—if you were to become a patient, like Lezlie, with a serious illness or injury.
> - What do you think would be your greatest worry in terms of the changes you knew your condition could impose on your loved one?
> - List one or two people you could call on to help you and the other person make it through the hard times of such a change.
>   Now put yourself in the position of Owen, a family caregiver for your loved one.
> - What type of condition that your loved one might incur would be the greatest challenge to your relationship as it now stands? Why? (i.e., what values and behaviors have seemed to sustain the "core" of the relationship during other challenges and changes)?
>   Take a minute to reflect on these questions or have a conversation with a classmate about some things you would hope to have available to you to help you maintain the relationship.

These types of exercises can help you imagine the challenges and concerns patients and their closest resources are facing. At the same time, the conclusion that their experience will be exactly as you imagine yours must be avoided. A more appropriate stance is to sympathetically acknowledge that there are serious challenges most people face in their relationship when one person in it is changed by illness or injury. This recognition is extremely important because all too often the health of family or other caregivers has been ignored to the detriment of everyone involved, especially when the new situation requires an intense, long-term (or even lifelong) commitment.

You may ask how important it is for you to gain an understanding of the caregivers' situation. The answer is "extremely important." At the time this book is being written, the U.S. Department of Health and Human Services estimates that family and friend (called *informal*) caregiver services will be one of the biggest changes this society will see during your professional careers:

> Unpaid informal caregivers, primarily family members, neighbors and friends, currently provide the majority of long-term care services. Informal caregiving will likely continue to be the largest source of direct care as the baby boomer generation retires, with estimates of informal caregivers rising from 20 million in 2000 to 37 million in 2050, an increase of 85 percent.[7]*

---

*From estimates developed using the National Long-Term Care Summary, Caregivers Suppl., and the National Health Interview Survey, Office of Disability, Aging and Long-Term Care Policy; 2002.

The authors have observed that most family caregivers rise to the occasion with remarkable courage, good spiritedness, and if all else fails, resignation. Still, study after study reveals that the everyday reality of life for most family caregivers begins with the belief that they are saddled with unbounded obligation by virtue of their wedding vows and commitments as parent, spouse/partner, son, or daughter, or "only living relative."[8]

The frequent occurrence of stress-related disorders among family caregivers is understandable and extremely disquieting. The rising incidence of serious physical injury from lifting or lack of good judgment because of exhaustion is rarely considered by policy makers.[9] This problem is so serious that beginning in the late 1990s the clinical literature began to address caregiver health status as a separate health care problem, recognizing, for instance, that caregiving had become an independent risk factor for death among elderly caregiver spouses, 75% of whom were women.[10] Family members or other informal caregivers who drop out because they literally cannot take it anymore face acute guilt for abandoning their loved one and often are rewarded with banishment from their own dwindling sources of community support. If you pull up the words "caregiver services" on the internet, you will discover a burgeoning new industry of counseling and other professional services being offered (at a price, of course) to caregivers who can afford to buy them. Even those services are geared largely to families who meet the profile of a family unit consisting of a husband, a wife, and their children. On a slightly more positive note, there seems to be an increasing awareness among community and nonprofit organizations of the need to address what is happening to caregivers who cannot afford to buy relief, support, or other services. All things considered, persons facing or in caregiving situations often do so with trepidation, and those who through illness or injury have occasioned the need for care have grounds to be anxious about whether they can weather the winds of change ahead.

Can We Face the Uncertainties?

Both of the questions we've been discussing in this section contain situations with elements of uncertainty. However, this theme is so fundamental that we now turn to uncertainty and ask you to consider it directly. At some time in every recovery or adjustment process, a patient's uncertainties loom before him or her (Figure 7-2). And whenever that happens, the reverberations race through close personal relationships. As a young child put it to one of the authors, "My sickness is like a ghost that hangs around our house. I'm doing OK, then it can creep up on me and 'Pow!' because I can't see it coming. When that happens everybody has to change their plans." His condition was characterized by roller coaster-like exacerbations and remissions, keeping everyone in suspense about what would be possible for all of them from day to day.

One persistent theme is uncertainty about the future. A patient's worry about the unsettling effect of uncertainty on close personal relationships manifests itself in many ways that health professionals must be prepared to interpret and try to respond to respectfully. Behavior changes or comments by the patient will give you clues.

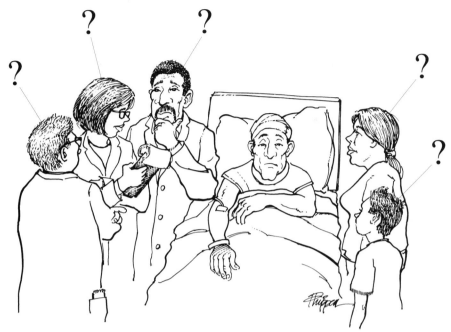

FIGURE 7-2: Uncertainty is a problem every patient faces during the recovery or adjustment process.

For example, a young woman who is reticent to undergo follow-up tests to check whether or not she remains free of her disease may be experiencing uncertainty about what another episode of treatment would mean for her family. It is easy for you, the health professional, to mistakenly conclude she does not care about her health. A man who has believed he was receiving good care in the past suddenly may question your competence when he no longer sees the positive results that previously were realized. His anger may be rooted in a growing uncertainty about whether he will be able to participate in an important event in his family's future. Only through conversation with him will you be able to sort out all the sources of the anger that appear directed solely at you. A patient's request for reassurance can come from a concern about her uncertainty regarding how to prepare family members, partners, close friends, work associates, and others in important relationships with her for what is going to happen. Patients who have dark doubts about what lays ahead may ask a different question, although not always as directly as stated here: "Will *you* be present to see me through this situation, whatever the outcome?" To this you can respond by assuring the patient that you and your colleagues will do everything you can for her or him. But such a question should also be an opportunity for you to gently explore whether this qualm is coming from uncertainty—uncertainty about whether persons important to the patient will be there at some critical juncture or whether they will be able to make it through their ordeal without your skilled assistance. In a sincere effort to encourage and support patients, you should provide them with as much certainty about their status and your judgment about the course to come as your own information and role allow. At the same time you should exercise due care not to give false information or instill false hope if you, yourself, are uncertain regarding the answers to their questions. The desire to comfort patients by providing false certainty will lead to their feeling of distrust or betrayal in the long run.

Concerns springing from uncertainties about the patient's current condition often are expressed by the extended family, friends, and other loved ones. Responding appropriately to queries from third parties—whether family, friends, or close associates—about the patient's situation should be motivated by your desire to be a positive influence in sustaining their relationship. It is an opportunity to practice your respect for the patient within the context that means the most to him or her. Of course, if the questions are about the patient's diagnosis, prognosis, or other patient-related matters, you do not have the prerogative to share this information except under certain circumstances that we describe here. Currently in the United States, the Health Insurance Portability and Accountability Act (HIPAA) regulations place serious legal constraints on what health professionals may share with anyone other than the competent patient, family members or others he or she designates to receive this information, and the health professionals directly involved in the patient's care.

The good idea behind HIPAA regulations is the serious concern that in today's health care system, patient information is shared with third parties ranging from family and friends to insurers, researchers, and others. The intent of the legislation was to protect the patient from unwanted or unwarranted invasions of personal privacy, especially regarding those types of information that may have a deleterious effect on his or her autonomy. The ethical foundation for keeping this information private is the age-old principle of confidentiality that long has been an important guide to professional judgment about disclosure of patient information and is an important indication of your respect for the patient.

Despite these legal and ethical constraints, it can be difficult to know where to draw the line on disclosing patient information so that the higher values cherished by the patient will be respected. While the constraints serve to affirm the importance of allowing the individual to be the owner of information about his or her health status, these disclosure guidelines can become especially burdensome among families and groups for whom the patient is not viewed as the appropriate recipient of such information or as the sole decision-maker for health care decisions. Sometimes communal approaches are deeply rooted in ethnic or other cultural practices, giving rise to uncertainties on the part of patients, their support groups, and members of the professional health care team if the patient is treated as the sole legitimate decision-maker. In another scenario, longstanding habits of who makes decisions for a couple, a family, or group also can raise uncertainties about who should speak for the competent patient. Consider an example of each type of situation:

> A 49-year-old Hmong male was dying of hepatic cancer. The patient was well known in the local Hmong community. He had emigrated from Laos with his family some years ago to this small Midwestern city and has become an influential advocate for the Hmong people living there. As many as 30 visitors occupied the visitor lounges and filled the patient's room to capacity at any given time. When asked if he approved of so many people, the patient said, "Oh yes. They are my brothers and sisters." The patient seemed apprehensive about talking to the physician when the latter tried to get him to talk about his wishes as his disease progressed. He said he could make no decisions without consulting with his family. Knowing that he would lose the ability to make decisions at some point in the near future, the health professionals watched intently to try to figure out who the key decision-maker, or decision-makers, should be. He slipped into unconsciousness and in a few days became short of breath. The health professionals thought it appropriate to consult someone about a decision as to whether the patient should be resuscitated if he stopped breathing or his heart stopped. Since they had no way to determine a designated spokesperson, they chose two of the older men whom the team recognized as being at the patient's bedside every day. But as soon as the discussion began, the room became crowded as the other visitors pushed closer. Murmurs arose every time the interpreter conveyed to the two what the physician had said. The two old men wore their suspicion and confusion in their deeply creased faces.
>
> After a long group consultation one of the men stepped forward and said they did not understand many things but they wanted to be present when the patient died. At this point, the primary physician decided to make the patient a "no code," meaning that the patient would not be resuscitated. As he lay dying the extended family began chanting, lit candles, and performed various rituals around him. Their activity continued for some time after he died.
>
> The health professionals involved in the patient's care talked about this situation for a long time afterwards. They were convinced that neither the patient nor the old men had sufficient certainty about what they were expected to do in this strange environment. Obviously the use of a skilled interpreter helped some, but a high level of uncertainty persisted.
>
> ▶ What would you like to know about the patient and these members of the Hmong people that might help you in caring for this patient and sustaining the relationships present at the bedside?
>
> ▶ Make a list of these items in one column on a sheet of paper. In a second column next to each one, indicate how you might go about getting information.
>
> ▶ Should the health care institution be responsible for providing you and other health professionals with resources that will increase your certainty about how to respond in this kind of situation?

Recall the discussion in Chapter 3 on cultural humility that requires ongoing self-reflection and critique as life-long learners. If we are willing to continue to reflect on what we need to know in order to provide patient-centered care, we will be better equipped to provide more certainty to a patient regarding his desire to honor his cultural practices and those of his loved ones.

A second occasion for high uncertainty can arise in situations where longstanding habits, not cultural and ethnic beliefs, appear to be the basis of relational behaviors. This case is an apt example:

Oscar works in a chemical processing plant, his occupation since he was a teenager. He didn't get the chance to finish high school because his dad died in a plant accident and he had to become the breadwinner for his mom and three siblings. He says that one of his biggest accomplishments, which "woulda made my dad proud!", was to get his GED in the evening school offered through the plant. His youngest brother, Walter, lives with him and has since their mom died about 20 years ago. Walter was let go from school after the sixth grade on the basis that he was "slow," though Oscar always doubted this "diagnosis." Oscar thought a better explanation is that when Walter lost his baby teeth, his adult teeth never came in. When he tried to talk, the other kids laughed and made fun of him, calling him "grandpa" since so many of the old people in this impoverished town were without teeth or dentures. Walter was in his middle teens by the time anyone mentioned the possibility of dentures to Oscar. A social worker at the local community clinic helped to get the dentures for Walter, but to this day, his childhood experiences have left scars on his personality and self-esteem. Whenever he makes even a small mistake, he suffers, calling himself a "dumbbell." Fortunately, since receiving dentures his pronunciation, nutrition, and appearance have improved.

Oscar was able to get Walter on at the plant, and Walter has done well there. In fact, over the years the other guys have grown used to his self-effacing personality, have come to appreciate his hard work and big heart, and know that there's more to him than may meet the eye initially. Oscar watches out for him, too, menacingly confronting anyone who treats Walter disrespectfully.

Over the last several months, Walter has been wheezing, and Oscar notes that he is going to bed earlier and earlier, always with some lame excuse. Some of the guys ask Oscar if Walter is OK because he seems so short of breath and is sweating so much. Oscar finally convinces Walter to go to the company clinic. The nurse practitioner who sees Walter and Oscar allows Oscar to stay with Walter while he undergoes tests. However, when the tests come back, the physician asks Oscar to leave the room and shares the bad news with Walter that he has emphysema. He explains that it is in its early stages and the physicians think that he may benefit from entering a clinical trial of a medication that they hope will help relieve the progressive deleterious symptoms of the condition. Walter is paralyzed by this news, saying that Oscar will have to make that decision and insists that the doctor tell Oscar everything he has just said. Oscar listens authoritatively, saying he will take responsibility for making the decisions about what will happen next, and declines the offer of a social worker who would be willing to talk with the brothers. He refuses the literature about the study. They both just laugh when the young physician asks if they would like to talk with a chaplain about this. But later, while Walter is filling out some paperwork, Oscar confides to the nurse practitioner who had seen them together on their initial visit that he knows the physician disagrees with his making the decisions, and he is frightened he might make the wrong one.

The health professionals are uncertain about what to do, too, understandably reluctant to turn over the decision-making authority to Oscar for a decision that is so important to Walter's life and well-being. To the health professionals, Walter is a competent, middle-aged adult, even though both he and his brother seem to assume that Oscar will make the decisions.

▶ If you were one of the health professionals in this situation, can you think of ways you might bring more certainty into these brothers' understanding of why the health professionals are hesitant to accept the decision-making arrangement?

▶ What additional information about their relationship would you want to know that might help decrease the health care team's uncertainty about how to proceed?

The dynamic between Walter and Oscar sometimes can be observed among older patients in marriage relationships. Their conviction that the husband "is the boss" and makes the decisions is all that some couples can fathom. For a husband suddenly to be left out of the information loop and lose his decision-making authority role may be extremely disorienting to both parties, adding a new level of uncertainty to an already difficult period in their life together.

What can health professionals do? Family meetings approved by the patient or a request by the patient that someone else be the decision-maker (or have a heavy hand in it) become avenues through which you can proceed with higher certainty about including someone other than the patient in specific clinical discussions and decisions. Documenting such patient requests in the patient's clinical record signals to other members of the health care team why you are relying on a partner's, son or daughter's, spouse's, religious leader's, or another's role in decisions about the competent patient's health care regimen, and may also help your professional colleagues know how to approach the various members in the relationship. Although rejected by Oscar and Walter, the intervention of a social worker, chaplain, or psychiatrist often helps all involved to gain a higher level of confidence before making momentous decisions.

Whatever the uncertainties for a patient or those close to the patient, you can attempt to help them move more knowledgeably and confidently through their questioning, especially in those areas related to health care. One of your judgment calls will be to determine other health professionals on the team who can be effective advocates for the patient when the patient's and caregivers' uncertainties reach beyond your own areas of expertise.

Having reviewed some important questions patients and their loved ones face, we turn in the next section to economic challenges they all face and how these challenges affect their relationships.

PERSONAL RELATIONSHIPS AND HEALTH CARE COSTS

In today's health care arena, at least in the United States, many patients' relationships will be dramatically impacted by costs associated with health care–related expenses. The authors of *Uninsured in America: Life and Death in the Land of Opportunity* paint a sobering and well-documented profile of the many ways that illness (physical and mental), injury, and caregiving act as portals into what the authors call the "death spiral." The death spiral is their metaphor "for the deep changes taking place in American society as the demarcation between rich and poor … hardens into a static barrier between the caste of the healthy and the caste of those who are fated to become and remain sick."[11] Their conclusion is that, except for the very wealthiest today, persons in relationships touched by serious illness or injury are forever more vulnerable to severe financial duress. This may come about by the cost of the initial health care episode, the necessary changes in employment made by the person or family caregiver, or the decreased likelihood of being able to find health insurance coverage for future conditions and ongoing maintenance. An adult's values may include that of being a good provider for those dependent on him, but the loss of opportunity to earn money for a time (or permanently) may be compounded by the high cost of his or her medical and other health care bills. The patient who decides to make a highly desirable change in life direction or lifestyle with a loved one may feel prohibited from doing so by the reality of the desperate financial distress the illness or injury has caused.

Their stress may express itself in depression or cause a patient to make health care choices you do not understand. It is well known that many instances of so-called "noncompliance" on the part of patients are occasioned by the cost of medications, treatments, devices, or services. A patient needs to weigh those goods against that same money being spent for food, housing, or other necessities for themselves and their children or others dependent on those resources.

As a health professional, you are in a good position to be an advocate on behalf of patients and their family or other caregivers. What does advocacy entail in such a situation?

1. Inform patients and their caregivers of available institutional resources (e.g., social workers) who can help them maneuver through the often confusing web of bureaucratic procedures they must traverse in order to receive essential services.
2. Be attuned to community services patients, families, and others in caregiver relationships with the patient may be able to access.
3. Educate yourself regarding the basic language and concepts of health care financing and how it operates in your area of professional expertise so that you can contribute to discussions and strategies about it in areas relevant to your practice. Attend educational conferences or in-service sessions addressing these areas of your professional practice.
4. Document instances in which you are forced by inadequate or unjust policies to say "no" to interventions or services you know will strengthen the relationships most critical to the patient's quality of life. For example, in the United States, Medicaid, Medicare, or private insurance reimbursement practices often control

the number of days the patient is eligible for treatment, placing professionals in an untenable position. Judiciously gathering empirical data regarding treatment effectiveness and patient outcomes can assist policy makers in creating cost-effective approaches to care.

5. Work directly with your colleagues and professional organizations to influence legislation or other policy in your institution, state or province, and nationally.
6. Implement innovations in your workplace to address the strengths and weaknesses of cost-containment policies.[12]

In short, while many of the family's financial burdens will remain outside of your sphere of responsibility or influence, these steps can be taken for you to be a positive force for them and for all coming down the road in similar situations.

RE-VALUING RELATIONSHIPS

Having reviewed some questions and problems patients and their loved ones face, this final section of the chapter ends on a positive note, turning to the enrichment that can be realized in relationships touched by adversity (Figure 7-3).

Many people faced with illness or injury discover that it prods them to reflect on the value of their relationships. You will sometimes be brought into the patient's thoughts or plans as the person reflects about things done and left undone in regard to his or her relationships.

⊚ REFLECTIONS

Although it is difficult to place yourself in a future situation, try to reflect on the following:

- If you learned that you had a serious medical condition that would likely lead to your death in, say, the next year or so, do you think there are relationships you would like to mend or enrich?
- Can you name a particular relative or friend that you'd probably spend more time with?
- Are there things you'd like to say to someone?
- Are there relationships you would now feel free to shed?
- Are there old friends, relatives, colleagues, or associates you would want to call or go to visit?

This reflection may give you a glimpse of the urgency with which you might invoke the help of your health professionals if you thought they were a resource for fulfilling one or more of your relationship-related goals.

It is not unusual that longstanding breaches with friends or loved ones may start to distress the patient and stir the desire to make amends. Of course, not all patients engage in trying to renew or strengthen such relationships. Sometimes a past trauma weighs so heavily on a patient or family member that they never fully recover from it, and their relationship remains mired in anger or grief. At other times, the illness or injury brings out behaviors that may have their source in deeper burdens the person has been carrying. One such woman who suffered a severe back injury from a

FIGURE 7-3: Often adversity can lead to renewed energy and commitment to personal relationships. *(© Corbis.)*

serious car accident (but recovered physically) told one of the authors, "The pain's gone, the mobility's restored, but I can't get over the feeling of being shell-shocked. It is starting to affect my partner Joyce, and our relationship is taking the brunt, but I can't shake the dread." With counseling, this patient was able to identify a source of her "shell-shocked" feeling that the injury had released; together she and her partner were able to survive this challenge to their formerly strong relationship. Fortunately, there is hope that today our increasing understanding of depression and other mental illnesses and of profound delayed responses to serious earlier trauma (post-traumatic stress syndrome) will provide an escape for many more people who in the past have been dragged down by these burdens.

The good news, too, is that most people do recover or adjust sufficiently to take stock of what is really important in their lives. A young couple may decide their differences aren't that important after all and try to make a new life together. A man who felt he was too busy for golfing may decide to take the opportunity to resume regular golf games with his long-time buddies and the camaraderie that they enjoy. An older woman may decide to move out of a secure but harsh job environment to find a new position where she believes she will find more support and her impairment will be more accepted.

Religious beliefs and images can help provide meaning to the patient's experience and aid in healing or adjustment of close relationships. The following is one example. You may be familiar with the words in Psalm 23 found in the Hebrew-Christian scriptures. There is a portion that reads, "He [God] makes me lie down in green pastures. He leads me beside still waters; He restores my soul." Herman, a middle-aged man with colon cancer, said that this was God's way of getting him to "lie down" so that his soul would be restored enough for him to get his relationship with his children back on course. While many people would have a hard time thinking of colon cancer as a "restoring moment," the health professional used this man's religious image to support the patient through trying periods. Later she heard the man laughing with a son who was saying he hoped he wouldn't have to be knocked off his feet in order to take care of what was important!

The stories of a difficult situation becoming the springboard to a new release into life are legion. Sometimes patients will ask your advice or even intervention, and at times you may feel you are faced with a dilemma about what to say or how much to get involved. A good general rule of thumb is to be mindful of the nature of respectful health professional and patient relationships. You have been gaining some ideas about that as you have read and reflected on the chapters in this book. Some helpful guidelines for maintaining appropriate professional boundaries are discussed in more depth in Part Five. However, any written guidelines also assume you recognize that whatever you can reasonably do will mean a lot to that patient. The result is that often you will have the satisfaction of watching patients or former patients use their conditions, however unwelcome they were initially, as opportunities to think things over and start afresh, in the process rejuvenating or bringing new perspectives to their close relationships.

SUMMARY

The personal life of the patient exists in a web of activities and relationships that help to provide status, meaning, support, and a sense of belonging to this person. The most immediate relationship for most people is their family; therefore, showing respect for the patient and assessing the challenges facing the patient means thinking about how his or her predicament affects the family and vice versa. The fragility of relationships in general often is increased by the fears and realities facing patients, their loved ones, and other supporters. Sometimes they see interest and support falling away; they may suffer from the changes that are taking place and from the uncertainties that lay ahead. Financial burdens are almost always an added stress. In all instances, the patient's responses are influenced by those closest to him or her. In turn, those near the patient become enmeshed in the concerns, new responsibilities, and changes. Those who become family or other "informal" caregivers represent a growing group of persons who can be identified as at-risk for injuries, burnout, and other debilitating conditions, and require the health professional's respect and considered attention. The good news is that illness or injury also may become an opportunity for relationships to draw on their past strengths and find renewed vitality and vision. One of the most critical and ultimately satisfying contributions you make as a professional is to engage in behaviors that express respect for everyone in the patient's circle of key relationships.

REFERENCES

1. Albertson SA: *Endings and beginnings: a young family's experience with death and renewal*, New York, 1980, Random House.
2. Purtilo R: The story of David. In Haddad AM, Brown KH, editors: *The arduous touch: women's voices in health care*, West Lafayette, IN, 1999, NotaBell Books/Purdue University Press.

3. Lee C: *Women's health: psychological and social perspectives*, London, 1998, Sage Publications.
4. Zuckerman C: 'Til death do us part: family caregiving at the end of life. In Levine C, editor: *Always on call: when illness turns family into caregivers*, New York, 2000, United Hospital Fund of New York.
5. Akin C: *The long road called goodbye: tracing the course of Alzheimer's*, Omaha, NE, 2000, Creighton University Press.
6. Surman OS: *After Eden: a love story*, New York, 2005, iUniverse.
7. Dept. of Health and Human Services Committee: *The future of long-term care in relation to the aging baby boom generation, Report to Congress*, May 2003, p. 38 (report online) http://aspe.hhs.gov/daltcp/reports/ltcwork.htm. Accessed April 29, 2006.
8. Purtilo R: Social marginalization of persons with disability. In Purtilo R, Have HAMJ ten, *Ethical foundations of palliative care for Alzheimer disease*, Baltimore, 2004, Johns Hopkins University Press.
9. Levine C: The loneliness of the long-term care giver, *N Engl J Med* 340:1587-1590, 1999.
10. Schulz R, Beach S: Caregiving as a risk factor for mortality, *JAMA* 282(23):2215-2219, 1999.
11. Sered SS, Fernandopulle R: *Uninsured in America: life and death in the land of opportunity*, Berkeley, 2005, University of California Press.
12. Purtilo RB: Thirty-first Mary McMillan lecture: a time to harvest, a time to sow: ethics for a shifting landscape, *Phys Ther* 80:1112-1119, 2000.

PART THREE

Questions for Thought and Discussion

1. If you were to lose the use of your lower extremities in an automobile accident, what would be the most difficult aspects of adjusting to this permanent change? What do you hope people would do to respect your situation?
2. Name some technologies and procedures that your profession uses to evaluate or treat patients. How do they affect a patient's dignity? For those that might have demeaning aspects, what can you do to help maintain respect toward the patient during the application of these procedures?
3. A patient asks you if she can bring her friend to treatment with her. You know that this patient has been asking a lot of questions and seems to be very anxious. When the friend comes, she starts asking you some of the same questions that patient asked you previously. You want to honor the patient's privacy and so are hesitant to respond. The friend states, "You know how anxious she gets. I just want to be able to reassure her, and I can't do that without knowing what is going on."

    What can you do in this situation to sort out what is going on? What steps can you take to show this patient and her friend respect in spite of your concerns about privacy?
4. A single woman in her 60s comes to you with symptoms you know are related to the stress of her position as caregiver for an elderly parent who has Alzheimer's disease. You know the best thing for her is to have some respite from the care of her father. You first ask her about other family members who might share her responsibility, but she claims to have none who are willing or able to help share her burden. Her situation seems perilous to you, and you begin to think of a perfect society where she would not be stuck in this seemingly endless and intense situation. List all the things you can think of to design an environment for her and her father so that both are able to realize the respect they deserve.

PART FOUR

RESPECT THROUGH COMMUNICATION

Chapter 8: The Patient's Story
Chapter 9: Respectful Communication in an
Information Age

Just as history does not exist in nature, but is created in the telling, so, too, autobiography and the patient's case history emerge out of interactions, which mean that they are at the same time both less and more than the "facts" of the case.[1] Chapter 8 focuses on how we understand our patients by examining the ways the patients' stories are created. Illness and injury are milestones in patients' lives. The clinical record is one place where the experience of the patient is set into words by individuals other than the patient, words that are shared with the whole health care team. The format, syntax, perspective, and language we use to tell the patient's story deserve your attention as much as the content. It becomes apparent that it is not enough to merely describe the chronology of events that bring patients to us.

You will want to understand why things happened the way they did, what meaning the patient gives to the experience, and what the patient expects from you.

To come closer to understanding the meaning your patients give to their experience, you will depend on your ability to communicate. The most immediate "tool" you have available to you for respectful interaction is your own communication, whether that tool is used verbally or nonverbally. What you say, how and when you say it, and how you communicate nonverbally through gestures and other types of physical messages will set the tone for everything else that happens in the relationship.

Chapter 9 focuses on components of respectful interaction in verbal and nonverbal aspects of communication. As you read and reflect on all the types of messages you give and receive, think back to Part One, especially to the parts of those chapters addressing values and culture. It is almost certain that you will work with colleagues and patients from countries and backgrounds different from your own. These differences are evident as we attend to patients and listen to

143

what they choose to include in their stories and what is left unsaid. Consider how the challenge of communicating both verbally and nonverbally, face-to-face or from a distance is enhanced and influenced by these factors.

REFERENCE

1. Greenhalgh T, Hurwitz B: Why study narrative? In Greenhalgh T, Hurwirtz B, editors: *Narrative based medicine: dialogue and discourse in clinical practice*, London, 1998, BMJ Books.

THE PATIENT'S STORY

CHAPTER OBJECTIVES

The student will be able to:
- Distinguish between the different "voices" encountered in the telling of a patient's story
- Identify some of the literary forms used in health care communications
- Describe two of the contributions of narrative to respectful health professional and patient interaction
- Discuss what a health professional can learn from a patient's account of illness or injury in a poem, short story, or pathography
- Relate a patient's narrative to his or her own experiences, values, and beliefs
- Discuss how literary narratives about patients' and health professionals' experiences apply to actual clinical practice

When you have mouth sores you think very carefully before even trying to take a bite of food; even something as innocuous as a yogurt smoothie is like swallowing a handful of nettles. This also happened to be the time when my hair truly fell out. Because I couldn't eat my weight had dropped alarmingly. I happen to be one of those people who look a wreck when I have a mere head cold; I look horrible out of all proportion to my symptoms. This time when I looked in the mirror I was truly alarmed. This was not a case that the Look Good-Feel Better people could solve.

—J. Hooper[1]

Human beings experience illness, injury, pain, suffering, and loss within a *narrative,* or story, which shapes and gives meaning to what they are feeling moment to moment.[2] One may say that our whole lives are "enacted narratives." Another way to understand this is to think about life as an unfolding story. Narration is the forward movement of the description of actions and events that makes it possible to later look back on what happened. And it is through that backward action that we are able to engage in self-reflection and self-understanding.[3] Illness and injury are milestones in a patient's life story. "The practice of medicine is lived in stories: 'I was well until…'

'It all started when I was doing…' are common openings of the medical encounter."[4] Much of this book has emphasized that health professionals are called into a particular relationship with patients because of the importance of the illness experience or serious injury. The medium of that relationship is the patient's story.

This chapter will help you grasp the importance of paying attention to the unique and personal story of a particular patient's life beyond the more general suggestions we have offered so far. In other words, we focus here on the idea of enacted narrative. Because the final focus of all of our efforts in health care is the patient, the insights that narrative analysis can offer to health professionals are important. We highlight how different voices or perspectives offer different stories of the patient's predicament. We briefly explore some of the basics of narrative theory and apply it to health care communications, such as textbooks, scientific journal articles, and the medical record. We include some examples of narrative literature to give you an opportunity to read and think about poetry and short stories that speak to patients' and health professionals' experiences. The chapter closes with a reminder that you also bring a unique and personal story to the professional and patient encounter and that you both participate in the creation of the continuing story of your lives.

WHO'S TELLING THE STORY?

When a patient enters the health care system, regardless of the place of entry, an exchange of stories begins. It might be hard for you to consider the patient's "history" portion of the history and physical examination to be a kind of story, but it is. So are the entries in a medical record and the scientific explanation of a particular pathologic condition in a textbook. Even within the medical record, for example, a "diverse collection of individual voices as well as interactions or viewpoints" exists that constitutes the single entity of the chart.[5]

Montgomery has convincingly argued that all knowledge is narrative in structure. She claims that medicine is not as much science as it perceives itself to be,[6] but this could easily apply to all of the health professions. She views the physician and patient encounter in terms of a story. The patient tells the story of an illness or injury, which she notes is an interpretive act in that the patient chooses certain words and not others and reports some incidents and not others. The physician then interprets the story and translates it into a list of possible diagnoses. Frank suggests that the physician's story is guided by the notion of "getting it right." "Diagnostic stories are about getting patients to the appropriate treatment as quickly as possible."[7] From the patient's perspective, however, getting it right may or may not be what counts. For example, a patient who has a chronic illness such as multiple sclerosis might have a story that is guided by figuring out how to cope with the unpredictable nature of the disease. So, at a minimum, we have two different notions of what the physician's response should be in terms of the patient's hopes and expectations.

The Patient's Story

One way to highlight the different ways that the same story can be viewed is to look at it from various perspectives. For example, how is a cerebral vascular accident (CVA) seen from the perspective of the patient, the medical record, and a medical textbook? Before we look at these different perspectives, consider the most basic differences in language here regarding what we call the neurovascular injury in question, a *cerebral vascular accident* or, in common language, a *stroke*. Think of all the metaphoric meanings of the word "stroke" that are stripped away by the use of the clinically sterile term: cerebral vascular accident. Now consider how health professionals distance themselves even further from the patient's experience by replacing "cerebral vascular accident" with the acronym "CVA." We will return to the patient's perspective with a personal account of a man who had a stroke. He recounts his experience in the past tense. This is common since most patient stories are recollections.[8] The following is an excerpt from a much longer account of the stroke that changed this person's life:

> ...all I knew was that I had a raging headache, and then, the next morning, I could hardly move.
>
> It was just another Saturday morning when I found myself in bed, alone and unable to get up at home in Islington, north London. My wife, Sarah Lyall, a journalist, was in San Francisco. It was odd to be on my own and odder still to be so helpless, but I was in no pain, and, in retrospect, I realise that I was barely conscious. Downstairs, the grandfather clock was chiming the hour: 8 o'clock. I could see that beyond the heavy maroon curtains it was a lovely day. I was supposed to drive to Cambridge to visit my parents. So, it was time to get up. But I could not move my left side. My body had become a dead weight of nearly 15 stone. I thrashed about in bed trying to sit upright, and wishing Sarah were with me. I experienced no anxiety—just irritation and puzzlement.[9]

Obviously, the patient/author is British, so some of the language may be unfamiliar, such as his reference to his weight as "15 stone." A stone, a measure of weight, is approximately 14 pounds, so at the time he had his stroke he weighed 210 pounds. Weight can also be measured in kilograms. Thus, we have an immediate example about the differences in words and terms that all mean fundamentally the same thing. Also, the description is written in the first-person voice. *Voice* is the personality of the writer coming through the words on the page. Voice can give the reader an indication of the uniqueness of the person who is speaking in the text. When a writer uses the first-person voice, it feels as if the writer is talking directly to the reader.

⊚ REFLECTIONS

Besides the obvious differences in language, what did you notice first about the patient's story? He claims he was not anxious, just irritated and puzzled.
- Would you expect this type of reaction?
- What sorts of emotional reaction, if any, did you have to the patient's story?

This is probably not the first time the patient told the story of his stroke, although it could be the first time that he actually wrote about his experience. In the telling and retelling of landmark experiences such as the trauma associated with a stroke, "the narrative provides meaning, context, and perspective for the patient's predicament. It defines how, why, and in what way he or she is ill. It offers, in short, a possibility of *understanding* which cannot be arrived at by any other means."[10] When a patient begins to tell you the story of his or her illness, you might be able to discern whether this is a familiar, often told story or if the patient is still trying to figure out what happened and make sense of the experience.

The Medical Record

Beginning with the patient's direct experience of the trauma that he has undergone, let us move forward in time to a different setting and interpretation of what is happening to him. We will assume that the patient was eventually discovered and taken to a hospital. In a hospital, one of the vehicles for communication between health professionals who care for a specific patient is the medical record, or chart. The "chart" might be handwritten or can be a file on the computer. How might the patient's story continue in the medical record? Here are two typical entries, the first from the nurses' notes and the second from the medical progress notes. Assume that they were written on the day after the patient was admitted to the hospital.

> **Nurses' Notes–7/18/07:** Impaired verbal communication R/T aphasia 2° to cerebral vascular accident.
>
> **9:00 A.M.**
>
> **S:** "Where's my book? Where's my book?"
>
> **O:** Pt. tearful and keeps repeating above statement. No books found in bedside stand. Pt. then picked up wallet from over-bed table and opened it to a picture of him and his wife. Pt. pointed to picture and repeated the above phrase. Calmed down when reassured wife was on way to hospital. Unable to use L arm. Ate breakfast independently. Poor appetite.
>
> **A:** Pt. appears frustrated and stressed due to inability to find the right words to express himself.
>
> **P:** Continue to support pt.; consult with speech, occupational, and physical therapy as needed; encourage as much independence as possible; remind pt. to attend to L arm and leg affected by sensory alteration.
>
> **Physician's Progress Notes–7/18/07:** Dx: R hemisphere hemorrhagic infarct.; Pt. stable; echo, CXR, MRI; contact speech/OT/PT for rehabilitation assessment.

⊚ REFLECTIONS

- What do you notice first about this version of the patient's story?
- Do you understand all of the terms and language?
- Does this more objective rendering of the patient's illness give you different insights into what you can do to help the patient?

Clearly, there is a difference in how the patient and health professionals describe what is going on. In Chapter 9 we discuss the use of jargon in health care and how it serves a useful purpose of facilitating communication between health professionals but also works to distance patients from caregivers. The jargon in these sample entries from a fictitious medical record almost becomes impenetrable to a novice in the official language of health care. Did you understand all of the terms and abbreviations? What is "aphasia?" Did you know that "R/T" means "related to," that "echo" is shorthand for "echocardiogram," and that "CXR" is an acronym for "chest x-ray?" Although the patient describes his experience of having a stroke in the first person, the medical record refers to him in the third person. He is now "Pt.," shorthand for "Patient." In the last few sentences or phrases describing the "objective" component of the nurses' notes, the "patient" is completely removed as the object in the account. We will discuss point of view in more detail later in this chapter. It is sufficient here to note the type of voice used in writing and the implications of using a particular voice. Third-person voice distances us from what is going on in the narrative.

Consider one more version of the patient's story, this one even further removed from the personal experience of a CVA. In a current medical diagnosis textbook, the clinical signs and symptoms of an intracerebral hemorrhage are described as follows:

> With hemorrhage into the cerebral hemisphere, consciousness is initially lost or impaired in about one-half of patients. Vomiting occurs very frequently at the onset of bleeding, and headache is sometimes present. Focal symptoms and signs then develop, depending on the site of the hemorrhage. With hypertensive hemorrhage, there is generally a rapidly evolving neurologic deficit with hemiplegia or hemiparesis. A hemisensory disturbance is also present with more deeply placed lesions. With lesions of the putamen, loss of conjugate lateral gaze may be conspicuous. With thalamic hemorrhage, there may be a loss of upward gaze, downward or skew deviation of the eyes, lateral gaze palsies, and pupillary inequalities.
>
> Cerebellar hemorrhage may present with sudden onset of nausea and vomiting, disequilibrium, headache, and loss of consciousness that may terminate fatally within 48 hours. Less commonly, the onset is gradual and the course episodic or slowly progressive—clinical features suggesting an expanding cerebellar lesion. In yet other cases, however, the onset and course are intermediate, and examination shows lateral conjugate gaze palsies to the side of the lesion; small reactive pupils; contralateral hemiplegia; peripheral facial weakness; ataxia of gait, limbs, or trunk; periodic respiration; or some combination of these findings.[11]

What does this final version of the patient's story tell you? The authors of the medical text are not concerned with a specific patient who has a CVA. The description is general, one written for health professionals, hence the use of highly technical terms, and one that can be applied to all patients who suffer a stroke. The symptoms are described as a matter of clinical, scientific fact, not of personal experience. You might be thinking, "Perhaps this is not all bad. A general description helps a health professional learn what to expect when a patient has had a cerebral hemorrhage." The danger lies in accepting the textbook description as "fact" or the truth as opposed to just one more interpretation of what a CVA is and means to individual patients. To assist you in scrutinizing the narratives you encounter in clinical practice, turn now to some basic concepts from narrative theory.

AWARENESS OF LITERARY FORM IN YOUR COMMUNICATION

When you see a poem on a page, even if you do not know anything about poetry, you recognize it as a poem because of its form and structure, i.e., the way it looks on the page. Because it is a poem, you also know that the particular words the poet chose are important. In poetry, every word matters. It is unlikely that you look at the writing in your textbooks, even this one, in the same way. Yet, any type of written communication (whether on paper or digital) has a form and structure, subtle or obvious. By paying attention to these aspects of the various types of writing you encounter in clinical practice, you can develop an appreciation for how language is used and its impact on your thinking and behavior. Two assumptions from narrative theory applicable to narratives encountered in health care are that narrative language is not transparent and does not reflect the whole reality of what is going on.

Narrative Language Is Not Transparent

The language of narrative does not function like a clear glass that lets messages be directly sent from sender to receiver. In other words, it is not transparent.[12] No language is neutral or "colorless." This is true of any narrative whether it is a story, a case study, or an article in a scholarly, professional journal. Scientific writing (this includes the writing on a patient's medical record) does not call attention to itself the way language does in a poem, play, or novel. As you saw in the sample entries in the medical record of the patient who had the CVA, there were no metaphors, similes, or figures of speech. The nurse did not write, "I walked into the room and found the patient sobbing his heart out." Yet, professional writing is based on and created in a particular context. The closest we get to an emotion in the nurses' notes is in the phrase "Pt. found tearful," but there is no mention of grief, loss, or the depth of his sadness, just a statement of fact or observation.

In Chapter 9 you will discover that one skill you must learn in your professional preparation is to write in this manner to communicate as a professional. Robert Coles describes an interaction with one of his teachers when he was in medical school. Although it involves physicians-in-training, it is applicable to all health professions. "He remarked that first-year medical students often obtain textured and subtle auto-biographical accounts from patients and offer them to others with enthusiasm and pleasure, whereas fourth-year medical students or house officers are apt to present cryptic, dryly condensed, and, yes, all too 'structured' presentations, full of abbreviations, not to mention medical or psychiatric jargon. No question: the farther one climbs the ladder of medical education, the less time one has for relaxed, storytelling reflection."[13] How and what one writes about the patient's story of illness or injury is a choice and should be a conscious one. Although you need to learn enough jargon to know what colleagues are saying, you don't have to be limited by it. Rita Charon,

FIGURE 8-1: A health professional listening while a patient shares her history. *(© Corbis.)*

a general internist trained in literary theory, doesn't begin patient interactions with a battery of questions (Figure 8-1):

> I find that I have changed my routines on meeting with new patients. I simply say, "I'm going to be your doctor. I need to know a lot about your body and your health and your life. Please tell me what you think I should know about your situation." And patients do exactly that—in extensive monologues, during which I sit on my hands so as not to write or reflexively call up their medical record on the computer. I sit and pay attention to what they say and how they say it: the forms, the metaphors, the gaps and silences. Where will be the beginning? How will symptoms intercalate with life events?[14]

Language Creates Reality

Rather than reflecting reality, language creates reality.[12] For example, without thinking very much about it, most health professionals would say that a patient's history in a medical record states the case as it is. In other words, the history is simply recorded observation. Yet the language used actually creates the reality of the case insofar as it frames the kinds of questions we ask about it, how we seek answers, how we interpret what we find, and sets limits on what we observe or even consider. Refer back to the structure of the nurses' notes. Did you know what the letters *S, O, A,* and *P* that preceded the nurse's entries meant? The SOAP charting method is a common way to record information in clinical records. The words being abbreviated by SOAP are *subjective* (usually a direct quotation from the patient), *objective* (the health professional's observations or description of the situation), *assessment* (the health professional's interpretation of the situation), and *plan* (actions to be taken to solve the problem presented).[15] The opening step in SOAP charting, subjective, is a rare occurrence in the medical chart. The health professional seems to actually record what the patient said at a particular point in time. But even the inclusion of a direct quote from a patient is filled with interpretation. The health professional chooses which quotes to include and then proceeds to use the quote as a springboard for the rest of the entry. Furthermore, the whole structure of SOAP charting requires one to think of patients as individuals with problems that need professional resolution shaping the way we look at what is important or not.

Language can also be used to exclude others. A clinical ethicist noted this manipulation of language on medical rounds:

> As I began to watch this process more carefully, it became apparent that the physicians spoke a language which was quite understandable when they thought the ethical issues were fairly clear and where there would probably be some consensus but resorted to high code when they felt uncomfortable with the decision(s) before them or when there was dissent in the group.[16]

So when things were easy and comfortable, everyone spoke the same language. When things got tough, the physicians switched to a language that allowed them to distance themselves from the discussion and allowed them to dominate it as well.

The use of extremely technical language, or "high code," creates an atmosphere that prevents lay people from participating in the conversation. In addition, scientific language and information are more highly valued than what the patient has to say.

> Witness the time devoted on rounds to discussing serum magnesium levels as compared to the time spent discussing the patient's experiences. When the patient's narrative (variously called "subjective," "qualitative," or "soft" data) conflicts with laboratory or radiographic findings (considered "objective," "quantitative," "hard" data), the narrative is usually given the lesser weight; it might well be ignored or minimized and the patient attacked for being a "poor historian."[17]

Although the language may vary from profession to profession, generally speaking the health professional's language will prevail.

CONTRIBUTIONS OF NARRATIVE TO RESPECTFUL INTERACTION

Health care practice is a rich metaphor for so many archetypal human dramas, featuring such riveting themes as life and death, loss and hope, and love and hate. All play out in different scripts, some meaningful and others trivial, each experience providing its own opportunity for wonder at the infinite capacity for human invention. There is an increasing emphasis on the use of literature, a specific type of narrative, in health professional education. The premise is that studying literature about illness, death, or caregiving will help you, the student, relate more personally to patients, hear patients' stories more clearly, and make decisions that reflect a humane appreciation of patients' situations.[18] Reading novels, stories, and poetry is a means of participating imaginatively in other lives; it encourages you to construct your own stories in relation to the ones you are reading. Consequently, you will come to know yourself better, too.

Literary Tools

Narrative literature, and by this we mean language used in an intensified, artistic manner, can be used to offer a fresh way for you to understand the encounter between health professional and patient. You can use some simple literary tools such as point of view, characterization, plot, and motivation to examine narrative literature, and as you have seen, the usual types of narrative writing in health care communication, such as the patient's chart.

Point of View

This is a good place to begin because it gives you an immediate sense of who is speaking to you through the poem or story. As you think about point of view, here is a simple question to get you started: Who is the narrator of the piece? In a medical record, the point of view is always third person. Health professionals talk about the patient in the third person, even avoiding pronouns whenever possible; that is, the patient is referred to as "Pt." not as "him" or "her." In the excerpt from *Current Medical Diagnosis and Treatment,* the point of view is that of an omniscient narrator, but one who is almost invisible. The personal voice is deeply hidden in scientific and professional writing, yet it is there.

Characterization

Also in good narrative, characters bring their whole intricate selves to the story. For instance, if the character in a story or a drama is a physical therapist, you will also learn that he is a son, maybe a husband and father, a friend, a softball coach, and a religious man. As the narrative unfolds, you appreciate how multiple, often conflicting, interests and identities figure in the twists and turns of his motivations and decisions. You follow along, getting the feel of his prejudices, fears, passions, and pains. Then, if you are lucky, the magic of transference will take you on a journey into the story and eventually into the byways of your own life, but from some new and different angle. The lived quality of narrative is what makes it plausible. "I could be him," feels the reader. "I've been there, too." On the other hand, some characterizations can cause discomfort, which can teach us about our "unspoken, unacknowledged, and often unknown fears, biases and prejudices."[19] Learning about what makes you uncomfortable is equally valuable as who or what you identify with in a novel, short story, or play. All of this knowledge has implications for your interactions with patients who may be similar or very different from you.

Plot and Motivation

Narratives of clinical interest tend toward plot in their structure rather than the more basic narrative of a simple story. In his oft-cited work, *Aspects of the Novel,* E. M. Forster explains the difference between a simple story and a plot: "in a story we say 'and then—and then…' in a plot we say 'why?'"[20] Why do the people in a particular clinical narrative make certain choices and act in specific ways? You can examine the motives of the individuals in clinical narratives in the same way that you can those of characters in a short story or novel. Once again, you may have to try harder to find motivation in clinical narratives because so much work goes into hiding the feelings or emotional reactions of health professionals. Even emotional outbursts by patients are written to appear objective and "clinical." Consider the "plan" portion of the SOAP note presented earlier in the chapter: "Continue to support pt.; consult with speech, occupational, and physical therapy as needed; encourage as much independence as possible; remind pt. to attend to L arm and leg affected by sensory alteration."

⊚ REFLECTIONS

- What are the motives of the writer, in this case the nurse?
- Is there any indication of the feelings or emotional reactions of the nurse?

Poetry

Literature written from the patient's perspective is particularly helpful to health professionals to gain insights into the experience. Poetry is one form of literature that deliberately calls attention to the specific words in the poem as well as how the words are placed on the page. There are many definitions of poetry, but the following description of poetry perhaps captures it best: "Poetry gives pleasure first, then truth, and its language is charged, intensified, concentrated."[21] The following poem explores the patient's experience with a colostomy. We suggest that you read the poem at least twice before reading the questions to help you appreciate it.

A RARE AND STILL SCANDALOUS SUBJECT

From Susan Sontag's *Illness as Metaphor*

The title of my confession
is "Colostomy." The word,
cured and salted,
sizzles on my tongue.

This is shame:
standing naked at the sink,
unsnapping the adhesive flange
from my abdomen.

I couldn't have imagined
the stoma, the opening,
red glistening intestine.
Peristalsis moves it like a caterpillar, hatched
from a visceral cocoon.

My life depends on the stoma,
which insists on gratitude,
gurgling, "Listen to me,"
but I place my hand over it,
even now when I am alone.
—R. Solly[22]

After you have read through the poem, you should be able to recognize who is speaking, what his situation is, and to whom he is speaking.

These are just a few questions to help you begin to understand the poem and find meaning to take away to help you in clinical practice.

> ⊙ REFLECTIONS
>
> - Before reading on, take each stanza in turn. What mood is the author trying to convey?
> - Refer to the poem's title, "A Rare and Still Scandalous Subject." What does the title mean and how does it set the tone of the poem?
> - What is it like for the narrator of the poem to live with a colostomy?
> - Why is the poem a "confession?"

Short Stories

A short story should be complete, which means is should have a beginning, a middle, and an ending. Stories should also have proportion, that is, the parts of the story should be in proportion to one another. Generally, more time is devoted to the beginning than the ending. Finally, a story should be compact. Every incident in a story must point to a solution, favorable or unfavorable, to the problem introduced at the beginning of the story.[23] The same literary tools that apply to poetry also apply to fiction. It is important to understand that the narrator in both poetry and fiction is not necessarily the author. Authors can create narrators who are more or less involved in the story. Consider the following short, short story about a nurse and a patient on an intensive care unit in psychiatry.

NADINE'S SECRET

The women in the psychiatric adult intensive care unit slept down one hallway of the L-shaped floor, the men down the other. At the point where the two hallways converged, the night shift staff usually pulled a card table out of the day room so they could sit in the intersection and watch both hallways. The first patients to arise in the morning were the smokers who walked down to the card table to get a light. Sometimes the patients would pull chairs out of the day room and sit in silence with the psych techs while they smoked their first cigarette of the day.

As head nurse of this unit, I was often there very early and very late. One particular morning I arrived before it was light to meet with one of the night nurses before she went home for the day. As I stood exchanging whispered small talk with the night staff, a door opened down the women's hallway. Nadine was the first patient up this morning. She emerged from her room and slowly made her way down the hallway to us. Nadine was a middle-aged woman who had been diagnosed with manic-depressive psychosis. On admission, she was in a full-blown, flamboyant manic phase. She had maxed out several credit cards, hadn't slept for days and was picked up for disorderly conduct when she refused to leave a bar at closing time. When the police brought her to the emergency room, still in a red sequined cocktail dress, she was singing loudly at breakneck speed. Now with medication she was subdued, at least in demeanor. However, she still wore the vestiges of her former outrageous self by applying make-up every morning as though she was going to appear on stage.

For a moment, it looked as if Nadine was naked as she walked towards us, but as she got closer I could see the faint outline of a flame-orange baby-doll nightgown. The nylon was so thin that it was essentially transparent except for ruffles around the low-cut neckline and arms. She wore gossamer orange panties that were no more than two triangles connected by string. As Nadine leaned forward with a cigarette hanging from her mouth she said, "Got a light?" I was momentarily speechless as one of the psych techs lit her cigarette.

"Nadine," I began, "I'm afraid you won't be able to wear that nightgown around here."

"Why?"

"It's just not appropriate. You cannot wear it here. You'll have to wear something else that's not so sheer."

"All my nighties are like this. I like them bright, cool, and sexy."

"If all your nighties are like this then you will have to wear a patient gown to sleep in and wear outside of your room."

Nadine paused and smoked. She leaned against the door and seemed to be completely at ease, even though the two psychiatric techs and I could see everything—her sagging, ample breasts, the pouch of her stomach over the top of the bikini pants, her pubic hair. Nadine rolled her eyes and sighed. She ran her fingers through her disheveled hair that was dark at the roots and bright red on the ends from the dye she used during her manic phase.

"Those patient gowns are ugly. Come on. I'm not hurting anyone. Besides, my butt will hang out in the back," Nadine countered.

I was ready for this argument. "You can wear two patient gowns. Put one on the regular way and the other like a coat to cover your backside."

I heard some of the male patients rousing from sleep so I knew I had to move quickly. I did not want Nadine standing out in the hallway dressed like that when the male patients came out of their rooms. I opened the linen closet and got out two gowns. "Here," I said in my most professional voice. "Put out your cigarette and put these on in the bathroom."

"You know what?" Nadine said over her shoulder as she slouched to the bathroom. "You're no fun."

The next morning, Nadine was again the first one up. I was pleased to see that she had on the requisite patient gowns, front and back. She pulled a chair out of the day room, sat down, and yawned loudly. A few minutes later, three male patients made their way down the hall to the communal bathroom. The noise of the toilets flushing and water running inevitably woke the rest of the patients on the unit. As the women patients awoke and opened their doors, the scene down their hallway was like some badly colorized version of the film *Night of the Living Dead*. One by one, every female patient shuffled down the hall in various stages of drug or sleep-induced stupor decked out in neon shades of green, red, purple, yellow, fuchsia, blue, and orange transparent baby-doll nighties and matching bikini pants. Although the nighties were of similar style and size, the women were not. Some of the women barely fit into the flimsy gowns, others swam in them, the bikini pants held up by a hand as they walked to the bathroom.

Some of the early risers on the men's side of the hall ran back to their rooms and pulled their roommates out of bed to come see the sight. Eventually, the staff and all of the male patients stood at the end of the hallway and dumbly watched this garish procession. Nadine smiled slightly and said, "Got a light?"[24]

---

⑨ REFLECTIONS

- From this short, short story, what do you know about the narrator of the story?
- Did she or he treat Nadine with respect? Why or why not?
- What emotions and reactions is the author trying to evoke in you and how is this accomplished?
- Do you have any insights into what the main characters are thinking?
- Would it change the story if you had specific knowledge about what Nadine is thinking? How?

The story form of narrative expands beyond the basic facts of most health care interactions into the experience of the event creating an opportunity for reflection on your reaction to challenging patients.

Illness Stories/Pathographies

A third type of literary narrative is the pathography, a form of autobiography or biography that describes personal experiences of illness, treatment, and sometimes death. "What it is like to have cancer," or "How I survived my heart attack," or "What it means to have AIDS" are examples of the typical subjects of pathography.[25]

Refer to Judith Hooper's description of her experience with chemotherapy after breast cancer surgery, which opened this chapter. Hooper's pathography would probably be characterized as an "angry pathography," even though it is laced with sarcastic humor. In angry pathographies, the author expresses frustrations and disappointments with the health care system in general and with particular programs or health professionals. The cartoon by Miriam Engelberg is another form of a pathography in which she uses humor to address the often taboo subjects of cancer (Figure 8-2). She is satirizing the most common form of pathography, the testimonial type, in which they offer advice and guidance to others who are faced with the same disorder or problem.[26] Pathographies offer you yet another type of narrative to help you understand your patients and their struggles.

WHERE STORIES INTERSECT

After exploring all the various ways a story can be told, you might wonder: "What is the true story?" The health professional must listen carefully to the patient's story but also understand that the patient does not know the "whole truth" either; the patient is not always accurate. There are clearly differences between the patient's experience and the health care professional's explanation of the experience. So how do we get coherence, if not the true story? "The patient and physician [health professional] are writing the story of the clinical encounter together."[27]

FIGURE 8-2: The F.O.L. Gene. *(From Engelberg M:* Cancer made me a shallower person: a memoir in comics, *New York, 2006, Harper Paperbacks.)*

Frank affirms the dialogical nature of narrative:

> We tell stories that sound like our own, but we do not make up or tell our stories by ourselves; they are always co-constructions. Stories we call our own draw variously on cultural narratives and on other people's stories; these stories are then reshaped through multiple retellings. The responses to these retellings further mold the story until its shape is a history of the relationships in which it has been told.[28]

What if we approached the interview process as "building" a history rather than "taking" a history from a patient? Building suggests collaboration and the positive outcome of mutual work rather than taking something from the patient and making it your own.[29]

Summary

Literary explorations of the subjective and interpersonal responses of patients, family members, and health professionals to the tensions encountered in health care settings can engage you in your own personal questions and reflections about your response to similar situations in your clinical practice. Narrative, in all of its forms, offers a way of seeing the deeper, subtle nuances involved in your interactions with patients, families, and peers, thereby improving the chances that the opportunities for showing them due respect are not missed or behaviors misguided.

Your role in your patients' stories will vary from assisting them to recover to witnessing their deaths. Whatever roles you take, recall that you also bring your own unfolding story to the relationship. You will build a story with each patient you encounter that then becomes another moment forming the narrative of both of your lives.

REFERENCES

1. Hooper J: Beauty tips for the dead. In Foster P, editor: *Minding the body: women writers on body and soul,* New York, 1994, Anchor Books.
2. Donald A: The words we live in. In Greenhalgh T, Hurwitz B, editors: *Narrative based medicine: dialogue and discourse in clinical practice,* London, 1998, BMJ Books.
3. Churchill LR, Churchill SW: Storytelling in the medical arenas: the art of self-determination, *Lit Med* 1:73-79, 1982.
4. Hatem D, Rider EA: Sharing stories: narrative medicine in an evidence-based world, *Patient Educ Couns* 54:251-253, 2004.
5. Poirier S and others: Charting the chart—an exercise in interpretation(s), *Lit Med* 11(1): 1-22, 1992.
6. Hunter KM: *Doctors' stories: the narrative structure of medical knowledge,* Princeton, NJ, 1991, Princeton University Press.
7. Frank AW: From suspicion to dialogue: relations of storytelling in clinical encounters, *Med Humanit Rev* 14(1):24-34, 2000.
8. Robinson JA, Hawpe L: Narrative thinking as a heuristic process. In Sarbin TR, editor: *Narrative psychology: the storied nature of human conduct,* New York, 1986, Praeger.
9. McCrum R: The night my life changed. In Greenhalgh T, Hurwitz B, editors: *Narrative based medicine: dialogue and discourse in clinical practice,* London, 1998, BMJ Books.
10. Greenhalgh T, Hurwitz B: Why study narrative? In Greenhalgh T, Hurwirtz B, editors: *Narrative based medicine: dialogue and discourse in clinical practice,* London, 1998, BMJ Books.
11. Tierney LM, McPhee SJ, Papdakis MA, editors: Gonzales R, Zeiger R, online editors: Current Medical Diagnosis and Treatment-2006. In Aminoff, MJ: *Neurology,* McGraw-Hill (website): http://www.accessmedicine.com.
12. Donley C: Whose story is it anyway? The roles of narratives in health care, *Trends Health Care Law Ethics* 10(4):27-31, 39-40, 1995.
13. Coles R: *The call of stories: teaching and the moral imagination,* Boston, 1989, Houghton Mifflin.
14. Charon R: Narrative medicine: attention, representation, affiliation, *Narrative* 13:261-270, 2005.
15. Weed LL: Medical records that guide and teach, *N Engl J Med* 278:593-600, 652-657, 1998.
16. Rogers J: Being skeptical about medical humanities, *J Med Humanit* 16(4):265-277, 1995.
17. Coulehan J: Pearls, pith, and provocation: teaching the patient's story, *Qual Health Res* 2(3):358-366, 1992.
18. Davis C: Poetry about patients: hearing the nurse's voice, *J Med Humanit* 18(2):111-125, 1997.
19. Wear D, Aultman JM: The limits of narrative: medical student resistance to confronting inequality and oppression in literature and beyond, *Med Educ* 39:1056-1065, 2005.
20. Forster EM: *Aspects of the novel,* New York, 1927, Harcourt, Brace.
21. Drury J: *Creating poetry,* Cincinnati, 1991, Writers' Digest Books.

22. Solly R: *A rare and still scandalous subject.* (Unpublished. Reprinted with permission of the author.)

23. Mueller L, Reynolds JD: *Creative writing: forms and techniques,* Lincolnwood, IL, 1992, National Textbook.

24. Haddad A: Nadine's secret. In Haddad A, Brown K, editors: *The arduous touch: women's voices in health care,* West Lafayette, IN, 1999, Purdue University Press.

25. Hawkins AH: *Reconstructing illness: studies in pathography,* West Lafayette, IN, 1993, Purdue University Press.

26. Engelberg M: *Cancer made me a shallower person: a memoir in comics,* New York, 2006, Harper Collins.

27. Bishop JB: Creating narratives in the clinical encounter, *Med Humanit Rev* 14(1):10-23, 2000.

28. Frank AW: From suspicion to dialogue: relations of storytelling in clinical encounters, *Med Humanit Rev* 14(1):24-34, 2000.

29. Haidet P, Paterniti DA: "Building" a history rather than "taking" one: a perspective on information sharing during the medical interview, *Arch Intern Med* 163:1134-40, 2003.

RESPECTFUL COMMUNICATION IN AN INFORMATION AGE

CHAPTER OBJECTIVES

The student will be able to

- Compare and contrast models of communication
- Describe basic differences between one-to-one and group communication
- Identify four important factors in achieving successful verbal communication
- Assess three problems that can arise from miscommunication
- Discuss two voice qualities that influence the meaning of spoken words
- Identify two types of nonverbal communication and describe the importance of each
- Describe how attitudes and emotions such as fear, grief, or humor affect communication
- Give some examples of ways in which time and space awareness differ from culture to culture
- Discuss ways to show respect through effective distance communication
- Identify seven levels of listening and describe their relevance to the health professional and patient interaction

After surgery last May, my first memory upon awakening in the ICU was a feeling as if I were choking on the ventilator, and of desperately wanting someone to help me. I could hear the nurse behind the curtain. I lifted my hand to summon her, only to realize I was in restraints, immobilized. I felt as if I were being buried alive. Lacking an alternative, I decided to kick my legs until someone came. This worked. The nurse came and suctioned me briefly, then disappeared behind the curtain. Still afraid and still feeling as if I needed more suctioning and the presence of another near me, I kicked again. She returned, this time to lecture me on how I mustn't kick my legs.

And then she left.

—S.G. Jaquette[1]

TALKING TOGETHER

By about the age of 2 years, a child makes all possible phonetic sounds, and the audience, totally captivated by the clucks, coos, chirps, and gurgles, provides encouragement for this baby babble. However, by the age of 4 years, a child knows that only certain sounds evoke a response from adults. Thus, the child begins to repress some sounds and mimic adults in combining sounds to form words. In this way, the highly complex, intricate skill of language is acquired, and an important bridge to relationship is built.

Patients rely on verbal communication to try to explain what is wrong or seek comfort or encouragement from health professionals. Yet they may have difficulty with the language itself, with finding the right words, or they may literally be unable to speak and have to resort to gestures, such as the woman in the opening scenario of this chapter. Unable to use words to convey her needs, the woman in the scenario spoke the only way she could—she kicked her legs.

The greater responsibility for respectful communication between you and a patient lies with you, although both must assume responsibility. By examining interdependent components of effective communication, you will gain insight into this critical area of human interaction. Health professionals rely on verbal, nonverbal, written, and electronic communication to share information, plan care, and collaborate with others on the health care team.

In your work as a health professional you will be required to communicate verbally with a patient to: (1) establish rapport, (2) obtain information concerning his or her condition and progress, (3) confirm understanding (your own and the person with whom you are communicating), (4) relay pertinent information to other health professionals and support personnel, and (5) instruct the patient and his or her family. Periodically, you are expected to offer encouragement and support, give rewards as incentives for further effort, convey bad news, report technical data to a patient or colleague, interpret information, and act as consultant. Naturally, you will be more comfortable with some activities than with others, according to your own specific abilities and experiences. Nevertheless, all health professionals should be prepared to perform the entire gamut of communication activities.

Verbal communication is instrumental in creating better understanding between you and a patient. However, this is not always the result. You will often be able to trace the cause of a misunderstanding to something you said; it was probably the wrong thing to say, or it was said in the wrong way or at the wrong time. The way words travel back and forth between individuals has been the subject of a great deal of study in the communication field. Several models have been proposed to graphically describe what happens when two people exchange the simplest of words.

MODELS OF COMMUNICATION

Although the following quotation focuses on the exchange of information between the physician and patient, the same can be said of all health professionals as they communicate with patients.

It is revealing to examine how this flow back and forth between physician and patient is shaped, what is revealed or requested, when, by whom, at whose request or command, and whether there is reciprocal revelation of reasons, doubts, and anxieties. When we look at the medical context, instead of a free exchange of speech acts we find a highly structured discourse situation in which the physician is very much in control. Some patients perceive this sharply. Others more vaguely sense time constraints and a sequence structured by physician questions and terminated by signals of closure, such as writing prescriptions.[2]

Communication understood in this way involves the transfer of information from the patient to the health professional so that a diagnosis or plan for treatment can be made. The focus is on the "facts" and generally begins with a question about what brought the patient to the health professional. However, once the initial complaint is stated, there appears to be little time or attention devoted to other patient-centered concerns.[3]

Think of some reasons this is problematic. For example, the first complaint that a patient mentions may not be the most significant. More important, the patient may take a health professional's hurried rush through a discussion as an overt sign of disinterest and disrespect. As one older patient observed, "The doctor acted the whole time like he was double parked on the busy street outside his office."

Most interactions with patients take the form of "interviews" rather than a conversation or dialogue. Health profession students take great pains to learn this interview technique designed to reveal, by the process of data gathering and elimination, the patient's health problem. The interview becomes a means to an end, the end being a diagnosis, problem identification, and treatment plan. This end may not be the one the patient is seeking. It could be that the patient's primary goal is for a knowledgeable person to really listen and understand. This variance in goals is especially evident when the patient is terminally ill or is struggling with a chronic condition. When health professionals interact with patients to plan for end-of-life care, the idea of an interview does not seem appropriate, but the need for "end-of-life conversations" does.[4] When patients have a chronic condition, the problem has already been identified and cannot be cured. Thus, an interview technique whose aim is to find a problem and resolve it is inappropriate in chronic care.

Furthermore, by strictly following the interview model of communication, the health professional effectively controls the introduction and progression of topics. This pattern of communication involves the use of power and authority but remains largely hidden from awareness. Patients may literally be unable to get a word in edgewise during the time they have to speak with health professionals.

Imagine yourself changing your view of communication to one of a dialogue or conversation so that you can focus your attention on different aspects of the process such as minimizing the disparities in power and creating opportunities for true understanding between you and the patient. Even including questions and prompts like, "Tell me more about that," or "What have you tried that helps?" offer greater opportunity for communication than mere "yes" and "no" types of questions. Figure 9-1 conceptualizes communication, both verbal and nonverbal, as the bridge between you and

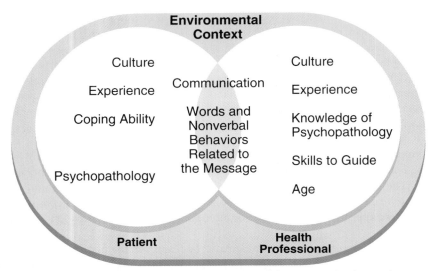

FIGURE 9-1: Essential and influencing variables of the communication environment. *(From Keltner NL, Schweke LH, Bostrom CE:* Psychiatric nursing, *ed 4, St Louis, 2003, Mosby.)*

a patient. The model also includes some of the primary and secondary cultural characteristics introduced in Chapter 3 that influence what each party brings to the dialogue. All of these factors (and others not listed in the figure) have an impact on the interaction.

THE CONTEXT OF COMMUNICATION

Figure 9-1 places the two parties who are communicating within an environmental context. Where, with whom, and under what circumstances the dialogue or conversation takes place can have a profound influence on the process and outcomes of the interaction. Clinical encounters between you and your patients are, according to Arthur Frank, a particular form of dialogue: "Most of the particularities generate tensions: stakes are often high for both parties, time is often limited, intimate matters are being broached between comparative strangers, power differentials intrude, and—not last but enough—both parties often have idealized expectations for what should take place."[5]

Thus, the internal context of this exchange between you and the patient sets it apart from everyday conversations. The external environment also has an impact on the process and outcome of your dialogue. Because of technology, you may find yourself communicating with the same patient in a variety of contexts (e.g., face-to-face in a clinical setting, talking on the telephone, or corresponding via e-mail).

Face-to-Face or Distant

If someone is standing or sitting right in front of you, the type of interaction is very different from what occurs on the telephone or through an e-mail message, discussion board, or chat room. What varies most between face-to-face interactions and those that occur across distances is proximity and the degree of relative anonymity. When we are in direct personal contact with another person, there are fewer places to hide our fears and discomforts. In fact, knowing this, some health professionals specifically choose areas of practice in which they will have little direct contact with patients.

When you have the opportunity to meet face-to-face with a patient, all of the possible ways of communicating can be engaged. Each sense can be a source of information about the other. This explains, in part, why the exchange is that much richer and, to some, more frightening than those that take place from a distance.

We will discuss various forms of "distant" communication tools later in this chapter. During your career there is a good chance you will use all sorts of devices to communicate with patients. Perhaps at some time in the future, a holographic, computer-generated version of yourself and the patient will virtually "interact" with each other. Face-to-face interactions with health professionals will continue but will be more and more supplemented by phone and online health communication (Figure 9-2).

Surveys show that patients want to be able to email their clinicians to get test results and ask questions.[6] Online communication with patients has many positive attributes such as the verbatim record of the transaction between patient and health professional.

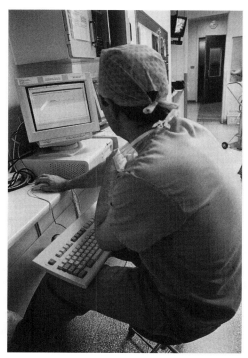

FIGURE 9-2: Online communication with patients has both its advantages and its drawbacks. (© Corbis.)

However, email is not well suited to urgent problems nor does it contain the nonverbal components of communication that are crucial to understanding.

One-to-One or Group

Before you begin any type of interaction with a patient, you should make sure the patient knows who you are and what you do. This sounds so basic that it hardly seems worth mentioning. However, some health professionals are so focused on getting on with the diagnostic examination or asking questions that they forget the introductions. Of course this is not necessary if you are seeing a patient often. If you have met before, but there has been some time between your interactions, it does not hurt to reintroduce yourself and explain your role. In addition, always wear your name tag with your name and professional role clearly displayed.

If you are meeting a patient for the first time, be sure to use his or her full name. Do not presume to address a patient, unless the patient is a child, by his or her first name until the patient gives you explicit permission. Ask the patient how to pronounce his or her name if there is any doubt about the correct pronunciation. The 6-year-old niece of one of the authors was highly insulted when her pediatrician continually mispronounced her first name after being corrected. The child said, "How would she like it if I kept saying her name the wrong way?" So even children notice this lapse in respect.

After you introduce yourself, tell the patient what you do in a few sentences. It is helpful to practice this explanation with a sympathetic audience such as relatives or friends who will tell you if you are being too technical or confusing.

Having established this initial rapport, you can now devote your attention to the patient before you and vice versa. We will address matters such as facial expression, gestures, and touch later in this chapter. All of these nonverbal forms of communication may override verbal messages, and this is especially obvious in a face-to-face interaction.

Working with an individual patient is far different from working with a group of patients. You will have the opportunity to interact with groups of patients or patients and their families or friends in addition to individual patients. Thus, it is important to become knowledgeable about group functioning because much of what you plan for and deliver may be accomplished through a group process. To have a constructive effect in a group setting you must be familiar with how a group influences individual behavior and the forces that operate in any group. The groups you interact with as a health professional may be spontaneously formed for a short period of time, such as a group of diabetic patients currently on the unit who come together for instruction about their diet, or they may be groups that will interact for longer periods of time, such as a support or therapy group in a rehabilitation setting. You will also work with interdisciplinary groups or peer groups in clinical practice. We focus here on the behavior that occurs when any group interacts and how you can improve the functioning of a group process whether you are the facilitator or a group member.

Group functioning in this setting has a social orientation and work orientation. For example, you socialize with members of your work group over coffee or during lunch breaks but also engage with them in setting patient goals during a team meeting. You chat with a group of patients when you meet them in the TV lounge but are aware that in the next hour you will be working with them as a support group or treatment group. In addition, groups appear to go through various stages of development, and the behaviors during each can help you understand group process:

▶ Stage 1—The "orientation," or "groping," stage. Members ask: What are we doing here? What is our purpose? If you are working with a group of patients, it is important to identify the specific goal of the group or what is to be accomplished in a specific time frame. In this initial phase of the group process, members are usually highly reliant on the leader. When you are in the leadership or facilitator role, you can do a lot to increase the effectiveness and decrease the anxiety and confusion of the group by clearly providing structure.

▶ Stage 2—The "griping" stage. Members of the group express, either openly or covertly, frustration and anger with the group process. This phenomenon seems to symbolize the group members' struggles to maintain their own identity and still be part of the group process. Much of this irritability will be directed at the group leader, so if you are in this role, be prepared. It is important to remember that this hostility is not personal, but part of the normal growth of the group.

▶ Stage 3—The "grouping" stage. If the group survives the second stage intact, members will move on to identify more with each other and the task of the group. They will begin to feel a sense of togetherness and shared purpose.

▶ Stage 4—The "grinding" stage. The group is then able to focus on the task at hand. This fourth stage is marked by problem-solving behavior and cooperation to achieve their individual and shared goals.

Of course, not all groups move through these stages in a straightforward manner. Group composition can change, disrupting the growth process. Also, in the frantic pace of contemporary health care, groups come and go quickly; therefore, many times, little cohesion can be achieved. In other words, you may find yourself constantly working in the "groping" stage of group development, with your role remaining one of providing guidance and structure.

REFLECTIONS

- Think of a group you have recently been in. What was its purpose?
- What role did you take in the group process?
- What behaviors did you note that indicated you were in each of the stages?

Institution or Home

In Chapter 2 we discussed a variety of environments in which patients receive care today. Whatever the environment in which you encounter patients, for social, psychological, and financial reasons, there is a strong tendency to medicalize the setting. So even in settings such as a skilled nursing facility or the patient's home, medical props and devices shape the atmosphere. It is evident to health professionals who work in patients' homes that they are viewed as guests, at best, or intrusive strangers, at worst. Home care places the health professional on the patient's turf. Communication in the home care setting is shaped by that environment. Health professionals are more deferential, more attuned to asking before doing. Other health care environments, such as intensive care units or emergency departments, do not even pretend to be "home-like" or welcoming to patients. The sights, sounds, smells, and urgency of these high-tech environments have a profound impact on patients, particularly because this environment is often foreign and threatening. Consider this excerpt from a poem involving a mother who gets her first glimpse of her child in critical care in a hospital.

> INTENSIVE CARE
>
> *... I am called.*
> *But nothing prepares me for what I see, my child*
>
> *in her body of pain, hooked to machines. Grief*
> *comes up like floodwater. Her body floats on a sea*
>
> *of air that is her bed, a force field of sorrow*
> *that pulls me to her side. I touch pain I know*
>
> *I have never felt, move into a new land*
> *of nightmare. She is so still. Only one hand*
>
> *moves, fingers oscillate like water plants risking*
> *the air. Machines line the desks,*
>
> *the floor, the walls, confirm the deep pink*
> *of her skin in rapidly ascending numbers. One eye blinks. ...*
> —L.C. Getsi[7]

◎ REFLECTIONS

- If you were to enter this patient's room and come upon this mother, what would your first words be?
- How would this institutional environment impact communication?
- What might you do to minimize the strangeness of the surroundings?

Sensitive communication depends on an appreciation of the effect of the environment on what transpires between you and the patient.

CHOOSING THE RIGHT WORDS

The success of verbal communication depends on several important factors: (1) the way material is presented, that is, the vocabulary used, the clarity of voice, and organization; and (2) the tone and volume of the voice.

Vocabulary and Jargon

As we note in Chapter 8 the descriptive vocabulary of the health professional is a two-edged sword. A student must learn to offer precise, accurate descriptions and must be able to communicate to other professionals in that mode.

Technical language is one of the bonds shared by health professionals among themselves. In contrast, highly technical professional jargon is almost never appropriate in direct conversation with the patient. It cuts off communication with the patient. It is imperative that you learn to translate technical jargon into terms understandable to patients when discussing their condition or conversing with their families. Only in the rarest instances are patients schooled in the technical language of health care sufficiently to understand its jargon, even in today's world of the Internet, television, and other health care-related resources. Even when the patient happens to be a health professional, it is important to use easily understandable language when talking about what is happening with him or her. Do not assume that the therapist or nurse who is your patient is conversant in all areas of health care. Take a cue from the health professional who is your patient regarding technical language and only use terms and words introduced by the patient.

Although we have been stressing that a dialogue or conversation model of communication is preferable, there are some distinct cases in which direct, simple questions are more appropriate. In a study of caregivers who worked with patients with Alzheimer's disease, a "yes/no" or forced choice type of question (e.g., "Do you want to go outside?") rather than an open-ended question (e.g., "What would you like to do?") resulted in more successful communication.[8] Family caregivers of patients with Alzheimer's disease also found that using simple sentences was more effective than other communication strategies, such as slow speech.[9]

Thus, as always, the general rule has exceptions, and you will have to assess what types of questions work best with each patient. Of course, the way to respectful communication is to try as much as possible to talk to patients as equals (because that is what the majority of patients want) while remaining flexible in your style to meet individual patients' needs.

Problems from Miscommunication

Several problems arise when miscommunication occurs because the health professional is unable to communicate with the patient in terms understandable to him or her.

Desired Results Are Lost

The health professional attempts to receive the patient's complaints verbally. Often the descriptions are too vague or too difficult to classify. Rather than continue to work to understand the symptoms and their significance for the patient, the health professional immediately turns to the more objective criteria of laboratory and other diagnostic findings and bases treatment programs on experience described in the literature or derived from a large number of other patients. This "miss" in communication all too often inhibits the results the health professional wished to achieve and could have achieved, had effective communication with the patient been established.[10]

Once again, when the health professional viewed the interaction with the patient as merely the transfer of information, the opportunity for true discourse was lost.

Meanings Are Confused

Another common area for miscommunication is when the health professional and patient are both using the same word but ascribe different meanings to it. In a qualitative study of diabetic patients and their physicians, it was found that different conceptions of the term "control" affected the ability of patients and their physicians to communicate effectively.[11] Although the physicians in the study acknowledged the numerous physical, psychological, and social obstacles to treatment, they did not focus on these aspects of the disease when they interacted with patients. Rather, they focused almost entirely on managing blood glucose numbers. This led to a great degree of frustration on the part of the patients.

Doubt Arises About the Health Professional's Interest

Another problem that can result from using technical language is that the person to whom you are speaking will not be convinced that you really want to know how he or she feels. In addition, your choice of words can unintentionally hurt the patient. For example, after her first prenatal visit to the doctor, a pregnant teenager reported to her friends, "The doctor wanted to know about my 'menstrual history.' I didn't know what that was. Finally, I figured out she was talking about my periods. Why didn't she just say that? I felt so stupid."

When the health professional persists in using "big words" or technical language, the patient may interpret this as a sign that his or her problems are not important. The complexity and impersonality of a health facility will undoubtedly be communicated to the patient if health professionals are unwilling to explain carefully to the patient, in understandable terms, his or her condition and its treatment. The amount that is accomplished within any allotted period of time, rather than the actual amount of time spent, will convince the patient that the health professional really cares. If the patient cannot understand what is being said, very little will be accomplished.

The mastery of appropriate vocabulary, then, includes being able to communicate with your colleagues but at the same time being willing to converse with patients in words they can understand. You will, in essence, need to become "bilingual," translating from professional terms to common everyday language. When this is accomplished, the patient will be able to do what is requested, will respond accurately to your questions, and will more likely be convinced that you care about him or her.

Clarity

In addition to using words that are too technical for the patient to understand, a health professional may not speak with sufficient clarity to free the patient from uncertainty, doubt, or confusion about what is being said. What is the difference between the two? Lack of clarity can result if you launch into a lengthy, rambling description of situation, not realizing that the patient was lost at the outset. Even a highly organized, technically correct, and objectively meaningful sentence can be unclear if it is poorly articulated or spoken too softly or hurriedly. Lack of clarity can result when patients become preoccupied with one particular facet of what you are saying and consequently interpret everything else in light of that preoccupation.

It is surprising to some students that patients may be too embarrassed to ask them to repeat something, and so patients rely on what they think they heard. Patients are sometimes hesitant because they are a bit awed by you as the health professional and so try to act sophisticated instead of asking you to repeat what you said. Patients may be awed primarily because they realize that health professionals have skills that can determine their future welfare and that, regardless of their influence in the business or social world, they are at your mercy in this situation. Some ways to help enhance the clarity of your communication include the following:

Explanation of the Purpose and Process

Clarity begins with helping the patient understand why you are there and what you plan to do. As we mentioned earlier in this chapter, you first establish the purpose of your interaction when you introduce yourself and explain your role. This general introduction should be followed by a statement of the purpose of this particular encounter (i.e., what is going to take place at this time and why). Thus, you and the patient know what the goal of the interaction is from the start. Because the patient may be tired or uncomfortable, it is also helpful to state at the outset how long the interaction will take and what the patient will likely experience (e.g., "The head of this instrument may be a little cold at first when it touches your skin," "When you get up on the table we will ask you to roll onto your side," and "Ring this bell if you feel any discomfort."). Questions the patient asks will then help you decide what more you need to say.

Organization of Ideas

Think ahead about how you are going to present your information. You can quickly confuse a patient by jumping from one topic to the next, inserting last-minute ideas, and then failing to summarize or to ask the patient to do so. Failure to systematically progress from one step to the next toward a logical conclusion is usually caused by: (1) your own lack of understanding of the subject or of the steps in the procedure or, (2) ironically, a too-thorough knowledge of the subject or procedure. The former causes the patient to have to grope for the relevant facts, whereas the latter causes the speaker to overlook points that are obvious to him or her but not to the listener. In either case, it is advisable to organize the description of a procedure or test into its component parts and then to practice describing it to a friend who is not familiar with the procedure. That person will be able to identify any obvious steps that have been omitted. Complicated information should be broken down into manageable chunks so that the patient is not overwhelmed by everything that follows. This is especially true when the information involves bad news.

Augment Verbal Communication

Verbal information and instructions alone are not always adequate to assure clarity. Written notes or instructions, diagrams, videotapes, and nonverbal demonstrations are highly desirable adjuncts to the spoken word because they may help the person organize the ideas and information more fully.

Tone and Volume

Paralinguistics is the study of all cues in verbal speech other than the content of the words spoken. Although paralinguistics is considered part of the realm of nonverbal communication, we will discuss tone and volume here because they are so closely connected to the content of speech. Sometimes a person's voice or volume belies his or her words. Any vocalized sound a person makes could be interpreted as verbal communication, so besides your words you will communicate "volumes" with the tone, inflection, speed, and loudness of the words you use.

Tone

Each of us tries to communicate more than the literal content of our messages by using different tones of voice of the same spoken message. An expression as short as "oh" can be used to express anger, pity, disappointment, teasing, pleasure, gratitude, exuberance, terror, superiority, disbelief, uncertainty, compassion, insult, awe, and many more. Try this exercise with "no," "yes," and other simple words or phrases to fully grasp the rich variety of meanings a word can convey when you vary the tone and inflection.

Tone is a voice quality that can actually reverse the meaning of the spoken word. When the patient's response is puzzling to the health professional, the latter should be alert to the tone in which the patient communicated a message or reacted to a statement. For example, if the patient asks, "Am I going to get better?" the health professional can inadvertently confirm the patient's worst fears by answering in a not-too-convincing tone, "Yes, of *course* you will."

REFLECTIONS

Give several meanings to the simple question "What are you doing?" by varying the tone in which it can be spoken. Try to mimic the tones of the following people: (1) a man telephoning his wife at midday; (2) the man's wife, who has just caught their 2-year-old son writing on the living room wall with a purple crayon; and (3) the 2-year-old son trying to make up to the mother after being scolded.

Volume

Tone and volume are closely related voice qualities. An angry person may not only spit out the words indignantly but may also alter the volume of the message. For instance, it is possible to communicate anger either by whispering words through gritted teeth or by shouting them.

Voice volume controls interaction in subtle ways. For instance, if one person stands close to another and speaks in an inordinately loud voice, the listener invariably backs away. On the other hand, a soft whisper automatically causes the listener to move closer. Thus, literally and symbolically, the volume of the voice does control distance between people.

Whatever you say, you must make certain that the patient can hear you. An easy way to assess if you are speaking loudly enough is to ask the patient to repeat instructions rather than just solicit "yes" or "no" responses. Make sure the patient can see your face when you speak, as some patients need the physical cues of your expression and the movement of your lips to understand what is being said.

CHOOSING THE WAY TO SAY IT

Your educational experience will provide you with the right words, but you will send many other messages to patients in addition to the spoken word. The most basic of nonverbal forms of communication is the manner in which you think, feel, or act— your attitude. We will begin our discussion of attitudes by presuming the inherent good in one another. We presume an attitude of mutual trust and respect. Most health professionals maintain a caring attitude toward patients, and their way of speaking to them helps to communicate this genuine concern. On rare occasions, however, you may feel anger or disdain for a patient. In Chapter 18 we address some types of patients who present a challenge in this regard.

Attitudes and Emotions

One variable that is frequently overlooked and has considerable impact on the exchange of information is the patient's emotional and mental state and attitudes. Examples are anger or fear that complicate communication and the management of his or her condition. If you want to effectively communicate with a patient, you must be knowledgeable about his or her mental state. You do not have to perform an exhaustive mental status examination to determine a patient's ability to comprehend, his or her orientation to the task at hand, or his or her ability to follow directions. You can obtain this information as you interact with the patient. If there is any doubt as to the patient's overall mental state and ability to process information or respond to questions, you can use one of the screening tools to assess general mental functions such as the Mini-Mental State Examination developed by Folstein et al.[12] or the Mini-Cog screening test, which combines two tests: recalling three unrelated words and a clock drawing test.[13]

The attitude or feeling that a health professional has toward the patient will help to determine the effectiveness of spoken interaction too. Attitudes and emotions that are commonly encountered among health professionals are fear, grief, and a sense of humor.

Fear

Patients are often afraid for many reasons. Fear may present itself as stony silence, clenched fists, profuse sweating, or an angry outburst. Patients may not recognize the emotion that they are experiencing as fear, so you must be watchful for the signs of fear and do your best to help reassure the patient.

The specific situations in which health professionals' fears arise are just as numerous as those for patients. How will your fear manifest itself during spoken communication? Fear can arise when the health professional is inexperienced or the patient is threatening in some way. In the following exchange from Samuel Shem's satire "Mount Misery," a new psychiatric resident interviews just such a patient:

> "So, Dr. Dickhead, tell me about yourself," Thorny said.
>
> Uh-oh. Surely this was backward—*I* was supposed to be asking about *him*. "I'm the new resident." I felt a sharp pain in my palm. I was clutching my key ring so hard the keys were biting into my flesh. "You?"
>
> "Got here a month ago from New Orleans. My daddy's rich, made a fortune burnin' trash down Cancer Alley. Calls himself the Burn King of the Bayous. I did okay till I was eighteen, 'n' got sent north to Princeton. Lasted about three months. You look kinda tentative, Doc. Scareda me?"
>
> I was, but I wasn't going to let *him* know it. "Nope."[14]

The patient, Thorny, began this exchange by putting the physician on the defensive. No one likes to be called an obscene, derogatory name. Furthermore, the patient took control of the interview process. Finally, the patient brought direct attention to the fact that the physician was scared. Here was an opportunity for the physician to be honest with the patient and acknowledge his fear. By denying his fear, he amplified its presence, and it remained a roadblock to communication. Of course, it is not prudent to announce to all patients when you are fearful. Patients count on the confidence and courage of health professionals. So as with all things, you must consider your relationship with the patient and the circumstances that would suggest disclosure of fear and other emotions.

Grief

Sharing your sorrow or tears with a patient or family member is often deemed "unprofessional." However, letting a patient know how deeply you feel about their situation is not always inappropriate. If you remain too stoic, patients may think you don't care. Striking the right balance between some distance and sharing grief are evident in the following account of a struggle by a neurosurgical resident when she has to tell a patient he has a terminal brain tumor:

> I sat down and delivered the news. I hinted at the ultimate implications of his diagnosis, but I didn't want to hit this too hard too soon. I wanted to give him some time to digest the shock of the unexpected. I looked at his wife, his infant daughter, and at him. He nodded his head, slowly, calmly. I wanted to provide them with some hope so I started, reflexively, to enumerate all the treatments he could receive that would give him the best possible chance. I reassured him that he was young and healthy, which would put him in a more favorable category.
>
> I felt I had done enough talking at that point, so I stopped and sat in silence, a natural invitation for questions. I looked at the three of them. His wife was starting to cry, silently.
>
> Then, without warning, I started to cry, too, then sob, interrupting the silence. My usual calm professional demeanor had broken down. I was struck by a harsh paradox: the vision of this young vibrant family sitting with me in the present, clashing with my

knowledge of biology and how this tumor was about to change their lives. I could see the future too clearly.

The patient continued to look at me, stoically, nodding his head. He exhaled audibly and then thanked me. I didn't deserve much thanks, though. I worried that my unbridled outpouring of grief had wiped out any shred of hope. Chances are that if the surgeon is bawling, the prognosis is dismal. I calmed down, hugged his wife, and left the room, passing his friends in the hallway and looking downward to shield my face. I walked straight out to the hospital garage and drove right home.[15]

 REFLECTIONS

- Since the prognosis was bleak, the message that the neurosurgeon related was accurate but was it appropriate?
- Would the patient necessarily lose all hope?
- What might be another outcome of the neurosurgeon's expression of grief?

Humor

A subtler, often effective way of dealing with a problem or hiding fear is through the use of humor. Health care settings can be full of banter, laughter, and jokes, some of which serve useful purposes, whereas others are destructive. Humor can be used wisely to help patients cope with stress related to their illness and accompanying problems.

In communication between the patient and the health professional, joking and teasing can be used constructively to (1) allow the person to express hostility and anxiety, (2) permit exploration of the humor and irony of the condition in which he or she is placed by illness or injury, and (3) reduce tension. Shared humor and a good laugh can often defuse anxiety in tense situations and open up connections between you and the patient. The following story by a psychiatrist highlights the mutual benefits of humor:

> I had one patient in therapy for a year who was completely bogged down in inappropriate guilt, always ready to take the blame for anything that happened to anybody anywhere in the world. She was, as usual, castigating herself, when I interrupted with, "You know, I don't mind the things you have done to the economy. I don't even mind the fact that you're responsible for high inflation. I don't even mind the taxes you cause me to pay. But I'm just madder than hell at you for causing it to rain the past three days."
>
> There had been a sharp intake of breath when I started. Her worst fears had been realized: *I* blamed her too! The seconds ticked by. First there was a small smile—just a twitch of the lips, really—then a grin, followed soon by a giggle, then a guffaw—which I joined. We literally laughed until we cried.[16]

In the preceding situation, the psychiatrist was an experienced health professional and knew the patient well. Both of the components, experience and familiarity or a bond with the patient, and good timing need to be present for humor to be therapeutic and not destructive. The same psychiatrist compared humor to nitroglycerin: in the proper hands it serves a useful purpose, but in the wrong hands it can cause great harm.

The inexperienced health professional and the lay person are often shocked by the openness with which patients joke about themselves. For instance, patients whose legs are paralyzed often joke about rubber crutches and icy surfaces, both of which are real threats in their present situations. Persons with disfiguring injuries call themselves "freaks." Their joking helps to alleviate their anxiety about these problems. Patients with temporary or permanent sexual impotence also joke a lot about sex. It is helpful to recognize their joking as one means of expressing very difficult thoughts and emotions.

The use to which humor is put will determine whether it fosters respectful interaction or is a poor substitute for direct confrontation. "When used appropriately, humor can have positive psychological, communication and social benefits, as well as positive physiological effects."[17] When used inappropriately, such as making fun of patients who are challenging or are perceived to be responsible for their own health problems, humor can be hurtful and disrespectful. Although you may witness derogatory jokes about certain groups of patients, you should not join in, and you should remember that this is unacceptable behavior.

COMMUNICATING BEYOND WORDS

In this section we turn our attention beyond vocal utterances designed to engage us in dialogue and conversation to consider all the additional (or substitute) ways we enter into communication with patients and others. Collectively these means are often referred to as *nonverbal communication*. In a systematic review of the literature from 1975-2000 of studies of office interactions of patients and physicians, the following nonverbal behaviors were positively associated with health outcomes: head nodding, leaning forward, direct body orientation, and uncrossed legs and arms.[18] All of these nonverbal behaviors and others that follow are easy to adopt so that they become second nature when you interact with patients.

Facial Expression

Earlier in this chapter, you were asked to consider the variety of messages conveyed by altering the tone and volume of the spoken word "oh." It is possible to omit the word altogether and, with only a facial message, convey a variety of emotions.

Eye contact generally communicates a positive message. There is a powerful, immediate effect when we gaze directly at another person. If two people genuinely like each other, they will position themselves so that they look into each other's eyes. The distance between them as they face each other further communicates how they feel about each other. Distance as a form of nonverbal communication is discussed later in this chapter.

Even without eye contact, the rest of the face reveals many things. The presence or absence of a smile and the genuineness of a smile are all clues to a person's emotional state. Grimaces from pain, the vacant stare of a child with a fever, or the bland affect of a depressed patient provides important information that speaks volumes without the use of any words. Your own facial expression need not be somber, but should be friendly and open. This is preferable to an overly cheerful demeanor that does not permit a patient to express his or her true feelings.

Facial expressions are reinforced by other information. Nonverbal messages meant to show the health professional's authority are enhanced if the health professional is standing over the patient. Since our facial expression is "connected" to the rest of what we are trying to convey, the patient looks at it all as one configuration of messages.

Gestures and Body Language

Gestures involving the extremities, even one finger, can suggest the meanings of a message. Consider the mother who folds her arms when a child begins to sputter an excuse for coming home late, the man who clenches his fist, or the adolescent girl twisting a lock of her hair. What unspoken messages are they sending? Refer to the patient scenario that opened this chapter. Because the patient had no other way of communicating her fears and her need for the presence of the nurse, she kicked her legs. The nurse misinterpreted the patient's gesture and left her alone not only feeling like she was suffocating but also chastised like a recalcitrant child.

Unlike the nurse in the opening scenario, many health professionals develop the skill of truly reading the meaning of the gestures and behaviors of patients. In more than one study, staff members in nursing home settings have demonstrated the predictive value of certain changes in nonverbal behavior in patients and the development of acute illness. One study found that the nursing assistants' documentation of signs of illness preceded chart documentation of acute illness by an average of 5 days.[19] Another study noted that the highest positive predictor values were for lethargy, weakness, and decreased appetite, each of which correctly predicted acute illness.[20] Understanding subtle and obvious gestures is an important component of learning respectful communication.

Physical Appearance

Stereotypes are formed from outward appearances. In some instances, a person tries to adopt a stereotyped manner of dressing or speaking in the hope of being identified with a particular group.

Some health professionals adopt a stereotyped manner of dress (the uniform) to be identified easily within the world of health care. The "uniform" may include clothing, a patch, a pin, a cap, or a name tag or badge. Certain instruments also identify the person: the nurse's stethoscope dangling from the neck or the laboratory technologist's tray.

However, some health professionals today are engaged in a controversy over uniforms. One group prefers to shed the symbols of their profession and to approach each patient on a more person-to-person basis. This group bases its argument partially on studies suggesting that patients, especially children, react negatively to a uniform. The other group defends the traditional uniform, arguing that it is a quick means of identification and serves as a positive stereotype in matters as simple as gaining admittance to a patient's room. Some patients actually feel more comfortable with a uniformed health professional who is about to begin a procedure that would be inappropriate in a social setting. Further, the uniform is often designed for durability and movement and may therefore be more desirable than clothing designed for less rigorous wear. Finally, it is a relatively efficient, economical mode of dress. Those on both sides of the argument agree that it is not the uniform alone but what the person in the uniform does that ultimately determines how a patient interprets the health professional's actions.

Besides clothes, other factors contribute to a person's physical appearance. Grooming is often a controversial subject because hairstyles and facial hair, the amount and type of makeup worn by women, and body piercings are so dependent on current styles. Some professional people resist rigid rules that define physical appearance because they feel it is very important to express their individuality through their appearance. Others are less concerned that compliance with regulations governing physical appearance will damage their individuality.

 REFLECTIONS

- What types of dress or identification do you think most likely convey respect to patients? Why?
- Conversely, what type of appearance would not convey respect?

Touch

For a child, a touch holds great significance: Aladdin produces a genie by touching the magic lamp; Cinderella's coach appeared at the touch of her fairy godmother's wand; and handsome princes awaken beautiful, bewitched princesses with their kisses. Adults, too, give touch great symbolic meaning in everyday conversation. They promise to "keep in touch," are "touched" by a tender scene in a film, and accredit the hostess with having "a special touch" for hospitality. Despite all this, many of us come from a predominantly nontouching society.

In all societies, individuals come into physical contact with each other all the time, but the context is crucial; that is, they tend not to put their hands on each other except in well-defined rituals. However, upon entering a health facility a person who dislikes physical contact may have to allow himself or herself to be palpated, punctured with needles, squeezed, rubbed, cut, and lifted.

These unusual touching privileges are granted to health professionals by society. Licensing of health professionals is primarily a protection against the charge of unconsented touching *(battery)*. In Chapter 11 you will learn about the boundaries, including physical ones, that must be maintained, even when legitimate touching is recognizable as part of the therapeutic encounter.

Fortunately, the comforting touch is usually regarded as legitimate, and you have in it a powerful tool for communicating caring (Figure 9-3). The effects of a caring touch are sometimes observable in the patient. For example, you may observe one or more of the following: a lowering of the patient's voice, a slowing and deepening of

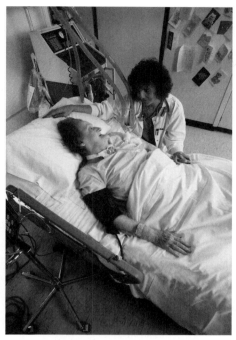

FIGURE 9-3: A health professional who uses touch in an appropriate manner communicates caring to his or her patient. *(© Corbis.)*

the patient's breathing, or a spontaneous verbal response like a sigh or "I feel relaxed." A physician who was seriously ill commented on how much rubbing his back meant to him: "The nurse giving a back rub was so incredibly important to me. It was profoundly human—an act of caring. Even with painkillers, there's suffering and pain. Those back rubs were … somebody affirm[ing] that I mattered."[21]

People pick up signals conveyed by your manner of touching. This is often related to your appearance, the speed and ease with which you move, and the quality of your touch. The sensation received by the patient when his or her arm is lifted by the health professional's cold, clammy hand sends quite a different message from the gentle support of a warm, dry hand. The reassuring hand resting on a patient's shoulder sometimes speaks more loudly than the kindest words. Patients should be touched with respect for the person who lives inside the body being manipulated. Even if our touch is less than perfect, perhaps a bit clumsy, patients are generally deeply grateful for being handled with care by another.

Patients will be much more aware of this touching than the health professional, who has become used to touching patients. The experienced health professional probably has so firm a concept of his or her good intentions that the question of inappropriateness or improper familiarity never arises. However, touch, as one form of nonverbal communication, does involve risk. It may be a threat because it invades an otherwise private space, or it may be misunderstood, but the risk, properly undertaken, should yield favorable results.

Proxemics

Proxemics is the study of how space is used in human interactions. For example, authority can be communicated by the height from which one person interacts with another. If one stands while the other sits or lays, the person standing has placed himself or herself in a position of authority (Figure 9-4).

Height is sometimes an unwitting message to a patient when the person is confined to a bed, a treatment table, or a wheelchair. In many instances, the relationship would be improved if the health professional would move down to the patient's level.

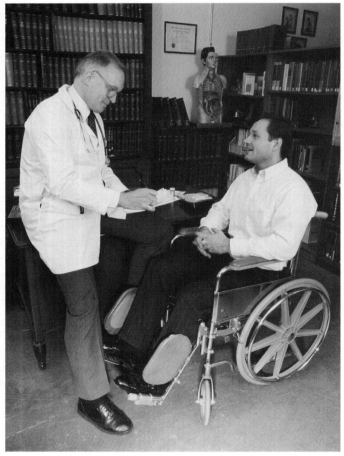

FIGURE 9-4: Standing over a patient in a wheelchair is inappropriate nonverbal behavior. *(© Getty Images/18164.)*

An important rule for respectful interaction whenever you are talking to a patient is to sit down. This signals to the patient your willingness to listen and gives the impression, even if this is not true, that you are not going to rush through your time together.

Another aspect of proxemics is the distance maintained between people when they are communicating. In his now classic *The Hidden Dimension,* an intriguing book that explains the difference in distance awareness among many different cultural groups, anthropologist Edward T. Hall defines four distance zones maintained by healthy, adult, middle-class Americans.[22] In examining these zones, you may also be better able to understand how they differ from those of other cultural and socioeconomic groups. Dr. Hall stresses that "how people are feeling toward each other at the time is a decisive factor in the distance used." The four distance zones are as follows:

1. Intimate distance, involving direct contact, such as that of lovemaking, comforting, protecting, and playing football or wrestling.
2. Personal distance, ranging from 1 to 4 feet. At arm's length, subjects of personal interest can be discussed while physical contact, such as holding hands or hitting the other person in the nose, is still possible.
3. Social distance, ranging from 4 to 12 feet. At this distance, more formal business and social discourse takes place.
4. Public distance, ranging from 12 to 25 feet or more. No physical contact and very little direct eye contact are possible. Shopping centers, airports, and city sidewalks are designed to maintain this type of distance.[22]

Health professionals perform many diagnostic or treatment procedures within the personal and intimate distance zones. You may have to invade the patient's culturally derived boundaries of interaction, sometimes with little warning. Consider, for instance, the weak or debilitated patient who comes for treatment and must be helped to a treatment table. To get the patient on the treatment table, you might have to "embrace" the patient and, in some cases, actually lift the patient to the table, deeply invading his or her intimate zone.

When you work with an ethnic or cultural subgroup outside of your own experience or travel to other parts of the world, culturally defined uses of space are readily apparent. It can be disconcerting to the average untraveled American abroad to be given hotel directions by a stranger who nearly embraces him or her or to observe men kissing and hugging and women strolling along arm-in-arm.

However, you need not travel abroad to experience uneasiness about distance zones; you will encounter members of the global village, with distance zones different from your own, in the health facility in your own community. The patient who clings to you or refuses to talk unless he or she is nearly in your lap may be confused or insulted if you unwittingly withdraw. In addition, you may become aware of some things that you did not expect to be part of the interaction. For instance, body odors become more apparent when you are working at close range. In mainstream American society in which a man or woman is supposed to smell like a deodorant, a mouthwash, a hair spray, or a cologne, but *not* a body, it is not surprising that some health professionals find the patient's body odor offensive, sometimes nauseous; some admit that it so repulses them that they try to hurry through the test or treatment.

Patients will respond to the health professional's odors, too. An x-ray technologist confided to one of the authors that one of her biggest shocks while working in a mission hospital in India came when her assistant reluctantly admitted that patients were failing to keep their appointments because she "smelled funny," making them sick. The "funny" smell turned out to be that of the popular American soap she was using for her bath.

Bad breath is a problem. What constitutes "bad breath?" It is *not* necessarily the smell of garlic, onion, tobacco, or alcohol. Its definition depends on who is asked the question. The health professional who is unwilling to try to go beyond his or her own culturally derived bias of distance awareness (with its accompanying distance zones for interaction) will have difficulty in communicating with many patients. While working at close range, your reaction to body and breath odors will affect interaction. Most patients are far too ill or preoccupied with their problems to have sweet-smelling breath, and others are not aware that they are being hustled out quickly because of the salami sandwich they had at noon.

Adhering to a patient's need to maintain an appropriate distance reinforces the patient's ability to feel secure in the strange new world of health care institutions. By handling distance needs respectfully, you are helping the patient to find himself or herself in the sometimes frightening vastness of the unknown health care environment into which he or she has been cast.

Differing Concepts of Time

A culturally derived difference that affects nonverbal communication is how people interpret time. The right time and the correct amount of time are relative, depending on one's cultural perspective. One aspect of the time dimension that directly affects the patient and health professional interaction is the scheduling and maintaining of appointments with patients. Most health professionals are punctual and expect their patients to be the same. In fact, the health facility operates each day on a schedule. Harrison points out that "punctuality communicates respect while tardiness is an insult." However, "in some other cultures to arrive exactly on time is an insult (it says, 'You are such an unimportant fellow that you can arrange your affairs very easily; you really have nothing else to do.'). Rather, an appropriate amount of tardiness is expected."[23] You may find that a patient is scheduled to arrive at "10 o'clock health-professional time" but arrives instead at "10 o'clock patient time," feeling no need at all to explain or apologize.

The amount of time spent in rendering professional service may also vary from one culture to another. How should a given amount of time (one-half hour) be spent so that the patient benefits most? By middle-class American standards, you should greet the patient briefly and begin treatment or a test without delay. If you rush in setting up equipment, the patient may interpret it to mean you care enough to hurry. When the treatment is over, the patient usually leaves immediately.

However, in some cultures, if the treatment does not begin as soon as the patient arrives, it does not matter as long as it will eventually be done. Rather than rush into the procedure itself, you should first inquire about the weather, the family, and other things that may be important to the patient, sometimes spending ten minutes in this way.

During the actual treatment or test, you may hurry, but goodbyes must not be short and rushed. One of the authors worked in an African village where she was expected to slowly enter the room, then greet the patient for a few minutes. The treatment or test could begin immediately after that, but at no time could she rush around the room. To rush while the patient remained seated was an unspeakable insult that could only mean that the health professional believed herself more important than the patient.

These examples give you an idea of the rich variety of ways in which time may have to be organized within different cultural contexts to convey respect toward the patient and others.

Other problems arise for the American health professional. We practice in a culture in which the idea of organizing patients' time on a "first come, first served" basis seems correct. However, in some cultures, this time-dependent criterion is not considered a just method for determining priority among patients who arrive for treatment. Who should be treated first if the patients with 9:15, 10:00, and 10:15 appointments all arrive at 9:15? Should the man scheduled for 9:15 be first? Or should the oldest of the three be first? The man or woman? The sickest or the highest-ranking official of the three in that tribe or community? The way in which you handle this situation will greatly determine your success in cultures other than those that are considered mainstream.

Ways of operating within and indicating time, then, are highly relative. The few examples presented only skim the surface of differences in time awareness among different cultures. As mentioned in Chapter 3, you should always take possible differences into consideration when working with people whose cultural backgrounds are different from your own, recognizing that both distance and time awareness are deep seated and culturally derived. A person usually is not consciously aware of how he or she interprets time and distance, and so neither factor is easily identified as the cause of misunderstanding. Clearly, culture influences the interpretation of verbal and nonverbal communication in terms of time or distance.

COMMUNICATING ACROSS DISTANCES

Much of the literature regarding communication between the patient and health professional has taken for granted that the two parties are within close proximity of each other. In many cases today, because of the mobility of society and technological developments, health professionals and patients can communicate across great distances. In addition, you may work with colleagues on the same complex patient problem and yet geographically be in two different cities. All of the techniques to enhance communication in general apply to communication across distances, but they must be adapted to the special demands created by miles between a patient and health professional instead of inches.

Written Tools

Written communication includes information about diagnostic tests and evaluation observations, progress notes about patients, instructions to patients to perform activities, informed consent documents, and surveys to obtain information from patients about services rendered. Whatever the reason for the written communication, there are distinct advantages to its use over verbal communication. Written communication has the advantage of visual cues. The reader has control over the pace of absorbing the information and can reread the information any number of times. However, written communication demands a high degree of accuracy. All written communication should clearly state and define the reason it is being sent. The content should be well organized. Clarity and brevity are also hallmarks of good written communication. The vocabulary must be fitting for the recipient. Studies of informed consent forms indicate that these forms generally do not give patients a clear understanding of the proposed treatment. Although Institutional Review Boards are supposed to guarantee that consent forms they approve are readable and understandable, study after study demonstrates that consent forms are written at too high a reading level.[24,25] In other words, if used alone they are *not* fitting for the intended recipient. Clear, concise written messages will be more easily understood and problems prevented if both verbal and written forms of communication can be used.

Voice and Electronic Tools

Since the telephone has become so much a part of our lives, you may not even notice how much you use it to communicate with patients. In an ambulatory setting, the phone may be your only contact with a patient between visits. It is best not to rely solely on this communication modality. It is especially important not to give bad news over the phone or try to explain a complicated evaluation finding or treatment plan. However, exchanging information or data such as blood glucose levels or electrocardiogram printouts electronically is an effective and efficient adjunct to other forms of communication.

Telephones can also be used to triage patient care.

> Telephone triage is the process by which a health care provider communicates with a client via the telephone and, thereby, assesses the presenting concerns, develops a working diagnosis, and determines a suitable plan of management. Determination of the seriousness of the situation will dictate whether the client can be cared for at a distance or whether a more comprehensive in-person evaluation is in order.[26]

Of course, as we noted above, use of the telephone to render care must be done cautiously, particularly when you determine what follow-up is needed.

Voice mail should be used with care. When you order a sweater from a catalogue over the phone or check your savings account balance, you generally do so with automated voice mail. But person-to-person communication that is so necessary to respectful care is missing when a computerized voice is on the other end of the telephone. However, a benefit of voice mail is the opportunity for a patient to leave a detailed message about a question or problem and avoid playing "phone tag" with health professionals.

E-mail is another form of electronic communication that is becoming more and more a part of health care practice. Although the following quotation describes the possible advantages of e-mail use in a physician's practice, the same applies to all health professionals.

E-mail between physicians and patients holds much promise and clearly has the potential to enhance the medical professional relationship. E-mail has the advantage of speed and convenience for both parties ... at the same time [it] allows correspondents to compose careful and structured responses. It is self-documenting. Used in conjunction with office visits, e-mail might allow patients and physicians to augment information or advice that was overlooked during a previous office consultation.[27]

Although e-mail may assist in communication, its use depends on the availability of a personal computer. Needless to say, not everyone has access to a computer. Even though it might appear at times that everyone in the world is on the Internet, the reality is that many people do not have access to this sophisticated technology.

According to proponents of computers and related technology in health care, the goal is to move to a "paperless" environment. As yet, this has not happened. "Despite the enormous popularity of computers and personal digital assistants, along with improvements in screen technology, mobile computing techniques, navigational and input tools, paper usage in the United States continues to increase."[28]

It seems that people still like to have a paper or hard copy of information in their hands on which to make notes or highlight important points. Although technology will continue to add new ways to communicate or complement old ones, face-to-face interactions remain critical to the success of health care and central to basic communication.

EFFECTIVE LISTENING

A considerable portion of a health professional's day is spent listening to patients and colleagues in person or over the telephone. Elizabeth Smith describes the following levels of listening and suggests that health professionals are usually involved in the more complex levels, cited first:

1. Analytical listening for specific kinds of information and arranging them into categories.
2. Directed listening to answer specific questions.
3. Attentive listening for general information to get the overall picture.
4. Exploratory listening because of one's own interest in the subject being discussed.
5. Appreciative listening for esthetic pleasure, such as listening to music.
6. Courteous listening because one feels obligated to listen.
7. Passive listening, as in overhearing something; not attentive to the matter being discussed.[29]

Most people lack the skills to listen effectively. If you are one of them, two goals for your further development are (1) to improve listening acuity so you hear the patient accurately and (2) to ascertain how accurately a patient has heard you. The first step to achieving these goals is to examine the reasons messages get distorted. Besides the often-overlooked but important possibility of a hearing deficit, there are at least three reasons a health professional or patient distorts a verbal communication:

Distorted Meaning

First, a mind set or frame of mind may distort meaning. It is the result of past experience. In this case, a person fails to listen to the spoken words or to note subtle individual differences because he or she is very sure of what the other person will say. A poignant example of people talking at and across each other and not really communicating in the health care environment is the following dialogue poem between members of the health care team and the mother of an infant in the neonatal intensive care unit:

THE PATIENT CARE CONFERENCE

"I just want them to show some respect for me … to understand that I'm her mother."

"What she has to understand is these doctors are busy; they can't stand around waiting for her to come and besides, she doesn't always understand anyway."

"I'm leaving here and I'm glad of it. I've never been anywhere they let the nurses talk back like they do here. In Alabama, the attending is the only one allowed to talk to the family and he does, so it's all coordinated. This group of nurses sides with the family and sets us up to be the bad guys."

"I don't leave often. If I go to the store, the nurses know when I'll be back. Don't they have some legal thing that requires my permission before they do things to her?"

"What you have to understand is we have talked to her. I heard Dr. Smith on the phone with her just the other night. He went over each of the possible outcomes. We can't help it if she forgets. Maybe she should call us to see what's going on. That might fit her schedule better. I'm sure whoever is on call could deal with her."

"Well, so the pulmonary guys said the lung was blown. We didn't ask that. Why are *we* always blamed for not telling her? She didn't ask the right service."

"He said changing her trach wasn't considered a procedure. OK. So what should I call those things I don't want them doing to her without me here?"

"What she has to understand is…"[30]

 REFLECTIONS

- Beneath the misunderstandings conveyed in the poem, what other communication issues are going on in the patient care conference?
- What are the attitudes of the health professionals described in the poem?

The patient's mother becomes just another mother in the neonatal intensive care unit, not a unique person with her own concerns and needs. Because the listeners, the health professionals, have made up their minds about what they will and will not hear, the mother's voice gets lost.

The Search for Familiarity

In addition to the risk that meaning becomes distorted, distortion can occur because most people tend to force an idea into a familiar context so that they can understand it quickly and ignore aspects of it that do not fit this context. This tendency is, of course, related to their mind set but is also a defense against possible change. It may be that a person's inability to accept new concepts is a result of a basic lack of self-understanding. Thus, the weaker or more ill-defined a person's self-image, the greater the need to resist ideas that are more complex or ambiguous.

The Need to Process Information at One's Own Rate

The rate at which incoming information can be processed varies significantly. This is partially, but not entirely, due to differences in innate ability. Overconfidence or too little confidence in predicting what will be said also determines whether a person will cease to process incoming information. If a person is overconfident, boredom settles in. If a person has too little confidence, he or she tends to become overly anxious and tune out the message. Active listening also requires undivided attention. If a person is distracted by too much sensory input, he or she will not be able to listen.

The rate and level of understanding at which you direct communication will alter the listener's ability to process the information. Thus, it is important that you have some knowledge of the patient's basic intelligence and past experience with a subject. The listener's set, the need to defend existing precepts, and the listener's innate intelligence both determine how accurately he or she will hear a message. Sometimes you will be the poor listener, and at other times the patient will be.

Taking all these factors into account, you cannot completely control how effectively a patient listens, but you can become a more effective listener. By simply restating what the patient has said, you can confirm part of a message before proceeding to the next portion of it. In addition, the following are some simple steps to more effective listening:

1. Be selective in what you listen to.
2. Concentrate on central themes rather than isolated statements. Listen in "paragraphs."
3. Judge content rather than style or delivery.
4. Listen with an open mind rather than focus on emotionally charged words.
5. Summarize in your own mind what you hear before speaking again.
6. Clarify before proceeding. Do not let vague or incomplete ideas go unattended.

The stakes are high when a patient is trying to communicate with you. Patients are often keenly aware of a lack of attention on the part of the health professional. In a study of patients who survived breast cancer, researchers asked why caring relationships failed. Patients felt that health professionals had a choice to "either receive the patient or not to do so." One patient in the study stated, "But she does not take the time, perhaps, to listen to patients. She has only got those fleeting moments for examining them."[31] Sometimes the patient's personality and fears may even cause the health professional to doubt the patient's information or dismiss it as a "somatization disorder," meaning that the patient's report of reality does not coincide with a medical explanation. This can lead to tragic results. For example, people in whom multiple sclerosis is eventually diagnosed are often first referred to psychologists for some form of somatization disorder.[32]

SUMMARY

The purpose of this chapter was to give you an overview of numerous components of respectful communication. You will communicate in many ways with your patients: in person and across the miles, verbally and in writing. It may seem impossible to pay attention to the context of communication, the words you choose, your attitude, and the nonverbal messages you send all at the same time. However, good communication is like any skill: it takes practice. If you are willing to truly listen to your patients, they will assist you in refining and improving your communication skills throughout your career in health care.

REFERENCES

1. Jaquette SG: The octopus and me: the nursing insight gleaned from a battle with cancer, *Am J Nurs* 100(4):24, 2000.
2. Smith JF: Communicative ethics in medicine: the physician-patient relationship. In Wolf S, editor: *Feminism and bioethics: beyond reproduction,* New York, 1996, Oxford University Press.
3. Byrne PS, Long BE: *Doctors talking to patients,* London, 1976, Her Majesty's Stationery Office.
4. Larson DG, Tobin DR: End-of-life conversations: evolving practice and theory, *JAMA* 284(12):1573-1578, 2000.
5. Frank A: From suspicion to dialogue: relations of storytelling in clinical encounters, *Med Humanit Rev* 14(1):24-34, 2000.
6. Grover F Jr and others: Computer-using patients want internet services from family physicians, *J Fam Pract* 51(6):570-72, 2002.
7. Getsi LC: Intensive care. In Getsi LC: *Intensive care—poems by Lucia Cordell Getsi,* Minneapolis, 1992, New Rivers Press.
8. Ripich DN and others: Training Alzheimer's disease caregivers for successful communication, *Clin Gerontol* 21(1):37-56, 1999.
9. Small JA and others: Effectiveness of communication strategies used by caregivers of persons with Alzheimer's disease during activities of daily living, *J Speech Lang Hear Re* 46(2):353-67, 2003.
10. Bergsma J, Thomasma DC: *Health care: its psychosocial dimension,* Pittsburgh, 1982, Duquesne University Press.
11. Freeman J, Loewe R: Barriers to communication about diabetes mellitus: patients' and physicians' different view of the disease, *J Fam Pract* 49(6):513-542, 2000.
12. Folstein MF, Folstein S, McHugh PR: Mini-mental state: a practical method for grading the cognitive state of patients for the clinician, *J Psychiatr Res* 12:189-198, 1975.
13. Lorentz WJ, Scanlan JM, Borson S: Brief screening tests for dementia, *Can J Psychiatry* 47(8):723-33, 2002.
14. Shem S: *Mount misery,* New York, 1997, Ballantine Publishing Group.
15. Firlik K: *Another day in the frontal lobe: a brain surgeon exposes life on the inside,* Random House, 2006, New York.
16. Chance S: *A voice of my own: a verbal box of chocolates,* Cleveland, SC, 1993, Bonne Chance Press.
17. Buxman K: Humor in critical care: no joke. *AACN Clin Issues Adv Pract Acute Crit Care* 11(1):120-127, 2000.
18. Beck RS, Daughtridge R, Sloane PD: Physician-patient communication in the primary care office: a systematic review, *J Am Board Fam Pract* 15:25-38, 2002.
19. Boockvar KS, Brodie HD, Lachs MS: Nursing assistants detect behavior changes in nursing home residents that precede acute illness: development and validation of an illness warning instrument, *J Am Geriatr Soc* 48(9):1086-1091, 2000.
20. Boockvar KS, Lachs MS: Predictive value of nonspecific symptoms for acute illness in nursing home residents, *J Am Geriatr Soc* 51:1111-1115, 2003.
21. Klitzman R: Improving education on doctor-patient relationships and communication: lessons from doctors who become patients, *Acad Med* 81(5):447-453, 2006.
22. Hall ET: *The hidden dimension,* New York, 1966, Doubleday.

23. Harrison R: Nonverbal communications: explorations into time, space, action and object. In Campbell JH, Hepler HW, editors: *Dimensions in communications: readings,* ed 2, Belmont, CA, 1970, Wadsworth.

24. Paasch-Orlow MK, Taylor HA, Brancati FL: Readability standards for informed-consent forms as compared with actual readability, *N Engl J Med* 348:721-6, 2003.

25. Tait AR and others: Improving the readability and processability of a pediatric informed consent document, *Arch Pediatr Adolesc Med* 159:347-352, 2005.

26. DeVore NE: Telephone triage: a challenge for practicing midwives, *J Midwifery* 44(5): 471-479, 425-429, 1999.

27. DeVille KA: Ethical and legal implications of e-mail correspondence between physicians and patients, *Ethics Health Care* 4(1):1-3, 2001.

28. Lui Z, Stork D: Is paperless really more? *Commun ACM* 43(11):94-97, 2000.

29. Smith E: Improving listening effectiveness, *Tex Med* 71:98-100, 1975.

30. Ogborn S: Patient care conference. In Haddad A, Brown K, editors: *The arduous touch: women's voices in health care,* West Lafayette, IN, 1999, Purdue University Press.

31. Arman M and others: Suffering related to health care: a study of breast cancer patients' experiences, *Int J Nurs Prac* 10:248-256, 2004.

32. Webster B: *All of a piece: a life with multiple sclerosis,* Baltimore, 1989, Johns Hopkins University Press.

PART FOUR

Questions for Thought and Discussion

1. In groups of three, have one student act as a patient with an injury, such as a fall off a ladder, have the second act as the interviewer trying to find out how the client was injured, and have the third student critique the interview process. Change roles three times so that all get to play each part. What works well and what does not?

2. Write out instructions for a simple procedure such as using a cane or giving a subcutaneous injection that a patient might carry out at home. Share the instructions with a classmate and see if he or she is unclear about any of the written instructions. What other modes of communication would make the instructions clearer? Work together to improve clarity.

3. Dennis is a 24-year-old man who has had surgery to control his epilepsy. Unfortunately, postoperatively he remains somewhat confused and apprehensive about healthcare settings. His wife brings him to your department, and you can see his anxiety. You must perform some tests on him that will not hurt him but will require his cooperation.
    a. What parts of this setting may be causing his anxiety?
    b. What aspects of your appearance may be causing his anxiety?
    c. What steps will you take to establish communication with him?
    d. How may his wife be helpful in facilitating effective "dialogue" between you and Dennis?

4. You verbally instruct an intelligent young businesswoman in the use of a home-treatment device and ask her if she understands what you want her to do. She assures you that she does. The next week when she returns, you discover that she has done exactly the opposite! You are dumbfounded.
    a. How will you react and what will you say when your patient glowingly reports that she did exactly what you said and you realize that she did exactly the opposite of what you said?
    b. List the possible communication reasons your patient failed to do what you asked of her.

5. Find a standard "case study" in a professional journal. Rewrite it from the patient's perspective.

6. You walk into the hospital room of a Russian woman to perform a procedure. You have not seen her as a patient before, but you know that she is new to this country and cannot speak any English. What will you do in this situation?

PART
FIVE

COMPONENTS OF
RESPECTFUL
INTERACTION

Chapter 10: Professional Relatedness Built on Respect
Chapter 11: Professional Boundaries Guided by Respect
Chapter 12: Professional Closeness: Respect at Its Best

In Part Five you have an opportunity to integrate many of the concepts you have encountered in this book so far. In Part One you were introduced to the centrality of the idea of respect in the health professions. You also were encouraged to reflect on your personal values and key institutional and societal forces that make up the larger value system in which health professionals work. In Parts Two and Three you focused on the parties who make health care a personal phenomenon—you and the patient surrounded by his or her loved ones and the health care team. Part Four provided you with an opportunity to learn how challenging it is to communicate with patients and others in a way that allows the deeper meanings of their situation and the health professional's role to emerge. In this part you will need to use everything you have learned from this book so far as the focus turns squarely on the particulars of the health professional and patient in their relationship.

Sometimes it does not appear so on the surface, but the relationship between you and a patient is significantly different from a friendship. When the similarities and differentiating characteristics are carefully defined and understood, you will enjoy the satisfaction of knowing that you, too, have achieved a habit of respectfully exercising the privileges of your role.

Chapter 10 describes some strong conceptual beams in the bridge that allow you and the patient to connect with each other in ways that allow you to meet the appropriate goals of your relationship: trust and trustworthiness, the importance of reassurance, attention to transference, a commitment to courtesy as a gateway to caring, skillful handling of dependencies in the relationship, and the desire to empower the patient toward his or her own goals. Chapter 11 discusses how establishing and maintaining respectful boundaries helps achieve the goal of comfortable closeness in your relationships with patients, distinguishing it from a friendship. In Chapter 12 you will have a chance to consider the ideal of professional closeness, the type of relationship in which respect is bountifully expressed.

PROFESSIONAL RELATEDNESS BUILT ON RESPECT

CHAPTER OBJECTIVES

The student will be able to:

- Describe how trust and trustworthiness give shape to the idea of respect between patient and health professional
- Assess the roles of competence and reassurance in strengthening the necessary connections between you and the patient
- Explain the phenomena of transference and countertransference in the health professional and patient relationship
- Contrast courteous behaviors with casualness and how each is perceived by the patient to bridge the gap of estrangement between you when you first meet and as the relationship develops
- Give some examples of what it means to focus on care
- Describe and compare detrimental dependence and constructive dependence in the health professional and patient relationship
- Distinguish contractual characteristics of the health professional and patient relationship from covenantal characteristics and evaluate the role of each

Of course the questions had to do only with illness. By the time he was through this young man would know all about her years in the sanatorium, about her hysterectomy, and about her damaged lungs—and that is all he would know. Laura was amazed to discover that she was struggling to make a connection on another level. In a hospital one is reduced to being a body, one's history is the body's history, and perhaps that is why something deep inside a person reaches out, a little like a spider trying desperately to find a corner on which to begin to hang a web, the web of personal relation.

—M. Sarton[1]

In this chapter you have an opportunity to take the insights you have gained from the book so far and put them together in the context of your relationship with patients. From time to time the authors have encouraged you to think about how you would respond to certain relationship challenges, but now you have the background to focus directly on the relationship. We have chosen to compare your situation to a bridge that needs strong supports because you and the patient always remain individuals, but your mutual goal is to be able to "bridge the gap" between you in ways that meet those goals (Figure 10-1).

Some characteristics described in this chapter are essential for any relationship to thrive. For example, trust and reassurance are fundamental. A psychological phenomenon called *transference* can always be a factor in how you view and respond to another person. At the same time, some characteristics of a professional relationship are unique, and at the end of the chapter we address the idea of professional caring, with two types of dependence and patient empowerment as foundational concepts. Having grasped the ideas presented in this chapter you will be prepared for the more in-depth exploration of this special relationship described in the rest of Part Five.

BUILD TRUST BY BEING TRUSTWORTHY

Trust is a basic support that gives shape to the idea of respect for persons. In the traditional physician-patient relationship, trust was thought to mean blind faith in the physician and the blind hope of the patient and family that everything would be fine if everyone did what the physician said. Until recently trustworthiness was just about all that health care providers had to offer. Until the beginning of the 20th century, a patient had less than a 50% chance of benefiting medically from an encounter with a physician. This total reliance on trust as the support beam allowing

FIGURE 10-1: The health professional and the patient always remain individuals, but their mutual goal is to be able to "bridge the gap." *(© Getty Images/16032.)*

the two individuals to "meet" meant that the doctor should be benevolent and protective toward patients.

Modern insights regarding the role of trust in human relationships are molding the understanding of the health professional and patient interaction. In the view of developmental psychologists, trust plays a central role in our developmental task of figuring out when to depend on others and when to be cautious. Viewed from a human development perspective, the focus shifts from the idea that Person A must venture out to trust the other person blindly, and without testing the strength of behaviors that warrant that trust, to the idea that Person B exhibits behaviors and attitudes that provide evidence for the trust (i.e., is trustworthy). The professional's proposals and responses should enable patients to feel secure and exercise their decisional capacity appropriately. But what, exactly, does trust entail in the health professional and patient relationship? In an article entitled "Engendering Trust in a Pluralistic Society," Secundy and Jackson observe that

> When a patient speaks of trust in a health care setting, he or she is essentially speaking about a comfort level, a feeling of safety, a belief that he or she can rely on people with power not to hurt or exploit him or her … Such positive feelings can ensure appropriate cooperation and compliance during the course of an illness. When such feelings are absent or ambivalent, the patient's behavior can influence outcomes negatively. There are several areas in which trust is relevant: The patient can trust or distrust the system of health care itself, the specific institution or setting in which health care services are being delivered, and the person or persons providing service or care.[2]

For trust to flourish, the patient must be convinced that he or she is viewed as something more than a symptom or an interesting medical case or a body part (Figure 10-2). Unfortunately, health professionals and institutions sometimes are insensitive to the messages they are conveying in this regard. For example, the "bone clinic," the "allergy clinic," the "heart specialist," and the "obstetrics nurse" all convey images of "things" rather than living, breathing human beings, and some have called this the phenomenon of "thinging." In it the patient is made to feel more valued for the "interesting thing" that he or she is bringing to the health professions setting than because of being a person with a human need.

Common sense suggests that patients should not trust you if you seem more interested in their diagnosis or symptom than in what these mean to their well-being as persons. To the extent that you recognize the mistake of "thinging" you will have taken a giant step in engendering a genuine bond of trust as the bond between you and the patient.

Competence and Trust

Competence is knowing what you know and are skilled to do, diligently striving to stay current on the research and management of conditions within your scope of practice, and being aware of your professional and personal shortcomings. It also includes being able to apply the communication skills discussed in the previous section of this book. You have learned that a patient's request for your services

FIGURE 10-2: Professionals' view of patients. *(From the Swedish translation of* Health Professional and Patient Interaction: Vård, Vårdare, Vårdad.*)*

usually is generated by the presence of a sign or symptom that manifests itself in the form of pain, lack of ability to function, or some other discomfort. In these instances a patient needs your professional skills and assistance in learning their diagnosis, what it means for their everyday life, and what they need to do to initiate and follow a treatment process. People also seek advice about staying healthy and preventing health-related difficulties.

In each instance the patient comes to you trusting that your professional training prepares you to competently address pertinent health-related needs and questions. Your role in the relationship is to be trust*worthy* through actions that demonstrate you are there to meet their reasonable expectations in ways you are professionally prepared to do. Their trust grows as you interact with them. Of course, as other parts of this book have emphasized, the challenge of being able to honor the patient's trust does not fall on your shoulders alone. In today's health care system, sometimes the policies determining your course of intervention seem to shortchange the patient. This does not relieve you of responsibility. Being trustworthy requires that you try to participate in the change of such policies whenever possible.

The delivery of competent care also almost always involves your collaboration on a team with professionals who have complementary skills and knowledge. Being trustworthy requires that you be an alert and active participant on the team. You should always tap the expertise of others more expert than you, deciding when it is in the patient's best interest to refer him or her to the care of such a person or group. If your professional role does not allow you to make the referral independently, an important component of allowing the patient's trust to be well founded is to know how to communicate the need for referral to whomever is in authority to do so.

Occasionally, health professionals find themselves in awkward situations knowing that the patient's trust might be based on unreasonable expectations. For example, consider the case of Mrs. Gleason, her family, and the team:

> Mrs. Gleason, a 70-year-old homemaker, has had amyotrophic lateral sclerosis (ALS) for just over a year. Mrs. Gleason and her family have gone on the internet and learned that ALS, also known as *Lou Gehrig's disease*, is a progressive neurological disease affecting all voluntary muscles of her body. Most patients become weaker and weaker until they die, usually of respiratory arrest. Mrs. Gleason has only a small amount of movement left in her legs but can get around in a wheelchair. She is in the hospital for treatment of pneumonia that is probably due to weakness of her swallowing muscles, allowing aspiration of her mouth contents into her lungs. Her weakness has accelerated since hospitalization, even though her pneumonia is responding to antibiotics. She is very discouraged, knowing that the aspiration will continue and that in her present state it is unlikely she will go home. Her family realizes she is probably past the point of her ability to live independently. They feel unable to care for her in any of their own homes but are afraid of the terrible effect it will have on her when she learns this news. They ask the physician, Jaime Sills, to do anything she can to reassure their mother that she will be OK.
>
> Jaime decides to request a reevaluation by speech therapy and occupational therapy with the goal of determining the maximum swallowing function she has necessary for eating and any possible way she might be able to function well enough in her activities of daily living to manage in her own home with home health care assistance and the family's periodic help. Both therapists are extremely guarded in their conclusions, believing that her potential for a return home is minimal. Jaime Sills calls a family meeting with Mrs. Gleason, the children, the nurses primarily responsible for her care, and the therapists. As the family feared, Mrs. Gleason is devastated, saying that she trusted them to help her and now they have let her down. The family, too, become assertive, telling the team that increasing her therapy at least would have given her some chance of a longer stay at home. No amount of reasoning about other alternatives open to all of them seems acceptable at this moment in time. Jaime Sills tells them that a social worker will be glad to work with them to further explore their options.

This situation was very uncomfortable for the health professionals who felt they had Mrs. Gleason's interests at heart but could not meet her and the family's expectations. In the end all you can do in such situations is to continue to search for ways to give the patient and family a basis for exploring new options open to them.

Honesty, Reassurance, and Trust

To be "assured" is to have a feeling of confidence and certainty. Reassurance helps restore that feeling when it is lost. No matter what their differences in other regards, all patients trust you to offer honest reassurance about what they can reasonably expect from their encounter. "Reality testing" is an important part of this bridge-building component. Although not all cultures treat the direct communication to a patient as the appropriate means of dealing with the patient's diagnosis, prognosis, or treatment decisions, the appropriate spokesperson on behalf of the patient expects honest reassurance. Even then a more general expression of reassurance must be directed to the patient. For example, you may be able to offer reassurance about ways to cope with a changing body or about resources available to help him or her adjust to the new situation. Chapter 6 recounts some major ways that life's "slings and arrows" can shake one's confidence in the way the world will respond and one's certainty about what is reasonable to expect in the future. The act of reassuring requires offering information that you can stand behind with certainty yourself, however minimal an effect you believe it will have on the patient. Reassurance may also take the form of your willingness to respond to difficult questions about areas that are causing anxiety for patients or their families.

◎ REFLECTIONS

Think of a time in your life when someone tried to reassure you.
- What did the other person say or do that worked?
- Can you recount an example of when someone tried to reassure you but it didn't work?
- Why did their attempts fail?
- Finally, have you ever been falsely reassured, only to find out later that the false or misplaced reassurance shook your trust in that person?

You can use these personal experiences with reassurance to help guide you when you are faced with a patient's or family's worries. Reassurance is a powerful bridge-building beam, giving the patient confidence to rely on your word and think differently about his or her situation. When your attempts at reassurance are unsuccessful, use your own experience of when others' attempts to reassure you failed. That can help you become aware of what might be going on in the mind of the patient. Further gentle probing may help to uncover the patient's cause for concern and give guidance to the direction your reassuring words or gestures should take. At the very least your reassurance that you are trying your best to work on their behalf in this difficult time for them is always appropriate. Your creativity about how to retain or regain their confidence in themselves and the relationship must be an intentional part of your work plan. Overall, in your practice you will find that the time and activities you devote to reassurance will be as varied as patients themselves, but it will always be worth your effort to express your respect in this manner.

TEASE OUT TRANSFERENCE ISSUES

The psychotherapeutic notion of *transference* can help you understand certain kinds of behavior some people might exhibit toward you when you enter into a professional relationship with them. Transference has its root in the theories advanced by Sigmund Freud and further developed by other psychologists who employ this term to convey the process of shifting your feeling about a person in your past to another person.[3] A young man, angry that his father "ruled with an iron hand," might conclude,

"Here it comes again!" and respond aggressively to the health professional as soon as he is reminded of his father. One of the authors knows a male nursing student who prepared extensively and carefully to provide care to his first obstetrics-gynecology patient. A part of the clinical evaluation was to conduct a personal exam on her. Upon entering the patient's room he said, "Good morning. I'm a student who is going to be your nurse today and I will be examining you." The patient took one look at this bearded, 6-foot-plus student and said, "Oh, no you're not! You look too much like my son, honey!" His supervisor who had just stepped into the room caught this woman's reaction and judged that to disregard the patient's discomfort would be a sign of disrespect. Instead she used the occasion as a teaching moment with the student, explaining that this type of transference sometimes happens. Everyone was relieved that this patient was reassigned to another student nurse.

Transference can be negative or positive. A negative transference interferes with trusting the support beams necessary for venturing confidently into a relationship. Examples are the aggressiveness of the young man and discomfort stimulated by the similarity of the student to the woman's son. For reasons patients sometimes cannot identify or express, their comfort level is low and guard is up. At the other end of the spectrum, positive transference, the good feelings a patient transfers to the health professional, can promote a well-working relationship.

It is not always easy to tell whether the transference will create a problem. A young nurse caught a new male patient staring at her very hard. Finally, he shook his head and said, "Man, I could have sworn my first wife walked in when you came into the room. The resemblance is startling!" Of course, this raised some questions—and the woman responded by saying, "Well, is that a good or bad thing?" He said, "Both!" So she was still in the woods on this one. She felt she had no choice in this case but to continue with the patient, watching for further signs that this man's association seemed to be affecting his responses and their relationship. (There were none, and the matter never came up again.)

The patient is not the only party in the relationship who experiences transference. *Countertransference*, the tendency to respond to a patient with associations of others in one's life, takes place every bit as often. A health professional may transfer feelings to the patient on the basis of name, physical appearance, voice, age, or gestures. Any one of these can increase the chance of countertransference. It is up to you to be self-aware about such associations and adapt your behavior to correct for any negative or other troubling responses you think might be issuing from your mental association of the patient with someone in your past or present relationships.

At the same time, total neutrality is not required. If you have served on a jury, you know that the lawyers try to select jurors whose past experiences and associations do not in any discernible way come into play when the facts of the case and the identification of the defendant and plaintiff are made known. A less rigorous standard is acceptable in the health professional and patient relationship. What is needed for maintaining a respectful relationship with a patient is to be aware that transference and countertransference take place and try to be aware of how they might affect the interaction. It may not be possible always to identify the person whom the patient is "seeing" in you or you are "seeing" in the patient.[4]

DISTINGUISH COURTESY FROM CASUALNESS

You might think that showing common courtesy to patients is such an obvious component of respectful interaction that it need not be discussed. However, nothing is too basic or obvious to consider if it provides a support beam for you and the patient as you bridge the gap between you and define what your relationship will look like. You can begin to see its importance in the simple dictionary definition of *courtesy* as "courtly elegance and politeness of manners; graceful politeness or considerateness."[5] It goes beyond "minding your manners" in a superficial sense because it requires doing so with dignity in the way you go about being polite. Patients take their initial cues about whether they matter as people from the courtesy they receive when they first come through the door (or, in the case of home health care, you go through theirs). Although we strive to go beyond courtesy to deeper understandings of care in the health professional and patient relationship, the patient's first, and often lasting, impression is connected to common courtesies they receive (or don't receive) from you. In this regard the work environment works best when it is a "consumer-friendly" environment.

As with many aspects of respect, you cannot generate a welcoming, courteous environment on your own. In every instance you will be a member of teams that schedule patient appointments, keep patients informed, collect fees, work toward making a diagnosis or carrying out a treatment plan, and conducting discharge or follow-up activities. Courteous conduct will vary depending on your type of work environment and the unique characteristics of your individual patient. For example, common courtesies in an ambulatory care clinic include greeting a person warmly, providing a safe place for them to hang a coat or umbrella, offering assistance with mobility challenges and completing forms, keeping the patient (and family member) informed about delays or necessary changes, being sure privacy is honored, and providing reading material and other calming distractions. But whatever your setting or the patient, the common denominator is that you pay attention to peculiarities and structure your approach so that the patient perceives you as one who participates actively as a model of courtesy in your workplace and sets high expectations of everyone else to do so. In a word, rudeness cannot be tolerated. It puts everyone, especially the patient, on edge and is a powerful deterrent to the good goals you want to accomplish.

 REFLECTIONS

Take a minute to reflect on the last time you visited a physician, dentist, or other health professional. Picture the environment as you first entered.

- What did you find there that led you to believe that you were welcome and that the staff had given some thought to what would make you as comfortable as possible?
- What signs of courtesy (or lack of it) did you encounter as you interacted with the staff?
- How could the environment and conduct of the staff be improved to make it a more commodious place?
- Now try to picture yourself being visited in your home by a home health care provider during your recovery from a serious accident. What courtesies do you expect?

FIGURE 10-3: "Hello, Nancy. I'm Dr. Simon McGinnis." "Hi, Simon! I'm Mrs. Kittery."

One common mistake health professionals make is to convey a casual, informal physical environment and casual informality with the patient, at the cost of what the patient perceives as courtesy. Patients and family members might have such a response if the waiting area of a clinic is messy, plants are in various states of withering, and chairs are at every angle in the room. Sometimes patients do not know how to interpret this casualness (Figure 10-3).

The casual informality of the team members from receptionist to you also creates an initial impression. If it is misinterpreted, a patient may push back, become wary, hostile, or show other signs that are making them feel they are being disrespected.

Some common mistakes a health professional can make occur when he or she: (1) tries to be amusing, drawing attention to herself and giving the idea that the patient should be having a good time (Figure 10-4); (2) quickly encourages the patient to establish a first-name-basis relationship, suggesting they can be informal with each other (see Figure 10-3); (3) lets the patient in on a "secret" or something very important in the health professional's personal life that the patient may not be interested in knowing about; or (4) as the relationship progresses, regularly spends extra time chatting with the patient and does little favors for the person in contrast to the treatment of other patients.

---

⑥ REFLECTIONS

Take time, again, to reflect on your own experience.
- Have you encountered a situation in the setting you focused on a few minutes ago—or some other situations as a patient—when you found the environment and behavior of the staff too casual and therefore a "turn off?"

Continued

---

⑨   REFLECTIONS—CONT'D

- List some ways that their attempts to establish a connection with you seemed superficial or in other ways were not working even though you knew the person had good intentions?
- What might you do to turn that behavior into more courteous conduct?

Your own experience can be a window into seeing more clearly why courtesy must be distinguished from an environment and conduct that substitute casualness for courtesy. The patient readily discerns that casual behaviors are being substituted for the deeper respect that courtesy reflects and that he or she hopes will be the basis for their relationship. A courteous professional person continually works at striking a balance between stiff reliance on correct manners and the imposition of a loose, casual physical and psychological environment that detracts from the seriousness of the situation for the patient. In other words, courtesy is one visible sign that the health professional "really cares" about the patient as a person.

CONCENTRATE ON CARE

Care is a concept so central to the identity of your professional role that your position is meaningless to others if you do not profess and express it. Sometimes it is a term used to distinguish human dimensions of a health professional's role from the real purpose of the encounter, namely treatment utilizing technology and technical skills. This distinction is misleading because patient care sometimes is best achieved by sophisticated technological means found in the ICU, the surgical suite, or the evaluation or diagnostic booth. *Technology* literally means nothing more than the application of scientific findings and allows the health professional to show care for the person's predicament by offering highly effective interventions from which everyone reading this book has benefited at some time. For instance, aspirin and penicillin are technologies, as are immunizations. Only when any technology is substituted for a respectful demeanor or actions designed to show deep respect for the patient and his or her family has a weak bridge-beam been substituted for the extremely secure one crafted with ingredients of care.

Care is a serious matter. Reich suggests that *care* means "paying attention"—it is not the warm fuzzy sentimentality so often expressed on the inside of greeting cards. True caring may become a challenge or even a burden. He points out that our lives and energies are expended on what we give our attention to, or put another way, what in reality we care about no matter what we may say to the contrary.[6] This is precisely what distinguishes sentimentality from a motivation to care: sentimentality stresses the awareness that a person has an emotion, whereas caring always requires involved concern about the person's well-being and action to address problems compromising it. The association of this deeper understanding of care with the idea of respect is highlighted by the Latin root word for respect, *respicere*, which means "to look at directly."

New insights into society's understanding about the basic function of care are emerging. For instance, Carol Gilligan's classic study of moral development in children

FIGURE 10-4: The Cheerful Tech. *(From Engelberg M: Cancer made me a shallower person: a memoir in comics, New York, 2006, Harper Paperbacks.)*

showed that girls and women tend to place their relationships at the center of their assumptions about the requirements for leading a good life. To care one must pay attention to specific demands and needs manifested in a particular relationship.[7] This does not mean that girls could not build a strong sense of self or be independent, but rather that an understanding of humans as essentially relational beings inform their moral thinking and choices. Additional studies have shown that these themes are not gender specific. The value of Gilligan's work with girls is that it helped to highlight that anyone who places the relationship into the center of decision-making will be deeply influenced by that variable alone in decisions about what is right or wrong in this situation.

Placing care at the core of the health professional and patient relationship is crucial when human suffering, anxiety, and other challenges to well-being are involved because expressions of care create a bond with the patient by reminding him or her that someone is paying attention, that he or she is not alone at such a time. The expression may be in the form of an attitude or disposition. Looked at from this perspective it is a moral character trait or virtue that should be valued, cultivated, and encouraged in health professional and patient relationships.[8] The bond also is strengthened by actual behaviors of health professionals towards patients and their families.

Caring Behaviors

Understandably behaviors that can be identified as caring behaviors are the subject of considerable attention in the health professions. As one of the authors has written elsewhere, the ultimate goal of the health professional's daily work is to find the caring response to each patient situation, and the very idea of a "response" suggests action based on experience, reflection, and knowledge.[9] A response is individualized and intentional. A response is different than a reaction, the latter being an immediate reflex when something catches one's attention. To what is the health professional responding? Perhaps the health professional is responding to the two elements that comprise all caring relationships: an understanding of the situation of the other and a commitment to the good of the other.[10] Part of the recent impetus for identifying caring conduct is the emphasis on measurable outcomes in health care interventions. Often patient satisfaction scales, one measure of a successful outcome, are designed to capture the patient's interpretation of what is perceived as caring conduct. This points to the fact that the health professions equate care with action more than with attitudes toward patients. We come back to specific types of action in Chapter 12 to describe in more detail how they fit into the ideal type of respectful relationship one can strive for.

The language and activity of caring might create a difficulty for health professionals too. We live in a sexist society in which traits associated with women often are devalued. It follows that nurses and many other professionals may find themselves treated as second-class citizens because their professional roles explicitly include caring and because they embrace conduct associated with caring. Caregivers and the persons receiving care may become devalued in the eyes of others, and persons needing care may feel embarrassed or reticent to ask for and accept it.[11] Despite these difficulties, the weight of evidence continues to support the idea that caring, in all of its dimensions, adds to the effectiveness of the health professional and patient relationship in a time when all too often efficiency is encouraged and unwittingly can be substituted for the caring attitudes and behaviors patients equate with compassion or empathetic involvement in their situation.[12]

Caring: The Patient's Perspective

A patient's perception of the difficulty he or she is experiencing often is quite different from that of the health professional. Earlier in this chapter we introduced the problem of "thinging" and how it undermines patients' trust. Patients are concerned primarily with what the problem signifies in terms of their daily lives, loves, and activities. Hardly ever is the technical aspect of what is wrong the governing factor. Health professionals are taught to look for the abstractive meaning of a condition: the chest sound, laboratory findings, x-ray films, the sight of the skin or tone of the muscle, and so forth. Contrary to this, the patient assigns a deeper *personal* meaning to the condition based on his or her understanding of the broader experience and effects of the condition. This is a good time to remind you that Chapter 8 describes how the patient's story (or stories) is the narrative he or she brings to the relationship and provides the clues to what this deeper personal meaning might be.

In John Updike's short story "From the Journal of a Leper," a young man begins his journal as follows:

> Oct. 31. I have long been a potter, a bachelor, and a leper. Leprosy is not exactly what I have, but what in the Bible is called leprosy (see Leviticus 13, Exodus 4:6, Luke 5:12-13) was probably this thing, which has a twisty Greek name it pains me to write. The form of the disease is as follows: spots, plaques, and avalanches of excess skin, manufactured by the dermis through some trifling but persistent error in its metabolic instructions, expand and slowly migrate across the body like lichen on a tombstone. I am silvery, scaly. Puddles of flakes form wherever I rest my flesh. Each morning, I vacuum my bed. My torture is skin deep: there is no pain, not even itching; we lepers live a long time, and are ironically healthy in other respects. Lusty, though we are loathsome to love. Keen-sighted, though we hate to look upon ourselves. The name of the disease, spiritually speaking, is Humiliation.[13]

 REFLECTIONS

- What physical and psychological experiences of the patient lead him to conclude that "the name of the disease is Humiliation"?
- What might you, in the name of care, do to begin to address his humiliation within the context of your professional relationship with him?
- What parts of his suffering seem beyond your reach?

His example is just one powerful reminder that in lived experience, a patient takes the clinical condition and places it into the larger context of meaning for his or her life. Your job is to address the condition, but always with the goal of building or maintaining the strong beam that brings the patient to the place of hoping for and needing your care.

ENCOURAGE CONSTRUCTIVE DEPENDENCE

People who seek your services to remain well or who become ill or injured are thrust into a new, unique relationship when they begin their encounter with you. Any relationship involves dependence on each other for certain expectations to be met. Even so, we seldom look the phenomenon of dependence straight in the eye when viewing the health professional and patient relationship, even though the type of dependence between you and the patient affects how satisfied each of you will be with the process and outcome.

The starting point for understanding dependence is to once again reflect on how different your two roles are, as well as factoring in your inclination to identify a patient with someone in your personal life or another patient (i.e., the possibility of countertransference). A major function of your role that has been emphasized so far in this book is that you are given authority by the patient to provide insight to him or her about staying healthy, evoke healing forces, apply appropriate technology, and other caring behaviors. Patients will have different responses to your authority depending on their own current needs and on the way they have learned to respond to other authority figures in their lives (e.g., transference). You, in turn, come to the relationship expecting the patient to respect your competence, be a partner in their healing or other health-related goal and, through these and other means, allow you to experience the gratification of having done your job competently. A patient probably does not fully understand his or her feelings toward you; they may be expressed as awe or deference, as vague admiration, as infatuation, or as resistance and hostility. To some extent, you can alter the patient's attitude and expectations if they seem to be interfering with the goal of the encounter. You must also work to help keep your focus on your role as a health professional.

Types of Dependence

To help you further develop your thinking in this area, consider two types of behaviors that rely on dependence: some situations seem bound for detrimental dependence (i.e., *over*dependence) and others, constructive dependence. You will encounter these types of dependence many times in the rest of this book, so note them carefully.

Detrimental Dependence

Detrimental dependence in any relationship usually is based on an intense sense of self-depreciation and the desire to find personal identity in relation to someone else. It develops when one person has a neurotic need to cling to another who either does not know how to control the amount of involvement between them, or needs the possessive aspect of the relationship, or both. They consequently become intimately entangled in each other's problems to the point that they are no longer helpful to each other, but they are unable to terminate the relationship gracefully.

One classic example of this relationship is that of wives who lose themselves in their husbands' work or vice versa. They claim no greatness for themselves and may feel they do not even *exist* apart from who they are in relation to their spouses. Concomitantly, the spouse is made to feel entirely responsible for the other's well-being.

The dependent person takes no responsibility for what happens. This dependence handcuffs both people to the relationship while each secretly, or sometime openly, blames the other for their mutual imprisonment. The result is continuing mutual overdependence.

When a patient or health professional is exhibiting behaviors that suggest this type of dependency need, that person will tend to neurotically clutch at the other person in order to realize the gains he or she believes lay in the relationship. A health professional may desperately need to be liked, either to prove his or her competence or simply to wield control over another person. Detrimental dependence may result if only one party exhibits the behavior, but it will undoubtedly result if both of them do. This dynamic is especially a challenge in longer-term health professional and patient relationships. Once the health professional and patient become overly dependent on each other, they will hesitate to end their engagement with each other, even after it becomes apparent that the patient no longer needs the professional services of the health professional. They may arrange to see each other outside the clinical setting. If the patient does not improve, he or she may begin to blame the health professional; by the same token, the health professional may accuse the patient of not wanting to improve. Such is the double bind of detrimental dependence. To illustrate one sobering example of what can happen, consider the case of Arthur Cranston, putting yourself in the position of the health professionals:

> At first, everyone thought Arthur Cranston was a delightful person. He was never late for his appointments, with you or others, cooperated thoroughly, and maintained a cheerful attitude in spite of his functionally debilitating symptoms. He began to telephone you between treatments, usually to ask a question in regard to his treatment regimen, but once you had answered the question, he hung on to chat.
>
> Naturally, everyone was concerned when after several treatments he received no relief from his symptoms. A meeting of the health care team was called, and the members tried to outline another approach with the hope that his functional status might improve. You learned at the meeting that he also had begun calling other members of the team, exhibiting the same behaviors you were beginning to find worrisome. Furthermore, you learned that he had been bringing small gifts to the others. You recall the time he brought in some donuts for you and your staff, a gesture that you appreciated, and you thought nothing more about it at the time.
>
> Now, after a few more weeks, his calls have become more frequent. He has also begun calling you at home, and you learned that the others have been receiving similar calls.
>
> Yesterday he telephoned while you were with another patient. You asked the clinic secretary to tell him you would call him back. The secretary did so. Later the secretary said, "Mr. Cranston said to tell you that he knows you are lying and just don't want to talk to him. He says he is coming over this afternoon and will wait in our receiving area until you have a few minutes. I told him you were pretty tied up this afternoon and asked if it was urgent. He swore at me and said, 'Of course it is'."
>
> When you returned his call, you realized that there was no urgency. However, he expressed his anger that you had "put him off."

▶ Discuss with a classmate what steps you will take to wean Arthur Cranston from this dependence on you (and the other health professionals).

▶ Does your plan maintain the trust he needs to have in you and allow you to treat him courteously?

▶ Describe the reasons your action is a caring response to his behavior.

A patient who enters the health care world with a desperate need for dependence on someone else becomes a challenge for everyone. The health professional's confidence and authority in matters related to his or her professional *role* engenders the initial dependence, and when it tips over into more than is appropriate or possible in that role, the task is to take an active part in helping the patient know the contours of that role. The next chapter takes up this challenge in more detail around the notion of professional boundaries.

Constructive Dependence

Constructive dependence is different. Each can identify a need from their individual roles as patient or professional, and fulfillment of the needs means establishing and honoring a special type of mutual dependence. The parties keep their focus on the appropriate goals of the relationship. They come together genuinely concerned, become personally (although not intimately) committed to achieving the goals of the relationship, and are able to terminate it when the patient's health-related goals are met and the health professional has carried out the necessary activities to achieve his or her team's goals relevant to the patient's health. Anything beyond that ceases to be mutually beneficial. This understanding about the terms of their involvement usually is easily established at their first meeting if they have a conversation about the patient's goals. If the relationship is more sustained, they are able to negotiate rough spots, aware that adherence to the goals must continue to inform their attitudes and conduct toward each other.

Constructive dependence enhances each individual's potential and is characterized by each accepting responsibility for his or her own "progress" in the relationship. Because the limits of the relationship are understood by both, there is no fear of rejection. However, at the core of constructive dependence is a paradox. The two people who trust and respect each other find that in their closeness they are able to allow each other freedom.

Constructive dependence as it applies to the health professional and patient relationship occurs when they come together acknowledging (though seldom as spoken acknowledgment) that the health professional wants to find satisfaction in applying professional skills, and the patient requires the services of a skilled professional. Both exhibit normal needs rather than the neurotic claims on the relationship that lead to detrimental dependence. Their involvement is personal and not merely a business transaction; they express to each other those feelings and opinions that can be shared within the limited professional setting. When the patient no longer requires the services of the health professional, there will be no regret about ending their relationship because each one has benefited from it, whether it lasted for 10 minutes or 10 months. To illustrate, consider the case of Mathilda Minier:

Mrs. Minier is a retired school teacher whose face and arms were severely burned when a camp stove exploded during a camping trip with her husband. Initially she was treated as an inpatient on the burn unit and now returns three times a week as an ambulatory care patient.

She gets discouraged at times but has an overall optimistic disposition despite the obvious physical discomfort and the cosmetic difficulties she experiences as a result of her accident.

On several occasions Mathilda Minier has telephoned you seeking reassurance that she is carrying out the home treatment procedures correctly. She speaks to the point and does not linger or make excessive small talk. Sometimes you have asked to call her back because you are with another patient. She does not mind and does not express annoyance or dejection. You know she deserves the reassurance and is reasonable in her extra demands on your time, though you also know that she is quite capable of carrying out the home procedures accurately.

On your birthday she sent you a birthday card at your home. Recently, upon learning that her ambulatory care schedule was about to end except for periodic checkups, Mathilda and her husband Oscar sent a beautiful large fruit basket to your department with a special note of thanks to you. You learned that a basket had been sent to other departments as well.

You realize what a bright spot she is in your schedule and on the way home this evening, you realize that you are going to miss her. You make a note to yourself to call her from time to time to see how she is doing, though you know that if she is like most other patients her life will become filled with other priorities and within a short time you will become engaged with other priorities as well.

▶ Write down five obvious differences between your dependence relationship with Mathilda Minier that distinguishes it from the one involving you and Arthur Cranston.

▶ Since both patients place some demands on your time and attention outside of the clinical encounter, what other behaviors of these patients cause you to be uncomfortable with Arthur's call for your attention and Mathilda's call for it?

▶ What aspects of your own dependence needs are being expressed in your responses to Mathilda? Can you identify whether they are indicators of a detrimental or constructive dependence relationship?

Having described the broad contours of how dependence influences your relationship with patients, we turn now to the final section of this chapter to examine your responsibility to help the patient remain in command of his or her larger life goals during the period you have a relationship.

RESPECT, CONTRACT, AND COVENANT

While a patient must successfully carry his or her share of responsibility for developing a constructive type of dependence, the health professional must take leadership in the process of building support beams that encourage the patient to exercise authority and autonomy in the relationship. Respect for the patient is partially realized through your acknowledgment of the patient's authority as a decision-maker in the health professional and patient relationship. Decision-making must be a shared decision-making.[14] In the United States and increasingly in other countries, informed consent formally acknowledges a difference in power between you and the patient and places the onus of responsibility on you to make the playing field more level through a process of "informing" and being sure the patient "consents" with as full an understanding as possible of what is in store. In doing so you both are in a better position of ensuring your respect for the patient's true preferences. This is the contract at the basis of your interaction, whether the contract is one you and the patient worked out individually or was signed upon admission to the institution in which you are employed. He or she then has legal authority to decide which turn in the path to take no matter what you say or what you offer.

At the same time, this contract between you and the patient is just the beginning. Everything you do reinforces or sets up barriers to the person's ability to be a free agent in this part of life. An ethicist, Bill May, suggests that thinking of ourselves as health professionals as being bound by a "covenant" includes the contract elements of mutual expectations and agreement but goes further. Covenants place people in a situation in which they not only provide goods but acknowledge being recipients of goods too. You can hear how a constructive dependency is one key for a covenant relationship to be held securely in place. This approach requires the professional to acknowledge all the benefits derived from health care practice and from the opportunity to be with a particular patient who arrives not only with signs or symptoms but also with talents, gifts, and histories. Therefore, an element of professional gratitude enters the relationship, empowering patients to do their best and encouraging professionals to go beyond the bare minimum of expectations that are agreed upon in a strict contract approach.[15]

A patient who is institutionalized and has lost control over many decisions in his or her life may still be able to command small details such as what to wear that day or when to eat, therefore expressing his or her individuality. Sometimes the loss of so many areas of decision-making is taken as a signal to both parties that the patient really should be treated like a baby, having everything done for him or her. This is just plain nonsense, but it is easy for everyone, including the family caregivers, to fall into that mode, and to do so out of a good faith attempt to help the patient. Family and friends also can be agents encouraging the patient and augmenting the health professional's efforts to counter unnecessary pampering. After a severe back injury, one of the authors suddenly realized how passive and discouraged she had become about the need to remain bedridden. This attitude was turned around by a close friend who sent a card with the following note:

> NOBODY HAS EVER SAID THE
> UNIVERSE CANNOT BE EXPLORED
> FROM A RECUMBENT POSITION.

Obviously this friend was tuned into the patient's growing sense of despair and feeling of powerlessness due to the persistent back pain and fear of reinjury. A simple gesture was enough to give her a new perspective on her period of being in a recumbent position! A patient who loses confidence in what he or she can still do is at risk of becoming immobilized more by discouragement than by the condition itself. The good news is that you in your role as a health professional can serve as a bridge builder so that the patient can traverse the gap between you in his or her steps toward empowerment.

SUMMARY

The test of all of the ideas presented in this chapter is the extent to which any of them support genuine respect toward patients, their families, and the ideals of the health professions. Professional relatedness builds on basic human relational characteristics such as trust (and how reassurance fosters it), sensitivity to the effects of transference and counter transference, attitudes and behaviors that engender the feeling that one is cared for and deserving of attention, an understanding of how dependence operates in a relationship, and the health professional's commitment to empowering the other person. Each is a necessary respect-beam that helps construct a bridge that can confidently stand up under the weighty decisions and situations that patients, their families, and you must traverse in your relationship.

REFERENCES

1. Sarton M: *A reckoning,* New York, 1978, Norton.
2. Secundy MG, Jackson RL: Engendering trust in a pluralistic society. In Thomasma DC, Kissell JL, editors: *The health care professional as friend and healer,* Washington DC, 2000, Georgetown University Press.
3. Freud S: *The ego and the mechanisms of defense,* New York, 1966, International Universities Press.
4. Northouse PG, Northouse LL: *Health communication: strategies for health professionals,* ed 3, Norwalk, CT, 1998, Appleton & Lange.
5. *The compact edition of the Oxford English dictionary,* vol 1(A-O), Oxford University Press, Oxford, England, 1971.
6. Reich WT: Care. In Reich WT, editor: *Encyclopedia of bioethics,* vol 1, ed 2, New York, 1995, Macmillan.
7. Gilligan C: *In a different voice,* Cambridge, Mass, 1982, Harvard University Press.
8. Romanella M, Knight-Abowitz K: The "ethic of care" in physical therapy practice and education: challenges and opportunities, *J Phys Ther Educ* 14(3):20-25, 2000.
9. Purtilo R: Professional-patient relationship III: ethical issues. In Post S, editor: *Encyclopedia of Bioethics,* ed 3, vol 3, New York, 2004, Macmillan.
10. Haddad AM: Leading students to care: the use of clinical simulations in ethics, *J of Pharm Teaching* 12(1):61-79, 2005.
11. Mahowald MB: Care and its pitfalls. In Haddad AM, Beurki RA, editors: *Ethical dimensions of pharmaceutical care,* Binghamton, NY, 1996, Hawthorne Press.
12. Benner P: When health care becomes a community: the need for compassionate strangers. In Kilner JF, Orr RD, Shelly JA, editors: *The changing face of health care,* Grand Rapids, MI, 1998, William B Eerdmans.
13. Updike J: From the journal of a leper, *The New Yorker* July 19, 1976.
14. Fried TR and others: Unmet desire for caregiver-patient communication and increased caregiver burden, *J Am Geriatr Soc,* 53:59-65, 2005.
15. May WF: Code and covenant or philanthropy and contract? *Hastings Cent Rep* 5:29-35, 1975.

PROFESSIONAL BOUNDARIES GUIDED BY RESPECT

CHAPTER OBJECTIVES

The student will be able to:
- Describe why the idea of professional boundaries is relevant to respect
- Distinguish a respectful, professional approach from one based on objectivity and efficiency alone
- Identify and discuss appropriate physical boundaries in relation to unconsented touching, sexual touching, and sexual contact
- Describe three types of situations in which maintaining emotional boundaries is crucial to avoiding "enmeshment"
- Identify clues that may alert you that your sympathy is becoming pity
- Define "overidentification" and its negative effects
- Describe what it means to "care too much"
- List five practical ways that professional boundaries can better be maintained

I remember the wintry day she called from a phone booth not too far from the office, barely hanging on. I got somebody to take me out to find her and bring her back to the office. I remember the moment when I realized that the absurd choice before me was to do grief work or find insulin. After a frustrating morning on the phone trying to find some public or private source of help—a struggle she was in no shape at the moment to handle—I took her to a drug store and bought the insulin myself.

I was feeling a bit of shame. There's an emphasis in our field now on maintaining proper boundaries, with the implication that those who do not are overfunctioning, co-dependent, and other compound words even more dreadful. Emotional disengagement was expected. Technically—though no one forbade it—it was not part of my job to go find people in phone booths or pay for their medicine. I was aware of stretching the limits of what I usually do.

—B. Jessing[1]

In this portion of the book, you have an opportunity to focus directly on the relationship with patients. The health professional in the above quote is struggling with the appropriate limits of her "professional" involvement with her homeless patient. She is an experienced health professional who knows she could overstep her boundaries, and in so doing, may cause more harm than good in the long run. Still, almost everyone can sympathize with her attempt to be respectful of her patient's desperate situation. As she suggests, her challenge is not only to show respect by honoring the *bonds* of the relationship but also its *boundaries*.

A good general rule is that the physical and emotional boundaries between you, the health professional, and patients must always be guided by the goal of facilitating a patient's well-being and maintaining profound respect in the interaction (Figure 11-1). As is the case with almost everything covered in this book, knowing the general rule does not necessarily help one with the complex human stories that face you in the line of work you have chosen. For one thing, relationships are dynamic, and there are changes in them with every encounter. As the authors of one article critical of boundary language correctly note, " 'Boundaries,' for us, is a metaphor that, like 'resources' leads to images of people as skin-bound containers with fixed contents or identities. This metaphor has implications for how subscribers to it view people and change."[2] Still, one has to appreciate the large body of literature that exists and the long tradition of behaviors that are considered appropriate for the type of relationship we are

FIGURE 11-1: Maintaining professional boundaries puts the goal of facilitating a patient's well-being at the forefront of the professional and patient relationship. *(© Corbis.)*

exploring here. Therefore, in this chapter we attempt to provide some more details and examples of what it means to maintain professional boundaries and why.

WHAT IS A PROFESSIONAL BOUNDARY?

A *professional boundary* is the usual way of talking about physical and emotional limits to intimacy and familiarity in the health professional and patient relationship. You have probably read accounts of health professionals losing their licenses or in other ways being sanctioned for engaging in sexual intercourse with patients or clients. The idea of sexual harassment includes conduct that falls short of direct sexual encounter but makes the other person uncomfortable by your comments or actions. We will briefly discuss this type of concern in a section that more broadly describes physical boundaries. Guidelines regarding emotional boundaries are designed to prevent psychological dynamics that are harmful to the patient or to you during the relationship. Most of these dynamics fall broadly into the category of detrimental dependence introduced in Chapter 10. We will discuss these, too. While studying this chapter bear in mind that some boundaries come from external sources (e.g., the time health professionals have to spend in the encounter) while others are internal (i.e., characteristics both health professional and patient bring to the encounter).

The guidelines for physical and emotional boundaries are derived from several sources. Some are from professional ethics codes; others are from laws. These in turn have grown out of the experience of health professionals and patients in the past. Sometimes the guidelines change based on insights from psychology regarding tensions that may arise from human needs for privacy, intimacy, and acceptance. Today studies of power within institutions and relationships add an additional component of understanding.

One way the wisdom of maintaining boundaries has been dramatized in the past is through the erroneous idea that being "professional" requires one to be aloof, objective, and efficient *at the price of good old personal warmth and affectionate conduct.* Sometimes this idea is suggested by the educational process, which correctly emphasizes the need to acquire competence and clinical judgment. But to suggest that professionalism also entails aloofness is a distortion of the highest goals to which we aspire and is often substituted for, rather than a sign of, competence.[3]

This notion of a strict dichotomy between personal and so-called professional qualities may have its origins in ancient philosophical and religious conceptions of healing based on the idea that healing requires the intervention of a mysterious, impersonal power. For instance, in ancient Greek legend, human life and death are in the hands of the gods who have some human traits but who also have powerful superhuman potential to defy tragedy and death at times. The God of the Israelites both smote and healed, but this healer's face was never seen and God's name could not be uttered. Unfortunately, these ancient sources do not instruct us well in how to behave today.

RECOGNIZING A MEANINGFUL DISTANCE

In human interaction, psychological and physical distance take on deep meaning, determined by the degree of intimacy it represents for both parties. At one pole, there may be a complete sense of separateness, and at the other there is the realm of togetherness that is highly personal, informal, and familiar (i.e., intimate). At any point along this continuum, certain behaviors are put into play, whereas others remain in the background. In health professional and patient interactions the degree of intimacy must be guided by the propriety and character of this particular type of relationship. A key is that the health professional must meet the reasonable expectations of the patient while not overstepping into too familiar ground, not remaining too aloof, and not abandoning the patient. However, the degree of distance ultimately also must take its reference point of meaning from the particular relationship. In Chapter 8 you learned that a patient's narrative unlocks doors to what the patient thinks and feels. Listening with care to this information will help you to be sensitive to the patient's needs, including those that may go beyond what you can respond to in your role. A health professional dare not place too great an expectation on the patient or his family for emotional support in times of the professional's own crisis. When the latter happens, the professional's dependence risks becoming detrimental to the patient, as the examples in Chapter 10 illustrated. The delicacy with which the boundaries of respect must be maintained are the impetus for many of the reflections on this topic, some of which we share here.

PHYSICAL BOUNDARIES

As a general rule we are a society that does not condone very much touching, especially among strangers. You may find a clerk in a store who physically touches the palm of your hand in returning change. You may be jostled in a crowd. Strangers may impulsively hug the man or woman next to them in the midst of an important sports event. However, the occasions when touching among strangers is socially sanctioned can probably be counted on the fingers of one hand. At the same time, many health professionals' tasks require them to be in physical contact with people who are their patients, and to do so respectfully. In addition, displays of affection expressed by a pat on the shoulder, a gentle hug, or other signs of support are behaviors you may be comfortable engaging in as a part of your interaction.

Because touching often is not socially condoned in a culture or particular social environment but can be a very effective means of establishing rapport or showing reassurance—and may be required for diagnostic or treatment regimens—the acceptable contours of physical contact between health professional and patient deserve your attention.

Unconsented Touching

The legal foundations of informed consent are some of the most basic societal acknowledgments that professional contact departs dramatically from accepted social norms of physical contact. Informed consent arose in part from the legal concept of battery. Battery acknowledges society's deep prohibition against unconsented touching. By giving informed consent the patient is saying, in effect, I give you—and others involved in my care—consent to stroke, rub, poke, or even puncture or cut me, depending on the scope of practice in your profession. Obviously the permission to make physical contact already puts the health professional and patient relationship into a special category where usual, socially acceptable distances are breached on a regular basis. This helps you to understand one important reason why we addressed informed consent in Part One, identifying it as the contractual basis of the health professional and patient relationship.

This right to make physical contact does not give you permission to automatically impose on a patient's sensitivities or dislikes regarding physical contact. Many cultural, social, and personal factors will come together to create a patient's comfort zone regarding physical contact, and you should be guided by a sensitivity to individual differences.

Sexual Touching

Some types of physical contact are deemed unacceptable in the health professional and patient relationship under any conditions, even with the consent of the patient or client. Under law you cannot make contact with a patient with an intent to harm him or her physically or psychologically. If you do, you will be charged with sexual or other abuse.

The type of touching that has received the most attention is physical contact delivered with an intent to excite or arouse the patient sexually. Although sexual intercourse is the most *verboten,* the prohibitions are not limited to it. For example, the American Medical Association's 2002 *Code of Medical Ethics: Current Opinions with Annotations* addresses the broader notion of *sexual misconduct.*[4] Why should it be forbidden if a competent, adult patient consents to or even seems to invite sexual contact? The strongest argument against this type of contact is that it betrays the reasonable expectations built into the essence of the health professional and patient relationship. Patients have a right to receive the best care possible without having to satisfy the professional's needs.

However, what about the idea that sexual activity between professional and patient may be taking place between two consenting adults? An objection to this argument is that sexual activity never is free from other types of claims on the other person, so that both patient and health professional may begin to alter the conditions of the relationship in light of the power of its sexual dimensions rather than the conditions under which a patient gave informed consent in the first place. In short, it is never considered fair that the patient would have to meet your need for sexual pleasure, sexual intimacy, sexual fulfillment, dominance in a relationship, or any other gain, no matter what the patient might believe will be gained.

Sexual Harassment

The importance of the idea that sexual distance must be maintained in public settings is being aired today in the notion of "sexual harassment." The U.S. Equal Employment Opportunity Commission (EEOC) defines harassment as unwelcome sexual advances, requests for sexual favors, and other verbal or physical conduct and includes activity that creates a hostile or unwelcome work environment for the person who feels "harassed." More specifically,

> Sexual harassment is a form of sex discrimination that violates Title VII of the Civil Rights Act of 1964. Unwelcome sexual advances, requests for sexual favors, and other

verbal or physical conduct of a sexual nature constitute sexual harassment when this conduct explicitly or implicitly affects an individual's employment, unreasonably interferes with an individual's work performance, or creates an intimidating, hostile, or offensive work environment. Sexual harassment can occur in a variety of circumstances, including but not limited to the following: The victim as well as the harasser may be a woman or a man. The victim does not have to be of the opposite sex. The victim does not have to be the person harassed but could be anyone affected by the offensive conduct. The harasser's conduct must be unwelcome. It is helpful for the victim to inform the harasser directly that the conduct is unwelcome and must stop.[5]

Most state licensing acts have provisions prohibiting such behavior by professionals, and many institutions include prohibitions in their policies. You will have ample opportunity to learn more about the particulars of the legal issues involved in this evolving area of the law. An important aspect of the issue of sexual harassment that has not been explored deeply enough is the harassment or other sexual behaviors that may issue from patients or their family members toward professionals. For example, one study of physical therapists reported that 63% of respondents had experienced some form of sexual harassment perpetrated by patients.[6] At the heart of the discussion is the degree of distance and quality of exchanges that must be maintained for respect to be expressed and for human dignity to flourish for everyone involved.

What About Dual Relationships?

In the past the typical belief has been that once a health professional and patient relationship formally has ended, two consenting, competent adults ought to be free to do whatever they please. This makes good intuitive sense on the face of it. We call your attention, however, to insights from literature on the dynamics of "dual relationships." Dual relationships are defined as those in which "[a] professional...assumes a second role with a client, becoming...friend, employer, teacher, business associate, family member, or sex partner. The dual relationship may begin before, during, or after the [professional] relationship." Dual relationships in the professions for the most part involve professionals who often rationalize their behavior, arguing that the situation is unique. "However, dual relationships are potentially exploitive, crossing the boundaries of ethical practice, satisfying the practitioner's needs and impairing his or her judgment."[7]

Friendships initiated after the termination of a professional relationship can be injurious to a former patient. Others warn that other relationships, such as business partnerships, can interfere dramatically with the professional's ability to be sensitive and appropriately objective in the professional and patient relationship.[8]

More research in this general area is needed. Current thinking about dual relationships is not conclusive. Not even all major health professions caution against it, especially once the formal relationship has ended. The American Medical Association's opinion on sexual misconduct addresses only current patient relationships, noting that a subsequent sexual or romantic relationship is acceptable if it does not permit the physician to "exploit trust, knowledge, emotions or influence derived from previous professional relationships," and many professions remain silent on the issue.[4] To take seriously the potential for harm to a patient or former patient is to err on the side of better judgment. Although an exception may present itself, a good rule is to honor physical and emotional boundaries with great thoughtfulness and care.

We turn, then, to three types of experiences in which maintaining emotional boundaries becomes a tool of respect in the health professional and patient relationship.

PSYCHOLOGICAL AND EMOTIONAL BOUNDARIES

Some specific ways the emotional responses and psychological attachments of the health professional or patient can interfere with respect for the patient can be summarized in the term *enmeshment*:

> ...the nurse who has become enmeshed often develops an emotional connection with or an emotional availability to the client that may be impossible to maintain over the life span of the client. This can ultimately lead to client feelings of anger or emotional pain and to a sense of abandonment. The process of enmeshment may also complicate provision of adequate care at a later time. This can occur if the patient sees the other care team members as not caring sufficiently or as providing inadequate care, in comparison with the nurse who is enmeshed.[9]

In these situations a self-conscious distance zone should be created to enable each person to gain or regain perspective on the appropriate nature of this public-sector relationship and the expectations each can reasonably have of it. Challenges include tendencies for sympathy to slip into pity, to over identify with the patient's plight, and to misjudge the scope and type of caring behaviors you should exhibit toward the patient.

The Slip from Sympathy to Pity

Emotional boundaries may have to clearly be set to maintain full respect for the patient if, in your attempt to respond well to her or him, you become so entangled in the apparent tragedy of the patient's plight that you begin to pity him or her. In *pity* one looks down on the other person. Once that happens it is impossible to think about the patient or act in a way that really serves the patient's best interests.

Most health professionals can name at least one type of illness or injury that profoundly affects them emotionally. Sometimes their feelings are so strong that they cannot bear to treat patients with that particular condition. For instance, you can probably think of a condition that would be so horrendous for you to have yourself that you would feel sorry to the point of pity for a person who has that condition. You might name cancer, severe burns, aphasia, or psychosis. Younger health professionals may have difficulty treating persons suffering from illnesses that affect young people, one factor ascribed to the phenomenon of "AIDS burnout" among young health professionals when AIDS first occurred among the young gay population of men in the 1980s.[10]

It is not at all unnatural for you to become periodically so involved in patients' situations that you take these problems home with you. Almost any health professional can recall the time he or she had trouble falling asleep or was moved to tears or laughter by a sudden tragic or joyful announcement touching a patient's life. There is, however, a significant difference between this depth of professional caring, which stimulates a purely human response, and fruitless or destructive enmeshment. The difference can be illustrated with the following case:

> Michael Anderson was admitted to the psychiatric ward of City Hospital after the police brought him there from the streets. The police found him unconscious in a doorway of a downtown office building. Michael is a 29-year-old alcoholic. His mother died when he was 12 years old, and he left home to live on the streets shortly after that. He recently learned that his father died of a heart attack shortly after he ran away from home.
>
> Craig Hopkins, a health professions student, is also 29 years old. His similarity to Michael Anderson, however, ends there. Craig Hopkins grew up in an upper-middle-class home and served as an officer in the Marines. He has never had close contact with an addict before, but he finds Michael very warm and human during his initial interactions. Michael is admitted to the detoxification unit where he will spend the next week or so. They both chat when Craig has a few minutes, and, over the next few days, Craig arrives at the conclusion that Michael has had more than his share of misfortune.
>
> The next day, when Craig goes into Michael's room, he finds Michael doubled up, writhing in agony. With a trembling voice, Michael tells him that the doctor has not given him anything to take the edge off his withdrawal from alcohol. To Craig's surprise, Michael grabs him by the wrist and pleads, "Please, please, I can't stand this agony. If you will just get me something to drink, just enough to make it over the hump, I swear I'll never touch another drop. If I can't get a little relief, I will kill myself. The doctor is a sadist."
>
> Craig Hopkins tears himself away and leaves the room. That night, however, he cannot sleep. He is haunted by the picture of an asthenic man who has survived the death of his parents but has succumbed to the bottle; he sees clearly the beads of sweat that clung to Michael's face as he spoke; he thinks that Michael is clearly all alone in the world; he is angry at Michael's physician for not making detox a little easier for Michael.
>
> The next morning a nurse motions to Craig to step into a quiet area of the unit. She says that Michael is in a restless sleep and experiencing some visual hallucinations. The nurse says, "I am telling you this because I can see you are assigned to Michael in 213. You've got to watch these alcoholics. They're all liars. They'll do anything to manipulate the staff to give them more of the stuff, so be on your guard."
>
> Craig remembers Michael's pleading eyes the day before and is overcome with a desire to make a sharp retort to the nurse's statements. He goes instead to Michael's room and deftly slips a half pint of whiskey into the drawer of the bedside stand and makes enough noise so that Michael stirs from his tortured sleep and sees what he is doing. He is not sure why he does this, but he knows it is important to quickly turn and leave.
>
> Try to think about where in this situation Craig's sympathy turned to pity, and why.

▶ What else could Craig have done to help alleviate the patient's suffering?

▶ Was it his professional duty to do anything?

We can see that he has reached the point where he is responding impulsively rather than with genuine caring because the situation is so painful to him. Such a feeling exceeds sympathy and is more closely related to pity. Because pity distorts the objective perspective necessary to resolve the real problem, he ceases to be of help. In fact, he may include himself among the patient's many problems.

Pity can be communicated to the patient in one meeting as well as over a period of time. Facial expression can instantly convey one's feelings. Quick nervous movements, coupled with a sudden departure, are sometimes correctly interpreted as expressions of pity. The desire not to talk about the patient's problem, and trite comments such as, "It'll be *fine*, I'm sure," can also be interpreted to mean, "Poor, poor you."

You cannot solve this type of problem arising from pity simply by enmeshing yourself more deeply into the patient's personal life. Of course, your pity is in response to a real need of a patient. What is called for is sympathetic acknowledgment of the person's problem, but also clarity that your professional role requires you to set boundaries on what you will be able to do to intervene constructively in his or her plight.

Overidentification

The second situation in which emotional boundaries and psychological distance must be maintained to assure mutual respect arises when you, the health professional, have trouble seeing the patient as a unique individual. The patient may so perfectly embody a stereotype that in your eyes he or she becomes the stereotype. The patient may so remind you of someone else that he or she becomes that person (see the discussion of countertransference, Chapter 10), or you may have had an experience so similar to the patient's that you believe your experiences to be identical. In all three instances such a reaction is called *overidentification* and is another variety of enmeshment. Because elsewhere we have discussed dynamics present in stereotyping and countertransference, we concentrate our discussion here on the third type of situation.

At first it seems a mistaken idea that having had similar experiences may actually hinder the effectiveness of a respect-based health professional and patient relationship. But everyone has had the experience of beginning to relate a traumatic (or exciting) event only to have the other person interrupt with, "Oh! I know *exactly* what you mean!" and then go on to describe his or her own story. One feels cheated at such times, thinking, "No, that's not what I meant, but you are more interested in telling me about yourself than in listening to me!" The way such overidentification works within the health professions can be illustrated in another case:

> Mrs. Garcia, an elementary school teacher, became interested in teaching language skills to hearing-impaired children after her third child, Lucia, who was born deaf, successfully learned to communicate by attending special classes for those with hearing impairment. Mrs. Garcia enrolled in a health professions course directed toward training teachers of hearing-impaired persons.
>
> During her clinical education, she was surprised and alarmed that some of the mothers requested that she not be assigned to their children. Finally, she approached one of the mothers whose child she had been working with and with whom she felt comfortable. "What's wrong?" she asked. "Do they think

I'm incompetent because I am an older student? Is it my personality? I want so much to help these children, and I can't understand what I'm doing wrong." The embarrassed mother replied, "Well, since you asked, I'll give you a direct answer. I don't feel this way, but some of the mothers think that you don't understand their children's difficulties because every time they start to tell you something about their children, you immediately interrupt with an experience that your child had."

▶ In your opinion, how might this situation have been handled to avoid Mrs. Garcia's natural tendency to overidentify on the basis of her own intense situation?

▶ Which parts of her response do you think exceeded appropriate professional boundaries?

Mrs. Garcia would benefit from recognizing that the tendency to overidentify is bound to be present because of her own situation. It will also be helpful to remind herself periodically that attempts to relate to the patient by pointing out superficial similarities between her own experience and theirs may be interpreted by the patient as her desire to talk about her own problem. Her basic task, and the task for all who encounter situations that lend themselves to overidentification, is to be on the lookout for the uniqueness of the other person's situation.

Caring Too Much

A third situation addresses the awkwardness that ensues when a relationship that began with appropriate boundaries has still led to circumstances signaling to you that a new set of boundaries must be established. This type of situation often is precipitated by genuine affection many people in health professional and patient relationships learn to feel for each other. The affection may spill over to, or be primarily directed to, the patient's family or other loved ones, too. One study suggested that professionals who have been brought up to view themselves as "caregivers" in the family may be more susceptible to overstepping this boundary than others because they become sensitively drawn into the other's life situation.[11] We identify some signs that affection, a positive component of the relationship, has spilled over into enmeshment and make some general suggestions about what can be done to rectify the situation.

Obviously, affection is more likely to develop in health care settings where longer-term professional relationships exist. One example of how a problematic dynamic can arise is illustrated in the following story:

Jack Simms has been an ambulatory patient at University Rehabilitation for 6 months. His affable, optimistic spirit has made him very popular with the staff. At 23 years of age, he was involved in a car accident in which his fiancée was killed, and he suffered a traumatic brain injury. Some health professionals have long suspected that Jack's optimism is a veneer for the deep sorrow and frustration resulting from this sudden, dramatic change in his life. However, attempts to encourage him to visit with the staff psychiatrist have been largely unsuccessful, a problem exacerbated by the fact that his insurance plan covers only 6 hours of psychiatric evaluation and treatment anyway. One day he tearfully tells Karen Morgan, a health professions student who has been treating him, that he is depressed and desperately lonely. Up to this point, their interaction has been full of banter and they have felt quite comfortable with each other. Karen does not divulge to the rest of the staff Jack's expression of depression and loneliness, but that night on the way home, she stops by a local pub where he has invited her to "come and have a drink" following work.

In the following weeks, she begins to visit him more often. She finds him attractive, they share common interests, and he is obviously happy in her company. During this time, however, Karen also leads her own private life, going on dates and interacting with a world of other people. However, Jack hangs around the clinic before and after treatments, and he counts the minutes until she arrives at the pub.

During her Christmas vacation Karen visits friends in a distant city and has a marvelous time. When she returns, bursting with enthusiasm and eager to share her stories, she finds Jack sullen and angry at her for staying away from him for so long. He has arranged for her to receive a present from him, which he plops angrily on the clinic desk. He says, "That's for you. Take it if you want." Then he leaves the clinic angrily.

Jack's reaction indicates that he feels Karen has betrayed their relationship and abandoned him. He has now reached the point where someone he thought was a friend has "rejected" him. Karen, who acted in good faith on her feelings of warmth and affection for Jack, has thus unwittingly fostered detrimental, rather than constructive, dependence. Her subsequent attempts to explain her sudden withdrawal may have profound, lasting negative effects on Jack. Instead of being a friend and confidante—maybe eventually a lover—as he had hoped, she will become just another of a long line of rejections he has experienced. He has relied on her more than she had intended or was able to manage.

There are no sure and fast rules about how to proceed when genuine affection and enjoyment of the other is present in the relationship. Many of the warning signs of detrimental dependence discussed in Chapter 10 can be useful. In fact, the most powerful antidote to enmeshment is the health professional's strong personal identity and the presence of a satisfying personal life.[12] Periodic reexamination of your own motives and conduct or others' assessment of your relationship can help too. Although it is important to maintain a professional demeanor, you will best be served by showing genuine warmth and affection but always tempering that with awareness that the other person's needs and wishes may exceed or differ from your own. Periodic reflection on the conduct you are observing is wise.

MAINTAINING BOUNDARIES FOR GOOD

The three cases above illustrate that trying to maintain respectful boundaries will serve everyone's interests best. We have made a few suggestions about how to do that and conclude this chapter by going through each case once more to make more specific comments for your consideration and reflection.

When Sympathy Turns to Pity

Craig Hopkins responded to Michael Anderson because he pitied him. However, patients abhor pity, even if it serves some small immediate purpose. Pity is destructive and belittling to the patient, who eventually will recoil from it.

Many patients who become objects of pity are suffering and do not know how or when to limit personal revelations when they find a professional person with a sympathetic ear. You can monitor the extent to which patients reveal confidences by simply asking if they really want to tell so much. Health professionals in general are in no position to solve most of the patient's personal problems unless they are trained to work in a psychiatric setting. A guideline is that if you are not professionally prepared for work in a psychiatric setting, you should readily refer the patient to someone—a chaplain, a psychologist, or a social worker—who is professionally skilled in providing this kind of assistance. The referral capacity is one of the strengths of a team approach to genuine care.[13] You would make a mistake by responding with a display of overwhelming emotion—pity, in this case—while failing to put the person in contact with other means of support.

Finally, in such situations, checking one's feelings with other professionals can be helpful. The incident between Craig Hopkins and the nurse is a case in point. She told him that Michael Anderson was simply manipulating the hospital staff, to which accusation Craig responded antagonistically. The nurse made a generalized statement that is often correct of such patients but could have been questionable in this particular circumstance. However, if Craig had listened to what she said, he might have gained a clearer insight into this patient or into others like him. Rather, he became defensive and was unable to listen objectively. In addition, he did nothing that might have helped the nurse attain a better understanding of Michael's situation.

When Overidentification Interfers with Caring

Mrs. Garcia's troubling personal feelings or biases stemming from stereotyping, countertransference, and overidentification surfaced in the patient and health professional relationship. Co-workers can be valuable when a health professional's close relationship with the patient prevents him or her from seeing the patient's situation clearly. They may view the situation from a different perspective and thus can provide insight into the trouble. When you refer a patient to someone else or share disturbing feelings with co-workers, you are maintaining a healthy, respectful boundary between you and the patient by bringing other people into the relationship.

Mrs. Garcia's effectiveness as a teacher was hindered by her own previous experiences, which led to overidentification. Overidentification, once it becomes a part of the health professional's thinking, cannot be easily erased. However, an important step toward adequate interaction is to keep a distance from one's own experience, only occasionally and thoughtfully sharing stories of similar experiences with the patient and his or her family. Respectful interaction is supported when you remember to listen closely for the uniqueness of the patient's experience and only then allow comparisons with your own experience. This conduct gives the patient an opportunity to describe fully his or her unique experience and express the feelings attached to it before you superimpose similarities. Then as you share your own ideas and judgments, the patient will begin to realize that your account reveals concern about and insight into his or her problem.

When a Professional Cares Too Much

Karen Morgan paid too much personal attention to the patient in an environment that invited more involvement with the patient, Jack Simms, than she wanted. With rare exceptions it is always wise for the health professional to refrain from visiting the patient in a social setting until absolutely certain that the patient's feelings and life situation are such that an injury to the patient's feelings and dignity will not result.

Another way to maintain constructive physical and emotional boundaries is to remind the patient of the real situation between them. A young man, for instance, should know that the health professional he adores is engaged to someone else. By discreetly sharing with the patient personal incidents from everyday life, you will be better able to maintain a "reality factor" in the relationship that will be helpful to both. It is the health professional's responsibility to give and receive pertinent personal information in such a way that workable limits are maintained in the relationship.

SUMMARY

This chapter promotes respectful interaction through your being aware of, reflecting upon, and willingly and intentionally acting within the constraints of the health professional and patient relationship. We have shown that the maintenance of professional boundaries is not achieved by employing a cold or impersonal approach. Indeed, such an approach may only increase a patient's conviction that he or she is not understood by you, the health professional. However, the line between behaviors and expectations in your personal and professional relationships can be stretched thin in some situations. Moreover, your physical attractions (and those of patients towards you), your emotional responses, and your personal experiences sometimes present themselves as challenges. You are faced with the opportunity to carefully structure the individual situation so that the dignity of both you and the patient is respected. The next chapter emphasizes situations in which the complementary and exciting challenge is one of creating a comfortable, appropriate closeness.

REFERENCES

1. Jessing B: Back to square one. In Haddad A, Brown K, editors: *The arduous touch: women's voices in health care,* West Lafayette, IN, 1999, Purdue University Press.
2. Combs G, Freedman J: Relationships, not boundaries, *Theor Med Bioeth* 23:203-217, 2002.
3. Swisher LL, Page CG: Professional development, competence, and expertise, In *Professionalism in physical therapy practice*, Philadelphia, 2005, Saunders.
4. American Medical Association: Section E-10: Opinions on the patient-physician relationship, *Current opinions of the Council on Ethical and Judicial Affairs*, Chicago, 2005, American Medical Association.
5. Equal Employment Opportunity Commission: EEOC-FS/E4: Facts about sexual Harassment: EEOC guidelines on sexual harassment 29 CFR 1604 11a. 93, January 1992: (website) http://eeoc.gov/types/sexual_harassment.html. Accessed Aug 7, 2006.
6. deMayo RA: Patient sexual behaviors and sexual harassment: a national survey of physical therapists, *Phys Ther* 77:739-744, 1997.

7. Kagle JD, Giebelhausen KB: Dual relationships and professional boundaries, *Soc Work* 39(2):213-220, 1994.

8. Nadelson C, Notman M: Boundaries in the doctor-patient relationship. *Theor Med Bioeth* 23:191-201, 2002.

9. Rich RA, Hecht MK: Staffing considerations. In Haddad A, editor: *High tech home care: a practical guide,* Rockville, 1987, Aspen.

10. Wachter RM and others: Attitudes of medical residents regarding intensive care patients with AIDS, *Arch Intern Med* 148:149-152, 1988.

11. Farber NJ, Novack DH, O'Brien MK: Love, boundaries and the patient-physician relationship, *Arch Intern Med* 157:2291-2294, 1997.

12. Davis C: *Patient-practitioner interaction: an experiential manual for developing the art of health care,* ed 3, Thorofare, NJ, 1998, Slack.

13. Cassel C, Purtilo R: Ethical and social issues in contemporary medicine, *Sci Am Med* ed. by D. Dale, WebMD, Inc: New York, Volume 1, 2005.

PROFESSIONAL CLOSENESS: RESPECT AT ITS BEST

The student will be able to:

- Describe the characteristics of professional closeness and why it is the optimal mode of respectful interaction between patient and health professional
- Discuss goodness in the form that it applies to the health professional's opportunity to contribute to the patient and society
- Identify the function of integrity in engendering the patient's confidence in the health professional
- Describe six guidelines for helping the health professional make good use of time spent with a patient
- List three types of "attention to detail" that convince patients of the health professional's respect for them as individuals
- Discuss health professionals' opportunity to foster professional closeness by their response to gifts from patients
- Identify five levels of intimacy and the appropriateness of each in a health professional and patient relationship characterized by professional closeness

It would be difficult for me to come up with a list of competencies I look for in a doctor, but I know when I have met one I will trust. Mark Kris, who heads the thoracic-oncology service at Memorial, was this kind of doctor. The first thing Mark did, after looking at my medical records and having me carefully retell the story of what had happened to me over the past few months, was to give me a thorough examination. This was the first physical I'd had since this drama began; everyone else had just looked at the x-rays and scans. After he finished, he asked me how I felt. It was the only time in these months that anyone had asked me that question. …

—A. Trillin[1]

This quote tells of one patient's brief relationship with a health professional that made an impression on her. Her reflection holds some clues you will recognize as professional closeness by the time you finish this chapter: she trusts him; she is convinced that she has his rapt attention and that he is applying his special skills to learn more about her; she seems to have no doubt about his respect for her as a unique individual or whose interests come first in this relationship. One might sum it up by saying that she has reason for high confidence that a good thing will come from this relationship and her participation in it. Not every encounter you have with patients will attain this level of refinement, but a committed and skilled health professional will always strive for it.

PARTICIPATING IN GOODNESS

Professional closeness is the optimal (and attainable) form of respectful interaction between a health professional and patient. It builds upon the type of relational bonds described in Chapter 10. It honors the boundaries explored in Chapter 11. But in reaching for professional closeness the health professional chooses to go beyond each of these bottom-line essentials of respectful conduct to express a robust faithfulness to high personal and professional ideals possible in the relationship. The goal is to be and act in ways that provide a substantive basis for the patient to have confidence in you (Figure 12-1).

Professional closeness shifts the attention from the must do's and must not do's to the joy of experiencing the goodness that your professional role allows you to share with others in the everyday practice of your profession. What is goodness? Everyone's experience of it will vary somewhat. We like this businessman's reflection on goodness after he had a reverse in his company's success and rebuilt the company on a values-based ethic similar to the ethic one finds in health professions writings. He found that

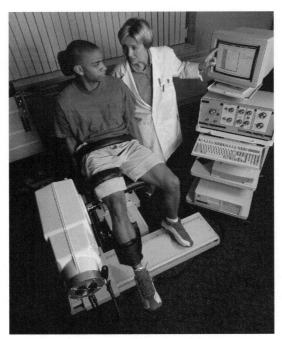

FIGURE 12-1: When the health professional works with the patient, it inspires confidence. (© Corbis.)

he and his employees were infused with a new passion for their work. They felt they were participating in something wonderful that went beyond the everyday routine of their particular tasks:

> Everyone has experienced a version of goodness, and you don't have to be pushed to the wall, like me, to find it: When you enjoy a work of art, thrill to a piece of music, feel that tingle in your spine when you read a passage in a novel … you have been touched by something outside of yourself. Remember when you fell in love? When things of this world grab you like this, in a way that we are inclined to think of as "deep," then you have been touched by goodness.[2]

Although we do not often think of being in love with our work or experiencing and sharing goodness through our daily conduct, there is the potential for that type of richness. Physical and emotional healthfulness is a cherished value in every culture. We participate in promoting that goodness as health professionals. Continuing to find work satisfaction year after year requires striving for the most value one can be in the role and the most value one can contribute and receive. Patients and families respond positively to that ideal in health professionals, making the former more willing to be participants in the process of their own healing and healthfulness. The next sections of this chapter provide you with insight into several commitments and practices you can employ to become a professional who encourages professional closeness in your relationship with patients and their families.

INTEGRITY IN WORDS AND CONDUCT

Integrity comes from the root *integritas,* meaning "wholeness." The cultivation of integrity is the commitment you make to yourself to temper your attitudes and conduct so that a patient can experience a high level of consistency between what you say and what you do. They can observe fittingness between their needs and your demeanor and actions, providing the evidence they need for them to confidently place their trust in you.[3] For example, you learned in Chapter 10 that patients look to you from the start for reassurance that the relationship is going to benefit them. But your attitudes and actions must be consistent with your reassuring words for professional closeness to develop. In the novel *I Never Promised You a Rose Garden,* the ward administrator tells Deborah, "It [the cold pack] doesn't hurt—don't worry." Those words sound like words meant to generate reassuring comfort and Deborah's willingness to cooperate with the health professional's plan. However, Deborah, who is undergoing treatments in a psychiatric hospital and is very frightened of what has already been done to her in the name of treatment, has exactly the opposite response. She thinks, "Watch out for those words … they are the same words. What comes after that is deceit."[4] Her situation illustrates that the words meant to be reassuring did not have the intended effect of engendering her confidence in the health professionals, because in the past, their conduct was not consistent with their words.

Integrity is not a character trait that only patients with long-term relationships with health professionals count on. Alice Trillin, the author of the quote at the beginning of this chapter was on high alert from the moment Dr. Kris began his examination. He won her confidence in a one-time interaction.

The patient's reliance on the professional's integrity also extends to his or her experience with teams. Teams were first designed to help coordinate care so that the patient could experience a kind of collective integrity across the system. However, today sometimes the patient's encounter with multiple members of a team breaks down confidence that there is "a plan" shared across units and among team members, and the patient experiences a fragmentation of services. The good news is that "[t]he culture of team care is a culture of interprofessional communication, with constant heads-ups and inquiries about what ought to be done with patients. In that sense, the culture of team care approximates the best that ethics seeks when it joins the team to help create the most humane and encompassing solutions(s) to the problems(s) at hand."[5] The potential for professional closeness is knitted into the fabric of teams, but in the end each individual on the team must strive to be sure that his or her own and the team's integrity is at work to help ensure that the patient's confidence is well placed.

INDIVIDUALIZING YOUR APPROACH

Professional closeness involves not only integrity but individualized care. Individualized care amounts to paying close attention to this unique person *and acting accordingly*. We do not know all the aspects of the exchange between Dr. Kris and the patient, Alice Trillin, but we do know she quickly became confident he was fully focused on *her* and not the last (or next) patient in his office waiting room (Figure 12-2). Many previous discussions in this book have provided information, insights, and examples of how you and the patient, each of you individuals bringing your hopes, expectations, and goals to the encounter, can negotiate the appropriate terms of the relationship. You have learned that any attitude, action, practice, or policy that allows the patient's well-being to take second place to some other end is a threat to the

FIGURE 12-2: The health professional who manipulates objects in everyday life is in danger of manipulating the patient in the same impersonal manner.

respect the patient deserves in this relationship and that your role is to protect that respect aggressively. In professional closeness, you take the opportunity to go beyond these basics, paying close attention to honor even the smallest detail to convey your awareness that this patient is unique from all others.

An often overlooked but extremely important expression of your respect is the way you handle a patient's scheduled time with you. Almost everyone struggles with effective time management, and health professionals are no exception. We elevate this issue to the level of suggesting that poor time management undermines patients' confidence that you care about them even if you know you do, thereby creating a barrier to professional closeness. At the same time, expending the energy to manage your work time signals that you are fine-tuning your caring behaviors. Several guidelines can help you:

Resist Cutting Corners

Your commitment never to cut corners in patient care unless it is absolutely necessary helps to keep you focused on fostering professional closeness. When you must take shortcuts, a patient is likely to maintain his or her confidence in you if you explain why you must give that person short shrift in this unfortunate circumstance.

Avoid Being a Slave to the Clock

A patient's confidence will remain high if he or she realizes you are committed to letting his or her situation guide your decisions rather than slavishly following the clock. It sometimes helps to remind the patient at the outset the amount of time you have to be with him and what you hope the two of you will accomplish in that time. Every health professional knows that on some days a particular patient needs some extra time to work through a problem, which can wreak havoc on a schedule. Then there are patients who for good (or poor) reasons are late or need to linger and make small talk, diverting your time and energy from other patients. Setting your time management against a backdrop of patient needs will help to mitigate the damage that necessarily occurs when no good solution can be found. Although some patients you have kept waiting will become impatient, your focused attention on doing all that you are able to do for them when their turn comes will create the conditions for professional closeness more readily than if you rigidly let the clock determine your day.

Make Time Serve You Well

Managing time with the goal of giving full attention to the patient can be aided by clues about how to act with the patient during the time you actually are together. Here are some hints:

1. Remove the person from areas where distractions are likely to impinge on your time together.
2. Sit down or in other ways convey your intent to give full attention to the person.
3. Refrain from calling attention to how busy you are. If there was an unavoidable delay in getting to the patient, explain why; if you cannot hide your distraction, explain that, too.

4. Approach the person slowly and graciously, even though you may have had to run to be on time for your appointment.
5. Look the person in the eye while conversing. A lack of direct eye contact communicates lack of interest.
6. Avoid looking at your watch. Place a clock at a place where you can be aware of the time without being obvious about it.
7. Protect the time that you have with the person. Let others know you are engaged and should not be disturbed. Turn off your cell phone or put it on vibration mode. The patient who is scheduled to spend 15 minutes alone with you but shares this time with 10 interruptions will feel more cheated than the one who enjoys 5 uninterrupted minutes.

Making time work to help maintain an attitude of respect and promote the conditions of professional closeness will be a challenge and perhaps an enigma for you, partly because of your curiosity and interest in so many wonderful things and partly because of the many external pressures competing for your energies.

LITTLE THINGS MEAN A LOT

An important way to enhance a patient's feeling of self-worth and confidence in the relationship, thereby enhancing the conditions conducive to professional closeness, is to acknowledge little personal details that too often go unnoticed. The poet William Blake noted, "He who would do good to others must do it in minute particulars." One of the authors recalls a student's journal entry just before graduation when he was reflecting on his own developing professionalism:

> I'd say one of the most surprising things I've learned about being with patients is that little things mean a lot! For instance, I have learned the importance of pouring a glass of water for a thirsty patient, listening to the 9th inning of a baseball game between parts of a treatment, laughing at something the patient says, wiping a nose. Perhaps these things sound silly to you.

On the contrary, this observant student was learning early in his now very successful career as a leader in his chosen field that "little things" count as expressions of deep respect for the patient as a unique individual worthy of the health professional's individualized attention. This attention is fertile soil upon which professional closeness can take root and grow. These little details take many shapes, but we remind you of a few common ones here:

Personal Hygiene

When a patient has a hygienic need, attention to it before any other activity or exchange will make him or her grateful. This is not to suggest that you need to wait on the patient with toothbrush, deodorant, and nail clippers in hand or that hygienic activity should in any way compromise time that should be spent utilizing professional skills. However, sometimes a simple act, such as providing a tissue when the patient needs one, makes the difference between an embarrassed and an attentive person.

Personal Comfort

A person sometimes experiences a certain amount of physical discomfort in a treatment, diagnostic, or testing situation. It is easy to forget how often we shift posture, scratch, blink, swipe, or shrug just to get comfortable; yet, there are conditions or techniques that prevent persons from performing these basic comfort functions. An extreme but instructive example is offered by Jean Dominique Bauby, the former editor of the magazine *Elle,* who suffered a brainstem injury that prevented him from any bodily movement whatsoever except to blink, but left intact all of his sensations. This severe condition is called *locked-in syndrome.* Mr. Bauby leaves an incredible memoir of his experience, achieved by blinking words with his left eye. Imagine his situation:

> This morning, with first light barely bathing Room 119, evil spirits descended on my world. For half an hour, the alarm on the machine that regulates my feeding tube has been beeping out into the void. I cannot imagine anything so inane or nerve-racking as this piercing beep beep beep pecking away at my brain. As a bonus, my sweat has unglued the tape that keeps my right eyelid closed and the stuck-together lashes are tickling my pupil unbearably. And to crown it all, the end of my urinary catheter has become detached and I am drenched. Awaiting rescue, I hum an old song by Henri Salvador: "Don't you fret, baby, it'll be all right."[7]

There are many ways a patient, even one with severe physical limitations such as Mr. Bauby, can be made more comfortable; they may involve straightening or cleaning the patient's glasses, wiping away sweat, supporting the person's arm while drawing blood, or running for an extra towel.

Many times patients are not asked simple questions such as whether the room temperature is OK, and if not, what can be done to make the person warmer (or cooler).

 REFLECTIONS

- Have you been stuck in a situation where you could not get comfortable?
- What did you have to do to get assistance in remedying the situation?

You can remember that situation as a starting point of your own imagination when you are with patients. Asking "Are you comfortable?" or "Is there anything else I can do for you while I am with you to make you more comfortable?" will always be appreciated.

Personal Interests

Almost everyone has some area of interest, whether it be a hobby, job, family, or other focus. Showing interest in the person does not require probing unduly into his or her personal life, something we warned against in Chapter 7. Some patients will want to chat about life outside of the moment, and others will not. At the same time, asking an inpatient about the noon menu, complementing an ambulatory care patient on something he or she is wearing, reminding a teenager that her favorite rap artist has a special show on TV that night, and spelling Mr. Schydlowski's name correctly on his appointment slip count as appreciated attempts to personalize care. Birthdays and holidays are important occasions to recognize a person (Figure 12-3). If you think that he would enjoy the attention, on Mr. Arnold's birthday, write "HAPPY BIRTHDAY, DICK ARNOLD" in bold letters on the schedule board or let other staff know so that they can acknowledge it, too. You will think of other expressions of this type of respect to put into everyday action.

Expanding Patients' Awareness

If you have been confined to a home, hospital, or other institution, you know how quickly one loses track of time and becomes out of touch with the rest of the world. By sharing an incident observed on the way to work, reviewing a play seen the evening before, or taking the patient to a window to see a child and dog playing together, you can extend the patient's environment beyond the immediate area, bringing him or her into contact with the outside world. One of the authors once brought apple blossoms into a four-bed room in an extended care facility only to have two of the residents burst into tears, saying they missed the smells of spring more than anything since being forced to make this their permanent home. This simple act opened the door to a discussion about springtime memories and moved the health professional into more of a position conducive to developing professional closeness.

None of the types of detail discussed above legitimately can be substituted for your provision of the technical professional services you are uniquely qualified to offer the patient. Alice Trillin's portrayal of her physician was deeply infused with evidence that the confidence she had in him grew in large part from the thoroughness with which he reviewed her past record, listened to her current assessment of her situation, and performed a physical examination. In the end, the health professional who is fostering a relationship of professional closeness remembers to do things a friend or attentive associate might think to do, but he or she never substitutes

FIGURE 12-3: A birthday is an important occasion to recognize a person.

personal detail for the one thing the patient can count on getting only from the professional because of his or her knowledge and skills. Your professional uniqueness provides an opportunity for the goodness of health to be realized or fostered through this special relationship.

RESPONDING TO GIFTS

Professional closeness creates the occasion for some patients to want to express gratitude to you. It is a sign that you have helped them to catch hold of the potential for their lives in the situation they find themselves in, and they feel confident in your ability to respond well to their wish to express their gratitude.

How you respond will help to support your relationship of professional closeness with a patient. It is not unusual for the professional to encourage and compliment the patient for his or her work toward the goals set. But sometimes the same professionals are unprepared for the patient's compliments or the offering of gifts. If the patient compliments you, accept the compliment graciously. Appropriate gifts also can also be accepted from patients or families with an expression of your genuine pleasure at their thoughtfulness. How does a professional know that the gift is appropriate?

The idea of "gratuities"—the accepting of gifts from patients or families—long has been discussed in professional ethics codes, oaths, and other thoughtful writings in the health professions because sometimes patients do want to express genuine gratitude for the help you have given them, but other times they are trying to curry favor with the health professionals. Looking first at the cautionary side, a general rule is to avoid accepting gifts the patient may be using as a means of trying to unduly ingratiate himself or herself.[8]

Refusing gifts can be taken by the patient or family as a sign of disrespect if in good faith they wanted to say a heartfelt "thank you." However, if you are concerned the gift will influence you to give disproportionate time or attention to the patient or in other ways to upset the finely tuned attitudes and behaviors that allow you to show equal respect to everyone, self-respect requires you to refuse it. The rule of proportionality—letting the gift be fitting for the occasion—is a general guideline to follow. If you feel uncomfortable with the size, nature, or timing of the gift, you should follow your instincts in graciously refusing it, always acknowledging to the giver that you appreciate the thought that went into it. One approach that may help is to suggest a small token of appreciation (e.g., a box of candy) that can be shared with your colleagues, thereby diffusing the more highly personal focus of the gift offered to you.

 REFLECTIONS

The following is a list of gifts that over the years the authors have been offered by patients and or their families. Which of the following do you think you would be able to accept without concern for its effect on your relationship with the patient or other patients?

- A bouquet
- Two tickets to a sold-out event the author and her husband wanted to attend, worth about $100 each

---

Continued

---

(9) REFLECTIONS—CONT'D

- Candy
- A gold Cross pen and pencil set
- A Christmas package containing a book
- An envelope with $5.00 tucked into it
- An envelope with $500 tucked into it
- Home cooked food/cookies
- A green jade ring set in gold
    What further questions do you want answered about the appropriateness of these gifts beyond the "message" they may portray due to their estimated monetary values?

In summary, by making a patient aware that you know their intent was to thank you, and then responding in a way that preserves your high ideals of professional acceptability, you have provided an environment that allows their confidence in you to flourish. The respect you show through these actions, when carried out in a spirit of genuine caring for the person, will support a relationship of professional closeness.

MISTAKES AND MAKING APOLOGY

In recent years, a significant literature in the health professions has emerged on the topic of the response of health professionals to a patient when a mistake related to the patient's care is made by individual professionals or due to a systems error in the health care institution. The number of deaths and serious injuries that occur in the United States each year alone is staggering. One major report estimated about 200,000 deaths per year.[9] Mistakes that have serious negative consequences for the patient are not a matter related to attaining professional closeness. Grave injury due to ignorance, negligence, or the willful imposition of harm fall below the bottom line of acceptable conduct and should be dealt with swiftly according to laws and policies governing the practice of health care. Patients or their families must be informed and appropriate restitution made. One current positive outcome of this increased visibility of this problem is a greatly enhanced focus on the necessity of and strategies for preventing grievous mistakes.[10]

The part of the larger discussion on mistakes that does warrant your thoughtful reflection in regard to professional closeness are accidents that do not cause serious direct physical harm to the patient but nonetheless are the result of carelessness or ignorance by an individual professional or a defect in the checks and balances of the institution. Examples are the administration of a wrong medication or wrong dose of a medication but in a situation where there are no obvious untoward results to the patient, or performance of a benign evaluation procedure intended for another patient. Accidents with minor or temporary harm due to failure of appropriate safety measures, for example, could also be included. In one way or another the patient was put at risk, inconvenienced, and made to participate in ways not designed to benefit him or her.

It is a good time to remind you that the value of professional closeness is that both health professional and patient are able to freely participate in working toward the type of goodness called *healthfulness*. But the health professional's knowledge of a mistake creates a breach in the bond of trustworthiness upon which the patient's confidence rests, not known to the patient even if it has been observed and reported by others. Can this glitch go unacknowledged to the patient?

There are rare times when to disclose this type of information to a patient and family may have such dire negative consequences for that patient's well-being that respect for the patient requires remaining silent, giving up all hope of reaching professional closeness in this relationship. There are two reasons nondisclosure must be reserved for only the rare situation:

First, the patient has a right to know and to engage the health professional or others in discussion about why such an occurrence took place. Any resulting loss of confidence in the health professional, short-lived or long-term, is the patient's prerogative. Your acknowledgement of the mistake is a first step that gives the patient an opportunity to begin not only to restore trust but also to rebuild his or her confidence in you on the way to (or way back to) professional closeness. Your honesty about the matter is the essential rock-solid foundation of truthful facts required for the patient and you to take that first step.

Secondly, the health professional's lack of attention to this type of breach has a deleterious personal effect. In a word, your integrity is at stake. You can hide the information from the patient but not from yourself. The courage to acknowledge the mistake in a profession that rewards your competence, accuracy of judgment, and the ideal of care is extremely painful for most. Bad news of any kind is difficult to share with a patient who is counting on you to help, and the humility required to own up to a mistake adds to the burden of the task. But without taking that step, you can't get back to integrity as a standard bearer of your professional identity.

Once disclosure (i.e., "I made a mistake.") is made, saying "I'm sorry" or in other ways apologizing for the action also is necessary. This person-to-person exchange puts you on even ground where the two of you have an opportunity to focus together on your relationship.[11] The next steps will depend a lot on what the nature of the mistake was and the consequences for the patient. Sometimes you or your institution may make financial restitution for the harm the patient perceives was done. At other times the patient is comforted to know that your mistake will lead you or your institution to take steps to try to prevent such occurrences in the future. In the end, you have done the work necessary to provide an opportunity for professional closeness with this patient to build or be restored.

INTIMACY CONSIDERED

Also at the core of professional closeness is the challenge of finding a comfortable level of intimacy with an individual patient, testing it against your understanding of the appropriate focus and goals of this type of relationship and honoring practical boundaries that should be maintained. Several years ago the authors found a capsule summary of intimacy levels to the extent that intimacy is expressed through conversation. These levels still seem relevant and helpful for your consideration in this matter:[12]

1. *Level 5:* Cliché Conversation: This is polite but almost impersonal conversation. The stranger who responds to your casual "How are you?" with a detailed description

of how he or she really feels is frowned on or, more likely, left to talk to himself or herself. This level of "niceties" is not intended to be an invitation to further involvement.

2. *Level 4:* Reporting Facts: Although this goes beyond cliché politeness, almost nothing personal is revealed. Only general information about subjects such as baseball scores, fashion, or a book is invited or offered.

3. *Level 3:* Personal Ideas and Judgment: People venture to give some information about themselves. You might find yourself in this type of conversation with someone sitting on the plane next to you or while you are in a long queue waiting to purchase tickets. There is an invitation to more engagement with the person but not involvement at a deeper level of personal investment.

4. *Level 2:* Feelings and Emotions: Only people who basically trust each other can be expected to engage at a level of feelings and emotions. Sharing at this level takes place between, say, friends, or among people who work together. The speaker wants to be understood, and the content of the conversation invites a response from the listener.

5. *Level 1:* Peak Communication: Profound mutual trust and honesty are shared at this, the deepest level. There is an expectation that the listener will share at an equally intimate level and that the conversation is only one means to deeper personal involvement in the ongoing lives of each other. Not many human interactions take place at this intense level. Old friends, lovers, family members, and the occasional other person are the major parties to this type of involvement.

These five levels of intimacy in conversation are valuable touchstones because they suggest accompanying behaviors and emotions appropriate to different types of situations.

⊚ REFLECTIONS

- What levels do you think are appropriate in the health professional and patient relationship? What levels are never appropriate? Why?
- Try to give an example of each level from your personal experience.

We believe that the health professional and patient relationship will include conversation at levels 5, 4, and 3 as means of getting started and learning some important things about the patient's history and current condition. Obviously your involvement goes deeper. The deepest intimacy at level 1 communication goes beyond the scope of the professional and patient relationship. The trust that appears at level 2 can support the patient's confidence in sharing happiness, sadness, and other emotions when the patient's or family's situation merits such response.

Some health professionals are uncomfortable with expressions of a patient's or family's emotional distress. In previous chapters you learned a wide range of fears and other worries that patients and their families may bring to their relationship with you. Without saying a word, you easily can prevent a patient from expressing his or her emotional distress; a "don't-tell-me" smile, an "I'm-too-busy" shrug, a "you're-above-that-kind-of-thing" wink, or a pleading "I-won't-know-what-to-do-if-you-cry" look will deter the most distressed patient or family member, but this response does not foster the patient's confidence and compromises the goal of professional closeness.

Knowing that your opportunity to develop professional closeness includes being prepared to respond to emotional distress, several guidelines may assist you for such incidents:

- Identify that the patient or family member has an emotional or feeling-level problem. This is not always easy to do because he or she, often afraid and embarrassed, may have clever means of disguising true emotions. What does he or she really feel? Is it anger, hurt, or fear?
- Verbalize to the person the emotion he or she appears to be expressing by saying the following: "Mr. Lee, you seem sad today," or "Mrs. Cerosi, I think you must be angry about something. Am I right?" The patient may readily admit to the emotion. If your guess is wrong, the patient may blurt out what he or she is really feeling.
- Try to help the person find a means of expressing emotional distress that is acceptable for the situation and, if necessary, refer him or her to a professional who can help to address the emotional suffering associated with the situation.

In short, each member of the relationship will seek a comfort level of intimacy for the encounter. Using your insights into the nature of the health professional and patient relationship will be one guide that helps all involved. Your goal of maintaining the relationship at a level that will allow all members to feel confident in their shared tasks is another. Your thoughtful response to the intimacy issue helps to assure the patient that he or she is fully respected as a human being. Under these conditions professional closeness is more likely to develop.

Summary

Professional closeness puts you in touch with the larger goodness that you are a part of when you optimize the potential of the health professional and patient relationship. This chapter highlights conditions under which the patient's confidence is high that partnering with you will help achieve his or her health-related goals. Your integrity and willingness to individualize care through sensitive attention to detail are essential components. Your willingness to deal graciously with gifts and to apologize for mistakes humanizes the relationship further. Your gentle guidance in regard to the appropriate depth and form of intimacy in this type of relationship exemplifies your motivation to keep the parameters and goals of the relationship on a clear course.

References

1. Trillin A: Personal history: betting your life. *The New Yorker* January 29, 2001.
2. Chappell T: *Managing upside down,* New York, 1999, William Morrow.
3. Beauchamp H, Childress J: *Principles of biomedical ethics,* ed 5, New York, 2001, Oxford University Press.
4. Greene H: *I never promised you a rose garden,* New York, 1964, Holt, Rinehart & Winston.
5. Burck R, Lapidos S: Ethics and cultures of care. In Mezey M and others, editors: *Ethical patient care: a casebook for geriatric health care teams,* Baltimore, 2002, Johns Hopkins University Press.
6. Eisenberg L: Good technical outcome, poor service experience: a verdict on contemporary medical care? *JAMA* 285:2639-2641, 2001.

7. Bauby JD: *The diving bell and the butterfly*, New York, 1997, Alfred A. Knopf (Translated by J Lagatt).

8. Purtilo R: *Ethical dimensions in the health professions*, ed 4, Philadelphia, 2005, WB Saunders.

9. Kohn KT, Corrigan JM, Donaldson MS: *To err is human: building a safer health system*, Washington, DC, 1999, National Academy Press.

10. Institute of Medicine: *Crossing the quality chasm*, Washington, DC, 2001, National Academy Press.

11. Purtilo R: Special editorial: beyond disclosure, seeking forgiveness, *Phys Ther* 85(13): 1124-1126, 2005.

12. Powell JS: *Why am I afraid to tell you who I am?* Chicago, 1969, Argus Communications.

PART FIVE

Questions for Thought and Discussion

1. Mr. Zorowsky has been treated for several weeks by Ms. Montgomery, a young intern at the local ambulatory care clinic. On her birthday, he slips her an envelope as he goes out the door. When she opens it, she finds a birthday card and a check for $50.
   a. What questions would you have to answer to interpret the significance of this gift?
   b. What problems may arise in the patient and health professional relationship if she returns the money?
   c. What problems may arise if she keeps the money?
   d. How, if at all, would your thinking change about this situation if the check had been for $25,000?
2. Name three virtues you think are the most important for ensuring respectful interaction between a health professional and patient. Why do you choose these as more important than others?
3. M.K. is a patient you initially found very enjoyable to be around. However, recently this patient has been taking every opportunity to touch you. Today it was a pat on your buttocks. You are starting to feel extremely uncomfortable around M.K. What steps should you take to bring this unacceptable behavior to a halt?
4. You have become friends with another health professional who works with you. Your friend tells you that she is thinking of going on a date with a patient who was just discharged a week ago. You both were part of his treatment team. She asks you, "Do you think there is any reason I shouldn't go? I really like him. Actually, he asked me out before he was even discharged. I told him we should wait." As a friend and a professional, how would you respond to her question?

PART SIX

RESPECTFUL INTERACTION: WORKING WITH PATIENTS EFFECTIVELY

Having studied the basic foundational pieces of respectful interaction, you now have an opportunity to apply your learning to several types of patients you will see in the course of your professional career. We have chosen to address them by age group, over the lifespan, being mindful that individual differences often outweigh the similarities we are emphasizing in these different age cohorts.

Part Six begins with Chapter 13, highlighting the challenges and joys of working with newborns, infants, and toddlers. Understandably, the family is a key element of consideration for these age groups. Chapter 14 moves the focus of your attention to school-age children and adolescents.

In Chapter 15 we discuss your interaction with people who become patients during young adulthood and the "middle years." Only in recent times have these life periods been given more than a cursory glance, and we share some of the insights that researchers and others are finding.

Chapter 16 examines key issues related to working with the older population. Of all age groups this one is increasing more in diversity and size worldwide than any other group. No matter what your chosen field, you will have occasion to work with persons who have lived a long time.

Throughout the lifespan, the person who becomes a patient is faced with many of the challenges we have been discussing so far. You have a substantial role in respectfully helping them to meet those challenges.

RESPECTFUL INTERACTION: WORKING WITH NEWBORNS, INFANTS, AND TODDLERS

CHAPTER OBJECTIVES

The student will be able to:

- Discuss how families serve as bridges to respectful interaction with newborns, infants, and toddlers
- Identify five realms of family health that can lend insight into family and patient dynamics
- Make several suggestions that will help support healthy functioning of the family during a child's illness
- Distinguish some basic developmental differences that need to be considered in one's approach to newborns, infants, and toddlers
- Discuss in general terms Erikson's sequential view of the psychological development of infants and toddlers
- List some everyday needs of the infant that may help explain an infant's response to the health professional
- Describe the steps showing how consistency of approach usually builds trust in an interaction with infant patients
- Describe five types of play, and show how each can facilitate respectful interaction with a pediatric patient
- Describe how the toddler's developing need for autonomy enters into the health professional and patient relationship

I mean, this is not, you know, a piece of machinery that...we want to make work. It's, it's a child and he, you've got all those dynamics of mom and dad, and grandma, and brothers and sisters. And, and you know, all of those things need to be, are, are just as important, just as important as whether that kid is breathing or not. ...Part of the recovery of the child depends on, and their future depends on, dealing with these issues too. Because of the attachment that the family has for that child.[1]

All health professionals will interact with newborn, infant, and toddler patients at some time, although most health professionals do not work solely or even primarily with these groups. These patients must be treated with the respect they deserve as unique individuals like everyone else. Furthermore, the opportunity they are given to experience human dignity and support in their time of illness, injury, or other adversity can become a resource to help them manage future difficulties.

Most of us take for granted that a newborn will live into his or her 7th or 8th decade of life. This has not always been so and is presently not so in many developing countries. At the start of the 20th century in the United States, more than half of reported deaths involved persons 14 years of age or younger. Today, the average infant mortality rate is 6.8 infant deaths per 1,000 live births.[2] However, the decline in infant mortality rate overall is not shared equally by all groups. Mortality is still higher for infants and children in poor families with poor living conditions. The mortality rate for black infants is more than twice that for white infants. Better opportunities for good initial health care and overall longevity in white groups point to deep, internal health disparities, the consequences of which must be reckoned with.[2] Demographic observations such as these suggest the types of health problems you will most commonly encounter in very young patients. Both health professionals and patients will benefit from your skillful and knowledgeable approach to patients in young age groups.

This is the first of several chapters that will examine your interaction with patients across the lifespan. It begins with the family as a focus of care and then moves to working with new parents and newborns, infants, and toddlers. The section on growth and development includes information that applies across childhood and adolescence as well, although working with each age group has its own challenges. Provided here is a wide range of relevant topics concerning interaction with young patients that should provide a basis for more in-depth exploration in your other coursework during your professional education.

HUMAN DEVELOPMENT AND FAMILY

In the past in mainstream health care in the United States, treatment focused exclusively on the patient as a solitary individual. It was not commonplace to attend to families as the focus of care. Today we see how important it is to care for patients, especially children, in the context of their families: the family is implicitly and explicitly recognized as a critical social unit surrounding and influencing its members and, in turn, being influenced by its members. We will begin by discussing the evolving concept of "family" in contemporary society. If you are to work with families as collaborators in maintaining the health of children and in the care of ill, injured, or disabled family members, then you must understand how families define themselves, how they function, and how best to interact with them.

Family: An Evolving Concept

The term "family" has been defined in a variety of ways. How would you define family? It is safe to say that your notion of what constitutes a family is influenced by your values, culture, and professional perspective. For example, a sociologist may define a family in terms of its socioeconomic status, or a psychologist may focus on the interpersonal dynamics of individuals who claim family ties. The most common type of familial bond is through spousal and blood relationships. However, none of these definitions is sufficient to describe the types of relationships and arrangements that make up the modern family. Current statistics suggest that family size and the number of two-parent families is decreasing while the number of single-parent families is increasing. Only 13% of all U.S. households consist of married couples with children in which the husband is the sole wage earner. Dual-career couples with no children represent 25% of the population, and families with two wage earners and children represent 31%.[3] Families may include several generations of blood kin, a mix of stepparents and children, or a combination of friends who share in household responsibilities and childrearing. One area of growth in family units is same-gendered parents with adopted children. Society is being forced by scientific and social advances to redefine what is meant by "family."

Thus, an inclusive definition of family is warranted, one that allows the members of a family to define themselves as a family unit and acknowledges the variety of cultural styles, values, and alternative structures that are part of contemporary family life. In fact, families define a unique culture; that is, a unique behavioral complex that is socially created, readily transmitted to family members, and potentially maintained through generations.[4]

To work with families, you also must understand how families function. There are numerous family theories describing how families operate, and how they respond to events both internal and external. Most health professionals use a combination of family theories in their work with children and their families, but all have in common the fact that the focus of health care shifts from the individual member who is ill, injured, or disabled to the family as a unit of care. We will focus on a particular method of viewing the family—the family health system approach.[5] According to this approach, care is directed toward five processes: (1) interactive, (2) developmental, (3) coping, (4) integrity, and (5) health. The story of Ian will help you by showing how the family health system model applies to a particular child and his family.

> Ian was a low-birth-weight infant with short bowel syndrome. Short bowel syndrome is characterized by maldigestion, malabsorption, dehydration, electrolyte abnormalities, and both macronutrient and micronutrient deficiencies. Owing to new medical and surgical treatments, the survival rate is 73%.[6] Ian will require long-term *parenteral nutrition*; that is, he will not be able to take food orally and will be dependent on parenteral nutrition (PN) to provide the bulk of his nutritional needs. Ian is the first child of Dylan and Adrianna Chapel, both in their early twenties. After a stay in the neonatal intensive care unit, Ian was sent home with his parents, who have provided care since that time with the help of a home care agency and a nutritional support company. The Chapels do not have other family members nearby. The majority of Ian's care falls to them.
>
> Ian is now an active 2-year-old. Mrs. Chapel is the primary caregiver during the day and most evenings. Mr. Chapel works as a paralegal in a law firm and attends law school at night. The Chapel's insurance coverage is through a group plan at the law firm where Mr. Chapel works.

Assume you are assigned to work with the Chapel family during an on-site educational experience with the home care agency providing primary care. The goal of your interaction with Ian and his family is to help promote family adaptation to his chronic condition (short bowel syndrome) and to empower the Chapels to develop and maintain healthy lifestyles. By reviewing the five processes listed earlier, you can get a picture of the family's functioning and possible areas for intervention.

The Interactive Process

The *interactive* process of the family is composed of communication, family relationship, and social supports.[5] In your assessment of the interactive process of the Chapel family, you will explore the types of communication patterns they use; the effect of Ian's illness on the communication of the family both internally and externally; the types of relationships within the family; and the quality, timing, amount, and nature of social support they receive. Open communication should be encouraged. One aspect of care could be to assist the Chapels in mobilizing the informational and emotional support they need to cope with Ian's illness. Because the Chapels do not have family support in the immediate community, they may have to rely on informal support systems, such as friends and co-workers, and formal support systems, such as respite care agencies, to assist them in the care of their child. Perhaps there are other children who have short bowel syndrome or who have to rely on parenteral nutrition in the community. The caregivers of such children may have or could form a support group to help troubleshoot common problems and offer advice.

The Developmental Process

Assessment of the *developmental* process includes the family developmental stage and individual developmental stages. The Chapels, as a family, are in the second stage of family development as described by Duvall in his classic work.[7] Stage II of the family life cycle involves integrating an infant into the family unit, accommodating to new parenting roles, and maintaining the marital bond. Ian is moving from infancy to becoming a toddler, and soon he will be interested in his environment and want to explore it. Ian will become increasingly mobile and develop language during this stage. (You will be introduced to basic development needs of toddlers later in this chapter.) All of this is influenced by the presence of his chronic condition. Therefore, it would be appropriate for you to assess how well these developmental tasks are being achieved. You could instruct the Chapels about the developmental milestones Ian should achieve and the tasks involved. For example, Ian needs freedom of mobility to learn to walk, so his nutritional solution could be placed in a backpack to allow him to move freely. Children with short bowel syndrome may also require frequent visits to the bathroom throughout the day when the time comes for toilet training. To decrease the Chapels' frustrations, you could plan ahead for this next developmental milestone and work with them to plan a structured routine that is consistently implemented and results in success for all involved, especially the child.

There is some evidence that about 10% to 15% of children with short bowel syndrome will experience neurological or developmental delays.[8] Thus, you will also want to watch for possible developmental delays to plan for early therapeutic interventions.

The Coping Process

Coping has been identified as problem-solving, adaptation to stress and crisis, and management of resources.[5] In your work with the Chapels, you should assess their ability to handle stress and the impact that Ian's illness has on everyday activities.

 REFLECTIONS

Which of these questions would most help you show respect for the Chapels' predicament?
- Has Ian's illness caused a change in the family's life plans? For example, did Mrs. Chapel plan on returning to work outside the home after the birth of her son?
- If so, can the family adapt to the loss of income or are support services available to allow Ian to be cared for during the day so that Mrs. Chapel can work?
- Were the Chapels intending to have several children? Have Ian's care needs changed this?
What else do you want to know in order to care for the Chapel family?

Overall, you would want to assess how the family deals with crises in general.

You can support the Chapels' coping processes by offering advice on the progression of the illness, discussing the normal feelings of frustration and guilt that accompany the care of a chronically ill or disabled family member, and offering resources to help the family cope more effectively, such as respite care and other support groups. Can you think of others?

The Chapels will also have to cope with financial difficulties. Even with the best health insurance, there are lifetime limits on coverage; in addition, there are many out-of-pocket expenses related to the care of a child with this diagnosis. Although most children experience small bowel adaptation over time and can be weaned from parenteral nutrition, most children require numerous surgeries, including an intestinal transplantation.[9] Thus, the Chapels may be facing years of out-of-pocket expenses and expensive hospital stays, procedures, and medications. This kind of financial pressure can be very stressful for any family.

The Integrity Process

This process of family life involves family values, rituals, history, and identity.[5] These aspects of the family process greatly affect its behavior. Family rituals, one facet of the *integrity* process, provide a useful framework for assessing threats to a family's integrity. Family rituals include celebrations and traditions such as activities surrounding birthdays, religious holidays, or bedtime routines for children (Figure 13-1). Suggestions for evaluating family rituals include assessment of the following[10]:

▶ Does the family underutilize rituals? Families who do not celebrate or mark family changes such as birthdays, deaths, anniversaries, and so forth may be left without some of the benefits that accompany rituals such as bringing the family together or marking changes in life and family roles.

FIGURE 13-1: The process of family life involves family values, rituals, history, and identity. (© *Getty Images/84116*)

▶ Does the family follow rigid patterns of ritual? In families who are inflexible, things are always done the same way, at the same time, and with the same people. Families who are rigid do not respond well to necessary changes that disrupt routines and rituals occasioned by illness and injury.

▶ Are family rituals skewed? A family with skewed rituals tends to emphasize only one aspect of family life (e.g., religion) and ignore others. For example, a family might spend all of its time celebrating with the father's side of the family on religious holidays and ignore the different rituals cherished by the patterns practiced on the mother's side.

▶ Has the ritual process been interrupted? For example, the birth of a disabled or chronically ill child may threaten family identity and permanently disrupt family rituals. In the case of the Chapels, they have elected to stay home for traditional family holidays because almost all holidays involve a focus on food. For the foreseeable future, Ian cannot tolerate most food orally, so the Chapels will have to consider what this interruption in ritual means to their life together and may have to develop other rituals at holiday time that do not focus so prominently on food.

▶ Are the rituals hollow? Rituals that are performed just for the sake of performing them have lost their life and may be stressful for the family rather than a source of joy and strength.

In addition to changes in ritual that occur over time in families, many role changes also occur, particularly when chronic illness or impairment is involved. For example, Mrs. Chapel has become the primary caregiver. She may or may not have expected to take on this role. Essential interventions include helping the Chapels redefine major family roles and maintain their new responsibilities.

The Health Process

The final process of family experience is related to *health*. This process includes health status, health beliefs and practices, and lifestyle practices.[5] You would want to assess the family's definition of health and how they define the health of the individual members.

 REFLECTIONS

- Besides the responsibilities involved in caring for a child who requires parenteral feedings, what do the Chapels do to maintain their own health?
- How do the Chapels deal with health problems? To whom do they turn?

Interventions in the area of health process include education, encouragement, and counseling regarding the short- and long-term aspects of Ian's care. In summary, the situation of Ian and his parents illustrates the family health system as one useful approach to the care of families and children. The family health system applies to all families, whatever the composition and stage of familial development. You are encouraged to explore other models of working with a family and their effectiveness in achieving optimal family health. Regardless of the model you choose, it is clear that family relationships are an important consideration in understanding the conduct of any patient and for developing an effective mode for respectful interaction with that patient. Care can best be accomplished if it is considered a collaborative venture between the family and the health care team. The components of family-centered care in Box 13-1 provide a context for recognizing the family's central role.

Legally, the parents or another formally appointed guardian are the voice of the young child, except in rare instances in which the state intervenes to protect the child from caregivers who the state judges are not acting in the child's best interest. The most grievous situation results when there is growing suspicion or knowledge that the patient is a victim of child abuse or neglect. In the case of a dysfunctional family in which abuse is suspected, however much you may empathize with the family's suffering, you must turn your attention to the protection of the victimized child. The Child Abuse Prevention and Treatment Act (CAPTA), originally passed in 1974, has been amended several times. The most recent amendment and reauthorization is the Keeping Children and Families Safe Act of 2003 (Public Law 108-36). CAPTA mandates reporting child abuse and neglect in all 50 states and provides support for community-based grants to prevent child abuse and neglect.[11] A good general rule

---

BOX 13-1

COMPONENTS OF FAMILY-CENTERED CARE

1. **The family unit is the focus of attention.**
   Family-centered practice works with the family as a collective unit, insuring the safety and well-being of family members.
2. **Strengthening the capacity of families to function effectively is emphasized.**
   The primary purpose of family-centered practice is to strengthen the family's potential for carrying out their responsibilities.
3. **Families are engaged in designing all aspects of the policies, services, and program evaluation.**
   Family-centered practitioners partner with families to use their expert knowledge through-out the decision- and goal-making processes and provide individualized, culturally responsive, and relevant services for each family.
4. **Families are linked with more comprehensive, diverse, and community-based networks of supports and services.**
   Family-centered interventions assist in mobilizing resources to maximize communication, shared planning, and collaboration among the several community and/or neighborhood systems that are directly involved in the family.

From National Resource Center for Family-Centered Practice and Permanency Planning, www.hunter.cuny.edu/socwork.

---

is to be suspicious of maltreatment when reports of the history of the child's injuries do not coincide with physical findings. Furthermore, you must become acquainted with appropriate reporting procedures for persons in your chosen profession. The procedures vary from state to state. Parents and others caregivers who maltreat children are deeply troubled. Your support of policies and practices that address maltreatment of children as a family affair is a valuable contribution to society.

In summary, in spite of the occasional problematic family situation, the family is usually a sound and reliable bridge to building better understanding of the needs of infants, toddlers, and young children. We now direct your attention to the growth and development of the child, another important factor in working with pediatric patients.

Useful General Principles of Human Growth and Development

Development occurs in numerous ways—physical, emotional, and intellectual—and all aspects of development affect one another. Although professionals often talk about growth and development simultaneously, growth can be thought of as quantitative, and development can be thought of as qualitative. We will address growth first. Human growth proceeds in accordance with general principles of (1) orderliness, (2) discontinuity, (3) differentiation, (4) cephalocaudal, and (5) proximodistal and bilateral. Each is instrumental in helping you understand what occurs in the growth process, when, and why.

Orderliness

Growth and changes in behavior usually occur in an orderly fashion and in the same sequence. Thus, all fetuses can turn their heads before they can extend their hands.

Almost every child sits before he or she stands, stands before walking, and draws a circle before drawing a square. Most babies babble before talking and pronounce certain sounds before others. Likewise, certain cognitive abilities precede the next. Children can categorize objects or put them into a series before they can think logically.

Discontinuity

Although growth is orderly, it is not always smooth and gradual. There are periods of very rapid growth—growth spurts—and increases in psychological abilities. Parents sometimes speak of the summer that a child grew 2 inches. Many adolescents experience a sudden growth spurt after years of being the ones with the smallest stature in their class.

Differentiation

Development proceeds from simple to complex and from general to specific. An example of differentiation in the infant is seen in an infant's ability to wave his or her arms first and later develop purposeful use of his or her fingers. Motor responses are diffuse and undifferentiated at birth and become more specific and controlled as the child grows. Beginning motor activity in the toddler involves haphazard and unsystematic actions, progressing to goal-directed actions and specific outcomes.[12]

Cephalocaudal

Cephalocaudal development means that the upper end of the organism develops sooner than the lower end. Increases in neuromuscular size and maturation of function begin in the head and proceed to the hands and feet. After birth, an infant will be able to hold its head erect before being able to sit or walk.

Proximodistal and Bilateral

Proximodistal development means that growth progresses from the central axis of the body toward the periphery or extremities. Thus, the central nervous system develops before the peripheral nervous system. *Bilateral development* means that the capacity for growth and development of the child is symmetrical—growth that occurs on one side of the body occurs on the other side of the body simultaneously. These principles apply throughout the lifespan, from infancy to old age.

Theories of Human Development to Guide You

Development can be discussed from a cognitive, identity, sexual, or psychosocial basis. We focus primarily on cognitive development because it entails how a person perceives, thinks, and communicates thoughts and feelings. Some time is spent on psychosocial development because of the profound impact this has on the health professional's interactions with patients. Although this chapter focuses on the cognitive and psychosocial development of the infant and toddler, the same theories are applicable to the school-age child and adolescent discussed in Chapter 14.

The manner in which a child learns to think, reason, and use language is vital to the child's overall growth and development.[13] Traditionally, health professionals have based their interventions with children on the stages of cognitive development described by Jean Piaget (1896-1980).[14] Piaget's theory is a logical, deductive explanation of how children think from infancy through adolescence. Piaget described the earliest stage of cognitive development as *sensorimotor*. At this stage, infants take in a great deal of information through their senses. Tactile and verbal stimulation and auditory and visual cues can have positive, long-range results. The early beginnings of cognitive development can be stimulated by talking to the infant and by face-to-face interactions.

Piaget labeled the cognitive abilities of toddlers as *preoperational*. Toddlers learn to think and understand by building each new experience upon previous experiences. Miller summarized Piaget's depiction of the cognitive stage of toddlers in terms of egocentrism (seeing the world from a "me-only" viewpoint), rigidity of thought ("Mom is always right"), and semilogical reasoning ("my dog died because I was a bad boy").[15] Children in this stage are confused about cause and effect, even when it is explained to them, and think in terms of magic (e.g., wishing something makes it so). However, more current researchers refute Piaget's beliefs and claim that he may have underestimated the cognitive abilities of toddlers. These researchers suggest that children have far more potential to understand complex illness concepts than they have previously been given credit for.[16] Thus, some toddlers may be capable of appreciating the perspective of another and adapting their behavior accordingly. Others propose that, rather than viewing the toddler as incapable of thinking a certain way, one should view him or her as a novice. Children have much less life experience than adults. Thus, when children gain experience through chronic illness, for example, or perform tasks involving their own expertise, they can demonstrate adultlike performance and more sophisticated thinking and reasoning.[17] The debate in the area of cognitive development is ongoing. For example, evolutionary developmental psychology, which takes into account genetic and ecological mechanisms that affect development as well as the effect of cultural contexts, has recently added voices in the discussion regarding variability in development.[18,19] The various ideas of developmental theorists are important to explore because they have direct implications for how best to work with young children.

As with cognitive development, there are numerous stage/phase theories about the psychological and social dynamics of child development. Development, seen this way, is a process or movement. "Movement from potentiality to actuality occurs over time and in the direction of growth and progress. It is not surprising, then, that most conceptualizations of development incorporate the notion of improvement— of 'better' more integrated ways of functioning."[20] Almost all stress the importance of bonding or forming attachments as the primary developmental task. No one has done more to promote this idea than Erik Erikson, a psychologist who, in the 1950s and 1960s, proposed eight stages of psychosocial development.[21]

According to his theory, the development of trust (shown in Chapter 10 to be fundamental to the effective patient and health professional relationship) is one of the tasks facing the child in all relationships. He or she is engaged in a process that will affect his or her ability to engage in respectful interaction with everyone. During infancy, the child is introduced to trust and begins to experience (or to not experience) its power.

The psychosocial development of the toddler involves acquiring a clearer sense of himself or herself that is separate from that of the primary caregiver, becoming involved in wider social relationships, gaining self control and mastery over motor and verbal skills, and developing independence and a self-concept. Later in this chapter, we spend time considering specific examples of how you can effectively interact with infants and toddlers by anticipating the developmental tasks specific to their age group. A caveat is warranted at this juncture about developmental stages. All stage models are just that—models—and it is difficult to place a child in a specific stage merely by chronological age. Stages are only a way to describe an ongoing process.

EARLY DEVELOPMENT: FROM NEWBORN TO INFANT

Between the first day of life and the first day of kindergarten, development proceeds at a lightning pace like no other. Consider just a few of the transformations that occur during this 5-year period:

- The newborn's avid interest in staring at other babies turns into the capacity for cooperation, empathy, and friendship.
- The 1-year-old's tentative first steps become the four-year-old's pirouettes and slam dunks.
- The completely unself-conscious baby becomes a preschooler who not only can describe herself in great detail but also whose behavior is partially motivated by how she wants others to view and judge her.
- The first adamant "no!" turns into the capacity for elaborate arguments about why the parent is wrong and the preschooler is right.
- The infant, who has no conception that his blanket came off because he kicked his feet, becomes the 4-year-old who can explain the elaborate (if messy) causal sequence by which he can turn flour, water, salt, and food coloring into play dough.

It is no surprise that the early childhood years are portrayed as formative. The supporting structures of virtually every system of the human organism, from the tiniest cell to the capacity for intimate relationships, are constructed during this age period.[22]

The Normal Newborn

The anticipation of the birth of a child is fraught with emotions ranging from joy to fear. In economically developed countries the birth process has largely moved from the home to the hospital. Many hospitals attempt to duplicate the comforts and familiarities of home by designing birthing suites complete with a DVD player and rocking chair. With the move to shorter lengths of stay for a normal delivery, it is unlikely that you will have much opportunity to work with these tiniest of patients unless you choose to work in labor and delivery or neonatology.

The normal newborn is highly vulnerable but also amazingly adaptable to the new environment outside the womb.

The newborn period ends at the first month of life. After that, newborns are called *infants*. Newborns have many needs, especially when health problems are present at birth. They also are human beings worthy of full respect. The field of neonatology, especially the intensive care of newborns, deserves consideration because it stretches our concept of what a "newborn" is.

Life-Threatening Circumstances

New technology is always changing the possibility for survival in the neonatal intensive care unit (NICU). Smaller and smaller neonates who have had shorter gestations in the womb are seen in NICUs. Many variables enter into survival for these tiny patients. Sometimes a neonate who weighs more than the fragile neonate in the next isolette is the one who does not survive. Each year tens of thousands of babies are born too early and too small and end up in a NICU. In each case, parents and physicians share a common goal—to make each baby healthy. New medical technologies are saving babies who until only recently would have died. Unfortunately, the costs can be staggering, and the result may be a baby whose future is limited by debilitating health conditions. With little or no preparation, parents are being asked to decide when the technology is doing more harm than good. It is interesting to note that in retrospect, many parents do not identify involvement in decision-making. In Pinch's longitudinal study of parents' experiences in the NICU, "Parents recalled that possibilities or alternatives were seldom offered to them. They were simply told what the professionals were required to do, what the baby needed, or what was suggested as the best treatment."[23] Thus, respectful interaction with parents and these fragile newborns requires that you take extra care to inform them about the progress and status of their children.

Moving into Infancy

When working with an infant, you will be in a position to make independent clinical judgments about his or her best interests and to observe the interaction between parents and their new baby. Happily, the parents almost always provide the primary supportive bridge between you and the infant patient, interpreting the baby's expressions, babbles, and postures and providing insight into how continuity of approach to the infant can be maximized. During this time, parents have to learn cues from their infants, and sometimes you can teach the parents as well as learn from the parents' comments and behavior.

The needs of infants sometimes are difficult to determine because these patients lack substantial verbal skills to express their wants and needs. (Even adults sometimes have great difficulty asking for what they need.) Professionals who rely on a patient's ability to ask for what he or she needs take a narrow view of needs assessment.

INFANT NEEDS: RESPECT AND CONSISTENCY

There are two contexts by which to view the infant's needs. The first focuses on the stage of psychosocial development that we have already discussed and the second on immediate concrete needs such as the need for a drink of water, food, pain relief, or a diaper change. You have an opportunity to demonstrate respect for the infant by responding effectively to each type of need. Remember that parents often have explicit ways of doing things for their infant that can help too. For example, parents may hold the infant in a certain way, play a favorite game such as pretending to sneeze or rubbing the baby's back that will, at a minimum, help calm the infant while you look for other reasons for the infant's distress.

A primary approach is characterized by the three "C's": *consistency* in approach, *constancy* of presence, and *continuity* of treatment. Consistency is especially important because it builds trust (infant self-confidence) through the following steps:

1. An infant's need exists.
2. The infant exhibits generalized behavior.
3. The caregiver responds.
4. The need is satisfied.
5. The need recurs.
6. The infant predicts the caregiver's response.
7. The infant repeats previous behavior.
8. The caregiver responds in a consistent manner.
9. The need is satisfied.
10. The infant's trust toward the caregiver develops.
11. The need recurs.
12. The infant is confident that the caregiver will respond appropriately.[24]

Of course, infants do have different temperaments, which will create differences in responses to you, the health professional. These individual differences are welcomed by health professionals because they support the belief that humans are unique, each deserving of unique respect.

Everyday Needs of Infants

By now you should have discovered in this book that the "solutions" to challenges during interaction with patients sometimes are concrete and mundane and dictated by common sense. Fussy, irritable, crying infants are in the position of becoming the least liked (and probably least cared for) patients on the pediatrics unit. Crying is one way infants try to communicate distress. More likely than not, because of the infant's age and stage of development, this distress is related to a concrete, immediate need. Respectful interaction with infants in distress requires careful attention to several types of detail.

Comfort Detail

Small children most often become irritable when they experience physical discomfort. Careful attention to comfort is key to their sense of well-being. This becomes all the more reason to check for factors that could lead to discomfort whenever possible. It is too easy to assume that a baby's crying or other belligerence is because he or she is a fussy or cranky baby. Examine the bed shirt, diaper, and crib sheets.

ⓢ REFLECTIONS

Which of these questions should the health professional ask?
- Is the bed shirt, diaper, or crib sheet wet from urine, sweat, or a spilled medication?
- Are they wrinkled and creating pressure spots?
- Does the baby have abrasions, punctures, or other bodily tenderness that cause contact pain? Is tape pinching the baby or has an intravenous line infiltrated?
- Check the ears, nostrils, and throat. Is something lodged in one of them?

Continued

REFLECTIONS—CONT'D

- Are the infant's throat and mouth dry? Check the medical record.
- What did the baby eat and when? Is he or she taking fluids?
- Is he or she hungry or thirsty, perhaps?
- Is he or she having some predictable side effect from a medication?
- What other comfort questions can you name?

Health Professional Detail

Discomfort can also be caused by what you are wearing or doing.

 REFLECTIONS

Think about the kind of clothing and adornments such as name tags that you wear in clinical practice.
- Is your uniform scratching the baby? Is the color or design too complex?
- Do you have on jewelry that scratches, scrapes, or pinches?
- Are your hands clammy and cold?

Your conduct is like a mirror to the young child. If you are anxious or uncomfortable with caring for an infant, the infant will sense it.

In addition to the immediate discomfort you may cause an infant by inattention to these details, a more persistent negative response could be a sign of deeper discomfort. A good general rule is to remain consistent, approaching the infant similarly in each interaction in hopes that the familiarity itself will be a comfort. Also, watch how the infant interacts with others, especially those who appear to be successful in calming him or her. Try altering your approach to match those that seem to help the infant.

Environmental Detail

Like all of us, infants have various comfort zones, which include temperature, space, and other environmental factors. Look about the room that you are currently occupying and imagine it is one that includes an ill infant.

 REFLECTIONS

- Is the room quite warm?
- Is the infant sweaty or clammy?
- Are there new noises in the area from nearby construction, an open window, or a newly placed monitor?
- Are there different smells in the air because of painting in the hallway or a new disinfectant used by the cleaning staff?
- Where is the crib placed? Try placing it in another position or placing the infant in a different position in the crib. Is he or she exposed to open spaces on both sides of the crib or is one side against the wall? Try alternatives to this arrangement.
- What else do you notice about the environment that could have an impact on an infant's well-being?

In short, you should be attentive to the behavior of the young patient and to the people who are associated with his or her care. Responsiveness to infant needs is generally best met during this developmental phase through predictable interaction. Infants, like all humans, are unique beings with various temperaments and their own histories and responses to environmental input. It is critical that you pay careful attention to detail when you assess a disturbed infant's needs.

EARLY DEVELOPMENT: THE TODDLER

Much of the material related to respectful interaction with the infant patient and his or her family can be applied to the child past the stage of infancy into other stages of childhood and adolescence. As a child grows, however, some new challenges confront both parents and health care providers. This is especially true of the toddler, a child in a difficult and challenging stage of development for all involved.

A review of Erikson's stages shows that the young patient's psychosocial tasks in moving from infancy to becoming a toddler and then an older child focus on becoming one's own "self," separate from others.

Respect for a toddler can be enhanced when the child actually asks for what he or she wants. Of course, sometimes the toddler will have difficulty making himself or herself understood and may be embarrassed by his or her own awkward attempts to act grown up. Especially important to the child is the need to succeed at "adult" tasks (which include anything new, from the early tasks of learning how to walk and to feed oneself, no matter how long it takes).

Play is an important vehicle through which a toddler patient's sense of worth can be fostered. According to developmental psychologists, play may be the child's richest opportunity for physical, cognitive, language, and emotional development. Freiberg states that there are several types of play, any of which can be encouraged as part of treatment or other aspects of interaction with the child. These include the following:

- *symbolic play*, used by children to make something stand for something else, such when the young patient "becomes" the more powerful health professional by wearing the health professional's clothes or stethoscope
- *onlooker play*, which involves watching others, such as when the health professional entertains the child or when the child observes others at play but does not participate
- *parallel play*, which is side-by-side play characterized by activity that is interactive only by virtue of another's presence (the participation by observation and side-by-side types of play may help to decrease a young patient's loneliness, even though he or she cannot fully interact with others) (Figure 13-2)
- *associative play*, which involves shared activity and communication
- *cooperative play*, in which rules are followed and goals are achieved (associative play and cooperative play are generally beyond the capabilities of the toddler)[25]

TODDLER NEEDS: RESPECT AND SECURITY

Attention to personal detail outlined in the section on infants applies to interaction with the toddler as well. Fortunately, in most cases toddlers can verbalize their basic needs ("Me hungry," "Me go?" "More," or "No") and express their curiosity by

FIGURE 13-2: Parallel play can be encouraged as part of treatment or other aspects of interaction with a child. (© *Corbis.*)

pointing to something and asking, "Dis?" Their illness, the intimidating surroundings, or their shyness, however, may make young children even more reticent than most patients to make their needs known in this direct manner. They often show their feelings of insecurity about what is happening to them by being cranky or acting overly fearful and demanding.

Children, like all patients, tend to regress when they become ill. Having so recently moved out of infancy, toddlers sometimes return to infantlike behavior. You need to be aware that this is a normal tendency and that you should not condemn young patients who do not "act their age." In the following story, a nurse tells of a toddler with Burkitt's lymphoma, a particularly fast-growing cancer, who was not doing well and was essentially silent:

> …I don't know how I knew this, but something said to me that he needed to be held right then. I asked him if he would like to rock in the rocking chair, and of course he didn't answer but he did not resist when I picked him up. We sat in that rocking chair

for an hour and a half, and I could feel him settling in. I had on this knit sweater with a print, and when he finally sat up I laughed and said, "Jason, you've got waffles on your face!" He said, "I know, I've got them on my knees too." That was the first time he spoke, and after that we couldn't shut him up.[26]

A combination of gentle support for age-appropriate behaviors and tender care, such as holding and rocking, can encourage the toddler to feel more secure.

SUMMARY

This chapter has presented an overview of a variety of theories that seek to explain how human beings develop biologically, psychologically, and socially over the lifespan. The progression from infancy to early childhood is shaped by the environment, the most important element of which is the family. As an infant becomes a toddler, he or she starts taking steps, literally and figuratively, toward a lifelong journey that is unique to each child. Recognizing the uniqueness of the child as an individual as well as the product of a developmental phase will help you to better understand the many dimensions in which respect can be conveyed, and the success of the your interactions will be maximized.

REFERENCES

1. Pinch WJE, Spielman ML: Ethics in the neonatal intensive care unit: parental perceptions at four years postdischarge, *Adv Nurs Sci* 19(1):72-85, 1996.
2. U.S. Department of Health and Human Services, Centers for Disease Control and Prevention: *Births, marriages, divorces, and deaths: provisional data for 2005,* 54(20):4, July 21, 2006. (website) http://www.cdc.gov/nchs/data/nvsr/nvsr54/nvsr54_20.pdf.
3. Rae SB: Whose child is this? Defining the mother in surrogate motherhood arrangements, *J Women's Health* 3(1):51-64, 1994.
4. Sparling JW: The cultural definition of family, *Phys Occup Ther Pediatr* 11(4):17-28, 1991.
5. Anderson KH: The family health system approach to family systems nursing, *J Fam Nurs* 6(2):103-119, 2000.
6. Quiros-Tejeira RE and others: Long-term parenteral nutritional support and intestinal adaptation in children with short bowel syndrome: a 25-year experience, *J Pediatr* 145(2): 157-63, 2004.
7. Duvall EM: *Family development,* ed 5, Philadelphia, 1977, Lippincott.
8. Beers SR and others: Cognitive deficits in school-age children with severe short bowel syndrome, *J Pediatr Surg* 35(6):860-865, 2000.
9. Neuhaus P, Pascher A: How successful is intestinal transplantation and what improves graft survival? *Nat Clin Pract Gastroenterol Hepatol* 2:306-7, 2005.
10. Imber-Black E, Roberts J, Whiting R: *Rituals in families and family therapy,* New York, 1988, Norton.
11. *Keeping children and families safe act of 2003, child abuse prevention and treatment amendment,* Public Law 108-36, 108th Cong., 2003.
12. Puskar KR, D'Antonio IJ: Tots and teens: similarities in behavior and interventions for pediatric and psychiatric nurses, *J Child Adolesc Psychiatr Ment Health Nurs* 6(2):18-28, 1993.
13. Mott S, James S, Sperhac A: *Nursing care of children and families,* ed 2, Reading, MA, 1990, Addison-Wesley.
14. Piaget J: *Six psychological studies,* New York, 1964, Vintage.
15. Miller SA: *Developmental research methods,* Englewood Cliffs, NJ, 1987, Prentice Hall.

16. Rushforth H: Practitioner review: communicating with hospitalized children: review and application of research pertaining to children's understanding of illness, *J Child Psychol Psychiatry* 40(5):683-691, 1999.

17. Yoos HL: Children's illness concepts: old and new paradigms, *Pediatr Nurs* 20(2):134-140, 145, 1994.

18. Geary DC, Bjorklund DF: Evolutionary developmental psychology, *Child Dev* 71(1):57-65, 2000.

19. Suizzo MA: The social-emotional and cultural contexts of cognitive development: neo-Piagetian perspectives, *Child Dev* 71(4):846-849, 2000.

20. Clark MC, Caffarella RS, editors: *An update on adult development theory: new ways of thinking about the life course: new directions for adult and continuing education,* San Francisco, 1999, Jossey-Bass.

21. Erikson EH: *Identity and the life cycle,* New York, 1959, WW Norton.

22. Shonkoff JP, Phillips DA, editors: *From neurons to neighborhoods: the science of early childhood development,* 2000, Washington, D.C., National Academy of Sciences Press.

23. Pinch WE: *When the bough breaks: parental perceptions of ethical decision-making in NICU,* Lanham, Md, 2002, University of America Press.

24. Schuster CS, Ashburn SS: *The process of human development,* Boston, 1986, Little Brown and Company.

25. Freiberg KL: *Human development, a life span approach,* ed 3, Boston, 1987, Jones and Bartlett.

26. Montgomery CL: *Healing through communication,* Newbury Park, CA, 1993, Sage.

CHAPTER

14

RESPECTFUL INTERACTION: WORKING WITH CHILDREN AND ADOLESCENTS

CHAPTER OBJECTIVES

The student will be able to:

- Distinguish some developmental challenges that need to be considered in one's approach to children beyond the toddler stage into adolescence
- Discuss in general terms the key developmental tasks of children and adolescents
- Describe how the five types of play introduced in Chapter 13 are relevant—or not relevant—to respectful interaction with older children
- Describe how a child's developing need for successful relatedness enters into the health professional and patient relationship
- Make several suggestions that will help minimize the disequilibrium of the family during a child's illness
- List some compelling reasons for giving respectful attention to an adolescent's desire to exercise authority in regard to health care decisions and describe legitimate limits on that authority
- Describe behaviors in adolescence that can lead to long-term health problems

When I was seven, my father who played the violin on Sundays with a nicely tortured flair which we considered artistic, led me by the hand down a long, unlit corridor in St. Luke's School basement, a sort of tunnel that ended in a room full of pianos. There, many little girls and a single sad boy were playing truly tortured scales and arpeggios in a mash of troubled sound. My father gave me over to Sister Olive Marie, who did look remarkably like an olive.

—P. Hampl[1]

Much of the material related to respectful interaction with the infant or toddler and his or her family can be applied to older children. As a child grows, however, some new challenges confront the child, parents, and health care providers. Therefore, in this chapter we add some dimensions to the groundwork we laid in Chapter 13 to highlight some of the most important differences as well as focus on the situation of adolescent patients.

THE CHILDHOOD SELF

A young child's psychosocial tasks in moving from infancy to childhood focus on the need to recognize that one has a "self," separate from others, but that ultimately many aspects of that self must survive and thrive in relationships with others. Therefore, much activity and energy are focused on being different from others at the same time that much is invested in learning how to be accepted by others and having some say in relationships. As we address later in this chapter, these tasks become paramount during the adolescent years, but the fundamental building blocks begin much earlier.

NEEDS: RESPECT AND RELATING

Writer Annie Dillard poetically describes the first part of the child's developmental task, that of becoming a "self" different from others. She recalls it this way in her autobiography, *An American Childhood:*

> I woke up in bits like all children, piecemeal over the years. I discovered myself and the world, and forgot them, and discovered them again. …I noticed this process of awaking and predicted with terrifying logic that one of these years not far away I would be awake continuously and never slip back and never be free of myself again.[2]

Children, in general, want to make it alone and have learned not to accept the full dependence of infancy and the toddler years, but yet are not really independent either. When they become patients, like most people, they regress. The dependence side of the scales tips heavy, and the good fit of selfhood that the child is slipping into suddenly escapes. In this confusing never-never land of being neither infant nor fully child nor adult, children must try to reestablish some sense of equanimity and self-identity during their time of being patients.

Most children beyond the toddler years have learned to communicate verbally and have many more experiences upon which to rely compared with an infant or a toddler. Thus, their resources for effective relating are greater than those in their earlier years. School-age children are capable of leaving the security of their families and the familiar setting of home to enter new worlds, such as the piano class described in the opening to this chapter. Sister Olive Marie is one of many authority figures, such as teachers, coaches, and other role models, with whom the child will interact. However, for the most part health professionals present types of authority that are often unfamiliar to the child. Family and school authority figures usually do little to prepare him or her for the health professions setting and its unique challenges and choices.

Play and Toys

Play appropriate to the child's age and social development can be an important vehicle to help ease the tension he or she is feeling about being able to relate to the people in the health care setting. In Chapter 13 we introduced five types of play and suggested that at the toddler stage and immediately beyond it children are comfortable with symbolic, onlooker, and parallel play. However, as the child grows, associative play, which involves shared activity and communication, and cooperative play, in which rules are followed and goals are achieved, become the norm. Some older children who become patients will regress to an earlier stage, but many will be able to assume roles at the higher levels of play, which will allow them to act out their predicament of being in such a new situation. For example, associative play can involve playing "hospital" with a professional or family member, and assuming the powerful role of the nurse or someone else in charge, thereby revealing children's own anxieties and how they perceive their situation. Clues to how they think their tension could be eased may be revealed in their attempts to minister to the play partner who has now become the patient. Cooperative play can involve table games, card games, or sports, using their participation and mastery as an effective way of relating.

Young patients often play with toys, too, so that a truck, doll, puzzle, or other object may be an effective means of helping to establish a relationship. At the same time, children can be very sensitive about being "too old" for certain types of toys, so health professionals and others must think carefully about which toys to offer.

School Issues

When children of school age become patients, health professionals are faced with additional challenges. Even a short illness or injury may mean a disruption in school attendance and may not only put the child behind in schoolwork but also can have devastating consequences socially. During the school years children organize most of their relational activity around family and school; therefore, they are at risk of being "out of the action" in every way when removed from the educational environment. At the very least you should be aware of this loss and show interest in his or her school-related activity if, indeed, any is being carried on at the moment.

Most children with chronic illnesses or long-term disabilities will receive special attention regarding education through the school system itself. Disability can be defined as a long-term reduction in ability to conduct social role activities, such as school or play, because of a physical or mental condition. A significant portion of children, estimated to be 7% of all those younger than 18 years, have experienced some degree of disability.[3] The percentage of minority children with disabilities is somewhat higher: 8.2% for blacks, 10.6% for American Indian/Alaskan Native and 11.8% for Hispanic/Puerto Rican.[3] The Americans with Disabilities Act (ADA) prohibits discrimination on the basis of disability in employment, state and local government services, public accommodations, commercial facilities, transportation, and telecommunications.[4] You can find out about the different components of the ADA at http://www.usdoj.gov/crt/ada/adahom. The Individuals with Disabilities Education Act (IDEA) (formerly called *Public Law 94-142* or the *Education for all Handicapped Children Act of 1975*) requires public schools to make available to all eligible children with disabilities a free, appropriate public education in the least restrictive environment appropriate to their individual needs (20 U.S.C. 1400 *et seq.*). However laudatory this is, the law does little to address the accompanying problems that sometimes arise: able-bodied children may be cruel toward peers who have medical conditions, parents may believe that their child is not getting care as good as they would like or disagree with the individualized education program that has been developed for their child, teachers may feel that they do not have enough time to devote to the needs of all the children in their classrooms, and children with serious but not permanent conditions may not qualify.[5] When you come into contact with families who are trying to work through some of these issues, you can often encourage them as well as direct them to the appropriate resources when problems arise. For example, if parents disagree with the individualized education program, they can request a due process hearing and a review from the state educational agency if applicable in their state.

In short, during the school-age years a child's feelings of self-worth and experiences of relatedness usually are tied to school. Any means by which you can convey sympathy for the child's predicament and respect for his or her capacities will enhance the child's fragile identity and self-esteem and help ensure success in the relationship.

Family—A Bridge to Respectful Interaction

All of the family dynamics described in Chapter 13 apply as the child grows older. The growing child, however, does present some additional challenges to the family and health professional working with the family.

It has been noted that the child's desire to become more independent is one of the major developmental tasks of this growth period, while at the same time he or she may feel extremely lonely and insecure when illness strikes. The family often is torn between wanting to support the child as an independent "big girl" or "big boy" while being attentive to his or her needs. They may also be dismayed by the child's obvious regression or respond to their own feelings of guilt for the child's illness with overprotectiveness. Your awareness of their struggles and needs is essential if you are to be successful.

Respect for the child's input, especially when his or her opinions seem to differ from those of parents, is essential, too. Although developmental psychology has often used age as an indicator of competency, this view is being challenged and replaced by the principle that social experience is a more reliable marker of maturity and decision-making ability.[6,7] Many policies now acknowledge the importance of listening to children, even if their opinions do not govern legally. For example, the prevailing feeling is that children usually know when they are seriously ill and can handle difficult information about their health and future prospects as long as they have the support of their families. In an era when health professionals and patients are trying to find better ways of setting humane limits on treatment, children's insights into appropriate limits sometimes are overlooked, even though they know when they have reached the place where they cannot tolerate any more interventions. Children often are aware of their parent's anxiety, opposition, or denial, and they try to act as referees among family members or between health professionals and family. Children can participate in a meaningful way in discussions about their health care (Figure 14-1). "The challenge is to provide appropriate techniques that neither exclude nor patronize children. Notions of children's incompetence are reinforced by methods that oversimplify and 'talk down' to them."[7]

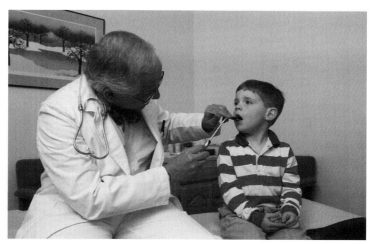

FIGURE 14-1: The health professional should listen to what the child has to say during an exam. (© *Getty Images/18191.*)

In addition, brothers and sisters of the ill child are also affected by the stress such illness creates in the family. In a study of the siblings of hospitalized children, the brothers and sisters noted stress that included feelings of loneliness, resentment and fear, and positive feelings of resilience, such as lessons learned and independence.[8] You can help siblings cope by providing support and information. Anything the health professional can do to keep the supportive context for siblings alive is well worth the effort. You can also help by trying to keep family disequilibrium at a minimum while acting primarily as an advocate for the child.

This balancing act sometimes is easier said than accomplished. The following story from one of the author's experiences highlights how such a dilemma can arise. As you read this case, think about your reasons for wanting to share the information about this child's condition with him or wanting to withhold it.

When John was 6, he fell from a swing, had some joint pain of the lower left extremity, and was unable to fully extend the knee. Numerous radiographic studies were completed, and results were largely normal. However, John could still not fully extend his knee and continued to complain of tenderness. Finally, a magnetic resonance image (MRI) revealed a lesion that turned out to be non-Hodgkin's lymphoma (NHL). John received combination chemotherapy and appeared to be in remission for several years. As John has gotten older the physician who has followed John and his family has grown somewhat concerned about his mother's overprotectiveness. Although it was less noticeable when he was younger it has been the topic of conversation among the professionals when he and his mother have come to the clinic. For instance, she mentioned that she still dresses John and accompanies him almost everywhere.

John is now 9, and during a follow-up visit to the oncologist, it is discovered that he has a recurrence of NHL. Although the prognosis for children with NHL has improved, the outcome for children with recurrent NHL remains bleak.[9]

John is re-admitted to the hospital for treatment. John had always asked many questions about his treatment, and so it seems odd to the nurses and others that he is uncharacteristically silent on the matter of his illness now, even though his condition continues to worsen. His mother visits for a minimum of 6 hours every day and warns everyone that John is not to be told that he has a recurrence of cancer.

During the last week, John has had several serious episodes. Last night he had a cardiac arrest and was resuscitated. The resident physicians and nurses would like to put him on a "no code" status so that if his heart stops again he will be able to die peacefully. They also would like him to know the seriousness of his illness and that he has cancer, because they think he has a right to know he is going to die.

Today the physician approached John's mother about whether John could be told about his illness. She flew into a rage and threatened to move John to another hospital immediately if they did not promise to never tell him under any circumstances. Although the health professionals know she has a legal right to remove him from the hospital, few of them think she actually will. Their opinions on whether he should be told are now divided.

▶ If you were a member of the health care team treating John and his family, what would you do at this point?

▶ What would telling John about his illness accomplish?

Several suggestions may help you to decide what to do when you are faced with dilemmas concerning how much information to share with child patients:

1. *Make your own position clear* to yourself and to the patient's parents. Do you believe the child is able to handle information about his or her condition? Why or why not? Under what conditions would you feel morally bound to disclose relevant health information to this child? Under what conditions would you withhold such information, even if you believed that doing so could increase the child's distrust in you?

2. *Explore the resources available in your health care setting* to support families as they work out their anxieties and difficulties. As one author notes, "The purpose is … to support, not supplant, the family. An atmosphere of acceptance and assurance allows each family to manage their own lives and to arrive at a solution most adequate for them."[10]

3. *Present information in a way the child can understand* with ample opportunity for questions and explanations from the child in his or her own words about what has been discussed.

In summary, a child brings to the health care interaction hopes, fears, and dreams that reflect his or her need to establish autonomy and initiative as a "self" while maintaining the security of relationships with family, friends, and others. The delicate balance between being an individual and being part of relationships that is difficult under the best of circumstances is further challenged by illness or other incapacity. The efforts of health professionals and family alike are required for successful adaptation or recovery. The benefit is that within a context of respect for the child as a unique individual, health professional and family will be able to work together to meet the patient's best interests.

THE ADOLESCENT SELF

The word *adolescent* means literally "to grow into maturity or adulthood." During the later stages of child development, all children are thrust into the difficult position of having to show industry and individuality in the larger world, to assert who they are, to command authority in some areas, and to explore the mysteries of developing sexuality. "Adolescence typically is defined as beginning at puberty, a physiological transformation that gives boys and girls adult bodies and alters how they are perceived and treated by others, as well as how they view themselves." [11]

Early and Late Adolescence

Most psychologists and others writing about adolescence divide it into two stages, early and late, each with developmental tasks. Early adolescence lasts for about 2 years and is characterized by growth spurts, maturing of reproductive functions and sex organs, increased weight, and changes in body proportions. These profound changes understandably may have profound psychological results.

Anyone who is around early teens knows that their self-images govern everything they do. The teen years are a time of intensely seeking one's "self." In its extreme form, the self is the way the body looks and nothing more. However, for many teens the absorption with the self goes beyond bodily appearance alone. Adolescents are generally concerned with fitting in with their peers. They will try various roles in an attempt to integrate their developing social skills with goals and dreams.

This early period of adolescence is so unsettling that psychologists and others have described it as a period of adolescent turmoil. However, other researchers indicate that adolescence may not be as fraught with emotional issues as has been previously thought. In an ethnographic study of early adolescent girls, both popular and not so popular, the findings revealed a close relationship with parents and certainly not the trauma and stress suggested by common discourses (or myths) about adolescence. Teachers, parents, and health care professionals may expect trouble from adolescents due to or attributed to "raging hormones," but in this study the trauma did not materialize.[12] At a minimum, there is clearly asynchrony between physical development and psychosocial maturation that may be the source of some conflict and also in part offers an explanation for the number of teen pregnancies and instances of sexually transmitted diseases.

After this period of rapid and profound change, young people move into late adolescence. Here self-identify fully emerges as they practice the various roles and responsibilities they will assume as adults. Some adolescents do not move on to this stage of development because they literally do not survive. In 2004, black males 18-24 years old had the highest homicide victimization rates in the United States.[13] The differences in the leading causes of death between white and black adolescents is one indication of the profound impact the context of an adolescent's life can have on health and mortality. For example, adolescents in developing countries have to contend with poverty, starvation, and infectious diseases. Those in developed countries contend with obesity, sedentary lifestyles, violence, and eating disorders. Adolescents spend less time with family and more time in new environments such as work settings, peer relationships, and romantic relationships.

The impact of a peer's behavior on an adolescent is significant (Figure 14-2). In a study of 527 adolescents in grades 9 through 12, substance use (cigarette, marijuana, and alcohol use), violence (weapons and physical fighting), and suicidal behavior (suicidal ideation and attempts) were related to their friends' substance use, deviance, and suicidal behaviors, respectively. On the positive side, the more prosocial behavior of friends had a negative correlation with violence and substance abuse.[14] Other factors, such as family function, depression, and social acceptance, influenced adolescents' health-risk behavior as well.

NEEDS: RESPECT, AUTONOMY, AND RELATING

Autonomous decision-making raises some delicate questions for health professionals who work with adolescent patients because adolescents often want to aggressively assert their authority in decisions. It is not always clear whether adolescents are capable of making wise authoritative decisions. Only in recent years has there been an attempt to address the legal rights of adolescents. The most prominent view, referred to as the *Mature Minors Doctrine*, allows for parents or the state to speak on behalf of a minor's interests only as long as the minor is unable to represent himself

FIGURE 14-2: An adolescent's behavior is influenced by that of his or her peers. (© *Getty Images/590044.*)

or herself. Thus, the level of the young person's development emerges as a decisive factor. In keeping with the legality of the Mature Minors Doctrine, you can try to assess the maturity of an adolescent patient in regard to his or her ability to cope effectively with illness or injury. The question whether an adolescent is a "mature minor" must be decided by health care professionals independent of parental judgment.[15]

There are some compelling reasons to give decision-making authority to mature adolescents. Some adolescents would never consult a health care provider with a problem if they knew it would require parental consent before treatment. Also, in their developing autonomy, they would never share delicate information with the provider if they thought confidentiality would be violated. Coupled with the reluctance of adolescents to speak about risky behavior or other health issues, they often do not receive recommended and preventive counseling or screening services appropriate to their age group.[16]

Adolescence was often viewed as a relatively healthy time in a person's life. However, behavior patterns can change rapidly in adolescence and can include irregular dietary habits, lack of sleep, inactivity, experimentation with drugs, alcohol and tobacco use, sexual activity, and reckless driving. The connection between these behaviors and long-term consequences for health are being increasingly recognized:

> ...addiction to cigarettes usually begins in the early teens, and may be a prerequisite for illicit drug use in the short term, although other adverse health consequences in terms of respiratory and heart disease take years to develop; genito-urinary infections may produce acute symptoms, but asymptomatic chlamydial infection can result in subfertility many years later with a subsequent requirement for assisted fertilization; and a variety of psychological disorders, including obsessive compulsive disorders and anxiety states, have their onset at this time. However a degree of experimentation and risk taking seem to be an integral part of the transition from childhood to adulthood, and most young people come through this phase of life relatively unscathed. So the challenge to researchers and clinicians alike is to be able to identify those at most risk of adverse consequences, without interfering with normal development, and to evaluate possible interventions that will result in improved long-term outcomes. [17]

At the very least, programs to promote healthy lifestyles for adolescents should include information on nutrition, activity, stress management, family planning, prevention of smoking, alcohol and substance abuse, and the spread of sexually transmitted diseases. Adolescents should be involved in the design of such health promotion programs so that they are both age and culturally relevant.

Family and Peers—Bridges to Respectful Interaction

Families and friends should not be excluded from the health care interaction process for patients in this age group either. The aforementioned emphasis on the importance of the adolescent's autonomy and authority should in no way be seen as undermining the importance of treating the patient as a part of a family unit when one exists.

Most adolescents like to argue about adult rules, even those they accept. Listening to family exchanges about rules that the adolescent disagrees with often will provide insight into the conduct of the adolescent toward you, too. Also, the health professional should not assume that the adolescent's attitude toward parents means there is not a deep dependence on them or heartfelt caring from the family. Further assessment is needed to ascertain whether family disequilibrium is creating a breach in that support system.

Health professionals often benefit from including an adolescent patient's close friends and peers in interactions. Peer group activity is essential for identity formation, and all illnesses or injuries are jolts to the adolescent's identity. Getting to know an adolescent patient's friends by name, seeking their support, and trying to understand their feelings about the patient's condition can be helpful to all.

SUMMARY

In this brief overview of children and adolescents, the theme of respect revolves around at least two ideas—patient autonomy and effective relatedness. There are numerous ways in which the young patient will try to exert autonomy and find a way of relating with you effectively. By showing imagination—and at times, patience—you will have an opportunity to build a close and rewarding relationship.

One of the greatest challenges for you as a health professional is to think of the development of people from birth to adulthood as a continuum, with some moving along it faster than others. We have provided some guidelines that will help you think generally about people as they pause—then continue to pass through—older childhood and adolescence. The individual patient will present himself or herself as a unique individual still in the process of forming and refining an identity. You have a responsibility to be sure that, in the midst of activities such patients may engage you in, their health care needs are met. Having said that, we move ahead to the next chapter and the unique challenges associated with treating people in the adult years.

REFERENCES

1. Hampl P: *I could tell you stories: sojourns in the land of memory*, London, 1999, WW Norton.
2. Dillard A: *An American childhood*, New York, 1988, Harper & Row.
3. National Center for Health Statistics: *Limitation of activity, all ages, United States, 2000-2004* (website): http:// www.cdc.gov/nchs/health_data_for_all_ages.htm. Accessed July 10, 2006.
4. Americans with Disabilities Act of 1990, 42 U.S.C.A. § 12101 *et seq.* (West 1993).
5. Sullivan PM, Knutson JF: Maltreatment and disabilities: a population-based epidemiological study, *Child Abuse Negl* 24(10):1257-1273, 2000.
6. Christensen P, Prout A: Working with ethical symmetry in social research with children, *Childhood* 9(4):477-497, 2002.
7. Kellett M and others: "Just teach us the skills please we'll do the rest": empowering ten-year-olds as active researchers, *Children and Society* 18:329-343, 2004.
8. Fleitas J: When Jack fell down... Jill came tumbling after: siblings in the web of illness and disability, *MCN Am J Matern Child Nurs* 25(5):267-273, 2000.
9. Kobrinsky NL and others: Outcomes of treatment of children and adolescents with recurrent non-Hodgkin's lymphoma and Hodgkin's disease with dexamethasone, etoposide, cisplatin, cytarabine, and L-asparaginase, maintenance chemotherapy, and transplantation: Children's Cancer Study Group CCG-5912, *J Clin Oncol* 19(9):2390-2396, 2001.

10. Fleming SJ: Children's grief: individual and family dynamics. In Corr CA, Corr DM, editors: *Hospice approaches to pediatric care*, New York, 1985, Springer.
11. Call KT and others: Adolescent health and well-being in the twenty-first century: a global perspective, *J Res Adolesc* 12(1):69-98, 2002.
12. Finders MJ: *Just girls: the hidden literacies and life in junior high*, New York, 1997, Teachers College Press.
13. United States Department of Justice: Homicide trends in the U.S. (website): http://www.ojp.usdoj.gov. Accessed July 24, 2006.
14. Prinstein MJ, Boergers J, Spirito A: Adolescents' and their friends' health-risk behavior: factors that alter or add to peer influence, *J Pediatr Psychol* 26(5):287-298, 2001.
15. Cook R, Dickens BM: Recognizing adolescents' "evolving capacities" to exercise choice in reproductive healthcare, *Int J Gynaecol Obstet* 70(1):13-21, 2000.
16. Bethell C, Klein J, Peck C: Assessing health system provision of adolescent preventive services: the young adult health care survey, *Med Care* 39(5):478-490, 2001.
17. Churchill D: The growing pains of adolescent health research in general practice, *Prim Health Care Res Dev* 4:277-278, 2003.

RESPECTFUL INTERACTION: WORKING WITH ADULTS

CHAPTER OBJECTIVES

The student will be able to:

- Compare unique challenges of development in the middle years with those of childhood and adolescence
- Discuss the meaning of work for adults
- Discuss "responsibility" as it applies to the middle years of life and how it may affect the patient's response to health professionals
- Describe at least three social roles that characterize life for most middle-age persons and consider ways in which showing respect for a patient requires attention to those roles
- Discuss how stress enters into attempts to carry out the responsibilities of each of the aforementioned roles and some health-related consequences of stress
- List basic challenges facing health professionals who are working with a middle-age person going through a midlife transition

Here are some guidelines on how to be an adult, said the consulting editor at a magazine where I worked several years ago. "I wrote them in honor of your twenty-first birthday, which if I'm not mistaken is today." The man handed me a sheet of paper. The list began, "Adults always speak in a calm quiet voice. When angry an adult says, 'I think I must tell you that I am angry.'" The list ended, "Adults are very careful about the drains, and often have trouble walking on beaches: sometimes they cannot synchronize their legs properly to adjust for the sand. "

—A. Lamott[1]

WHO IS THE ADULT?

It may be true that of all the life periods, adulthood has been the least understood and least studied. It follows that health professionals will probably be least adept at interacting respectfully with persons in this age group. The relative ease with which health professionals generally approach adult patients does not ensure that the needs of a person of middle years will then automatically be better met. Although ease of initial interaction is an important ingredient in effectiveness, it is not in itself sufficient. If only there were an accurate list of what it means to be an adult. In fact, adulthood is far more complicated than youth.

A stereotype about adult life is that it is only a waiting period or holding place made up of work, establishing a family, or dealing with menopause on the way to retirement and old age. In reality, there is a wide variation in the type and timing of transitions and activities in adult life that is far richer than this stereotype suggests. For these reasons, it is important to examine some vital issues concerning life as an adult in this society.

Adulthood can be legally defined by chronological age or at the time a person begins to assume responsibility for himself or herself and others.[2] It can also be defined by achievement of certain developmental tasks such as being independent; establishing long-term relationships; establishing a personal identify in a reflective way; finding a meaningful occupation; contributing to the welfare of others or making a contribution to family, faith community, or society at large; and gaining recognition for one's accomplishments. Finally, adulthood can be defined in psychological terms, that is, by the level of maturity exhibited by a person. Mature persons are able to take responsibility, make logical decisions, appreciate the position of others, control emotional outbursts, and accept social roles. The opening quote pokes fun at the adult attribute of accepting minor frustrations with the seldom heard phrase, "I think I must tell you that I am angry," as if all adults remain calm and composed when they are angry. What it means to be an "adult" is a combination of many factors, the most important of which you will be introduced to in these pages.

NEEDS: RESPECT, IDENTITY, AND INTIMACY

Adult development is not marked by definitive physical and motor changes such as those seen in toddlers (e.g., learning how to walk), but it is full of challenging and largely unpredictable experiences. Adult life is marked by concepts such as midlife physical and emotional challenges and changes, generativity, and the empty nest, but not every adult has these experiences. We would be better able to predict the response of a 5-year-old to a major illness than we would that of a 30-year-old. In addition, there may be differences between the way middle age is experienced by men and women. Also, the specific point in history that a person enters adulthood may have profound implications for adult life. For example, many women who entered adulthood during the women's movement of the 1960s and 1970s had more opportunities regarding work and sexual freedom than the previous generation of women. Finally, development may also differ because of sexual orientation, race and ethnicity, class, and education, to name a few differences. Thus, no single theory is adequate to explain adult development. Even if we hold several variables constant (e.g., age and gender), it is still difficult to predict how two middle-age patients would react to the same diagnosis. Consider the example of Ms. McLean and Ms. Jeon, both of who have just learned that they have in situ cancer of the cervix.

🦢 Sara McLean, age 34, has a family history positive for cervical cancer. Her maternal aunt and older sister both died of cervical cancer. Ms. McLean has recently become engaged and plans to be married in 6 months. She put off committing to a permanent relationship and starting a family until she completed graduate work in clinical psychology. With the support of her husband-to-be, she had planned on balancing a career as a private therapist with raising a family. She is devastated when the oncologist presents information about the treatment of choice for her condition—a total hysterectomy.

Eunice Jeon, age 33, also has in situ cancer of the cervix. She has no family history of cancer and has always prided herself on her "hearty" family stock. All of her grandparents are alive and well. Ms. Jeon married her high school sweetheart the weekend after graduation. The Jeons have four children aged 5, 8, 10, and 12. Mr. Jeon is an emergency medical technician and plans someday to enroll in medical school after he finishes his bachelor's degree. Ms. Jeon works as a secretary/receptionist at the Catholic grade school her children attend. She is troubled by the diagnosis, but when presented with treatment options merely asks, "When can we schedule the surgery? I want to get this taken care of as soon as possible."

Both of these women's feelings and reactions are the result of their life experiences to this point, which in turn, are determined by their roles. In Ms. McLean's case, her response to the diagnosis is influenced by her roles as daughter, sister, niece, fiancée, and psychologist. Ms. Jeon's response is influenced by her roles as mother, wife, daughter, granddaughter, and receptionist. These life roles are only a few that we can ascertain based on the information presented in the brief cases. It is highly probable that both women have many more roles. Ms. McLean planned her life around finishing her education. Ms. Jeon's has revolved largely around her family. In short, just looking at their ages, it would be impossible to predict how Ms. McLean and Ms. Jeon will interpret this crisis.

Adult patients are generally more capable of entering into a professional relationship as an equal partner than younger people. Even though adult patients are better able to protect their own interests and make their wishes known, they are still worthy of the respect that we accord to younger, generally more vulnerable, patients. Respect continues to be one of the hallmarks of effective interaction as we work our way through the lifespan.

A developmental task unique to the adult is the development of a self-definition or identity. Identity has its roots in self-perceptions in relation to specific social settings. For example, after completing an educational program, a person may refer to himself or herself as "an engineer" or "a physical therapist." The professional role has become part of the person's identity. Identity provides continuity over time and across problems and changes that arise in life. Illness and injury invariably result in changes in the patient's identity as was previously mentioned in Chapters 6 and 7. So there is a sense of maintenance of self through identity and yet room for change to accommodate the vicissitudes of life.

Intimacy is another developmental task of the adult. According to Erikson, adult development is marked by the ability to experience open, supportive, and loving relationships with others without the fear of losing one's own identity in the process of growing close to another.[3] You were introduced to levels of intimacy in Chapter 12, illustrating that the type of intimacy experienced with family members, lovers, and friends is deeper and more involving than a degree of intimacy you might experience in other relationships. It is that deeper intimacy that Erikson is talking about. The major developmental facets of adult life are referred to repeatedly as we explore the social roles, meaning of work, and challenges of midlife.

Psychosocial Development and Needs

Maturity requires the acceptance of responsibility and empathy for others. The concept of achievement central to adult life can be defined in a number of ways. Some "midlife challenges" discussed later in this chapter seem to stem from a person's having adequately assumed responsibility and realized his or her achievement potential, whereas others arise when the individual has failed to do so.

A profile of a person in the middle years of life will necessarily involve a consideration of his or her sense of "responsibility." When we ask if someone is willing to "assume responsibility," we are concerned with acts that the person can do and has voluntarily agreed to do. Given these conditions of ability and agreement, we want to know whether the person can be trusted to carry out the acts, regardless of whether the agreement was explicit (i.e., a promise to abide by the terms of a contract) or implicit (i.e., a promise to provide for one's own children or parents). Underlying the idea of acting responsibly is an assumption that the individual *is* a free agent, i.e., one who is willing and able to act autonomously. Thus, a person coerced into performing an act is not considered to have accepted responsibility for it.

During the middle years, there is another aspect to acting responsibly: it involves having a high regard for the welfare of others. The adult must find a way to support the next generation by redirecting attention from him or herself to others. In other words, the adult learns to "care."[4] This involves empathy for the predicaments that befall others in life. The acts may flow from a free will, but the will must operate in accordance with reasonable claims and justifiable expectations of other people. The claims of society on a person peak during the middle years, so "acting responsibly" must be interpreted in terms of how completely the person fulfills the conditions of those claims. For instance, in Hindu culture, one stage of acting out karma involves active engagement in the affairs of family and business. Only when an individual has successfully completed these tasks may he or she move on to higher, more contemplative levels of existence.

One way to view the matter in our culture is to review the discussion of self-respect in Chapter 1. This basic value is among the most essential ingredients of "the good life." During the middle years, most people perceive their self-respect as being vulnerable to the judgments of others: one's self-respect at least partially depends on the extent to which he or she commands the respect of employer, family, and friends. This idea is related to our concept of "reputation": one commands respect by giving due consideration to society's claims. Hiltner notes, correctly we believe, that, to a large extent, even the personal values of the middle years must include a regard for others. For most, it is a highly social period when interdependencies are complex and pervasive.[5]

One factor distinguishing the contemporary person of middle years from like persons in other periods of history is that today some of the psychological components of adolescence are extended to a much later age than previously. Thus, a 30-year-old who feels some of the weight of societal claims placed on adults may still be financially dependent on his or her parents (or spouse), may still be in school, may be living in the family home, and may still be actively exploring sexual preferences and lifestyles. Adulthood sometimes involves people going back to previous developmental tasks such as establishing an identity if they didn't resolve these issues previously in late adolescence or early adulthood. For example, in a study of gay males in middle adulthood, the researcher found that "these men were facing issues befitting their chronological age (non-gay issues which had been worked on while leading a double-life) as well as unresolved identity issues from the past."[6] The key point of this study is that the subjects were initially working through the earlier stage of development rather than reworking earlier developmental issues that can occur throughout adult development.

Adults who have children might believe that they have moved through an adult developmental task of parenting children, only to find their children returning home after a divorce or unemployment. Therefore, a parent or parents who might have been rejoicing in an empty nest and time for each other may find their adult children under their roof once again and with grandchildren in tow. Furthermore, a significant number of women have delayed pregnancy until midlife and find themselves attempting to integrate childrearing, marriage, and recreational and work roles in their late 30s and early 40s. Thus, the delayed acquisition of independence, earlier physical maturation characteristic of modern cultures, pressures on young people to grow up fast, return of adult children to their parents' home, and delayed childbearing all complicate the traditional views held about progression through adulthood.

Social Roles in the Middle Years

There are several social roles that most fully characterize this period involving primary relationships, parenting, care of older family members, and involvement in the community in the form of political, religious, or other social or service organizations and groups.

Primary Relationships

It is almost always during the middle years that a person decides with whom lasting relationships will be developed. Fortunately, an increasing number of older people are also developing new relationships, but they are usually people who were able to sustain deep and lasting relationships in the middle years as well.

The primary relationship takes priority over all others, the most common type being the relationship with a spouse. Choosing a spouse or other permanent companion and becoming better acquainted (i.e., learning to know the person, discovering potentials and limits, similarities and differences, and compatibilities and incompatibilities) are processes interwoven with the more basic activities of eating, sleeping, acquiring possessions, working, worshipping, relaxing, and playing together.

Those who do not enter into a marriage relationship sometimes develop a deep and lasting involvement with a partner, often a friend or sibling. One of your first tasks of respectful interaction with a patient of middle years is to find out if there is a key person in his or her life and, if so, who that person is. This can be accomplished without unnecessary probing into the person's private life. Particularly in times of crisis the patient looks to that key person for comfort, sustenance, and guidance. However, sometimes the person you assume would be the most supportive is not. Consider the case of Mary Ogden and Pam Carlisle:

> Mary Ogden, age 61, is a retired, single teacher who is hospitalized for treatment related to severe diabetes. The entire small community where she has resided and taught for 35 years adores her. Through the years she has received numerous awards for community service. She is a cooperative, cheerful person, who, in spite of her illness, continues to be an inspiration to everyone. She is especially fond of Pam Carlisle, the head nurse on the unit where Mary is being treated.
>
> On the afternoon before Mary's planned hospital discharge, an unscheduled visitor comes to the nursing desk insisting to speak to Pam about a highly personal matter. The visitor is Agnes Ogden, an elderly lady who informs Pam that she is the older sister (and only living relative) of Mary. The visitor seems sincere and asks that Pam provide details of her sister's condition so that she might be better prepared to aid her with both her physical illness and personal affairs. Pam complies with her request, actually feeling relieved that there is someone to share this burden with her. The following morning Pam visits Mary's room and finds her profoundly irate for the first time. She informs Pam that she has not been on speaking terms with her sister for many years, that she considers her sister to be untrustworthy, and that she thoroughly resents her sister's having the knowledge of her personal affairs and illness. Mary develops a distrust of Pam and becomes depressed, agitated, and uncooperative.
>
> ▶ What could Pam have done differently to foster Mary's trust rather than to destroy it? What would you have done when Agnes came to you requesting information?
> ▶ Besides violating HIPAA regulations that protect Mary's privacy and confidentiality, Pam has also broken the trust that once existed between them. How might you rebuild the trust that once existed between you and a patient should such a breakdown occur?

Parenting

Caring for children often is a part of adult life. The gender role stereotypes traditionally assigned to mothering and fathering are breaking down in many families so that both parents share the whole range of parenting skills. The concept of parenting is being expanded, too: there is the "single parent," who provides the full care usually shared with another; same sex couples are parenting; and many children live within extended family situations in which parenting is shared by several persons.

Whatever the challenges of each model, all share the assumption that the child's welfare depends on the quality of parenting. The age-old recognition that a child's physical well-being depends on adult care is now buttressed by more recent assertions that the child's potential for fulfillment and satisfaction in later years is also determined in the earliest years of life that are strongly influenced by the parent. The least that can be said of parenting relationships is that they are among the most enduring and complex of human interactions (Figure 15-1). The health professional who fails to consider them respectfully neglects an integral part of the patient's identity.

Care of Older Family Members

Not only do many adults care for children as a part of their daily responsibilities, but they also care for their parents, parents-in-law, and other older friends and relatives. Middle-age adults are sometimes referred to as the "sandwich" generation. The decrease in premature death has resulted in a sharp increase in the natural lifespan. Thus, more people are living into older age. At the same time that the population of older people increased, the birth rate declined, resulting in a shortage of filial caregivers. Parent care is not limited to one age period of the caregiver's life but may span across several age periods in adult life.

FIGURE 15-1: Parenting relationships are among the most enduring and complex of human interactions. (© *Corbis.*)

The consequences of parental caregiving are not fully understood, but it clearly exerts an impact on adult life for an unpredictable amount of time, unlike child-rearing, which has built-in time limits of dependence and a progressive move to greater independence from the parent. Additionally, we are just beginning to appreciate the cultural differences that play a part in caring for elderly family members. For example, in a study of Mexican-American families and elder care, it was found that there is a clear sense of responsibility to care for the elder members of one's family.[7] Thus, women in this culture may go about readjusting their work obligations in different ways than women in other cultures. The cultural lens is essential for accurately viewing this role of adult life.

Political and Other Service Activities

Involvement in political and social organizations has traditionally been at a peak during the middle years. Responsibilities stemming from membership in such organizations are often second only to those of work if measured in terms of energy consumption and personal commitment. A sense of identity in the middle years depends heavily on belonging to such groups whether they be a political party, religious group, or service organization. Not only are these service activities a source of identity, they are also a vehicle for contributing to one's profession or community.

In summary, there are other sources of claims on adults, but attending to primary relationships such as spouses, friends, children, and parents and contributing to public initiatives constitute some highly significant ones.

Work as Meaningful Activity

Work, like family and adulthood, is a concept that can be variably defined. Work as meaningful activity can occur in a variety of settings and assumes many patterns. Therefore, the meaning of work and the responsibilities it requires will depend on the person's value system, expectations, and aspirations as well as the specific environment, job title, and position within a hierarchy. For some, work is performed primarily in the home; for a great many others, it entails a significant amount of time away from home. Adults in the middle years are judged to spend about half of their waking hours engaged in work. The kind of work they do largely determines their income, lifestyle, social status, and place of residence. Because of the amount of time and energy expended, the type of factual information one acquires over a lifetime is often influenced by the working situation (Figure 15-2). Studies of professional socialization suggest that, at least for white-collar and professional workers, the kind of work done also defines their worldview.

Work-related responsibilities still differ generally for men and women. You have undoubtedly observed what most women experience in their work roles: expectations on them include not only doing a job in the labor force as well as men but also maintaining the quality and amount of work performed in the home.

Women respond to these various needs or demands by trying to balance their impulse to care and the level of personal support available.[8] When the limits of caregiving are reached, something else has to give. In many cases, women make changes and adjustments in their employment in order to continue in the caregiving role.[9]

FIGURE 15-2: "I've learned a lot in sixty-three years. But, unfortunately, almost all of it is about aluminum." (*From* The New Yorker, *November 11, 1977, p. 27. © The New Yorker Collection 1977 William Hamilton from cartoonbank.com. All Rights Reserved.*)

Two types of responsibility are associated with the work role: (1) to do one's job well and (2) to fulfill the reasonable expectations of others (e.g., employer, peers, or family members). The professional relationship has the added dimension of helping: one is expected to help those who need professional services.

Work relationships are different from simple friendships in a number of ways, although the former can be lasting, deep, and complex. Moreover, there is not always clear separation of the two. The car pool phenomenon is an intriguing combination of how work and friendship roles become intermingled; here people who are grouped together for the purpose of getting to and from their workplace also usually engage in camaraderie over minutes or hours each week and sometimes more regularly than with their own family members. We have known some car pool members who interact as friends or acquaintances during the commute, then assume their "proper" workplace role with each other when work begins.

Your task is to assess how the patient views his or her work situation, what work means, and particularly the relationships in it. Whether a patient's work involves providing quality child care, laboring on the section crew to replace railroad ties, or presiding over a meeting in the executive suite, the work entails responsibility both toward a job to be done and toward other human beings. Treatment goals must be tailored to help the patient either carry out these responsibilities or to accept the fact that it is no longer possible to do so.

Those who work with adult patients in the areas of occupational health are keenly aware of the relationship among health, injury, or illness and the worker's role. Consider the following case:

> Masie Baldwin has worked as a nursing home aide for the past 15 years. She is the sole provider for her three children, one of whom has just started college. Although Ms. Baldwin has attended the mandatory in-service sessions on proper body alignment and lifting of patients, she has not always followed the proper procedure. Ms. Baldwin stated to her fellow workers more than once, "I'm big and strong. I don't like waiting for help or lugging out the lift to get patients up. I can get them up and out of bed without help." Unfortunately, while getting Mr. Collins out of bed, Ms. Baldwin injured her lower back and neck. Ms. Baldwin has been on worker's compensation leave for the past month and is now involved in a "work-hardening" program to determine if she is capable of returning to work in the nursing home. The health professionals working with Ms. Baldwin observe that she is highly motivated to return to work, but frightened of reinjury. Her confidence in her strength and sense of invulnerability has been badly shaken. During a particularly trying day in the work-hardening program, she tells her therapist, "If I can't work in the nursing home, I don't know what I'll do. It's the only kind of work I've ever done. All my friends are there."
>
> ▶ What "meanings" do you feel Ms. Baldwin gives to her work?
> ▶ How does her identity tie to her work roles?
> ▶ What are some of the challenges you might face in working with Ms. Baldwin?

We have emphasized responsibility in terms of relationships and work roles in the middle years and that self-respect during this period is determined in large part by meeting the justifiable expectations of others. However, self-respect unquestionably also depends somewhat on believing in and being true to oneself. Thus, the person of middle years who meets all of society's expectations can still be unfulfilled.[10] That, in fact, is precisely the plight of many people today who have not pursued personal interests and goals at all or very minimally. This situation can be viewed as an inability or unwillingness to assume responsibility toward oneself, and it contributes to the challenges of midlife that are discussed in this chapter. Accepting the consequences of one's own behavior is vital; all of us share, to some extent, the problem expressed by the motto on President Truman's desk, "The buck stops here." The sense of "being somebody," such an integral part of adolescence, must become more fully defined in the middle years. In this period, individuals are expected to be able to show more clearly who they are and what they are able to contribute to the welfare of loved ones and to society.

Biological Development during the Adult Years

In human beings the lifespan is thought to be about 110 to 120 years. In Western nations the average life expectancy is said to be 77.5 years, although this varies according to race and other variables (Black females, 76.1 years; Black males,

68.8 years; White females, 80.5 years; and White males, 75.1).[11] The 15 leading causes of death for all age groups are listed in Table 15-1.[11]

Cause of death varies according to race and sex, too, but this table should give you a general idea of the types of illnesses you will encounter most often with adult patients. Gradual physical decline is often associated with middle age, but this too is highly context dependent.

From adolescence on, human beings continue to grow and mature. *Aging* can be defined as "the sum of all the changes that normally occur in an organism with the passage of time."[12] Demographers, social scientists, and developmental psychologists consider middle age to be roughly between ages 35 and 65.[13] Aging, like adulthood itself, is complex and varies from one person to another. Aging also gives rise to feelings of anxiety in a way no other area of human development does. Failing intellectual or biological functions in the middle years can become a preoccupation for your patient. For example, during this period the pure joy of physical activity experienced in younger years may acquire a sober edge. One of us overheard a man who for years has enjoyed running just for the sport of it tell his friend, "Yeah, my running will probably guarantee that I live 5 years longer, but I will have spent that 5 years running!" Adults may also worry about changes in their mental capacities when they forget a name or misplace the car keys. Suddenly, forgetfulness is no longer something to be taken lightly but could portend more serious problems generally associated with old age.

Perhaps the anxiety that aging provokes is due to the close relationship most of us believe exists between biological development and illness, decline, and death.[14] Rather than view aging in this way, gerontologists have proposed the concept of *compressed morbidity*, which suggests that people may live longer, healthier lives and have shorter periods of disability at the end of their lives. The focus of health care then becomes one of prevention, health improvement for chronic disease, and

Table 15-1	Cause of Death
Rank	**Percentage of Total Deaths for Population of the United States in 2003**
1. Diseases of the heart	28.0
2. Malignant neoplasms	22.7
3. Cerebrovascular diseases	6.4
4. Chronic lower respiratory diseases	5.2
5. Accidents (unintentional injuries)	4.5
6. Diabetes mellitus	3.0
7. Influenza and pneumonia	2.7
8. Alzheimer's disease	2.6
9. Nephritis, nephrotic syndrome, and nephrosis	1.7
10. Septicemia	1.4

U.S. Department of Health and Human Services, Centers for Disease Control and Prevention, *National Vital Statistics Report*, 2003 (website): http://www.cdc.gov/nchs. Accessed August 15, 2006.

postponement of disability or death rather than cure.[15] In Chapter 16 we will discuss different views of aging and their impact on your interactions with older patients.

Stresses and Challenges of Midlife

"In terms of social roles, middle age is described generally as a time when the individual is a responsible member of society under pressure to coordinate multiple roles (e.g., spouse, worker, parent)."[16] The more responsibilities a person assumes, the more vulnerable he or she becomes to the symptoms associated with stress. Stress is recognized as a threat to the well-being of the present generation and will increase if steps are not taken to deal with it. Major problems associated with stress in adult life finally are gaining the attention of investigators, health professionals, workplace counselors, and religious groups.

Chapter 4 addressed some aspects of stress in students, and Chapter 7 suggests types of challenges faced by patients likely to produce stress at any age. Midlife stress is similar in its most general form. The specific sources differ, but the means by which a young person has learned to deal with stress will be carried into adulthood. One significant difference is that, in the middle years, no clearly defined end to some sources of stress—no "gracious exit" from an impossible situation—may be in sight. The stress attending next week's exam can be more easily managed than that arising from the realization that one has a stressful lifestyle in general.

Some stresses result from personal life choices. The responsibilities assumed in marriage and other primary relationships (e.g., childrearing, parent care, and work) all create stress, as do unemployment and some factors in the social structure itself. Each is discussed separately.

Primary Relationship Stresses

Marriage relationships during the middle years have been studied more extensively than other types of primary relationships, but it is reasonable to believe that all such relationships produce stress situations. Common sources of stress in the marriage relationship include nonfulfillment of role obligations by a spouse, lack of reciprocity between marital partners, and a feeling of not being accepted by one's spouse. Illfeld maintains that sources of stress that are damaging to the marital relationship are those of an ongoing nature instead of those of a discrete event. He further proposes that these common, mundane stressors in everyday life take more of a toll in suffering than does the impact of a dramatic life crisis.[17] Couples with children often experience stress around the departure of their children, leaving both (and not only the woman, as is often thought) with the "empty nest syndrome." The empty nest has traditionally been a gendered approach to theorizing about changes in midlife. In addition to the empty nest, women's middle age is often discussed in terms of menopause and new opportunities for activity and self-expression. For many women who work outside the home, the empty nest is not an issue of concern. Also, menopause is not universally viewed as the critical event of middle age that many popular authors claim it to be.[18]

A more violent expression of stress, the primary source of which may not arise from the relationship itself but is acted out within it, is spousal domestic violence.

Some persons involved in situations of domestic violence receive attention from self-help groups and other organizations, but not all do. They may well be present among your patients, exhibiting symptoms that deserve attention. For generations they have remained hidden and silent, victimized by the fear of stigmatization and having no place to go. Refuges, or safe houses, exist in many cities and sometimes also in rural areas. An increasing number of health professionals are volunteering their services for the treatment and rehabilitation of these women and men and their abusers.

Parenting Stresses

The tremendous responsibility associated with parenting also leads to stress situations in the middle years. Child abuse and neglect, which are increasing (or, perhaps, are being reported more systematically), are other tragic examples of what can happen when stress is not controlled. Most stress related to childrearing leads to less deplorable results, but nonetheless, it does take an immense toll on both parent and child.

Stress in Care of Elderly Family Members

Growing numbers of baby-boomers will experience the struggles of an aging parent. Assuming the parents of baby-boomers bore an average of two children, there are about 76 million parents of baby-boomers who are dealing with the acute and chronic disabilities of old age.[19] The average caregiver is a 46-year-old woman who has at least some college experience and provides more than 20 hours of care each week to her mother.[20] As previously mentioned, the majority of the burden for parent care falls on adult women. Many quit their jobs to fulfill the responsibility of caring for one or more elderly family members. Women caregivers also report strains on their own health that are a result of the stresses of daily caregiving. The most common health consequences of caring for an older, sick relative are higher levels of depression and anxiety. This often goes undetected and untreated. Add to this the other demands competing for these women's time and energy, and you can see how stressful parent care can be. The stress is often borne with considerable grace as adult children express the desire to care for their parents and the satisfaction and joy it brings them in concert with the burdens. Unfortunately, elder abuse, like spousal and child abuse, is on the rise. Much needs to be done in the way of effective social policy development to assist families in caring for their frail family members so that they do not reach the limits of their endurance.

Work Stress

For many individuals in the middle years, stress related to work is their primary stress, manifesting itself in a wide range of disorders. The source of stress may be job dissatisfaction in general, coupled with the notion that there is nowhere else to go. It may be that the job is basically satisfactory but that some component is an ongoing source of stress, such as a co-worker who is a continual "thorn in the flesh." Some jobs are in themselves highly stressful. One of the most studied high-stress jobs is a position in an intensive care unit. Another is work in an airport control tower.

These studies demonstrate that a job with high responsibility in which the consequences for a mistake are dire creates the highest stress. Boredom and repetition also create stress. Work-related stress can be a key factor in the development of serious health problems such as cardiovascular disease and alcoholism or other substance abuse problems.

A particular form of stress related to the work role is caused by the inability to hold a job or find one. In a society that rewards its members for paid work, the stress of working can be less threatening to health and well-being than the stress of being unemployed.

Thus, it becomes evident that the middle years, in which a person is in many ways at his or her prime, are also years of responsibility and stress. The burdens, although each taken alone may be a small constraint, sometimes have the overall effect of making the middle-age person feel exhausted and overwhelmed. Although these years are sometimes characterized as a plateau or holding pattern, they are much more varied than that: they are filled, instead, with alpine meadows, treacherous cliffs, cool blue pools, and swift undercurrents.

Doubt at the Crossroads and Midlife Challenges

The task of assuming responsibility and its attendant stresses, the great desire to achieve, or transitions in career, family life, and health condition may at some critical moment trigger an opportunity to take stock. The feeling accompanying the experience is most clearly expressed as doubt. It differs from the vacuous zero point of boredom and lacks the volcanic fervor of other types of stress. Doubt allows no rest; indeed, it is a relentless churning that nakedly reveals almost all the dimensions of one's life. The masks that have allowed the masquerade to go on, the clatter that has accompanied the parade, the walls that have kept fearful monsters from view, all suddenly evaporate and leave a pregnant silence. The self stands alone. Middle-age adults may wonder "Is this all there is?" and feel that "something is missing." Also, the focus on worldly aspirations may start to shift to more spiritual aspects of life and their place in the bigger scheme of things. Middle-age adults make more informed decisions about their futures.

The various transitions that are a part of adult life allow people to come to terms with new situations. Bridges conceptualizes a transition as a three-phase psychological process people go through: ending, neutral zone, and new beginning.[21] A transition begins with an ending. Something must be left behind to move to the next phase. A transition may be sought or thrust upon a person.

Consider the case of Tanya Zorski, who worked as a claims processor at an insurance company for the past 10 years. Recently, Tanya's employer merged with another company, resulting in "downsizing" or firing of many people in the claims department, including Tanya. Tanya's transition begins with the ending of her job. The next phase of transition is the neutral zone. After letting go, willingly or unwillingly, she must examine old habits that are no longer adaptive.[21] As Tanya begins to look for another position, she will discover that the computer skills that had been adequate at her old job are not marketable. Employers want people with experience in leading-edge computer programs, and Tanya does not possess these skills. During the neutral zone phase, people start to look for new, better-adapted skills or habits. People may take this opportunity to pursue a long-held dream. The final phase is the new beginning. Tanya decides to move into a new beginning in her life by pursuing a degree in nursing. She reasons that if she is going to invest the energy, time, and financial resources in learning new skills, she might as well do it in a profession that she has wanted to join since she was young.

▶ Do you anticipate working in the same job for your entire career?

▶ What would make you "shift gears" in your work, living arrangements, or location?

Although changes in midlife have often been labeled as a "crisis," perhaps the language is too strong. "Instead, perhaps, many individuals make modest 'corrections' in their life trajectories—literally, 'midcourse' corrections."[22] These corrections to one's life course are often the opportunity for growth. As is the case with Tanya Zorski, the more life-changing an event, the more likely it is to be associated with learning opportunities. "In fact, learning may be a coping response to significant life changes for many people."[23]

Regardless of whether a vision is being claimed or reclaimed, the adult's task is to prepare for the adjustments and challenges still to come.

WORKING WITH THE MIDLIFE PATIENT

This chapter deals almost exclusively with the psychosocial processes people face in their middle years. The fact is that life tasks associated with the middle years primarily are psychosocial ones.

The patient you encounter in his or her middle years who arrives at the health facility may be working to maintain health or is experiencing a physical symptom. Because the middle years are not "supposed to be" characterized by painful or other troubling physical symptoms, those patients may feel especially angered or confused by this physical intrusion into their work of being a responsible person and pursuing goals! A woman of middle years who was being interviewed recently in a seminar reported that she had "bow-and-arrow" disease. The doctor had told her that she had multiple myeloma, a bone marrow disease, but the fact that she heard "bone marrow" as "bow-and-arrow" probably more accurately expresses how many adults experience their illnesses or injuries. The idea of being struck down in one's prime and that of the "untimely" accident or death are often applied to this age group. The denial, hostility, and depression that patients feel about being so attacked are factors to which you should give your attention, whether your interaction occurs only once or extends over a long period of time.

Because psychological and social well-being are preeminent for people of middle years, treatment must be attuned to both. Of all the challenges described in Chapter 6, the loss of independence most epitomizes the overall loss experienced by the adult patient. Of course, the person's former self-image is threatened, too, but this is almost a direct outgrowth of the loss of independence. A patient who can no longer go about meeting the responsibilities expected of him or her and pursuing the numerous life goals now established will usually feel trapped, vulnerable, and frustrated. The primacy of these concerns in middle life should help you to understand why a patient seems overly concerned about having to get a baby sitter for an hour or having to be home at a given time or why he or she is willing to forego treatment rather than to take time from work for a trip to the health facility.

Furthermore, an adult patient experiencing acute stress poses special problems and challenges. Each one must be treated according to the particular manifestations of the stress. Part of the respect you must express is to assess physical or psychological symptoms that may be arising from stress. This, of course, must often be done with a psychiatrist or psychologist, but not always. Indeed, the skills of listening to the patient's narrative are tools to help you discern what is on a patient's mind. Listening may not only help to decrease his or her anxiety at the moment but may also enable you to make adjustments in schedule, routine, or approach that will further diminish it.

Many of the suggestions given throughout this book apply to all age groups. However, if you are alert to some of the central concerns and roles of middle life, you may well find that your success in achieving respectful interaction with the patient of middle years is heightened.

In the next chapter you have an opportunity to examine some changes that are faced by the person who has successfully lived through the middle years. As you will see, these changes involve some of life's greatest challenges, both positive and negative.

SUMMARY

Even though biological capacities begin to diminish in middle adulthood, adults generally have sufficient capacity for a personally satisfying and socially valuable life. The major life tasks for adults are to establish personal identity, develop intimate relationships, and feel and act on the desire to make a lasting contribution to the next generation through parenting, work, and public service activities. Although some people never resolve the issues that are brought into focus during the transitions of midlife, fortunately most do. Some emerge from the process with a new job, a new mate, or a new life view. The various aspects of adult development that were presented in this chapter are a sampling of the ways you can look at the complex process of how people grow and develop as adults with an eye to how these observations can help you to be respectful in your relationships with midlife patients and their families.

REFERENCES

1. Lamott A: *Hard laughter,* New York, 1980, North Point Press.
2. Bee HL: *Journey of adulthood,* ed 3, Upper Saddle River, NJ, 1996, Prentice Hall.
3. Erikson EH: *Childhood and society,* ed 2, New York, 1963, WW Norton.
4. Reeves PM: Psychological development: becoming a person. In Clark MC, Caffarella RS, editors: *An update on adult developmental theory: new ways of thinking about the life course: new directions of adult and continuing education,* San Francisco, 1999, Jossey-Bass.

5. Hiltner S: Personal values in the middle years. In Ellis EO, editor: *The middle years,* Action, Mass, 1974, Publishing Sciences Group.
6. Peacock JR: Gay male adult development: some stage issues of an older cohort, *J Homosex* 40(2):13-29, 2000.
7. Clark M, Huttlinger K: Elder care among Mexican American families, *Clin Nurs Res* 7(1):64-81, 1998.
8. McGrew KB: Daughters' caregiving decisions: from an impulse to a balancing point of care, *J Women Aging* 10(2):49-65, 1998.
9. Pohl JM, Collins CE, Given CW: Longitudinal employment decisions of daughters and daughters-in-law after assuming parent care, *J Women Aging* 10(1):59-74, 1998.
10. Moos RH, Billings A: Conceptualizing and measuring coping resources and processes. In Goldberger L, Breznitz S, editors: *Handbook of stress: theoretical and clinical aspects,* New York, 1982, Free Press.
11. U.S. Department of Health and Human Services, Centers for Disease Control: National Vital Statistics Report, 2003 (website): http://www.cdc.gov/nchs. Accessed September 10, 2006.
12. Matteson ES, McConnell ES, Linton AD, editors: *biological theories of aging in gerontological nursing: concepts and practice,* ed 2, Philadelphia, 1996, WB Saunders.
13. Brim OG, Ruff CD, Kessler RC, editors: *How healthy are we? A national study of well-being at mid-life,* Chicago, 2004, University of Chicago Press.
14. Mott VW: Our complex human body: biological development explored. In Clark MC, Caffarella RS, editors: *An update on adult developmental theory: new ways of thinking about the life course: new directions of adult and continuing education,* San Francisco, 1999, Jossey-Bass.
15. U.S. Department of Health and Human Services *Healthy People 2010* (website): http://www.health.gov/healthypeople. Accessed July 12, 2006.
16. Helson R, Sato CJ: Up and down in middle-age: monotonic and nonmonotonic changes in role, status and personality, *J Pers Soc Psychol* 89(2):194-204, 2005.
17. Illfeld FW: Marital stressors, coping styles and symptoms of depression. In Goldberger L, Breznitz S, editors: *Handbook of stress: theoretical and clinical aspects,* New York, 1982, Free Press.
18. Gergen MM: Finished at 40: women's development within the patriarchy, *Psychol Women Q* 14:471-494, 1990.
19. Sherman FT: This geriatrician's greatest challenge: caregiving, *Geriatrics* 61(3):8-9, 2006.
20. American Association of Retired Persons, National Alliance for Caregiving: *Caregiving in the U.S.A.* (website): http://www.caregiving.org/data/04finalreport.pdf. Accessed April 2004.
21. Bridges W: *Managing transitions: making the most of change,* Reading, MA, 1991, Addison-Wesley.
22. Stewart AJ, Ostrove JM: Women's personality in middle age: gender, history, and midcourse corrections, *Am Psychol* 53(11):1185-1194, 1998.
23. Zemke R, Zemke S: Adult learning: what do we know for sure? *Training Magazine* 32:31-40, 1995.

CHAPTER OBJECTIVES

The student will be able to:

- Discuss in general terms Erikson's assessment of the developmental tasks in the later years of life
- Describe the roles of friendship and family ties among older people and how these ties can have an impact on an older patient
- Compare and contrast at least two psychological theories of aging
- List some basic challenges to well-being that present themselves in old age and some ways to help older people meet such challenges successfully
- Describe how the health professional's attention to sensory impairment in older patients who require assistive devices can have a positive effect on the interaction
- Summarize the reasons an established time for treatment and a regular routine may be signs of respect toward older patients
- Discuss appropriate and inappropriate responses to a patient who has acute or permanent cognitive impairment
- List some values that may become highly prized among many older people, and suggest approaches that the health professional can use to optimize those values

I look at my mother. She's staring at the birds in the small cage across the room. Her rocker soothes her and her eyes close to slits. I take my thumb and trace her cheekbone. I rub the skin and watch it become young in my hands. The lines vanish, then reappear. Vanish, then reappear.

I remember being her young daughter, rubbing the rouge into her cheeks this way. She taught me how to find the bone and trace it. And then she placed the color on my finger and let me smooth it in. I could have stared at her forever. I still could.

My thumb moves softly from front to back, again and again. I watch the lines return and disappear. They will someday be the lines that already have begun to form across my own face.

—J. Dyer[1]

One of the challenges confronting anyone who attempts to speak of old people is to earmark exactly when old age begins, even though it is a time of life everyone will enter if they are fortunate enough to live past middle age. According to many statements on social policy, eligibility for financial and other supportive benefits begins at age 65, but the usefulness of this age as a distinguishing line largely ends there. In fact, people's feelings that they are "old" usually are much determined by the presence of sickness, disability, or other factors rather than simply by their chronological age. For the purposes of this chapter, terms such as "elderly," "old," and "aged" will refer to individuals age 65 or older. The older population numbered 36.3 million in 2004 (the latest year for which data are available). They represented 12.4% of the U.S. population—about 1 in every 8 Americans. By 2030, there will be about 71.5 million older persons, more than twice their number in 2000. People 65 and older represented 12.4% of the population in the year 2000 but are expected to grow to be 20% of the population by 2030.[2] Even though not all older Americans are sick, it is true that the average patient in a health care facility is likely to be older than 75 years of age. Additionally, the older population—the heaviest users of the health care system—will be far more diverse and will be women, especially among the oldest old, or people over 85.[3] Thus, if you work in an inpatient health care facility you will probably encounter older patients who will likely be women from diverse backgrounds.

Almost every generality advanced about the older person is quickly countered by an individual's personal experience with a chronologically older man or woman. However, some processes that take place in a person as he or she advances in years differ little from one individual to another. This chapter provides an overview of physiological and psychosocial changes, with a special emphasis on the psychosocial aspects of aging as they are relevant to respectful interaction. We urge you to study the burgeoning literature of aging further because the questions and clinical issues surrounding care of older patients are complex.

The days of "over the river and through the woods to grandmother's house" have disappeared in large segments of today's society. Indeed, grandmothers may be actively involved outside of the home in a work setting or in voluntary community work. She may be raising grandchildren while Mom or Dad works.

Older persons are among us in a variety of roles. The rapid societal changes taking place around older people give them greater opportunity for divergent roles than ever before. If they are unable to take advantage of these opportunities, as many are, then they are burdened with greater insecurity and more complex problems than were any of their predecessors. However, if they can make the best of these opportunities, their potential for an active and meaningful old age is excellent.

VIEWS OF AGING

"Aging is a highly individualized process that affects each person in unique ways. Aging is the result of the interaction among genetics, environmental influences, lifestyles, and the effects of disease processes."[4] This definition of aging is fairly straightforward, but there is much more to aging than mere physiological changes. Cultural and societal views of aging influence how you understand the aging process and how you work with older patients. The following are various views of aging, proposed by Gadow in 1980 and still relevant today, with some examples involving older patients.[5]

Antithesis of Health and Vigor

This is the negative extreme as far as views of aging go. Aging is the opposite of what we value most highly in our society—youth, vitality, strength, etc. This view is seen in health care when terms such as *degenerative* are used to describe physiological changes that accompany normal aging. Many elders view their health status as "fair to good" even with a number of degenerative conditions.

Unwelcome Reminder of Mortality

Death is more common in old age in the United States than it is in younger age groups. Thus, it is often seen as an expected part of older age and more "natural." "The effect of this view is that the more natural and acceptable mortality is thought to be for 'the elderly,' as they are sometimes called, the more unthinkable it is for the non-elderly, and the more elderly people are avoided as symbols of the unthinkable."[5] Thus, one of the major problems of working with older people is that we have not come to terms with our own aging and mortality. The presence of the aged is an uncomfortable reminder of the future that is in store for all of us. Health professionals sometimes react to this discomfort by trying to avoid such patients whenever possible.

Underprivileged Citizens

Ageism as a type of discrimination and demeaning behavior were addressed in Chapter 3. "Most people, including healthcare professionals, are more familiar with pathological aging than with healthy aging and tend to generalize and project expectation of pathology. Ageism is thus the composite of stereotypical beliefs and attitudes held about a group of people based on their advanced age."[6] In this view, old adults are not readily accorded the respect they deserve but are forced often to rely on the benevolence of society in an attempt to make up for past and continuing discrimination. Programs such as Medicare and Medicaid, "senior discounts," and special services for "senior citizens" are examples of programs designed to redress shortcomings in society's treatment of older people as full citizens. Because we live in a youth-oriented society, older people often seem to have little importance. What young people see or read in the media or hear from adults plays a critical role in shaping their perceptions of older people.[7] Thus, it is important to promote representations of elderly people in the full range of activities and health states that comprise old age.

Aging as a Clinical Entity

This view of aging sets it apart from other life experiences shared by all human beings. Aging is seen as a clinical entity in its own right, something to be studied and analyzed through research. The subspecialties of "geriatrics" in health care and "gerontology" in the social sciences bear witness to the trend of separating out the unique features of aging. Although considerable positive developments have come from this view of aging, such as recognizing the special strengths of older patients as well as deficits, the risk remains that older patients will be treated differently from younger ones merely because they are old. An example of this can be found in a study of the recommendations medical students give to older ($\geq$ 59 years) and younger ($\leq$ 31 years) women regarding breast-conserving procedures. Although research has determined equivalent results between breast-conservation therapy and modified radical mastectomy, the medical students ($N = 116$) were biased by patients' ages when making recommendations. "They recommended breast-conservation therapy for a significantly higher percentage of younger patients than older patients (86% versus 66%)."[8] When age is inappropriately used to determine treatment options, it is a form of ageism. Fortunately, new theories of social and psychological development show that some aspects of development can continue throughout the lifespan.

Older People as a Cultural Treasure

The most positive view of aging is to see people who have lived a long time as a source of wisdom and experience. Recent interest in obtaining oral histories from elders who have witnessed great and mundane historical events are evidence of this view. The past experience of elderly people is of value to younger generations and fits well with Erikson's theory about the later stages of adult development.

NEEDS: RESPECT AND INTEGRITY

Several basic psychological and social processes are evident in the widely divergent lifestyles of today's older people. Erikson proposes that the success with which an older person can make psychological and social adjustments will depend on his or her ability to meet the most basic psychosocial developmental challenge of old age—that of integrity. In this last stage of human development, the person "understands, accepts, and loves the life he [or she] has led."[9] The person "possesses wisdom" and is willing to share this wisdom with the younger generation.[9] The little girl and older man in Figure 16-1 perfectly illustrate this sharing of expertise across generations.

Health professionals are delighted, and sometimes awed, by an older person who expresses the breadth and depth of acceptance described by Erikson. These older people readily accept the psychological and social adjustments that confront them. However, some older persons despair of being old, the psychological and social adjustments of old age overwhelm them, and they find little from their past to support them in their present situation. Key psychological and social processes assist or deter older persons from achieving a sense of wholeness and integrity in old age. Some of these are discussed on the following pages.

The Psychology of Aging

One theory of aging, the disengagement theory, suggests that, even before their friends die, some people contribute to their own isolation. In Elaine Cumming and William Henry's 1961 book, *Growing Old: The Process of Disengagement*, the following broad points were made:

FIGURE 16-1: (© *1995 Joan Beard, from* Family: a celebration, *edited by Margaret Campbell, Peterson's [USA].*)

Starting from the common-sense observation that the old person is less involved in the life around him than he was when he was younger, we can describe the process by which he becomes so, and we can do this without making assumptions about its desirability. In our theory, aging is an inevitable mutual withdrawal or disengagement, resulting in decreased interaction between the aging person and others in the social systems he belongs to … [The individual's] withdrawal may be accompanied from the outset by an increased preoccupation with himself; certain institutions in society may make this withdrawal easy for him.[10]

They view disengagement as a normal process that occurs earlier for some than for others, depending on the person's physiology, temperament, personality, and life situation. Retirement, they propose, is society's permission for men to disengage, whereas widowhood serves the same purpose for women; the disengaged person eventually develops a high morale. Some of the postulates of the disengagement theory appear dated, such as the one regarding gender roles. Many critics, beginning in the 1970s, have questioned whether disengagement theory is a true or desirable indication of successful aging. The theory was one of the first attempts at a "grand theory" of aging and, as such, remains of interest to the field of gerontology.[11]

Contemporary theories of aging include the socioemotional selectivity theory (SST) that states that as people age, they become increasingly selective of their social partners in order to conserve energy and to regulate emotions.[12] Another new theory of aging is gerotranscendence, a shift in perspective from a materialistic and rational vision to a more cosmic and transcendent one. Gerotranscendence is the final step in individual maturation and toward achieving wisdom, a new construction of reality for the aged individual.[13]

Recently, healthy aging has been described as a lifelong process optimizing opportunities for improving and preserving health and physical, social, and mental wellness; independence; quality of life; and enhancing successful life-course transitions.[14] This definition of healthy aging requires that older adults work to overcome the natural losses that occur with age. As you can see, there is still considerable disagreement about what counts as successful old age. Older adults have defined healthy aging more simply as having the physical, mental, and financial means to go and do something worthwhile.[15]

 REFLECTIONS

- Can you think of some problems that could occur clinically if you and a colleague differed in your definition of "good" old age?
- What if your idea of healthy aging differs from that of your elderly patient? Identify some of the elderly people that you know.
- What theory best describes their attitudes toward relationships, gains or losses, etc.?

Friendship and Family Ties

The amount of contact older people maintain with their families and friends varies greatly. Many persons lose a valuable source of natural physical contact and companionship with the diminution of friendship and family ties, whereas others remain actively integrated into family and community circles. If you take time to assess how many of your patients' needs for physical contact are still being met by friends and family, you will understand a lot about their conduct during their time with you. It is not unusual for people to transfer their needs to health professionals once they have lost other contacts.

Friendships

Until the present ultramobile way of life in the United States, the acquisition of a single set of friends continued throughout early life and tapered off when one settled down in a community. One's job seldom changed during the entire period of employment, and, as a result, the community (and the friends therein) remained the same up through old age. In one sense, this is a secure mode of existence, but reliance on lifelong friendship carries with it the risk that, if these friends all die, the person will be left alone. Many people who have depended on lifelong friendships find it difficult to make new acquaintances at 70 or 80 years of age. Friendships have been demonstrated to influence a person's psychological well-being. An older person's attitudes toward friendships and the make-up of the physical environment play a role in the maintenance and development of friendships in old age.[16]

The older person's ability and desire to make new friends depend partly on the extent to which friendship has been considered an important individual value throughout life and therefore on the extent to which friendship skills have been cultivated. Another important determinant is the types of friendship the person established in younger years.

There are basically four types of friendship, which vary in number and importance over the years:

1. *Fusion* friendships, which are fused to or an integral part of other roles, such as those involving family or occupation, increase or decrease in importance according to the person's present situation.
2. *Substitution* friendships are those into which the person channels energies that formerly were directed toward someone or something else.
3. *Complementary* friendships develop from situations in which another role (such as that related to occupation) and the friendship are mutually supportive.
4. *Competition* friendships are those that compete with another role.[17]

Therefore, an older person whose fusion or complementary friendship, made at an early age, centered on his or her occupation, may find that after retirement the friend is very much alive, but their friendship is dead. Conversely, a substitution or competition friendship may thrive after retirement because energy directed elsewhere can now be devoted to the friend. In this sense, the basis of a friendship is an important determinant of its longevity. In working with patients, you can understand some important things by exploring who the person's friends are and how the friendships were generated and sustained.

Family

As we discussed in Chapter 13, the family structure is changing. Participation in that unit is one of the most lasting and significant roles a person assumes.

In married relationships or other long-term couple relationships, the history is that the couple usually had an opportunity to spend much time alone together. When children become a part of the relationship, attention is transferred to them, and in many families much of the communication for many years takes place in the presence of at least one child. For persons with no children, jobs often become the center of attention. Only after the children have left home or the working years end is the couple alone again. Their attempts to reestablish direct communications are sometimes futile, causing them to withdraw, literally or symbolically, from the family. Other couples find this to be an opportunity to engage in activities together that they put off in their younger years.

In the present oldest population, those 85 years and older, there are many married or formerly married people. Older men are more likely to be married than older women are. You may work with elderly women who are not prepared to cope with financial and other business affairs because in their youth it was considered improper for women to be thus involved. You may work with elderly men who have never had to prepare a meal or wash clothes because it was considered improper for a man to do "woman's work." The death of a spouse or partner can be extremely difficult for them. Sometimes they turn to children, nieces, or nephews for help. Elderly people often turn to siblings when they find themselves alone. A sibling has the added benefit of a shared history, as is evident in the following poem:

> HOMECOMING
>
> *I*
> *after 45 years*
> *of writing letters*
> *& calling, Estelle sent word*
> *to find a contractor—*
> *she wants a home*
> *built next to her sister*
> *the house, brick & modern,*
> *is an oddity—*
> *sits prominently among shotgun houses,*
> *cows, chickens, fish ponds, bait shops*
> *& trailer homes*
> *Celeste walks the clay red road*
> *to her Oakland-California-sister—*
> *they have forty-five years to catch up on*
> *II*
> *Estelle & Celeste talk of the other two sisters*
> *who died in their early 70s—*
> *bring out boxes of black & white worn photos*
> *Estelle rakes arthritic fingers*
> *through Celeste's hair*
> *conjuring memory*
> *she parts the white/yellow-stained strands—*
> *braids her sister's hair.*
> *—Andrea M. Wren*[18]

A discussion of aging and family relationships must include a look at who is most likely to provide support for older people in times of illness. Social support systems for people who are ill include both family caregiving that exceeds normal care or help and informal ones (friends, neighbors, or members of a religious or other type of community). As we discussed in Chapter 15, families provide the majority of care for older relatives. Many families struggle to provide this care as is evident in the following example.

> Dad may be desperately ill, demanding constant attention and unable to join the family and guests at dinner. Mom may be afflicted with Alzheimer's and can't follow a conversation. Grandma may be bedfast. And in as many cases as not, the woman of the house does the caretaking even though she is poor, busy with a job to stay above subsistence level, preoccupied with her own children, and untrained. In such circumstances— God forbid—there is no extra room for the ill or aged, and little patience or reason for hope. Caring in the home is still the great overlooked medical-social problem among all classes in the United States.[19]

It is no wonder then that this level of stress sometimes leads to elder abuse. Elder abuse can take several forms:

1. Rights violations—denial of basic rights to adequate medical care or decent housing
2. Material abuse—monetary or material theft
3. Physical abuse—covers a variety of practices from omission (leaving a nonambulatory person in bed for long periods of time) to commission (beating or injuring the person)
4. Psychological abuse—a situation in which the person is debased and intimidated verbally[20]

Elder abuse is often not reported because the older person (or others) fear retaliation or believe that nothing will be done to change the situation. Just as with a child whom you suspect is being abused or neglected, you are legally responsible in all 50 states for reporting suspected elder abuse. It is important to add, unfortunately, that elder abuse is not isolated to the home setting. Elder abuse can occur in institutional settings as well such as domiciliary homes, nursing homes, day care, or even hospitals.

Where "Home" Is

A major challenge for older people is to decide where to make their homes. Security, accessibility to services, transportation, and physical considerations due to bodily changes in aging are important variables. Reduced income and the desire to be near friends or relatives also often weigh heavily for people who have a choice of location. For older persons with functional disabilities or those who need more assistance with daily living activities than can be provided at home by family or professional caregivers, a nursing home becomes their last place of residence. Primary reasons for admission to nursing homes include Alzheimer's disease and osteoporotic hip fractures. About 90% of nursing home residents are over 65. Not all admissions to skilled nursing facilities are for the rest of a patient's life. Some elderly patients are admitted only for a short time for rehabilitation so that they can regain strength and function and return to their homes.

Chapter 6 addresses how changes associated with illness or injury are a challenge for any patient. You will benefit from bearing in mind that these same losses may have already occurred for the older person simply because he or she is old rather than because of illness or injury. The loss of a long-established place of residence, of consequence to anyone, is felt deeply by the older person because self-respect and the power to command the respect of others depend, in part, on independence. Although many patients experience the loss of independence as temporary, older people usually realize that each loss is a one-way street to more dependence. Moving out of one's home permanently symbolizes dependence with a capital D.

Each move of residence may have a greater significance for old people than for those of any other age group. For example, a woman who has been forced to move out of her long-established residence into her daughter's home and who then requires admission to the hospital for elective surgery that results in placement in a nursing home for rehabilitation certainly has grounds for feeling completely "undone" by the number of moves she has had to make in a short period of time. Thoughtful health professionals take these factors into consideration and are patient in helping the older person adapt accordingly. In fact, a key to respectful interaction with an older person is to promote as much stability in the place of residence as possible.

THE CHALLENGE OF CHANGES WITH AGING

In the following section, some major losses described in Chapter 6 are discussed as they present themselves as challenges to many older people today.

Challenge to Former Self-Image

There is ample evidence to support that we have the potential to continue to develop throughout our lifespan, and our self-esteem can remain high or even grow stronger in older years. Some recognize talents they never knew they had or refocus their energies on other hobbies or projects. Consider the following poem and the primary values that guide each woman's daily activities.

SOCIAL SECURITY

She knows a cashier who
blushes and lets her use
food stamps to buy tulip
bulbs and rose bushes.
We smile each morning as I
pass her—her hand always
married to some stick
or hoe, or rake.
One morning I shout,
"I'm not skinny like
you so I've gotta run
two miles each day."
She begs me closer, whispers
to my flesh, "All you need,
honey, is to be on welfare
and love roses."
—Barbara Lehr[21]

Some persons do not even notice the changes in how they look, seeing only what they want to see in the mirror (Figure 16-2). Unfortunately, other people cling not only to a former visual image, but begin to reject the changes brought about by aging. They see themselves as has-beens who are no longer valuable to society and cannot perform as they did in the past.

Retirement from a long-held job often poses a threat to self-image (and, subsequently, to self-esteem) in many older men and women. With almost all adults employed in the workforce at some time in their lives, more people than ever before will face the challenge of retirement. However, many predict that the baby-boomer cohort, which is steadily moving into late middle age, may not retire at the traditional age of 65 because of concerns about funding shortfalls in Social Security and

FIGURE 16-2: "…I haven't changed a bit …"

Medicare, possible cuts in government programs for the elderly, and cuts in traditional defined benefit pension plans which previously provided a fixed income during retirement. For most, retirement not only involves a substantial reduction in income but also signals a change in their daily activity.

As the person looks forward in time to retirement, a central issue becomes replacing time spent in work with other activity. Although work is only one part of the person's whole landscape of activities, it is a large part. The disappearance of work potentially leaves much of his or her landscape unfilled. At a minimum, retirement precipitates change in the person's whole activity pattern.[22] Four basic tasks seem to comprise essential post-job satisfaction: social activity, play, creativity, and life-long learning.[23]

To maintain their status as useful members of society, almost all old people need to be engaged in some kind of ongoing activity. This may be a job, a hobby, a volunteer service, or a club. In fact, the majority of volunteer hours are contributed by Americans beginning in midlife and continuing into old age in many areas that U.S. social policy fails to address adequately, such as the provision of basic human services.[24] Regardless of the activity chosen, they do need to have something to look forward to and to know that they are needed in a certain place at a certain time. Research suggests that involvement in volunteer activities may significantly improve the health and well-being of older people themselves through lower rates of depression, retention of functional abilities, improved physical activity, and cognitive activity.[25,26] However, not all older people are able to be involved in activities outside of the home, and there are some good reasons why:

1. They may be shy about meeting new people, particularly if they have maintained one set of friends and acquaintances for many years.
2. They may be too physically ill to participate in ongoing activities.
3. They may have no way to get to them.
4. They may not be able to afford to go.
5. They may be afraid to go out alone or at night.

One or more of these reasons may also prevent them from seeking ongoing health care!

Fortunately, as the average age of our society grows, older people will become involved in continuous activities. For example, politics is one area in which the older-than-65 population has gained a powerful voice. Political involvement facilitates progress in legislation regarding their own interests and provides a broader perspective for legislation regarding society as a whole.

Physical Changes of Aging

A high percentage of older people are remaining in good health longer than ever before. Perception is the process of making meaning out of experience, and largely depends on our sense organs. With aging, the efficiency of both information gathering and making sense out of the information declines for most people. Visual changes include declines in acuity, speed of focusing, and accommodation in vision. With aging, adaptation to darkness usually declines too. Hearing losses are greatest in the high-frequency range. There is a steady loss in perception of body movement, or kinesthesia. The older person may "adjust" to the losses gracefully. An example is an exchange that one of the authors had with her 92-year-old neighbor. As she walked into his living room, where the television announcer was blaring the Red Sox's latest play, she was surprised to see Tom planted in front of a blank screen. "Tom!" she shouted above the clamor, "There's no picture!"

"Picture tube went about a month ago!" he shouted back. "Can't see the screen anyway!" Tom, in spite of his good humor, would probably concede that the savings on the picture tube was not worth the price of failing eyesight. For people with sensory impairment, the start of each day must seem like, as Shakespeare put it, the "Last scene of all,/That ends this strange eventful history... /Sans teeth, sans eyes, sans taste, sans everything" (*As You Like It,* II, vii, 139). Your sensitivity to a patient's feelings about these losses can have profound effects on the extent to which the patient feels respected by you.

Understandably, attention to a patient's sensitivity about such matters and attempts to help an older person with sensory deficits prepare for the day are critical components of showing respect.

We will not discuss musculoskeletal or neurological changes in the aging process because many health professionals learn this elsewhere. Posture, balance, strength, endurance, and other physical expressions of aging will vary, but overall wear and tear on the body will affect everyone in their later years. On the other hand, exercise has a positive impact on human beings of almost any age. Regular activity can reverse the decreased mobility that contributes to disease and disability in old age.[27] Furthermore, exercise has been shown to promote modest positive changes in cognitive functioning in the aged.[28] Given demonstrated improvements in so many areas, a prescription for activity seems indicated for most elderly patients.

One way of dealing with all of the physical changes that are a normal part of aging as well as those that accompany chronic and acute illness and injury is to share experiences with others who understand what the person is going through. A wonderful example of this can be found in the field study of older women in a neighborhood beauty shop by Furman. Because few of us get to interact with older people who are not related to us, this glimpse into the social life of elderly women is particularly enlightening.

> Customers exhibit a capacity for laughing at themselves, at their aches and pains, and at their intense engagement in such matters. For example, Blanche and Carmela, along with Claire, find themselves discussing various surgeries that they've had, stimulated by the fact that Blanche recently had cataract surgery. They first compare notes on that type of surgery; Blanche then talks about the hysterectomy she had years back, and so forth. Rather spontaneously, Blanche breaks into this discussion by saying, "Look at us, talking about cataracts, hysterectomies, hospitals!" They all laugh in this moment of self-recognition and amusement at themselves.[29]

Your sensitivity to changes, offering the person opportunities to talk about illness and loss and especially what changes mean for his or her feeling of well-being, is an avenue to respectful interaction, too.

Mental Changes of Aging

In most respects, working with an older person is no different from working with a person of any other age. However, a few minor differences due to mental changes normative for all aging can enhance the health professional's success in working with older people.

All patients benefit from the security of a set schedule, and this may be especially true for many older persons. The security arises from the knowledge that, at least in this one small area, he or she is in control of the environment. Some older people continue to exercise complete control over the details of their existence, whereas others gradually lose this opportunity. Even if this control extends no further than the patient's telling the taxicab driver to hurry because he or she is scheduled to be in speech therapy in 13 minutes, that person's self-respect will have been bolstered by exercising this type of control.

More important, establishing a schedule may be a way of helping an older person maintain a proper orientation to the environment. Some institutionalized older people become confused about the time of day and the date because they have few clues to orient them compared with the person who works 5 days a week or a peer who has more ongoing routine activity.

Besides setting a time, you can state the time limit of a certain treatment or test. For instance, if an apparently disoriented old man will be in the testing situation for $\frac{1}{2}$ hour, he should be told this at the onset and at the end of the test. If he does not have a clock, one should be provided so that he can check the time in the interim.

An older person's sense of security, control, and orientation can be further enhanced if, in addition to being treated at the same time each day, the routine of the treatment or test is kept reasonably stable from one day to the next. If the treatment or testing situation varies significantly every day, the patient may feel that nothing about it is familiar; it may be an anxiety-producing experience every time the person reports to the health professional. Anxiety can greatly decrease the person's performance and have a detrimental effect on both the relationship with you and the patient's progress.

Establishing a routine does not imply that the treatment should be exactly the same each day. Monotony or boredom can be just as detrimental to the patient as anxiety. Rather, the ideal situation is a balance between the patient's need for stability and his or her continuing interest in life and need for stimulation.

INTERACTING WITH COGNITIVELY IMPAIRED OLDER PEOPLE

Cognitive impairment in the aged person can take many forms, and it is important that you study them in more depth than is appropriate to address in this book. However, impairment in one particular aspect of an elderly person's life, instrumental activities of daily living (IADLs), has been shown to be correlated with the presence of dementia and may be one of the early signs of cognitive changes.[30] If there is impairment in one the following four IADLs, a thorough mental status evaluation should be performed: (1) medication management, (2) money/financial management, (3) telephone management, and (4) transportation management. We engage you in a general discussion about cognitive impairment and provide some general guidelines for respectful interaction with people suffering from brain syndromes that directly affect thought and speech processes.

Acute confusion or disorientation can be caused by a variety of factors, such as an infection, a fluid or electrolyte imbalance, or a cerebral vascular accident. It is important to determine the cause of confusion in an elderly patient and not just ascribe it to "being old." The following case illustrates how critical it is to understand the genesis of a change in mental status in an older patient.

🐦 Family members brought an 81-year-old man, Abraham Steinman, who was in an acutely agitated and confused state, to the emergency department. The family stated that Mr. Steinman had gradually been getting more and more confused over the last few weeks and finally became violently disturbed earlier in the evening. He was admitted to the adult psychiatric unit because he was physically violent to the staff in the emergency room. The distraught family said he had never had an emotional outburst in his life and could not understand his behavior. The next day a careful physical examination revealed that Mr. Steinman had bilateral pneumonia and some signs of kidney failure. His confusion and agitation had only been a symptom of his physical illness.

▶ What action might have prevented the admission to psychiatry?

▶ Would the assessment and treatment have been the same if Mr. Steinman were 40 years old? If he were 20 years old?

For such patients, acute confusion can be continual and may be increasingly profound, although you can help diminish the patient's suffering from disorientation at any given moment. Often, a useful approach is to not support the older person's constantly confused ideas, unless correcting them causes him or her to become violent, further disoriented, or deeply agitated. If an old man thinks he is in a hotel, you should try to correct him using a gentle reassuring voice and manner. If he confuses you with someone else, his mistake can be corrected by showing him your name badge and repeating your name. Chances are that he will be less frightened if the people around him are willing to help him clear up his mind, if only for a few minutes. It is a good general rule of respectful interaction to correct the person. However, you should also remember to listen with interest and politeness to the patient. Listening will help you to determine the depth of the confusion, ascertain the wisdom of trying to correct it, and, in some cases, discern that the patient is making sense within a context not immediately evident.

The seemingly confused person should be treated kindly. Such treatment should never be condescending, but it should reflect the gentle authority that gives the patient a sense of security. If the confusion is the result of a disease such as Alzheimer's disease or another form of dementia, many of the same principles apply. Some additional strategies for communicating with patients with dementia are as follows: use broad opening statements or questions, try to establish commonalties, speak to them as equals, and try to recognize themes in what the patient is trying to share with you.[31]

Sometimes medications can help the patient relax or in other ways be more comfortable, although with elderly patients it is best to be cautious with the use of drugs. Goals must be adapted according to what patients can comprehend. Some patients may be unable to remember the simplest tasks from one testing or treatment period to the next and may never grasp the most elementary verbal instructions. Others, however, will be able to follow astonishingly complex procedures. It is your responsibility in such situations to approach each person as an individual and to not take for granted that all confused utterances are signs of organic brain changes.

In some cases, the confusion will increase no matter what is done. However, none of these complications should deter you from first attempting, in a kind way, to correct the inaccuracies. With a great number of patients, this humane act is the key to respectful interaction.

ASSESSING A PATIENT'S VALUE SYSTEM

The mechanics of adjusting a hearing aid, setting a schedule, or correcting a confused-sounding statement must all be done in a way that supports the older person's value system. Otherwise, the person is reduced to nothing more than an object to be efficiently manipulated. Chapter 1 listed some of the primary societal and personal values cherished by people in this society. Older people as a group can be expected to hold the same range and variety of values; no particular value can be ruled out automatically on the basis of age. However, the topics treated in this chapter can help you understand why so many older people adhere to some values more than others.

For instance, the primary good of self-respect will often be a more consciously prized value for older people because they perceive, correctly, that they are subject to loss of self-respect in an ageist society. Security, both financial and physical, may also be highly prized by older people because, again, for many of them the hold on it is more tenuous. Further, continued independent functioning is valued dearly when commitment to a nursing home is a threat or when activities that can be performed alone become increasingly limited. Listening for which values the older patient expresses as his or her most precious and then trying to set treatment goals accordingly will greatly enhance your success.

In working with older people, the most important challenge confronting you is resisting the tendency to stereotype them. Society's expectations of older people, many of which are inaccurate and outdated, are propagated through literature, television, and other popular media.

You can learn to appreciate individual differences among aged persons by increasing your contact with people who are older. Programs sponsored by churches, private organizations, and the government offer volunteer opportunities ranging from transportation to recreational activities to providing hot meals for homebound persons. In some cities foster care facilities and other institutions where older persons live welcome young people who are interested in volunteering their services or visiting older people. Whether through volunteer services, organizations, or contact as a health professional, your challenge is to develop an acutely discriminating eye for individual differences.

SUMMARY

Care of older adults must be based on a sound understanding of the physiological and psychosocial aspects of aging. The major developmental tasks of old age are to find meaning and satisfaction with life as it becomes more and more difficult to keep up with everything that goes on in a busy world. The chief goal of care is to maintain and support the patient's self-esteem by affirming his or her strengths and discovering hidden resources. By keeping in mind a patient's emotional and social needs, you can help him or her retain dignity and self-respect. The secret to respectful interaction with older people is to keep their age-related problems in mind while concentrating on their individuality.

REFERENCES

1. Dyer J: *In a tangled wood: an Alzheimer's journey,* Dallas, 1996, Southern Methodist University Press.
2. Administration on Aging: *Statistics on the Aging Population* (website): http://www.aoa.gov. Accessed September 23, 2006.
3. He W and others: *65+ in the United States: 2005* (website): http://www.census.gov/prod/ 2006pubs. Accessed November 9, 2006.
4. McConnell ES: Conceptual bases for gerontological nursing practice: models, trends, and issues. In Matteson ES, McConnell ES, Linton AD, editors: *Biological theories of aging in gerontological nursing: concepts and practice,* ed 2, Philadelphia, 1996, WB Saunders.
5. Gadow S: Medicine, ethics and the elderly, *Gerontologist* 20(6):680-685, 1980.
6. Rosowsky E: Ageism and professional training in aging: who will be there to help? *Generations* 29(3):55-58, 2005.
7. Wircenski M and others: Age as a diversity issue in grades K-12 and in higher education, *Educ Gerontol* 25:491-500, 1999.
8. Madan AK, Aliabadi-Wade S, Beech DJ: Ageism in medical students' treatment recommendations: the example of breast-conserving procedures, *Acad Med* 76(3):282-284, 2001.
9. Erikson EH: *Childhood and society,* ed 2, New York, 1963, WW Norton.
10. Cummings E, Henry WE: *Growing old: the process of disengagement,* New York, 1961, Basic Books.
11. Achenbaum WA, Bengston VL: Re-engaging the disengagement theory of aging: on the history and assessment of theory development in gerontology, *Gerontologist* 34(6): 756-763, 1994.
12. Frederickson BL, Carstensen LL: Choosing social partners: how old age and anticipated endings make people more selective, *Psychol Aging* 5:335-347, 1990.
13. Tornstam L: Transcendence in later life, *Generations* 23(4):10-14, 2000.
14. Health Canada. *Workshop on Healthy Aging* (website): http://www.hc.sc.gc.ca/seniors-aines/ pub/workshop_healthyaging. Accessed August 24, 2006.
15. Bryant LL, Corbett KK, Kutner JS: In their own words: a model of healthy aging, *Soc Sci Med* 53:927-941, 2001.
16. McKee KJ, Harrison G, Lee K: Activity, friendships and wellbeing in residential settings for older people, *Aging Ment Health* 3(2):143-152, 1999.
17. Riley MW: Friendship. In Riley MW, editor: *Aging and society: a sociology of age stratification,* vol 3, New York, 1972, Russell Sage Foundation.
18. Wren AM: Homecoming, *Afr Am Rev* 27(1):157, 1993.
19. Marty ME: The "god-forbid" wing, *Park Ridge Center Bull* 11(Sept/Oct):15, 1999.
20. Benton D, Marshall C: Elder abuse, *Clin Geriatr Med* 7(4):831-845, 1991.
21. Bolz B: Social Security. In Martz S, editor: *When I am an old woman I shall wear purple,* Watsonville, CA, 1991, Papier Mache Press.
22. Jonsson H, Kielhofner G, Borell L: Anticipating retirement: the formation of narrative concerning an occupational transition, *Am J Occup Ther* 51(1):49-56, 1997.
23. Vaillant GE: *Aging well: surprising guideposts to a happier life from the landmark Harvard study of adult development,* Boston, 2002, Little, Brown.
24. United States Department of Labor, Bureau of Labor Statistics: *Volunteering in the United States, 2006* (website): http://www.bls.gov/news.release/volun.nr0.htm. Accessed November 12, 2006.
25. Moen P: Reconstructing retirement: careers, couples, and social capital, *Contemp Gerontol J Rev Crit Discuss* 4(4):123-5, 1998.
26. Fried LP and others: A social model for health promotion for an aging population: initial evidence on the experience corps model, *J Urban Health* 81(1):64-78, 2004.

27. Buckwalter JA, DiNubile NA: Decreased mobility in the elderly: the exercise antidote, *Physician Sportsmed* 25(9):126-128, 130-133, 153-155, 1997.

28. Van Sickle TD and others: Effects of physical exercise on cognitive functioning in the elderly, *Int J Rehabil Health* 2(2):67-100, 1996.

29. Furman FK: *Facing the mirror: older women and beauty shop culture,* New York, 1997, Routledge Press.

30. Barberger-Gateau P and others: Instrumental activities of daily living as a screening tool for cognitive impairment and dementia in elderly community dwellers, *J Am Geriatr Soc* 40(11):1129-34, 1992.

31. Tappen RM and others: Communicating with individuals with Alzheimer's disease: examination of recommended strategies, *Arch Psychiatr Nurs* 11(5):249-256, 1997.

PART SIX

Questions for Thought and Discussion

1. If you were asked to propose policies and plans for a waiting room area for families of high-risk newborns in your institution, what would you suggest to the architects, decorators, and administrators? Why? What sorts of support services would you recommend for families in this situation?

2. You are the supervisor of an adolescent unit in a hospital. The patient, a 16-year-old named Sam, is very mature for his age, and you have found him to be very thoughtful. Sam has cancer that you know has metastasized. His parents have decided with the surgeon that he should have an amputation, although all agree that the hope of saving him completely from the spread of the disease is negligible. One evening you notice that Sam is very withdrawn. He says, "My parents and the doctor are going to cut off my leg, and they haven't even asked me what *I* think about it. I'd rather die than lose my leg."
   a. What should you do?
   b. To whom should you speak about this conversation? Why?

3. You are hurrying down the hospital corridor when you notice an acquaintance of your family, a bricklayer in his middle fifties. You express surprise at seeing him there because he has always been the picture of good health. He tells you that he has had a heart attack. Suddenly he begins to pour out a blow-by-blow description of the incident. As he talks, he becomes increasingly agitated and finally bursts into tears, sobbing, "It's all over. I'll never be able to go back to my job or anything. What am I going to do?"
   a. What can you say or do right then to calm this man's immediate anxious state?
   b. Will you report this incident? To whom and why?
   c. How can health professionals work together to treat the middle-age person's anxiety about the long-term effects of illness on family, job, and self-esteem?

4. What do you dread most about growing old? What do you look forward to most? How do you think an older person's role will have changed by the time you grow old?

5. An alert 92-year-old patient who has been in your care for several days arrives late for treatment one morning at your ambulatory care clinic. She explains that she missed her usual bus and had to wait in the rain and cold for the next bus to arrive. You begin to converse with her in your usual manner and very quickly realize that something is wrong; she does not answer your questions appropriately. Once or twice, she mentions her son (who you know was killed years ago in the service of his country), but her sentences are disconnected and incomplete.
   a. What possible reasons may there be for her apparent confusion?
   b. Where will you start in your attempt to diagnose her problem?

PART
SEVEN

SOME SPECIAL CHALLENGES

In this last section of the book we explore with you some special challenges you will face in your attempt to show respect for patients and their families.

Chapter 17 tackles the relevant considerations you will want to bear in mind while working with patients who are dying and their loved ones. Human beings' understanding of dying and death is shrouded in mystery and today is punctuated by our exposure to violence in the media and our personal lives. Death rarely is portrayed as "natural." Patients may bring specific fears related to their condition to the health professional and patient relationship—fears shaped by their personal experience and stereotypes. You have an opportunity to examine these issues and how they affect patients and their families. You will learn about priorities that you as a health professional can set for such patients to show them the respect they deserve.

In the final chapter, Chapter 18, you have an opportunity to examine some situations that many health professionals identify as difficult. Now that you have read and thought about different types of patients and situations, you have a good basis for thinking about disparities of power or status in the health professional and patient relationship and how role expectations may affect interactions. In each of the examples our goal is for you think expansively about your potential for respectful interaction in even the most challenging situations you will encounter.

RESPECTFUL INTERACTION WHEN THE PATIENT IS DYING

The newspaper near his chair has a photo of a Boston baseball player who is smiling after pitching a shutout. Of all the diseases, I think to myself, Morrie gets one named after an athlete.

You remember Lou Gehrig, I ask?

"I remember him in the stadium, saying good-bye."

So you remember the famous line.

"Which one?"

Come on. Lou Gehrig. "Pride of the Yankees?" The speech that echoes over the loudspeakers?

"Remind me," Morrie says. "Do the speech."

Through the open window I hear the sound of a garbage truck. Although it is hot, Morrie is wearing long sleeves, with a blanket over his legs, his skin pale. The disease owns him.

I raise my voice and do the Gehrig imitation, where the words bounce off the stadium walls: "Too-dayyy ... I feeel like ... the luckiest maaaan ... on the face of the earth. ..."

Morrie closes his eyes and nods slowly.

"Yeah. Well. I didn't say that."

—M. Albom[1]

This excerpt, from a book titled *Tuesdays with Morrie*, chronicles the last months of a man's dying as it is recorded through the pen of his friend and former student. Here you catch them in one of their many exchanges, the young man trying to make conversation and the dying one bringing the narrative back to the heart of the matter—his own unique experience of dying. Of all the challenges you will face, your work with people who are dying will provide some of the greatest opportunities to use your skills as a professional.

Terminally ill is a term that is commonly used to describe people who are dying from a pathologic cause. Like all labels, it allows people in this group to be identified easily according to their special needs. At the same time, we refrain from using it in this chapter in large part because it is like a double-edged sword: it can further remove dying persons from others' caring by the fact that they belong to a group that carries many negative assumptions with it. One difficulty with the term is its generality. Persons such as Morrie, who suffered from amyotrophic lateral sclerosis (commonly known as *Lou Gehrig's disease*), may live for many months or years. Another person with a different condition may die within days or weeks. Still, both are labeled terminally ill. Many health professionals, as well as others, immediately place both people on the "critical list." One of the authors remembers a friend who had lived for more than 10 years with a diagnosis of malignant lymphoma. He went into the hospital for his periodic blood test. A health professional who had come back to work after a 5-year hiatus greeted him cheerfully, "Are *you* still around?" She was apparently astonished that this "terminally ill" patient had not died long ago! The patient recalled that although he knew her intentions were good, her greeting led to the most severe depression of his entire illness. As with all types of patients, the key is to look for the distinguishing factors that make this person's situation unique, and respond respectfully to the needs that arise out of that individual person's experience. Toward achieving that goal, a first step toward any health professional's understanding of a patient's situation is to gain some general idea of how death and dying are viewed within the larger society.

DYING AND DEATH IN CONTEMPORARY SOCIETY

Children's experiences of dying and death have been studied in detail, highlighting some important differences in their understanding of and responses to dying and death compared with those of adults. We encourage you to acquaint yourself with these differences. However, we do not have the space to discuss them in detail here and therefore focus on patients who are past childhood.

Dying as a Process

Dying is first and foremost a personal event. Although individuals respond differently to it, one common thread shared by all is that they are going through a *process*. In addition, all persons share some awareness that the end of the dying process is the death event. What does this mean to a person? In the minds of many patients or their families, a known diagnosis and somewhat predictable range of symptoms make them feel robbed of the "natural" flow of life. The dying process feels unnatural, an imposition. A life-threatening condition generates new fears and concerns.

Fortunately, for others it is also an opportunity to conduct long-neglected business, put one's affairs in order, or pursue a postponed adventure. Anticipation of the death event, too, creates its own concerns, fears, and hopes, many of which are rooted in religious and philosophical understandings of life and death. For most people death remains perhaps the ultimate mystery.

How *do* we gain an understanding of death?

In almost all cultures, death stories are an integral part of the stories passed down from childhood onward. They are the "great" stories, the material of the myths, in a culture. Notice the role death plays in snuffing out an enemy (but not the "good guys") in the following popular Western fairy tales:

> Down climbed Jack as fast as he could, and down climbed the giant after him, but he couldn't catch him. Jack reached the bottom first, and shouted out to his mother, who was at the cottage door. "Mother! Mother! Bring me an axe! Make haste, Mother!" For he knew there was not a moment to spare. However, he was just in time. Jack seized the hatchet and chopped through the beanstalk close to the root; the giant fell headlong into the garden, and was killed on the spot.
>
> So all ended well. …[2]

> Then Grethel gave her a push, so that she fell right in, and then shutting the iron door she bolted it. Oh how horribly she howled! But Grethel ran away, and left the ungodly witch to burn to ashes.
>
> Now she ran to Hansel, and opening his door, called out, "Hansel, we are saved; the old witch is dead!"[3]

Many Western childhood portrayals of the dying-death continuum show no connection between the two. Both the health professional and patient may share beliefs about the "unnaturalness" of death rooted in many Western childhood stories. Of course, not all cultures have the same understanding of life and death. How might your relationship with a patient be different if, say, he or she grew up with the deep memory of this childhood story recounted by Mitch Albom, the author of *Tuesdays with Morrie* (whose conversations with his dying friend led him to read about how different cultures view death)?

> There is a tribe in the North American Arctic, for example, who believe that all things on earth have a soul that exists in a miniature form of the body that holds it—so that a deer has a tiny deer inside it, and a man has a tiny man inside him. When the large being dies, that tiny form lives on. It can slide into something being born nearby, or it can go to a temporary resting place in the sky, in the belly of a great feminine spirit, where it waits until the moon can send it back to earth.
>
> Sometimes, they say, the moon is so busy with the new soul of the world that it disappears from the sky. That is why we have moonless nights. But in the end, the moon always returns. As do we all. …[1]

As you can begin to discern, in today's great mix of patients you will encounter, it is an important first step to try to gain some understanding of how death is viewed by each of them. It will give you a starting place for your further deliberation about how to respect what they say, how they behave, and what their attitudes are toward various aspects of their interaction with you and others during their dying process. Having considered that, let us turn to additional insights that will help guide you in this situation.

Dying: Denial and Beyond Denial

It is often said that Western societies are death-denying. What can that possibly mean when all around us people are dying every day from illness, accidents, violence, old age, war, and other causes? Probably the best explanation is that although there is evidence everywhere of our mortality, we do our best to hold the inevitable at arm's length.

In many parts of Western culture, treatment of the dead body is one expression of a desire to deny death. The dead body is painted and dressed to make it appear alive, although a sign of life, such as a sigh or fluttering eyelash, would cause most people to rush screaming from the room. For the most part, however, denial has simply become more subtle. For example, a subtle denial of death is manifested in the incredible scenes of violence and killing viewed in films and on television, as Figure 17-1 illustrates.

FIGURE 17-1: TV's influence on the child's perception of reality. *(From the Swedish translation of* Health Professional and Patient Interaction: Vård, Vårdare, Vårdad, *p. 242.)*

Even young children are exposed: they see the culprit killed but know that the same culprit will be on next week's show, having adventures in dangerous places.

To the viewer, death must seem a very exciting and not very permanent condition. Another demonstration of this denial is illustrated by the response of many people to the AIDS epidemic. Although it affects all population groups, AIDS is still often treated as a disease confined to small target groups in society: a "them but not us" perception of who could die from AIDS.

There are some positive dimensions of the denial of death for the person who is dying and for her or his family. The function of denial and its limitations are expressed well by a woman examining her own experience of having lung cancer:

> Our fear of death makes it essential to maintain a distance between ourselves and anyone who is threatened by death. Denying our connection to the precariousness of others' lives is a way of pretending that we are immortal. We need this deception—it is one of the ways we stay sane—but we also need to be prepared for the times when it doesn't work. For doctors, who confront death when they go to work in the morning as routinely as other people deal with balance sheets and computer printouts, and for me, to whom a chest x-ray or a blood test will never again be a simple, routine procedure, it is particularly important to face the fact of death squarely, to talk about it with one another.[4]

As a health professional you often will be pivotal in determining how families will cope with their loved one's dying. Attentiveness to their need to deny the impending death or some aspects of it for a time can help them adjust to the momentous reality. At the same time, the case of Beth Rice illustrates how we may unwittingly encourage a family's unhealthy, prolonged denial:

> When Beth Rice, a woman with a diagnosis of chronic obstructive pulmonary disease, began to experience discomfort from her symptoms, the health professional advised her husband, "Better bring her to the hospital, where she can get better care!" Beth was admitted to the hospital, but, despite the best of care, the disease continued to run its debilitating course. The doctor then sent the patient to the intensive care unit, where she could get constant attention.
>
> In the intensive care unit, rehabilitation services were discontinued, and intensive care was implemented. Adult visitors were allowed to be with her for only a few minutes at a time. The nurses were kind, but firm, in restricting the family's visits. Eventually, the son and husband began to come less often, explaining to each other, "It's better for her, for there's really nothing more we can do for her, and she needs her rest." In addition, her two grandchildren were kept from her, as is the case in most intensive care settings. The adults rationalized this, too, saying, "It's better for them to be protected from this pathetic sight." When finally Beth lapsed into unconsciousness, the family realized that they had missed an opportunity to say goodbye to her as well as to fully admit how close to death she was.

All this was done by well-meaning, loving, grieving people who could not cope with the approaching reality of death and who believed that they were doing what was most helpful for Beth. The institutional barriers they faced further encouraged—and at times required—them to seriously restrict their time with their loved one.

 REFLECTIONS

- What do you think should have been done differently—by the families and by the institution?
- If you were involved in her case, what do you think you would have done to decrease their regret afterwards?

Often, families need assistance in figuring out what is going on and what they can do to support their loved one and each other:

> My husband, John, age 55, was handed his diagnosis of liver cancer by a newly graduated doctor—John's own had just retired. "As I'm sure you know," the young man had blushingly begun, and John said simply, "Yes." We walked out of the office holding hands and cold to the marrow.
>
> Near the end, I started looking for signs that the inevitable would not be inevitable. I watched a few leaves that refused to give up their green to the season. I took comfort in the way the sun shown brightly on a day they predicted rain—not a cloud in the sky! I even tried to formulate messages of hope in arrangements of coins on the dresser top—look how they had landed all heads up, what were the *odds?* I prayed, too, in a way that agnostics do at such times. Sorry I doubted you "dear God, help us now." I stood shivering on our back patio in the early morning with my mug of coffee and told whatever might help us that now would be the time … but my dreams betrayed me: John, shrunk to the size of a thumb, fell from my purse where I'd been carrying him and was stepped on. In another dream, I took a walk around the block and when I came back, my house was gone.[5]

Moving beyond denial toward a greater understanding is possible for many people, patients and family alike. One key is for them to become more familiar with their own feelings about and understanding of the death event itself. Jeremy Taylor suspected as much 300 years ago when he said, "In order to die well, look for death. Every day knock at the gates of the grave, then the grave cannot do you a mystery."[6] For many, however, knocking at those gates gives rise to fears and other responses associated with both dying and death.

RESPONSES TO DYING AND DEATH

Because nearly all of us dread the thought of gradual and certain loss, the news of a life-threatening diagnosis is almost always disquieting. In the next section you have an opportunity to think about three of the most common fears, followed by some other responses patients and families may have.

Fears of Dying

What would be your biggest fears if you learned that you were dying? Most people can vaguely imagine what they would dread most; once the diagnosis is made, however, harsh reality intrudes and forces them to become acutely aware of their real fears. A patient's previous notions about their particular disease or injury and the known experiences of others who have had it combine to create a vivid picture of what the patient believes to be ahead. The following are some of the most commonly expressed ones.

Fear of Isolation

The fear of separation from loved ones during dying becomes a reality for many. The story of Beth Rice, who was first admitted to a hospital and then moved to the intensive care unit, is not uncommon.

Many persons are aware of the practice of being admitted to the hospital to die or of having to spend the final period of their lives in a care facility. It is not unusual for patients who have had several admissions to the hospital during a lengthy illness to announce during one of them that they will never leave the hospital again, and often they are right. This awareness alters their response to those around them long before the final separation from life is imminent.

You will understand a patient better if you recognize her or his acute anxiety about being abandoned by both family and health professionals. The fear may be shown in comments such as: "They are starting to ignore me;" "My family is busy with other things;" "The nurses skipped my medication this morning, so they probably are giving up on me;" "They spend more time with the woman in the next bed, but of course they know I'm dying." This worry about being abandoned when facing the greatest, or at least the final, event of physical life can be your cue to lend extra support and encouragement. You can personally do little things to help the person gain greater self-understanding, even though the person cannot repay you with renewed functioning. If the person's friends and relatives are withdrawing, you can contact the institution's chaplain, social worker, or volunteer. These team members can help maintain a supportive atmosphere for a patient, and because they are institutional resources, they should be summoned without hesitation.

Fear of Pain

Fear of pain is also common in patients who are dying. Those who have known others who experienced a distressful end to life cannot be sure that their own dying will not be equally painful or worse. Fortunately, modern medicine has the potential to nearly obliterate the physical pain of dying, though it is still a challenge in some settings to get positive pain relief.[7] Hospice arrangements are explicitly designed to emphasize effective pain management. You should be mindful that, even in patients who have persistent pain, the experience of physical pain can be influenced negatively or positively by psychological states. For example, anxiety and depression have a heightened effect on pain, whereas distraction and feelings of security tend to diminish the suffering associated with pain.[8] Therefore the patient's suffering may be decreased by your compassion and caring.

Fear of Dependence

In previous chapters fear of the loss of independence during illness, injury, and old age is examined. The attention given to these issues should signify the importance of continued independence when the person is in the process of dying. With rare exceptions, such people face certain and increasing dependence. Proof that they have thought about this is shown in their expressions of astonishment at having reached a point in their symptoms they had previously felt would be totally unbearable. Indeed, everyone has ideas of what he or she believes to be the "outer limits": loss of bowel and bladder control; sexual impotence; inability to feed oneself, to communicate verbally, or to think straight; unconsciousness; or other loss. Awareness of your own worries about dependence in some area of functioning will make you better able to understand your responses to what is happening to a patient.

Some health professionals also have to deal with their own feelings of pity toward a patient's plight, a caveat we introduced in Chapter 11. A student said to one of the authors about a patient he was treating, "I think I'm able to accept his blindness and the fact that he can't talk anymore, but what gets me is that no matter what I do for him, he is going to get worse and worse and finally die. I feel so sorry for him that I can hardly stand to go into the room." Although feelings of pity are not uncommon for health professionals in this setting, they must be dealt with wisely.

What can you do when that happens? You were introduced to some alternatives in Chapter 11 when you were considering some detrimental consequences that can occur when your sympathy slips into pity. For instance, some health professionals have to ask a colleague to assume responsibility for a patient because they find a patient's condition so horrendous that the professional's effectiveness is hindered. It may be the best alternative in this difficult situation.

Patients' fears of isolation, pain, and dependence are basic, but there are other fears as well, such as the dread of suffocation and the fear that one's loved ones will not be adequately provided for. A person who dies suddenly in a car accident or plane crash or from a myocardial infarction may have long harbored these fears, but did not have a period of prolonged illness during which these fears surfaced. In the case of a long and progressively debilitating condition, sometimes you can help attend to the fears. For instance, a man who has had trouble openly expressing affection to his wife may be able to do so by sharing his fear that she will not be adequately provided for. An indirect means of communication, such as writing a letter or telling a friend how wonderful she is, serves a similar purpose. You can be instrumental in making suggestions to help such a patient carry out her or his wishes if you get a hint that the patient desires to do so.

In summary, during their dying process, people must rely on their own best inner resources and the support of family, friends, and health professionals to sustain them as they face their fears. Any hesitance, embarrassment, or disdain you show when a person expresses a fear will exacerbate the suffering associated with it.

Fear of Death Itself

Why are we so afraid of the death event? Not everyone is, of course, and different cultures treat the moment of transition from alive to dead differently, but for many it is not something to relish. There are many possible reasons why a person might dread being "dead and gone": separation from loved ones, unfinished business, concern for the welfare of those left behind, the fear of being totally alone in some other world or other uncertainties about what comes after death, and the dread of annihilation, to name a few.

Probably for many people the greatest fear arises from the uncertainty of death. It is not what we know but what we do not know that scares us. The mystery of death baffles us all, and we are left groping for meaning beyond that provided by our own knowledge and experience.

Death and Immortality

The majority of people are taught that after this life there is something else. But that assumption is by no means held by everyone, including many who are religious. The varieties of religious beliefs are many, and there are wide variations in interpretation of the relationship of this life to the next, as well as of the meaning of illness and suffering when a person is faced with a condition that threatens to end physical life as he or she knows it.[9] In his now classic work, historian Arnold Toynbee traces, from a historical perspective, the ways in which people have tried to circumvent the finality of death and achieve immortality.[10] These ways include the following:

1. *Physical countermeasures.* Physical life is prolonged by providing the corpse with food and drink, and, in some cultures, even wives when a man died. This practice was common in ancient times and still exists in some parts of the world.
2. *Fame.* The dead person's image is preserved in poetry or inscription. War monuments, memorial rolls, and names inscribed in tree trunks are all examples. Plato encouraged his followers to achieve immortality through the fame of heroic deeds or scholarly pursuit as well as through procreation.
3. *Procreation.* Immortality is achieved through one's offspring. An example of this is illustrated in James Agee's novel, *A Death in the Family.* When Jay Follet is killed, one sees him emerging again in the person of his son, Rufus. In a sense, Jay is reborn in his son. The possibility of physical "procreation" beyond one's physical lifetime is now possible with the availability of sperm banks and banks for storing fertilized ova ("pre-embryos").
4. *Passing down one's material treasures.* Family heirlooms, including monetary trusts, are constant reminders of their original owners, just as works of art, such as paintings or books, are reminders of their creators. Inanimate objects are the means of immortalizing a person.
5. *Submersion in ultimate reality.* Predominant beliefs in many religions, especially but by no means only those associated with Eastern religions such as Hinduism, propose that "death" is a process of birth and rebirth (e.g., reincarnation). The last step is not extinction but perfection, at which time one is absorbed into a "place" or into a "being" where complete unity of all beings is realized. Depending on the religion, the type of being one will become after physical humanhood and the

opportunity for the final step into ultimate unity may or may not depend on the type of life one lived on earth during the human "phase." In Islam one may be transported through several levels of paradise depending on the type of life one has lived.

6. *Resurrection of individuals.* Some people believe in the resurrection of souls only, whereas others believe that the actual human body will be restored. Most forms of Christianity believe in a literal, sudden bodily "resurrection" (sometimes referred to as the "rapture"), in which those—both dead and still living—who have lived holy lives will be immediately transported to heaven while others will be left behind forever to suffer the consequences of their sins. Other Christians have different versions of what it means to be "resurrected," although all share this basic belief.

Toynbee's six categories are useful for thinking about basic positions, but many groups (as well as individuals) combine aspects of these immortality-producing activities and beliefs. Recall the Arctic tribal belief cited earlier in this chapter that when a living being dies, its miniature self finds another kind of being in which to reside, including a place to rest while awaiting where to go next. The Ho-Chunk peoples (now known as the Winnebago tribe—made up of the Iowa, Oto, Missouri, and central Algonquian Indians residing in the Midwestern states) believe that by living a clean life and enduring inevitable suffering, death will come, but they will be reincarnated and eventually reach Heaven as a reward for their self-sacrifice on earth.[11]

You will meet individuals who talk with anticipation about "going to meet the Lord" while at the same time wanting to meet with their lawyers to be sure the bequest of their earthly belongings is in order. Knowing that any of these beliefs about immortality may influence the way an individual interprets the impact and meaning of his or her own impending death, you can be better prepared for comments from the patients or for rituals a patient and family engage in during the dying process.

REFLECTIONS

Before proceeding, go back over the six categories, and try to think about conversations you may have had with patients or others who hold each of these positions.
- Which ones do you hold, if any?

Death as the End

A significant number of people in today's society do not view death as a precursor of immortality in any form. This view finds artistic expression in Tom Stoppard's play, *Rosencrantz and Guildenstern Are Dead.* The two attendants, who believe through most of the play that they are accompanying Prince Hamlet to his death in Denmark, find out that, instead, they are going to be put to death. Upon realizing their fate, one of them reflects: "Death isn't romantic, death is not anything. ... Death is ... not. It's the absence of presence, nothing more ... the endless time of never coming back ... a gap you can't see."[12]

From this standpoint, you could interpret a patient's fear of death as his or her dread of separation from things he or she values or wants to be around to experience: family, springtime, a growing bank account. There may be regret over not being able to reach a special anniversary or not knowing who will win the Super Bowl this year. To this person, death is viewed as an infringement on the deep wish for continued life, or "being."

 REFLECTIONS

Try to construct a conversation you might have with a patient or family who does not believe in immortality.
• What themes are the most apparent?

All of these concepts about death can help you understand patients and their families when they share their feelings and ideas about death and how to prepare for it. When you can enter into such conversations with equanimity and express genuine interest in what the person wants or needs to say about death, you will be showing genuine respect for that person. Some specific methods are presented later in this chapter, but having now discussed basic sources of fear about dying that patients, families, and you and your colleagues may have, as well as common interpretations of the death event, let us turn to some other important responses besides fear.

Other Responses

Although the aforementioned fears associated with dying and the death event may become more sharply focused, and denial becomes one common way to respond at least initially, you can anticipate other responses as well. For many, the first response is acute shock or grief. Coping also will lead the person to respond with depression, anger, and hostility, bargaining behavior, or acceptance. In the 1960s, Elisabeth Kübler-Ross, a psychiatrist, introduced denial along with these additional responses as sequential "stages of dying"—a framework that has deeply influenced the approach taken by health professionals to dying patients in the subsequent years.[13] Today they are more generally viewed as a useful *range* of emotional-psychological responses a person may have rather than as sequential stages. Patients who go through a long process of dying are likely to feel all of them from time to time, and many times over. On one day, a woman denies her impending death; on another, she makes secret bargains with God about how long she will live; and on the following days she feels the relief of acceptance followed by a deep depression, and so on. Although the danger with any such framework is that you or your professional colleagues may tend to pigeonhole a patient according to the categories provided, we have found them to be a useful set of tools for thinking about what is happening to a person.

The patient's basic personality structure is an important factor in determining which kind of responses will predominate, too. How did the person deal with stress before learning that he or she had a life-threatening condition? Similar coping responses will probably surface in the present situation.

To further prepare yourself for working with such patients, we suggest you pause here to engage in a reflection on your own life.

REFLECTIONS

Try to think about how you respond to stressful situations in your life.
- Can you imagine what you might be like as a patient or family member faced with the challenge of a dying loved one?
- If you have in fact had to face it, try to recall your major types of responses.

Another resource you can use was mentioned in Chapter 8, in which we high-lighted how useful the writings of novelists, poets, essayists, and others can be. Many have recorded their experiences in this powerful situation, and it is to your advantage to avail yourself of these narrative accounts in preparation for your professional encounters with people who are dying.

Responses of the Patient's Family

The best and worst aspects of all family relationships are exposed when a family member is ill or dying. You will witness lifelong destructive patterns and the most intimate, loving characteristics of family relationships. The great majority of families are brought closer together by the experience, and their mutual support during this time is touching to observe. Despite this, for some health professionals, the members of the patient's family are viewed as intruders to be tolerated rather than as important people to be included. The experienced health professional knows that the family's presence may complicate the situation. At all hours of the day and night, they may ask questions, peek in on the patient, disrupt schedules, and aggressively offer suggestions. If the patient has not been told of the life-threatening nature of the condition, they whisper to you in doorways, trying to involve you in elaborate schemes to ensure continued deception. At the busiest time of day, they may stop you to tell you something, only to burst into tears.

Why is it important for them to be there? First, it is an absolutely critical means of coping with their own grief. Toynbee, at the age of 79, reflected on the sadness he experienced when his wife died, "That is, as I see it, the capital fact about the relationship between living and dying. There are two parties to the suffering that death inflicts; and in the apportionment of that suffering, the survivor takes the brunt."[10] The opportunity for a family member to be in the presence of a loved one who is dying usually is comforting to the family. The astute health professional recognizes the agony the family experiences in anticipation of the loss of their loved one. The family sometimes goes through a series of reactions called *anticipatory grief* that parallels the symptoms usually seen in the acute grief that follows a death. You can watch for symptoms of acute grief such as the family member's tendency to sigh, complaints of chronic weakness or exhaustion, and loss of appetite or nausea. In addition, a family member may be preoccupied with what a person looks like, express guilt or hostility, and change his or her usual patterns of conduct.[14] As a result, the family members' behavior in the presence of their loved one may appear altogether inappropriate for the welfare of the patient.

Except in extreme situations, family members should be an *integral* part of the treatment approach. Family members not only need comfort but also provide it; they need to receive communications about the patient's status but often are also the best source of information; and they need to do their own grieving but can assist both the health professional and the patient in theirs as well. Sharing decision-making power with the patient and the family is one way of helping them to maintain their dignity and almost always improves the quality of patient care during this period.

SETTING TREATMENT PRIORITIES

In addition to your role as one who tries to listen, understand, and respond caringly to the patient and family, several additional treatment priorities are appropriate when a patient is dying. They include information sharing with the patient and others, treating losses and fears described in the first part of the chapter, and helping patients maintain hope.

Information Sharing: What, When, and How?

What types of information do patients and families need to know? Start with the patient's diagnosis. Traditionally it was considered unwise and uncompassionate to tell a person that he or she had a condition that appeared to be life threatening. For the most part today in the United States, Canada, and many European countries, medical policies and practices support the position that a patient should be told of his or her diagnosis because the patient has a right to information about his or her health status. There is also a conviction that the duty not to harm is best realized by disclosure—the truth "sets free." The health professional's duty to protect the patient has been challenged by the idea that patients should have the opportunity to assume more say in the relationship, and to do so they must have all the necessary facts. In support of this, some states in the United States have passed laws that allow a patient to read the notations on his or her own medical record while other states permit the patient's lawyer to do so. Overall, the trend toward immediate access to formerly inaccessible information may eventually eliminate the question of whether or not a patient "ought to be told."

This trend toward openness is by no means shared universally or even by many of the cultures within the changing United States, Canadian, and Western European populations. At the very least, you must be attentive to clues you are receiving from the patient and family as to whether directly sharing this information with the patient is a culturally competent way to proceed. There may be an official spokesperson who should handle the situation, with or without your presence. Or other cultural norms may govern the way you will best be able to meet the intent of empowering and providing comfort to a patient through your honesty.

One consideration is the belief by many who advocate sharing the information about a patient's diagnosis and prognosis that they and their loved ones will figure it out anyway. For example, in *Endings and Beginnings,* a young woman's account of her husband's terminal diagnosis and eventual death, the author recalls that after exploratory surgery the doctor tried to be reassuring by saying they had found a "lymphatic tumor" but did not go on to tell them that it was an aggressive, life-threatening malignancy. In fact, that evening her husband reassured her that, since it was "lymphatic," it at least was not cancer. Their reassurance was short lived:

> That evening, as I left the hospital elevator … I was startled to have the head resident under Dr. C (the surgeon) turn to me and say, "Try not to worry; we'll do everything we can." It was clear there was much more going on than any of us was admitting.[15]

Following her encounter the young couple spent many days trying to verify the simple truth that he had something very serious. In reflecting on the whole course of his dying, the author remembers that period of uncertainty as one of the most painful for both of them.

Do patients figure it out? Probably some do, and some do not. Whatever combination of considerations make up the physician's decision, many are now telling patients with life-threatening conditions their diagnoses, usually in direct terms with emphasis on keeping communication channels open after the initial discussion.[16] In the end, there is no substitute for personalized, sensitive communication by all members of the health care team, initially and throughout the patient's course of interaction with them. Key to such communication is determining what information is shared, along with how and when it is shared.

⊚ REFLECTIONS

Before proceeding, pause to think about whether you would like to be told the news that you have a life-threatening condition that the physicians have just discovered. If you would want to know, try to imagine the physical setting, people you would hope were (or weren't) present, and key points you would want to know in this initial exchange.

- What would you like to have happen over the course of your dying that would most help you feel as if you were being treated with respect from the very start of your ordeal?
- What (if any) role would health professionals play in this process?

Sometimes health professionals think they have a responsibility to talk with a patient about the diagnosis, prognosis, or specific aspects of the situation only if he or she asks. This is a "responsive" posture insofar as discussion takes place only in response to a patient's direct questions: "Am I dying?" or "Is it inoperable?" or "What can I expect?"

Although being responsive always is a sign of respect, sometimes it is helpful to the patient if you are proactive. The key is to try to be attentive and ready to communicate those things he or she has a right to, and is ready to, know. Sometimes it is not within the boundaries of your professional role to communicate a diagnosis or prognosis directly, but you can always encourage this course of action with the physician or others whose legal/ethical responsibility it is.

Using words the patient really understands is imperative. Without this translation from medical/clinical terminology to everyday language, nothing will make sense in the conversation. In most cases, however, stopping there is rarely helpful to the person.

Talking with a patient and family about the patient's prognosis has its own challenges since almost always the prognosis is not known with absolute certainty. Sounding the death knell on a given date in the future understandably would be disastrous for most patients anyway. Today physicians often talk about probability: "You have a 50 percent chance of a 5-year survival." This approach allows certain information to be transmitted to the patient and may permit the patient to learn what usually happens to people in similar situations. At the same time, probabilistic information doesn't answer the key question of what, exactly, does this mean for *me*?

Finally, you should always listen to the patient's story with as much attentiveness as you can. Using all of the skills we introduced in Chapters 8 and 9 will be required in your work with dying patients. The patient who begins by asking, "Am I going to die?" may be asking, "Do I have metastatic cancer of the breast?" or may be asking, "Am I going to be dying in a slow, painful way for the next few months?" or "Will I lose my hair and grow weak like my Aunt Susan did?" or "Will I be slowly abandoned by my family and friends?" You will not be in a position to provide full assurance to counter every question a patient might have, but your attention to their questions will provide some relief to their anxieties because it will show that you are willing to leave communication channels open.

Treating Losses and Fears

Previous sections of this book emphasize the importance of recognizing and understanding the patient's challenges, especially those in the form of losses. Those experienced by people with life-threatening conditions can span the whole range discussed in Chapter 6. However, the patient in the following excerpt is facing the awesome prospect of losing everything associated with this worldly life, including physical identity. In *A Very Easy Death*, Simone de Beauvoir poignantly describes her mother, who has been dying from cancer over a period of several months:

> I looked at her. She was there, present, conscious and completely unaware of what she was living through. Not to know what is happening underneath one's skin is normal enough. But for her the outside of her body was unknown—her wounded abdomen, her fistula, the filth that issued from it, the blueness of her skin, the liquid that oozed out of her pores. She had not asked for a mirror again; her dying face did not exist for her. ... [17]

Many life-threatening conditions are accompanied by a gradual diminution of strength, endurance, control of movement, and sensory acuity. Helping the person and family adjust to each of the "little deaths" as they are experienced is a continuing challenge; your success depends on being attuned to the losses being suffered at any one time.

The fears outlined earlier in this chapter also call for your attention. For instance, you can "treat" (allay) the patient's fears of isolation by your presence. You cannot always assure patients that their loved ones will not "jump ship" when the going gets rough, because sometimes families do. Observing this tapering off of supportive relationships is often very trying for you, let alone the patient. Relationships are bound to be altered during this time; some friends and relatives disappear because of indifference, despair, or exhaustion, and those who do not become more cherished. Health professionals often are eventually able to ascertain who, among the many at the onset, will endure. Often, it is wise to begin providing your own support to those who you judge to be the most enduring so that the patient will continue to have a community of support as the condition progresses.

In addition to your attentiveness occasioned by the necessary performance of technical skills, you may choose, as do many health professionals, to stop in and see a patient briefly or to talk with the patient's family from time to time after treatment has been discontinued. Sometimes a telephone call to the patient's home after discharge is a great source of comfort and encouragement to all there.

Of course, these means of maintaining human contact can present some difficulties. Tension arises over the establishment of priorities. Spending extra time with this person may subtract from time left for others. Judgment must be exercised in deciding how to proceed so that other patients receive their fair share of time and attention. Furthermore, sometimes spending extra time with the patient outside of the treatment or testing situation may encourage overdependence on you for things you cannot now or eventually be there to provide. The general rule is to be compassionately guided, aware that the patient and family are in a time of great turmoil and need.

Sometimes "treatment" takes curious forms when a person is dying. The following case illustrates:

> When she was an internal medicine resident, part of her day consisted of making rounds with the attending medical staff. Each day for several weeks, one of the patients they saw was a withered wisp of an old woman who was now semicomatose in this stage of a long bout with cancer. The old woman had no known relatives and was never visited by anyone, but she lived on and on past the time the medical staff believed she would die. The group of physicians stood at the foot of the bed each day, studied her with bewilderment, read her medical record for signs of changes, said a few words to each other, and left. The resident believed that the old woman became tense during these discussions, and finally one day she mentioned it to her colleagues. They scoffed at the idea, saying the patient was too weak and too far gone to know what they were saying or that they were even there. The resident became increasingly troubled by the presence of this tiny patient, who was lying in what seemed to be a gigantic hospital bed. Finally, one time while on call, the resident was walking down the patient's corridor at 3 o'clock in the morning. For some inexplicable reason she was drawn into the patient's room. The woman looked no different than ever—very small, very alone, and very still. The resident shut the door, gathered the woman into her arms, and wept. Later that morning when the resident checked into the front desk, she was told that the woman had died at about 5 o'clock that morning.

It seems to us that the medical resident "treated" the patient with the human contact that the patient somehow needed to be released from her suffering. We know very little about the deep process of dying, but such acts of basic human caring may be the key to helping a patient face the unique challenges of the dying process.

Helping Patients Maintain Hope

When a patient is dying, the focus of hope will change over time, from a hope for cure to a hope for meaningful activities in the remaining life left to this person. His or her hope may be directed toward events such as seeing a loved one another time, visiting a favorite place, or hearing a familiar piece of music played.

Some hopes are less tangible: that one will be able to keep a positive spirit or sense of irony to the end; that one will be remembered and missed; or that a particular tradition will be carried on in one's absence. Previously sought long-term goals are put into perspective, and the patient focuses his or her hopes on the most important ones, knowing that some will no longer be attainable.

Families also adjust their hopes for what is possible given the new circumstances. As one husband wrote when he learned that his wife was not going to recover from her early bouts of ovarian cancer:

> There is a transition between the certainty of living and the acceptance of dying. When there is such acceptance, there is a kind of emotional purgatory. The cartoon character stands still in space beyond the edge of a cliff and awaits the fatal fall. That is where things were for us in early October. There were choices, however, even in this purgatory. They remained a moment to live in ... if only a moment. After that we will go on with our lives. Before it was over and before I began my desperate search for a new life, there would be a time for us as a family that was like none other. Most important was that we manage the pain. The first priority was comfort. The second priority was to get Lezlie back home not so much so that she could die there as that she could live there before she left.[18]

How can you help? Listen carefully to the patient and family express hopes and take seriously what the person says. Hope itself depends significantly on the attitudes of health professionals as well as on those of family and friends when the patient dares to disclose a hope. Your listening can help to maintain the person's feeling of worth and thereby provide a human context in which hopes may be expressed. Of course, health professionals can also often play a significant role in actually helping the patient realize some specific hope by making a few important telephone calls to the right people, by mentioning the patient's wishes to the family and others, or by other similar means.

In short, people faced with dying all hope that they will be treated kindly, that everything clinically possible will be done for them, and that meaningful human exchange will not disappear. You can do your best as a health professional to support those hopes.

PROVIDING CARE IN THE RIGHT PLACE AT THE RIGHT TIME

Partially in response to the movement in several Western countries to reexamine the health professional's role in assisted suicide and euthanasia, much attention is being devoted to improving the methods of care at the end of life. Both the site of such care and the timing and focus have been the source of discussion and policy. An important factor is the considerations arising from an improved understanding of physiological and other responses to pain or other disturbing symptoms associated with many life-threatening conditions, and where the interventions best can be delivered.

Hospital, Hospice, and Home Care

Many patients who are dying still do so in the hospital. This is an appropriate site for interventions that require technologies and specialties available in the hospital setting. However, today the hospice and home care settings have become viable alternatives for many patients during their dying. The most dramatic changes from the last century have taken place due to the rise of the hospice movement.

The modern hospice, which began in England and has spread to Canada, the United States, and many other countries today, has been a commendable attempt in recent years to provide treatment and care expressly designed to meet the needs of patients with life-threatening conditions and their families. Initially, hospice care was geared to the treatment of patients with cancer, but today hospice care is available for many other types of patients with irreversible conditions such as Alzheimer's disease, progressively deteriorating neurological conditions, and AIDS.

Hospice focuses on comfort measures when cure or remission is no longer possible. The hospice setting is characterized by interdisciplinary health care approaches. When there is a family it (and not the patient alone) is the unit of care. A 2004 study of family perspectives on end-of-life care in different settings showed significantly more favorable experiences of their loved ones dying in hospice than those whose loved ones died in hospitals. The authors concluded that this setting is far better equipped to provide symptom relief, communication with health professionals, emotional support, and the perception of being treated with respect.[19]

In some locations, home care is supported sufficiently by government and/or insurance plans to make this a viable alternative for families. Some hospices are actually "without walls"; that is, they are designed to provide services within the home with devices such as hotlines, care networks, and respite programs for caregivers. Churches and other organizations sometimes become involved in home caregiving arrangements.

You and your patients will benefit from your acquainting yourself further with the functions and structure of each of these settings and the hospice and home care alternatives available in the communities where you work. This will prepare you to inform patients of these options when it becomes appropriate and to be active in their information gathering process. You may even find yourself drawn to these aspects of health care and be one of the growing numbers of professionals working in the hospice or home health care setting.

Balancing Cure and Comfort Measures

From a clinical point of view, the treatment always must fit the situation. What constitutes "appropriate treatment" when a patient is dying?

In clinical practice focusing on people who have life-threatening conditions, the idea of palliation has played a central role. *Palliative care* (or, as it is commonly called, *comfort care*) traditionally was thought of as what health professionals can do when cure no longer is possible. In other words, it becomes appropriate when all else has failed. The problem is that from as early as the time of Hippocrates, there was a suggestion that if cure was no longer possible, the disease had gone beyond the "art of medicine" and should not be interfered with by the doctor. So all too often palliation meant that dying patients received very little care. At the same time, you can understand that the idea of palliative care is important because, applied appropriately, it allows you to have better insight into how to respond well to patients' fears of abandonment, pain, and other distress associated with the dying process.

Today the growing focus on appropriate end-of-life care has shed new light on what palliative care entails. Comfort care goes well beyond the traditional hand-holding at the bedside, as important as that continues to be. Comfort can be achieved for various patients through many varieties of intervention, such as painkillers, ventilators, dramatic surgical procedures, and psychological counseling, to name some. Moreover, there has been a rethinking of traditional medical, nursing, rehabilitation, and other health care specialties to include palliative as well as curative aspects in their realm of expertise. Within medicine this may include anesthesiologists, physiatrists, internists, pediatricians, geriatric specialists, and surgeons, all of whom often address chronic symptoms associated with dying. Along with this heightened consciousness and technology focus, there has also been a rethinking about the traditional assumption of a progression from "treatment" to "palliation" as the patient's dying ensues. Using cancer as a model, the Institute of Medicine in the United States proposes that treatment geared to cure and treatment geared to palliation do not progress in a tidy, linear way (Figure 17-2).

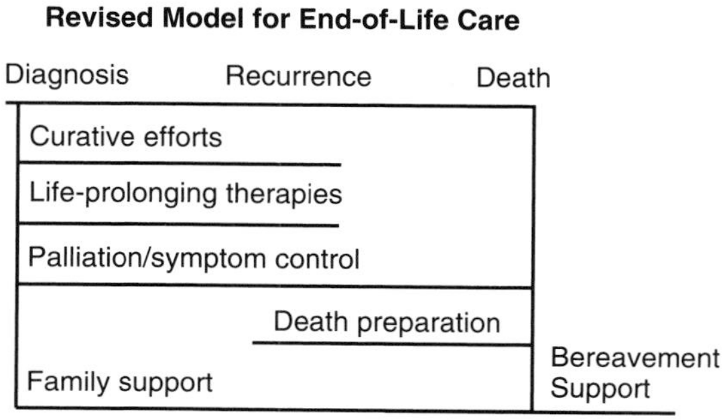

Revised Model for End-of-Life Care

Diagnosis	Recurrence	Death

| Curative efforts |
| Life-prolonging therapies |
| Palliation/symptom control |
| Death preparation |
| Family support | Bereavement Support |

FIGURE 17-2: *(From Field MJ, Cassel CK, editors:* Approaching death: improving care at the end of life, *Committee on Care at the End of Life, Institute of Medicine. Washington, DC, 1997, National Academy Press.)*

Different combinations of education about how to prevent deterioration or the appearance of new symptoms, responsiveness to rehabilitative needs, acute care interventions, and comfort measures all may remain appropriate from the beginning to the end of the patient's dying process.[20]

Other models that are fine-tuned to patients' and families' real needs also are being attempted. You are entering the health professions at a time when the attention devoted to these issues will assist you in doing a better job than your forbearers did in providing care for dying patients.

When Death Is Imminent

At some point in the course of an irreversible, life-threatening illness it becomes apparent that the person will die soon. Persons who do not suffer from a prolonged illness as such also face the moment of imminent death: the accident victim, the attempted suicide or murder victim, and the young person going into battle.

Individualized Care

The patient whose death is imminent should not be barraged with routine requests and procedures that no longer matter. As one woman sitting by her dying father's bedside asked dismayingly, "Does it *matter* if his bowels haven't moved on the last day he will probably be alive?"

Attempts to relieve pain by medication, massage, and other therapeutic means may have been started long before, and these should be continued unless the patient asks that they be withdrawn. Some people, if they know that they are experiencing the final days of their lives, find the torpor induced by heavy medication more troublesome than uncomfortable symptoms.

However, maximizing comfort goes beyond alleviating pain. It involves the relief of real or potential suffering. Suffering is a far more inclusive, personalized concept than pain, and your assistance in helping patients and their families have a final time together as free of pain and suffering as possible is a laudable goal. Families may do many things to try to provide a meaningful and peaceful transition. We have seen families who read to their loved one, bathe him or her, sing songs he or she loved, or fill the room with flowers. A friend of one of the authors sneaked her 2-month-old daughter up to the hospital room so that her husband could witness his wife nursing their child for one last time. A religious leader may be called in. The patient who has been nourished only intravenously for days or weeks may request that all medications and IVs be removed. Specific activities will vary from person to person. Health professionals can be facilitators by allowing the family and friends their final day together, remaining "on standby" if needed. This might mean breaking hospital rules and readjusting one's schedule. It also means knowing who should be called if the patient's condition worsens and death appears near.

Many people today do not have any customary rituals associated with the time of death, although you have a responsibility always to consider that a patient may have an urgent need to participate in a religious or other cultural act appropriate to his or her faith and beliefs. When they exist, respect requires you to alter your treatment procedures to honor them.

Saying Good-Bye

Many people find it difficult to say good-bye to a friend or other loved one who is going away. It is more difficult still when the person is dying—so much so that good-byes are seldom said, especially by the health professional to the patient and the patient's family. This is, however, something that you can do to show respect for the people and their situation when many other forms of interaction have been suspended. One psychiatrist offers this suggestion:

> What should be said is, I want you to know the relationship was meaningful, I'll miss this about you, or ... it won't be the same, I'll miss the bluntness that you had in help-ing me sort out some things, or I'll just miss the old bull sessions, or something like that. Because those are things you value. Now what does that do for the other person? The other person learns that although it's painful to separate it's far more meaningful to have known the person and to have separated than never to have known him at all. He also learns what it is in himself that is valued and treasured by [you]. And some of those underlying, corrosive feelings of low self-esteem that plague people are shored up. ...[21]

This encounter also allows the patient and his or her family to express similar feelings. There is often a real sense of closeness and gratitude felt toward the health professional, and to be able to show it is a great relief. In addition to what the exchange does for the patient and family, it is important to realize how much it can help in your own grieving. Giving patients and families an opportunity to express gratitude to you may sound odd, but it is one way in which some patients and families can be assisted in their own grieving. When they observe that the health professional receives his or her thanks humbly, they will appreciate this show of human caring.

Accepting Rejection If Necessary

Having outlined some ways in which good-byes and thank you's can be exchanged gracefully and meaningfully, you should also prepare yourself for the rare instances in which the patient and family reject your attempts to show respectful caring during this intense period of their lives.

Sometimes when a person is close to dying, he or she shuts out many people. Such a patient may not want to have anything more to do with you. There are many reasons for this:

▸ We have already discussed the great difficulty many people have with saying good-bye under such trying circumstances.
▸ There is the possibility that the person has accepted his or her death and no longer needs any people around. That such acceptance may occur has been well documented by those who have worked with a large number of dying patients. Although not necessarily so, it is more likely to occur when the approaching death has been preceded by a long illness.
▸ You are not as important as loved ones, and the little energy the patient has is reserved for them.

▶ The patient and his or her family may actually direct any anger they feel about the death toward you and other health professionals. The health professional who is the object of such anger may not even be the one who spent the longest or most significant time with the person, but rather the one who happened to be there at some crucial moment.

▶ You are inextricably linked to the whole setting in which suffering and the dying process have taken place. So much anguish may be associated with you and your professional environment that it is painful for the patient to be in your presence.

You should be prepared for the possibility that your final efforts and good intentions are neither wanted nor welcomed. On some occasions, you may feel hurt by these sudden or unexpected rebuffs and can do little more than forgive the person responsible for them. At times when hurt is present, support from your professional colleagues may become vital. Sharing feelings of failure, rejection, or bewilderment with an understanding colleague can be a balm for injured feelings and give you courage to try again in another such situation.

Summary

This chapter scratches the surface of considerations that can be helpful to you in your attempts to show respect in the extreme life situation in which death is approaching for a patient in your care. The patient needs your professional skills, your compassion, and your wisdom in this situation. At the same time you are confronted with your own uncertainties and fears about dying and death along with the irony that, no matter what you do, the end result for this patient will be death. Your part in making the remainder of life for a dying patient as rich and worthwhile as possible may be the motivation you will need to sustain that person and his or her loved ones.

References

1. Albom M: *Tuesdays with Morrie,* New York, Doubleday, 1997.
2. Jack and the beanstalk (a traditional English fairy tale). In *The Arthur Rackham fairy book,* Philadelphia, 1950, Lippincott.
3. Hansel and Grethel (a Grimm's fairy tale). In *The Arthur Rackham fairy book,* Philadelphia, 1950, Lippincott.
4. Trillin AS: Of dragons and garden peas: a cancer patient talks to doctors, *N Engl J Med* 304:669-701, 1981.
5. Berg E: *The year of pleasures,* New York, 2005, Random House.
6. Taylor J: *The whole works,* vol 2, New York, 1971, Adler's Foreign Books (edited by R Heber) (originally published in 1847).
7. Brennan F: "Pain relief is a basic human right": the legal foundations of pain relief, *J Palliat Care* 20:236, 2004.
8. National Consensus Project: *Clinical practice guidelines for quality palliative care,* Brooklyn, New York, 2004, [Pamphlet published by the National Consensus Project].
9. Burt RA: *Death is that man taking names: intersections of American medicine, law, and culture,* Berkeley, 2002, University of California Press.
10. Toynbee A, editor: *Man's concern with death,* New York, 1968, McGraw-Hill.
11. Thomas R: The Ho Chunk (Winnebago) people. In MondragÛn D, editor: *Religious values of the terminally ill: handbook for health care professionals,* Scranton, PA, 1997, University of Scranton Press.
12. Stoppard T: *Rosencrantz and Guildenstern are dead,* New York, 1967, Grove Press.

13. Kübler-Ross E: *On death and dying*, New York, 1969, Macmillan.
14. Balber PG: Stories of the living dying: the Hermes listener. In Corless I, Germino BB, Pittman MA, editors: *Dying death and bereavement: a challenge for living*, ed 2, New York, 2003, Springer Publishing.
15. Albertson SH: *Endings and beginnings*, New York, 1980, Random House.
16. Veatch RM, Haddad A: Veracity: dealing honestly with patients. In *Case studies in pharmacy ethics*, ed 2, New York, 2007, Oxford University Press.
17. de Beauvoir S: *A very easy death*, New York, 1973, Warner Books (translated by P O'Brien).
18. Surman O: *After Eden: a love story*, New York, 2005, iUniverse.
19. Teno JM and others: Family perspectives on end of life care at the last place of care, *JAMA* 291(1):88-92, 2004.
20. Field MJ, Cassel C, editors: *Approaching death: improving care at the end of life*, National Academy of Medicine Report, Washington, DC, 1997, National Academy Press.
21. Cassem NH: The caretakers. In Langone J, editor: *Vital signs: the way we die in America*, Boston, 1974, Little, Brown.

RESPECTFUL INTERACTION IN OTHER DIFFICULT SITUATIONS

CHAPTER OBJECTIVES

The student will be able to:

- Identify three potential sources of difficulties creating barriers to respectful health professional and patient interaction
- Discuss how disparities in power within the relationship can lead to anger and frustration on the part of all involved
- Identify attributes and behaviors of patients, such as manipulative, sexually provocative, or aggressive behaviors, that may challenge the health professional's ideal of compassionate care
- Reflect on personal expectations of what it means to be a "good" health professional and how this impacts interactions with patients
- Describe environmental factors that may contribute to difficulties in health professional and patient interaction
- List and evaluate guidelines for managing and, when possible, preventing difficult health professional and patient relationships
- List and evaluate techniques that can help to change a "difficult" working relationship and the surrounding environment

She asks for help and I have given it to her. She has been on various medications but nothing seems to work. She is a sad case really, and her anxiety seems to stem from a poor home environment. She gets anxious and then gets anxious about being anxious. I prescribe, but I know she will be back again in a short time. It would not be so bad if she tried to help herself.[1]

Many health professionals view working with dying patients and their families as one of the greatest challenges they face in health care. However, as you read in Chapter 17, working with patients who are dying can sometimes be full of joy as well as sorrow. Even though you might experience loss and grief when a patient you have cared for dies, there is often also an accompanying sense of satisfaction that you were able to make his or her death a little easier, a little less painful, or less lonely. There are other patient care situations in which you will not come away with a sense of satisfaction, but one of profound frustration. This chapter focuses on difficulties inherent in the health professional and patient interaction that have not specifically been addressed elsewhere in this book or that bear reemphasizing. We suggest that you refer to Chapters 10 through 12 to review the content on establishing relatedness, recognizing boundaries, and creating professional closeness. You will need to utilize all of these insights and skills in your work with patients who challenge your conceptions of what it means to be a "good" health professional. Moreover, you will have an opportunity to think about other factors that can create great frustration in the health professional and patient interaction, such as disparities in power and role expectations or an unsafe and negative working environment. We devote this last chapter to some summary statements about how to work more effectively with "difficult" patients and offer ways to effect change in "difficult" settings and situations.

SOURCES OF DIFFICULTIES

Generally, when you enter a relationship with a patient, you have good reason to expect that things will go well, or if there are problems, you expect that they can be resolved. However, there are situations in which even your best efforts cannot make things right. When this happens, a common response is to look for a place to lay the blame. For example, you might wonder what else you could have done for the patient, or you might reason that the patient was not ready for treatment, or you may become defensive and decide that the patient was disruptive, noncompliant, maladjusted, or any number of other negative labels. Difficulty relating to a patient may originate in the health professional, in the interaction itself, or outside of the relationship in the setting in which the interaction takes place.

Sources Within the Health Professional

As emphasized throughout this book, you bring a wealth of experiences, education, prejudices, and values to your interaction with patients and their families. All of these factors can affect how you react to a particular patient. For example, recall the discussion on transference and countertransference in Chapter 10: A patient may remind you of your third-grade teacher whom you particularly feared and disliked. This past experience can arouse intense emotional reactions in the present relationship. In addition, your personality and how you deal with stress will play a large part in how you manage patient care situations that are interpersonally difficult.[2] In fact, your personality, more than your professional or demographic background, may explain why you react negatively to some patients and certain situations and have little difficulty with others.

For the health professional, the most reliable indicator of a negative emotional response is an unfavorable gut response or sense of discomfort in encounters with a particular patient.[3] If you are attuned to monitoring your feelings, then you can try to assess how much anger, fear, or guilt you bring to the interaction and try to manage those feelings before trying to manage the patient. Certain key words and phrases can help you identify the emotion that is being triggered (Box 18-1).

After you identify the emotions, two questions often follow: "Why is this happening?" and "Where is this emotion coming from?"

Although it is a widely held belief, which has certainly been emphasized in this book, that health professionals should be nonjudgmental in their relationships with patients, it is a fact that some patients are more likable than others. More than

---

BOX 18-1

KEY WORDS FOR IDENTIFYING NEGATIVE EMOTIONS

Anger	Helplessness
Annoyance	Hostility
Apprehension	Hurt
Bitterness	Irritation
Boredom	Loneliness
Concern	Rejection
Disappointment	Resentment
Discouragement	Sadness
Emptiness	Worry
Fear	Anger at self: "I should have...,"
Frustration	"If only I had...," "I wish
Guilt	I had..."

From Herber CP, Seifert MH: When the patient is the problem, *Patient Care* 24(1):60, 1990.

---

45 years ago, Highley and Norris asked their nursing students to identify major "dislikes" related to working with patients. The types of patients the students disliked can still be found in clinical practice today. The students reported the following dislikes:

1. Patients who feel bad and complain after everything has been done for them.
2. Patients who are not clean.
3. Patients who will not do what the health professional asks them to, will not cooperate, will not obey the rules.
4. Patients who are extremely demanding.
5. Patients who can help themselves but insist on the health professional doing everything.[4]

The common denominator in these dislikes is that either the patients made the students feel guilty because of their dislike for the patients, or, because they were never satisfied, the patients made the students feel inadequate as nurses. In general, patients who do not affirm the health professional's identity, i.e., accept help and appreciate that help, are considered bad patients. The rejection of the health professional's help can easily be misread as rejection of the health professional. This rejection can take many forms, ranging from outright physical violence, to incessant demands, manipulative behavior, ingratitude, sexually provocative behaviors, or basic noncompliance with advice or treatment.

Because this study was conducted in the 1950s, the students might not have mentioned some problems people are more self-consciously aware of today, such as patients who make sexually explicit remarks that cause embarrassment or aggressive patients who frighten or sometimes even threaten or physically harm health professionals.

These findings lead to another factor that is characteristic of health professionals and can cause difficulties in patient interactions: high expectations regarding the ability to help. As you progress through your program of study to become a health professional, the ideal is reinforced: you should be able to function effectively in all patient situations, and you are solely responsible for the success or failure of these interactions. This may not be what your teachers or we wish to convey, but it is often what health professionals feel at the beginning of their careers. Thus, long before you have a full complement of skills with which to deal with difficult situations, you may blame yourself for failing to meet the needs of a challenging patient. Before jumping to self-blame for not meeting these unrealistic expectations, you need to recognize that many errors occur before full competence is attained, and even then you should continue to work at establishing realistic expectations of yourself as a health professional.

Your perception of the patient's socioeconomic status also can influence your reactions to a patient. You are encouraged to review the content of Chapter 3 regarding appreciating differences and recognizing discrimination. A perceived difference in socioeconomic status can have a profound effect on the health professional and patient interaction. Papper noted:

> The very poor may be viewed as undesirable unrelated to their ability to pay. Even when the physician has genuine concern for the economically disadvantaged, he may because of his own background, unwittingly regard the extremely poor as *different,* with a flavor of *inferiority included in the difference.*[5]

Papper's personal observation of his medical colleagues was substantiated in a research study by Larson, who presented nurses with case studies in which the patient was identified as middle or lower class, with a more or less serious and more or less socially acceptable illness. The specific findings of Larson's study indicate that persons ranked as "lower class" were perceived as relatively passive, dependent, unintelligent, unmotivated, lazy, forgetful, noncomprehending, uninformed, inaccurate, unreliable, careless, and unsuccessful.[6] We return to the findings related to socially unacceptable illness later in this chapter because this also leads to the labeling of a patient as difficult or undesirable.

Socioeconomic differences between patient and health professional can surface in values about cleanliness. Most health professionals are from the middle or upper-middle class and hold certain values about cleanliness and other "correct" ways of being in the world. They not only are unfamiliar with the ways of poor people, but hold them in disdain (Figure 18-1). Persons in lower socioeconomic groups may be so concerned about basic human needs, such as food and shelter, that they have little time or resources for luxuries such as bathing. It may appear that they don't care at all about cleanliness. Middle-class health professionals often, unconsciously, try to impose their values on patients concerning cleanliness. If neither the health professional nor the patient is aware of differences in socioeconomic status that generate values about bathing and hygiene, a struggle can ensue regarding cleanliness that is out of proportion to its importance in most patient care situations. Matters of hygiene are not the only issues that can escalate into battles with patients. Confrontation and power struggles should be avoided at all cost. Tactics for successful negotiation are outlined later in this chapter.

FIGURE 18-1: "You understand you're the sort of person I ordinarily wouldn't even speak to." *(From Wilson G:* Is Nothing Sacred? *New York, 1982, St. Martin's Press.)*

Sources Within Interactions with Patients

What makes a patient "undesirable?" Patients who sabotage or do not comply with treatment are generally labeled as problematic. Other types of behavior that commonly elicit a negative response from health professionals are violence, anger, or self-harm behaviors such as substance abuse. Kelly and May proposed a theoretical framework for the way health professionals conceptualize good and bad patients using an interactionist perspective.[7] According to this view, patients come to be regarded as good or bad not because of anything inherent about them or in their behavior but as a consequence of the interactions between health professionals and patients. Patients are not passive recipients of care but active agents in the interaction process. Kelly and May explain that patients have the power to "influence, shape and reject professionals' attempts to impose a definition on their situation, with profound consequences for nurse-patient relations and the professional task."[7] Even though Kelly and May focused on the nurse-patient interaction, their framework appears applicable to all health professionals and their reaction to withholding affirmation for the health professionals' roles.

As you can see from the list of dislikes that the students in Highley and Norris's study generated, the focus of the dislike easily moved from dislike for the consequences of inappropriate or unacceptable behavior to dislike for the patient. For example, patients with illnesses that are socially unacceptable often are labeled as difficult even if their behavior is a model of compliance. People with addictive disorders such as alcoholism or drug abuse are often viewed as unacceptable or bad patients. Even if a health professional views alcoholism as a disease rather than a behavior a patient should be able to control, the patient who has a problem with alcohol is commonly rejected by most professional personnel.[8] Patients who appear to be responsible in some way for their illness or injury such as obese patients or smokers are also labeled as less worthy of respect than patients who are "blameless" for their present health condition. All of these patients have one thing in common: either because of the nature of their health problems or the way they respond to the health professionals involved in their care and treatment, they withhold the legitimation that makes health professionals feel good about whom they are and what they do.

Thus, a large part of the label a patient receives depends on our role expectations of patients in general and of patients with specific characteristics. One of the most basic expectations of patients is compliance with agreed-upon treatment. Noncompliance is largely viewed in health care literature as a problem to be resolved: The problem is located in irrational patient beliefs that contradict scientific evidence or in patients' lack of knowledge or understanding.[9] Thus, we assume patients aren't following medical advice because they don't understand or have some misconception that prevents them from understanding. Major efforts, then, are directed toward getting patients to understand so they will comply. An alternative view of noncompliance focuses on the social context of patients' lives.

> Within this alternative social view, it cannot be assumed that non-compliance is simply a matter of patients choosing not to follow advice. Instead, it is recognized that choice may be severely constrained by the social circumstances in which patients live their lives. For example, is a female patient who lives in a violent neighborhood non-compliant if she fails to follow advice to walk around the block each day?[9]

If health professionals approach the problem of noncompliance by trying to understand the factors in patients' lives that mediate their cooperation, then efforts can be made to change those factors that are amenable to change or adjust treatment to meet the reality of a patient's life.

Sources in the Environment

As we noted specifically in Chapters 8 and 9, the health professional and patient interaction takes place in a particular context. At times the context can be the source of difficulty in an interaction. For example, if the environment is strange and frightening, the patient or health professional may react in a fearful or angry manner. For many patients, a health care facility can be an extremely threatening place. Taken in this context, even a simple activity such as bathing can be viewed as menacing.

Rader noted that for a person with *apraxia* (inability to execute purposeful, learned motor acts despite the physical ability and willingness to do so), *agnosia* (inability to recognize a tactile or visible stimulus despite being able to recognize the elemental sensation), and *aphasia* (loss of language function either in comprehension or expression of words)—symptoms often found in patients who have had a cerebrovascular accident—the standard nursing home bathing experience may be perceived as horrific. Consider these limitations, and place yourself in the patient's position.

> A person the resident does not recognize comes into her room, wakens her, says something she does not understand, drags her out of bed, and takes off her clothes. Then the resident is moved down a public corridor on something that resembles a toilet seat, covered only with a thin sheet so that her private parts are exposed to the breeze. Calls for help are ignored or greeted with, "Good morning." Then she is taken to a strange, cold room that looks like a car wash, the sheet is ripped off, and she is sprayed in the face with cold and then scalding water. Continued calls for help go unheeded. Her most private parts are touched by a stranger. In another context this would be assault.[10]

An environment can be equally strange and intolerable to the health professional. For example, we have noted in other chapters that, in community health practice, health professionals may go into the unknown realm of the patient's living environment. One of us recalls a home visit to a small, run-down house literally butted up against the back fence of the holding pens for cattle at the stock market. The smell of manure was overwhelming both outside and inside the house. The elderly woman who lived there (and the subject of the home visit for management of diabetes) seemed oblivious to the odor. In fact, she had just finished hanging a load of clean sheets on the line to dry in her tiny backyard!

Similar stresses can arise in a hectic and crisis-ridden environment. Patients who are kept waiting in an overcrowded emergency room or office are more likely to be frustrated and hostile to health professionals when they are finally seen. Understaffing often leaves health professionals feeling frustrated and dissatisfied as they attempt to meet the needs of too many patients with too little time and resources. Overworked staffs worry about the effect of stretching themselves too thin and the impact this can have on patient care. The physical and psychological exhaustion resulting from excessive professional demands that can drain you have been aptly dubbed "compassion fatigue."[11]

Other environmental factors that make care difficult include the aesthetics of a space, crowding, and climate. One of us worked in a large acute care pediatric setting during the hottest months of the year with no air conditioning. As the temperature rose during the day, so did everyone's irritability; children cried more easily, and co-workers snapped at each other for the slightest offense. Only with the setting of the sun and the resultant drop in temperature did the atmosphere on the unit cool down as well.

Some settings in which the health professional and patient interaction takes place are tense and unpleasant because of the personal dynamics of the individuals who work in them.

Disparities of Power

We have noted several times in this book that patients are placed in a position of diminished power upon entering the health care environment. The content in Chapter 6 specifically discusses numerous losses that patients face because of illness or trauma: independence, social status and responsibility, and expressions of identity often are taken away from people upon entering a health care institution, and all of these factors contribute to feelings of powerlessness. A common reaction to powerlessness is anger, and a common target of anger is the most accessible and least-threatening health professional involved with the patient.[12] Thus, students are often the target for a torrent of rage from a patient that has little to do with the student or his or her abilities. Very few studies have explored patients' perceptions of this inequity in power, but in one study of mental health workers and patients, both groups reported an awareness of the struggle to gain or retain power and control. Patients noted that when health professionals demonstrated respect, took time with them, and were willing to give them some control and choice in their own care, feelings of anger were reduced.[13]

Role Expectations

Because we are socialized not to use negative terms such as "bad," we substitute euphemisms to describe patients with the attributes listed above: they are described as disruptive, unmotivated, regressed, maladaptive, and manipulative. Patients who are perceived to be difficult to treat evoke intense negative-affective responses in the health professional that can work against establishing a positive, constructive relationship.[14] Furthermore, there is also a strong possibility that the professional's language exerts a powerful impact on thought and, consequently, action. Negative words lead to negative thoughts and actions regarding difficult patients. An example from rehabilitation medicine highlights the impact of language.

Most rehabilitation staff have encountered patients who resist their best efforts to engage them in therapeutic activities. These patients seem not to want to be in rehabilitation. They may view therapies as trivial, irrelevant, uninteresting, or too demanding, and they must be constantly coaxed to attend; if they do attend, they do not participate. Staff members become quickly frustrated with patients who do not share the "rehabilitation perspective" that places a high premium on attaining maximal independent functioning. The patient's lack of involvement produces slow progress, proving the patient's point that therapy is valueless. This further antagonizes staff members who, feeling professionally and personally offended, may diminish their efforts to engage the patient, thus producing a hostile standoff and virtually guaranteeing therapeutic failure. This is the fate of the "unmotivated" patient.[15]

Any patient behavior that is inconsistent with expected patient role behavior (read "good patient behavior") could negatively influence the care of the patient. Not only might you be tempted to diminish your efforts in the care of a difficult patient, but you might also resort to distancing yourself from the patient. Unfortunately, avoidance and distancing may result in the reinforcement of deviant behavior as a patient response to nonsupportive care. In extreme cases, health professionals have been known to respond to difficult patients with their own version of negative behavior. In a study of nurses by Podrasky and Sexton, vignettes describing a variety of negative patient behaviors were used to elicit the following responses describing actions these professionals would take or would like to take, including, "I have to keep myself from hauling off and whacking her one," "I would restrain her just a little bit too tight," and "I'd make her stay in the wet bed for a long while."[16] More profound and perhaps life-threatening consequences can result from a health professional's negative reactions to a patient. In a national study of transplant coordinators, a full 62% revealed a belief that a hostile or antagonistic patient should *not* receive an organ transplantation.[17] The irony and tragedy in such findings is that expressions of anger and frustration (behavior that can be labeled as hostile) may be a natural response by patients to chronic illness.

Most health professionals are able to control these kinds of strong emotional reactions and continue, at least marginally, to meet their obligations to the patient. The result is a sort of "grudging attention," i.e., the patient gets the minimal care that he or she needs and nothing more. Grudging attention occurs because of a combination of factors. Once a negative label is attached to a patient, it is difficult for health professionals to look past it and process other data about the patient. Negative labels often get "passed on" until a patient develops a bad reputation.[18]

It is as if we see only one aspect of the patient. Couple these stereotypes about the difficult patient with idealistic role expectations of ourselves as caring, nonjudgmental, and capable of reaching every patient, and the result is an interaction devoid of everything but going through the motions.

Although it is important to work toward the goals of acceptance and constructive problem-solving, sometimes the only solution is to do what you must for the patient and then leave. This is exactly what happened in the case of a sexually aggressive patient who made lewd propositions and repeatedly exposed himself to his caregivers. The health professionals in this case responded with grudging attention as follows:

> By now Mr. Leland was getting only the absolute necessities—no extras. After all, who wants to sit down and chat with someone who talks about nothing but his sex life—or yours? Once our professional responsibilities were met, we avoided Mr. Leland. He couldn't fail to notice this, and as a result his demands for attention become angrier and more disruptive.[19]
>
> ▶ If you were assigned to care for Mr. Leland and he continued to talk explicitly about sex after you asked him not to, what would be your next step?
> ▶ What are some possible negative outcomes of "grudging attention?"

Going through the minimal motions of care is a temporary, and not very effective, solution to a much larger problem. Often it results in guilt on the part of the health professional and can result, as in the case of Mr. Leland, in an escalation of the very behavior that led to avoidance in the first place. Although the following quote refers to nurses, the same can be applied to all health professions: "If patients interpret a nurse's manner as uninterested, or if they overhear pejorative comments, they fear that they won't be cared for adequately. It's as valuable to examine staff's behaviors as it is to understand a patient's motivations."[20]

DIFFICULT HEALTH PROFESSIONAL AND PATIENT RELATIONSHIPS

In this section, we introduce you to three patients who share some of the attributes that have been identified as undesirable or difficult by most health professionals. As you examine some of the character traits and behaviors of the three and the nature of the relationships between the patients and health professionals, perhaps you will gain insight into your own values and attitudes and begin to prepare yourself for how you will respond.

The Patient with a History of Substance Abuse

Consider the case of Alex Peterson and Claire Chui:

> Alex Peterson was admitted for treatment of a *Pseudomonas* infection of his sinus and respiratory tract. In addition, he had developed some bleeding from his nose after being seen by the ear, nose, and throat specialists at the outpatient clinic. Alex looked considerably older than his 24 years due to a history of intravenous drug addiction, several attempts at drug rehabilitation, and finally a diagnosis of AIDS. He had a history of petty theft, prostitution, and imprisonment. Alex seemed to enter the unit with the intent to harass the staff. Despite a slow but steady recovery from the infection that led to his admission, he endlessly asked for pain medication. The physicians on Alex's case could find no cause for Alex's pain or his constant demands for pain medication. A psychiatric consultation determined that Alex was competent but had a diagnosis of antisocial personality disorder. The health care team decided to decrease the amount of analgesics Alex could receive. Even though Alex was informed of this plan, he still asked any staff member he could find for pain medication. Other members of the team had warned Claire Chui, a medical technologist, that Alex would probably ask her for pain medication when she went to draw blood. She felt she was prepared for her interaction with Alex. She kept telling herself, "Just stick to business. Draw the blood. Be firm but gentle." She stated when she entered the room, "I am here to draw a blood sample." When Alex asked Claire for something for pain, she responded, "I will not discuss your pain medication with you." As Claire bent over to lower the side rail on Alex's bed, Alex seized Claire's wrist and said, "I won't let you go until you promise to get me something for this pain." Clair managed to wrest her arm from Alex's grasp and hastily left the room. Claire immediately reported Alex's actions to the unit supervisor and her colleagues. When the unit manager confronted Alex with his inappropriate behavior, Alex reacted with a shrug and said, "I didn't hurt her, did I? Why did she get so rattled?"[21]

▶ How would you describe Alex's behavior? In other words, how would you view Alex after this incident?

▶ Can you identify several reasons why the rest of the staff might not want to spend time with Alex?

▶ Put yourself in Claire's place for a minute and ask yourself how you would feel.

▶ Would you be able to work with a patient after an incident like this?

▶ If so, where would you start in communicating with him the next time you interacted with him?

Alex would be characterized as a difficult patient for several reasons. His background sets him apart from the health professionals who are trying to care for him. He has led a life on the margins of society. He has engaged in unacceptable social behaviors such as intravenous drug use and prostitution, which carry with them increased risk for AIDS. His diagnosis places him at risk for stereotyping and stigmatizing. Alex is anything but a model of cooperation in the health care system. Alex also falls into the diagnostic category of "antisocial," which includes the inability to regulate impulses, delay gratification, and relate to others except by intimidation and manipulation. (This explains why Alex cannot tolerate pain of any kind nor comply with the plan to decrease his pain medication. He tries the only methods he knows: constant verbal harassment, and, when that does not work, physical intimidation.) Alex is not respectful of the usual boundaries established between patient and professional. The final section of this chapter explores some specific techniques to show respect for Alex as a person while managing his antisocial behaviors.

The Patient Who Is Self-Destructive

Sometimes the most difficult patient is not the one who commits actions that are outrageous or inappropriate, but shrinks from constructive action and resorts to self-harm behavior such as that encountered in the case of Violet Mercer and Tina Kramolisch.

🦢 Tina Kramolisch worked evenings and weekends in a busy, urban emergency room as a technician while she finished her last year of professional preparation. Tina often commented to classmates that you really do not have a taste for what it is like in practice without the experiences you find in an emergency room. In fact, Tina felt as if she had seen it all and was quite proud of her ability to work with different types of patients in various levels of distress. However, after taking care of Violet Mercer, Tina wondered if she was ready to care for all types of patients.

Tina entered the holding area where Violet Mercer lay absolutely still on the examination cart under a sheet. When Tina said Violet's name, there was no response, so Tina gently touched the woman's arm. Violet flinched so violently at the touch that it startled Tina as well and she jumped back from the cart. Tina was even more shocked at how Violet looked. Violet murmured, "You scared me." The words were somewhat difficult to understand as Violet's lips were swollen and split in one corner. Violet had lacerations, contusions, and swelling all over her face. Tina had never seen anyone so badly beaten. Tina noticed old bruises and injuries all over Violet's body as she conducted her intake assessment. Tina knew the physician would have to confirm it, but she was also certain that several of Violet's ribs were fractured. Because Tina had been trained to work with women who had been abused, she knew the right questions to ask and did so. Violet admitted, very cautiously, that her husband, Donnie, had lost his temper and done this to her. Tina reported her findings to the nurse and physician, and they set into motion the services and protection the health care system can offer battered women. In fact, Donnie was being treated down the hall for a scalp laceration that Violet had inflicted as she tried to defend herself. The police who brought both of the Mercers into the emergency room were waiting outside Donnie's room to see if Violet would press charges. Tina was holding Violet's hand as the rib binder was put into place when the nurse entered the room and said, "The social worker can take you to the women's shelter after you talk to the police." Violet did not look up as she said in a flat voice, "I've changed my mind. I don't want to press no charges. I'll just go home with Donnie." Tina was speechless as she watched every effort to change Violet's mind fail. Tina felt hot tears of frustration and anger run down her cheeks as she watched Violet and Donnie walk out of the emergency room arm-in-arm.

▶ Why do you think Tina felt a combination of frustration and anger with Violet?

▶ What would your reaction be?

▶ Which of the two patients, Violet Mercer or Alex Peterson, would be more difficult for you to take care of after this encounter?

In this case, the perception of Violet Mercer as a difficult patient is of a whole different nature than that of Alex Peterson. Whereas Alex committed actions that were disruptive and inappropriate, Violet is compliant and willing to accept professional intervention—to a point. In Violet's case, the perception of difficulty rests to some extent on the invalidating effects of Violet's behavior on Tina and the other health professionals caring for her. In the eyes of the professionals, intervention in Violet's case should include more than merely suturing her cuts and bandaging her broken ribs; it should also include offering her a way out of an abusive, potentially life-threatening situation. When Violet fails to accept the help that is offered to her, the primary treatment goal is thwarted, and the health professional's role as a therapeutic agent is invalidated.

The Patient with a History of Violent Behavior

Many health professionals feel inadequately prepared to deal with patients who have a complex medical condition that is complicated further by a history of violent behavior. The case of Darrin Block and Austin Greder involves a seriously ill patient and behavior that is generally unacceptable in an acute care institution.

Darrin Block was an orderly on the surgical intensive care unit at an urban medical center. Because of the medical center's location in a large city, the intensive care unit got more than its fair share of victims of gunshot wounds. Most of these patients were African American, male, young, and unemployed and knew their assailants. Many were members of gangs and had to be admitted under aliases for their own protection. Austin Greder fit this description exactly. He was a 21-year-old high school drop-out who had been shot by a rival gang member. Although he lacked formal education, Austin was very bright. His major sources of support were his mother and a girlfriend. He was admitted to the surgical intensive care unit in serious condition, but had begun to recover, although his wound was not healing as well as the treatment team expected. Since his admission, the staff had referred to Austin and his numerous visitors as "nothing but trouble." Large numbers of visitors moved in a steady stream in and out of Austin's room even though the staff had told them about the restrictions on visitors in the unit. Austin's girlfriend, Alicia, had practically taken up residence in Austin's room. One time, Darrin walked into Austin's room and found him and Alicia involved in sexual activity. Darrin left in confused embarrassment, but was somewhat angry too. He did not expect to walk in on a sexual encounter and didn't feel he should have to apologize. After this incident, Austin became angry and abusive to Darrin, refusing to let him perform wound care and asking for one of the other staff members to care for him. To make matters worse, Austin told one of his friends what his alias was even though this undermined maintenance of security on the unit. Darrin believed that the right thing to do was set limits on Austin's behavior because things were clearly getting out of control. However, he was fearful of retaliation by Austin's friends outside of the safety of the hospital. He had heard more than one other staff member talk about being confronted in the parking garage by one of "these gang members."

▶ Put yourself in Darrin Block's position. What would you do the next time the patient refused wound care?

▶ What resources might there be in the hospital to assist Darrin in working with Mr. Greder?

All of these patients challenge the very notion of what it means to be a "good" health professional. They make us realize that, although we are generally able to effectively help patients, sometimes we fall far short even with our best efforts. There are some techniques that may help you in working with difficult patients of all types, and we also share some ideas about changing a difficult working environment.

SHOWING RESPECT IN DIFFICULT SITUATIONS

When patients are uncooperative, manipulative, angry, or help-rejecting, this is not a license to show disrespect toward them as persons. You will have to be responsive to your own feelings of disgust, fear, anger, and so forth, as well as manage patients' unacceptable behavior. An appropriate place to start is to show respect by initially refusing to believe that you are dealing with a person whose character is flawed. The behaviors and attitudes may be the result of a treatable or modifiable factor. For example, one of your first determinations is to make certain that the patient has received a thorough, understandable explanation of the treatment or therapy in question. The patient may also be unmotivated or uncooperative if he or she has not been shown the respect of participation in establishing personally meaningful goals. After these more obvious problem areas are explored and resolved and problems still persist, you can turn to the following types of behavior that have been found to be effective in working with difficult patients.

As a general rule for all types of difficult situations, structure and consistency in communication in every aspect of patient care is very important.[22] A key component of a deliberate, consistent approach is "setting limits." Setting firm limits is a part of setting boundaries with all patients but with additional safeguards given the extremity of the situation. By setting forth clear, consistent expectations in a nondefensive manner, you can help strengthen the patient's inner control. Be open to negotiation. Listen for opportunities to find out what is important to the patient. However, when you are involved in setting limits, respect for the patient must govern. You should ask yourself whether the limits you are setting are arbitrary—that is, do they stem from your need to be in control or to punish the patient—or whether the patient's welfare would indeed be best served by establishing external limits. Any plan to set limits should be agreed upon by all members of the health care team to avoid the potential for a patient to "split" the staff, i.e., divide staff into all good or all bad. To avoid division of the staff, good communication lines between all members of the team are essential. For example, the patient may use charm and flattery to manipulate some staff members but make disparaging and critical comments about their co-workers.[21]

It is also helpful to focus on a patient's unacceptable behaviors rather than on the patient himself or herself. This allows for open communication and avoids negative labeling that tends to stick to patients and obscure the real problem. One way to avoid negative labeling of patients is to be honest with them and tell them exactly how you feel. Again, your honest comments should be directed at the patient's behavior and not at the patient. This way you can share your reactions and still not humiliate the patient. Look for opportunities to give plenty of positive feedback for desired behaviors. Also, focus on the here and now rather than long-term aspects of behavior. If all else fails, a behavioral contract can be developed to focus on specific actions. A contract, sometimes called a *patient care agreement*, "outlines the expectations, plans, and responsibilities of the patient and the consequences for noncompliance."[22]

On a broader basis, you can encourage the development of an environment that is respectful of everyone. Such a setting encourages patients to ask questions and challenge the system's rules and practices. If just a single member of the health care team prompts the patient legitimately to question his or her care, the rest of the team could come to see the patient as "difficult." Having patients ask about the care they receive and make decisions about their care must be considered the normal, desired state.[12] The safety of health professionals should also be encouraged in a respectful environment. There must be practices and policies in place to give people like Claire Chui some protection from harassment, abuse, and so forth. You may find yourself in an environment that is amenable to change through education and support for staff. In fact, the support of supervisory staff in the form of validation and insight is an essential component of an environment that fosters positive health professional and patient interactions.

As you gain experience working with difficult patients in challenging settings, you can use this experience to effect change. However, if you find yourself in a work environment that routinely fosters negative stereotypes and lack of respect for workers and patients alike—and if there is little hope for improvement—the only resolution might be to seek another position rather than endure the stress that is inherent in that type of situation.

In summary, here are general guidelines for showing respect toward difficult patients, keeping in touch with your own values, and making the system more responsive to both:

1. Avoid the use of derogatory labels as a means of reducing your frustration or anger.
2. Remember that the caring function is as important as other interventions. Make an empathetic statement such as, "I know you must be frustrated or disappointed." This kind of response tells the patient that you understand that there is a problem and are sympathetic, which allows the patient to be less defensive.[23]
3. Set realistic expectations of your own power as a health professional to force compliance.
4. Do not expect to change aspects of the patient's situation beyond your control.
5. Take care of your emotional well-being. Select a time to talk the patient when you are able to be a good listener. Do not try to tackle problems when you are overly tired or busy with other concerns.
6. Try to help change the underlying social and institutional conditions or attitudes that lead to devaluing behavior by health professionals.
7. When interacting with an aggressive patient, "assure that exit is possible for both you and the patient; monitor your body language and tone of voice; avoid pointing your index finger or putting your hands on your hips in a threatening stance; avoid sarcasm or loudness."[20]
8. Work to affirm policies and practices that encourage respect of everyone while ensuring their physical and emotional safety.

Although all of your efforts as a health professional should be directed at acknowledging negative biases and keeping them in check, you may find that you cannot operate in the best interest of a given patient, no matter how much you try. If it comes to letting a patient go, be certain that you are referring him or her to a capable professional and not abandoning the person. Respect includes everybody, but as humans we come in all shapes and forms, so the wise health professional recognizes that difficulties with patients and situations will arise.

SUMMARY

This final chapter makes suggestions about respectful interaction with types of patients whom many health professionals find difficult to treat without negative feelings or behaviors intruding on the relationship. Sources may be the patient's personality and behavior, societal stereotypes, your own countertransference and learned behaviors, or the opinions of your peers. The environment in which the relationship takes place can also cause difficulties and add to frustration, anger, and other negative responses by both parties. Despite such challenges, your responsibility to show respect for the patient as a person remains and can be expressed through attempts to use behaviors that provide an opportunity to minimize the negative aspects of the relationship.

References

1. Shaw I: Doctors, "dirty work" patients, and "revolving doors." *Qual Health Res* 14(8): 1032-1045, 2004.
2. Santamaria N: The relationship between nurses' personality and stress levels reported when caring for interpersonally difficult patients, *Aust J Adv Nurs* 18(2):20-26, 2000.
3. Herbert CP, Seifert MH: When the patient is the problem, *Patient Care* 24(1):59, 1990.
4. Highley BL, Norris CM: When a student dislikes a patient, *Am J Nurs* 57(9):1163, 1957.
5. Papper S: The undesirable patient, *J Chron Dis* 22:777, 1970.
6. Larson PA: Nurse perceptions of patient characteristics, *Nurs Res* 26(6):416-420, 1977.
7. Kelly MP, May D: Good and bad patients: a review of the literature and a theoretical critique, *J Adv Nurs* 7:147-156, 1982.
8. Harlow PE, Goby MJ: Changing nursing students' attitudes toward alcoholic patients: examining effects of a clinical practicum, *Nurs Res* 29(1):59-60, 1980.
9. Russell S, Daly J, Hughes E, op't Hoog C: Nurses and "difficult" patients: negotiating non-compliance, *J Adv Nurs* 43(3):281-287, 2003.
10. Rader J: To bathe or not to bathe: that is the question, *J Gerontol Nurs* 20(9):53, 1994.
11. Leon AM, Altholz JAS, Dziegielewski SF: Compassion fatigue: considerations for working with the elderly, *J Gerontol Soc Work* 32(1):43-62, 1999.
12. Staples P and others: Empowering the angry patient, *Can Nurse* 90(4):28-30, 1994.
13. Breeze JA, Repper J: Struggling for control: the care experiences of "difficult" patients in mental health services, *J Adv Nurs* 28(6):1301-1311, 1998.
14. Gallop R, Lancee W, Shugar G: Residents' and nurses' perceptions of difficult-to-treat short-stay patients, *Hosp Comm Psychiatry* 44(4):352, 1993.
15. Caplan B, Shechter J: Reflections on the "depressed," "unrealistic," "inappropriate," "manipulative," "unmotivated," "noncompliant," "denying," "maladjusted," "regressed," etc. patient, *Arch Phys Med Rehabil* 74(October):1123, 1993.
16. Podrasky DL, Sexton DL: Nurses' reactions to difficult patients, *Image: Journal of Nursing Scholarship* 20(1):19, 1988.
17. Neil JA, Corley MC: Hostility toward caregivers as a selection criterion for transplantation, *Prog Transplant* 10(3):177-181, 2000.
18. Juliana CA and others: Interventions by staff nurses to manage "difficult" patients, *Holist Nurs Pract* 11(4):1-26, 1997.
19. Stockard S: Caring for the sexually aggressive patient: you don't have to blush and bear it, *Nursing* 21(11):72, 1991.
20. Nield-Anderson L and others: Responding to the "difficult" patient: manipulation, sexual provocation, aggression—how can you manage such behaviors? *Am J Nurs* 99(12):26-34, 1999.
21. Daum AL: The disruptive antisocial patient: management strategies, *Nurs Manage* 25(8):49, 1994.
22. Morrison EF, Ramsey A, Synder B: Managing the care of complex, difficult patients in the medical-surgical setting, *Medsurg Nursing* 9(1):21-6, 2000.
23. Baum NH: 12 tips for dealing with difficult patients, *Geriatrics* 57(11):55-56, 2002.

PART SEVEN

Questions for Thought and Discussion

1. You are in a patient's room performing a procedure. The patient, who has a type of cancer that is always fatal, has been told of his condition. While you are there, a man visiting a patient in the next bed begins to describe the horror of his wife's last days before she died of cancer. The patient becomes increasingly tense and finally begins to sob.
   a. What can you do to console or reassure this patient?
   b. How could you have helped to prevent this situation?
   c. Should you report this incident? To whom and why?

2. Under what conditions would your life seem no longer worth living? What course would you take to show respect for a patient whose life is very similar to these conditions?

3. If you were truly able to plan your own death (age, setting, cause, persons present, etc.), what would be your most preferable way to meet your death? Least preferable?

4. You are working in an outpatient clinic in an economically depressed area of the city. A disheveled woman comes in dragging three young children behind her. One of the children begins to whine that she is hot. You are in the receiving area and see the woman hit the child so hard the child falls to the floor and begins to scream. The woman looks at you in panic. You are already late for your next appointment. Your next patient is anxiously waiting to be seen and looks with scorn at the woman and you.
   a. What feelings does this scene trigger?
   b. You probably think there are some things you should do in this situation, but what would you really like to do?
   c. What does this teach you about the possible difference between your emotional and "professional" reaction to this extreme situation?

5. In a small group, brainstorm major "likes" related to working with patients. After compiling the list, look for the common denominator or theme. What does this tell you about your expectations of patients?

6. What types of difficult patient care situations make you (or, if you are still a student, do you *think* will make you) the most uncomfortable? Identify two or three concrete interventions you would take to effectively deal with the situations you identified.

7. What types of policies or guidelines can be developed to foster better relationships with difficult patients, such as patients who become physically or verbally aggressive? How would guidelines help? What sort of supervisory support would you find most helpful?

INDEX

Page numbers followed by *f* indicate figures; *t,* tables; *b,* boxes.